FRANCIS EDGAR WILLIAMS:
'THE VAILALA MADNESS' AND OTHER ESSAYS

Francis Edgar Williams

FRANCIS EDGAR WILLIAMS

"The Vailala Madness"
and Other Essays

edited, with an introduction, by
ERIK SCHWIMMER

THE UNIVERSITY PRESS OF HAWAII
HONOLULU

PUBLISHER'S ACKNOWLEDGMENTS

'The Vailala Madness' and 'Bull-Roarers in the Papuan Gulf' have been reprinted by courtesy of the Government of Papua New Guinea; 'The Natives of Lake Kutubu' and 'Trading Voyages from the Gulf of Papua' by courtesy of the Editor of *Oceania*; 'The Vailala Madness in Retrospect' (from *Essays Presented to C. G. Seligman*, edited by E. E. Evans-Pritchard and others) by courtesy of Routledge and Kegan Paul Ltd.; 'Sex Affiliation and its Implications' by courtesy of the Royal Anthropological Institute, London; and 'The Creed of a Government Anthropologist' by courtesy of the Australian and New Zealand Association for the Advancement of Science. While all the material has been reset, the typographical styles of the respective original publications have been retained. We are indebted for the map of Papua, showing the fieldwork areas of F.E. Williams, and for the Index, to Mme Andrée Gendreau of Université Laval.

CONTENTS

PART I

PART II

Contents

Contents

ILLUSTRATIONS

10

PART I

F. E. WILLIAMS AS ANCESTOR[1] AND RAINMAKER

by Erik G. Schwimmer

This book, and this essay, are above all an act of piety as, during my first work among the Orokaiva (Northern District, Papua), Williams' two books on that tribe were with me as an inexhaustible guide in my search for insight. As an ethnographer I found not only that Williams was rarely wrong, but also that he had an almost unfailing instinct for the focal areas in a culture. Unencumbered by the temporary obsessions of academic anthropology schools, yet always an inveterate professional, he could identify, in dialogue with the societies he studied, basic patterns of thought that served to make Papuans comprehensible to Europeans.

In this unique position of 'government anthropologist' in Papua from 1922 to 1943, Williams may well have spent more time on professional anthropological field work in New Guinea than any other man. He wrote four major monographs, all of which have recently been reprinted.[2] In addition there was a vast collection of shorter writings which are now in danger of falling into oblivion. The present collection is intended to make some of the most remarkable of these available to a larger public.

This republication of Williams' work is addressed, in part, to a new readership. In the past the anthropology of Papua New Guinea was virtually a white man's preserve. There were basically three kinds of public: romantic laymen who loved to read about what they presumed to be man in the State of Nature; the anthropological profession; and white public servants and missionaries with a practical interest in the country. This third category included Williams' employers. The Lieutenant-Governor of Papua, Sir Hubert Murray, had established the post of government anthropologist, because he wanted to know 'which customs you should preserve and which you should abolish'. He thought the best remedy against wrong decisions would be the study of 'the science of anthropology . . . so long as the student does not allow the claims of that science to prevail over the claims of duty' (Murray 1921).

As Papua New Guinea is becoming independent, this last-mentioned kind of public has certainly disappeared. The new

11

leaders of Papua New Guinea, however, have become potential readers, whose interests this kind of book should certainly serve. One may well ask what kind of service anthropologists can now till render in New Guinea and, in particular, what is the usefulness in reviving the essays of F. E. Williams.

With regard to 'applied anthropology'—the application of anthropological knowledge to social and economic development—a tradition of dialogue between the administration and the profession has been built up and will no doubt be maintained. In this sphere, paradoxically, the work of F.E. Williams may no longer be especially relevant. It certainly had a largely beneficent influence during the days of the Murray administration when Williams defended the traditional values of Papuan society against public servants and missionaries. But all this is now history. His writings on agriculture and education may have little to contribute today.

On the other hand, his ethnographic records of the people of the Purari Delta, the Gulf Coast, Lake Kutubu, the Orokaiva, and several mountain tribes have now become classics. They will undoubtedly be read by scholars both inside and outside Papua New Guinea for many generations to come, if only as monuments to a past way of life the positive achievements of which are a basis for ideological development in the future. On the basis of a wealth of precise facts, Williams admired Papua's mythology, art, drama, dance and systems of thought. He analysed them in much detail, and untiringly sought their meaning.

Over and above this, the present volume is intended to draw attention to Williams' theoretical insights in anthropology, which have been obscured by being unfashionable when first published. At the present time, his contributions to kinship and marriage, to magic and sorcery, to millennial movements and to the cultural use of mythology ought to be better understood, as scholars have begun again to ask many of the same questions, and Williams' unusually wide field experience equipped him to give some useful answers.

Though working mainly in the tradition of British functionalism, Williams expressed basic criticisms of this school towards the end of his career. He foreshadowed some of the methods of enquiry of the structuralist school that developed after his death. The works in the present volume have been chosen, not only for their ethnographic excellence, but also as documents to illustrate the assertions I have just made.

Williams was too deeply involved in fieldwork and in practical problems (including his many attempts to defend Papuan cultural traditions against their powerful detractors) to spend much time on theoretical exploration. His most innovative suggestions were at times made rather tentatively, as though he were still unsure of their theoretical consequences. Referring, in a preface, to his own masterly analysis of the social structure of the Morehead District (which one could not present nowadays without being typed as a slavish follower of 'French structuralism'), he wrote:

But I have essayed such an explanation in the case of the highly anomalous three-section and moiety organisation, because it seemed to defy any attempt at functional interpretation. I now regret having embarked upon the task, for I have spent innumerable days and weeks tacking about on a sea of difficult evidence, and when all is said and done I remain doubtful whether the conclusions, except in the most general sense, are to be relied upon, and indeed whether the work need have been begun. But this kind of enquiry has a fascination of its own and, once in, it is hard to withdraw (1936:ix).

In these circumstances I would do less than justice to Williams if I were to fabricate some theoretical system to which his works may conform. I shall therefore organise my remarks around the seven selections in this volume, taking each in turn, and elucidating some of Williams' favourite concepts as they occur. If a systematic approach to Papuan ethnography and culture should emerge, no harm is done. What would please me more would be to convey somehow the mode of thought of this man whose understanding of Papuan life was varied and subtle, dry, yet full of joy.

Francis Edgar Williams died in an aeroplane crash in the Owen Stanley Range in 1943 at the age of fifty years. We know little of his life except for the brief biography written by A.P. Elkin just after his death.[3] He was a Rhodes scholar (1915) and obtained a Diploma in Anthropology with distinction under Marett at Oxford (1922). In 1922 he became Assistant Anthropologist, Papua, and in 1928 Government Anthropologist. In 1933-4 he returned to Oxford on a Rockefeller Fellowship, in order to write a B.Sc. thesis, later published as *Papuans of the Trans-Fly*. Though Williams found this a most exhilarating year,[4] and he established close contact with the reigning functionalist school, this did not fully break his isolation, which was a necessary consequence of his independence of mind. The attitude of the British anthropological establishment towards him, as judged by reviews in *Man* (Hogbin 1936, Piddington 1938), remained kind but patronising; when he died, he did not rate an obituary in *Man*.

It is easy to say that his untimely death was an irreparable loss to anthropology, but Williams died at the end of his era: after the war the time of the great traditional ceremonies in Papua was over. His work stands as a monument to a culture that was rapidly being

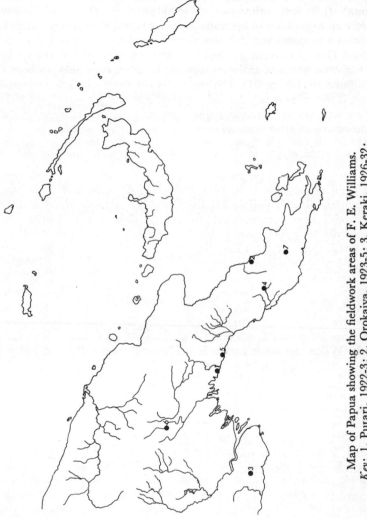

Map of Papua showing the fieldwork areas of F. E. Williams.
Key: 1, Purari, 1922-3; 2, Orokaiva, 1923-5; 3, Keraki, 1926-32;
4, Koiari, 1929-31; 5, Elema, 1923-37; 6, Foe, 1938-9; 7, Keveri, 1940.

transformed, and Williams' first experience of the 'new man' in Papua—'Mission Influence amongst the Keveri of South-East Papua' (his last ethnography, published posthumously)—was largely an expression of his nostalgia for a world that was passing. It contains a brilliant account of *vada* and much hilarious satire on the Oxford Group movement, but the key sentence of the report is: 'In eighteen years of anthropologising I have never been so bored' (Williams 1944/5, p. 91). His work has relevance for Papua in the future if the 'new man', the independent Papuan, chooses to rebuild his society on the foundation of the great achievements of the traditional culture which Williams knew and celebrated.

1. *Trading Voyages: Magic of Impersonation*

Our first selection is poignantly romantic, for the Elema turned to long trading voyages only after European pressure and their own millennial cult, the Vailala Madness, had led them to abandon their traditional mask ceremonies, and to develop a new institution, supposedly to 'make money' but probably as a substitute for their lost ceremonies. The trading voyages described here did not make money and were highly dangerous. Williams was chiefly interested in describing a special form of magic employed on these voyages.

Magic and sorcery were a special interest of F.E. Williams throughout his career. In an early, largely theoretical report on Orokaiva Magic[4a] he defined magic as the symbolic representation of a hoped-for result, which is felt to assist the realisation of that result. When the same action is performed repeatedly and judged efficacious, belief in the procedure develops. Long-established magical procedures tend to have at least one highly secret and mysterious component, often known only to specialists. Among the Orokaiva such occult components ('specifics') are mostly medicines

The magic of the Elema trade voyages was likewise in part a publicly known procedure, in part a secret component, known to the captain alone. Used to protect the voyagers against the malice of the sea *hevehe*, the secret, however, is often not a substance but a name used (inaudibly) in a spell. This name refers directly to the hero of a myth. While the myth will normally be fairly general knowledge among the Elema, the name that makes the magic efficacious is known only to those qualified to be captains.

What are the resemblances and what are the differences between these two kinds of magic? An important resemblance is that both systems ultimately depend on mythology. In the case of the Orokaiva this is often hard to establish, because (even if an informant is willing to talk about it) such a specific works jut as well if the user is ignorant of the mythological basis, and this basis is easily forgotten.

Indeed, as Williams says, a medicine's power may seem greater if it is wholly mysterious.

In one case Williams was fortunate enough to be able to trace the 'origin' of a specific. It was (1928: 204-5) a Binandere medicine for dogs, used to improve their ability to hunt pigs. On the upper reaches of the Gira river

> ... there is a large mass of rocks scored with curious grooves. These grooves are ascribed to the manmonster Totoima who used to sharpen his teeth on the rocks as a man sharpens his axe on a stone. Totoima was famous as a hunter of men, and accordingly any medicine obtained from the neighbourhood will be recommended, by association with the hunter, as a medicine for dogs. This association was made explicit by more than one informant.[5]

The mythological association of this symbolic representation is thus obvious. Williams notes that such medicines tended to be replanted elsewhere, and where this was done knowledge of the mythological association would obviously soon be lost. Yet belief in the potency of the medicine would remain.

There is a minor difference between Orokaiva and Elema magic in that in the former, mythology is used only in the genesis of magical procedures, but later becomes irrelevant. For the latter, knowledge of the connection between the secret names and the myths always remains essential.

Let us now consider in more detail the basis of the power of the Binandere dog medicine. Williams' informant pointed to the minute white hairs with which the leaf of the orchid was covered: 'Did they not call to mind the coat of a dog?' As Williams comments, 'the hairy coat of the leaf will not suggest the hairy coat of the dog unless there is always some one to point out the resemblance'. Here is clearly a case of the operation of Sir James Frazer's laws of homeopathic magic: Williams shows that Orokaiva always explained the efficacy of a magical agent by its resemblance or contact with the object at which it was aimed. We have seen, however, that such explanations do not reveal how the belief in the medicine's efficacy first arose. Williams argues that they provide us only with the 'pseudo-logic' by which people would explain its power once the original association had been forgotten.

This argument needs some clarification. It is sound to argue that Orokaiva magic is ultimately founded on the mythico-religious associations of certain powerful objects. Williams is therefore on firm ground when he rejects Frazer's theory of an evolutionary chain where there would be a magical stage preceding a religious stage.[6] In 1928, this was a point of some practical importance, as white administrators and missionaries based their disrespect for Papuan traditions at least partly on Frazer's kind of theory which would place the whites on a higher level on some imaginary evolutionary ladder, because the Papuans were supposedly at the 'magical stage'. It is possible, however, to reject Frazer's evolutionary theory, while still accepting that all magical associations are based either on similarity or contact. This is as reasonable as Saussure's theory, promulgated around the same time,[7] that all semantic associations in language are based on either metaphor or metonymy.

Such theories do not assert that resemblance or contact are sufficient to establish magical power, but that one or the other is necessary. We may ask whether the dog medicine could have remained in use if the practitioner did not *see the resemblance*. As Williams rightly says, if the 'original' resemblance is lost, the practitioner can, without harm, invent another one to satisfy a curious enquirer, but the fact remains that he resorts to either resemblance or contact as the basis of his explanation.

At this point let us return to the Elema case. If a magical association is founded, as a universal principle, on either contact or similarity, then what is the basis of a captain's use of a special secret name when he breathes an appeal to a mythical ancestor? The answer is that breathing the secret name does not suffice to make the magic efficacious. In addition, the captain must establish either similarity or contact between himself and the ancestor. He must impersonate him, he must imitate him; he must establish a relation of 'sympathy' between himself and the ancestor.

Williams regarded the magic of impersonation as a special case of sympathetic magic. It is by no means found everywhere, and in many other Papuan cultures it occupies a much less prominent position. Williams did not describe it among the Orokaiva, and though I did find evidence for it when I restudied that tribe,[8] it obviously played a minor role. Williams encountered it among the Kutubu, also in a minor role. He claimed, however, that in Elema magic, 'impersonation is the *leit-motif*'.[9]

Williams' interest in this form of magic was in part theoretical. As usual, his practical ideological purposes as 'government anthropologist' acted as a powerful stimulus to his theoretical acumen. Ideologically, his major commitment was to establish that the traditional achievements of Papuan culture were great enough to justify that the administration should treat them with far more respect than they did. Now it was clear to Williams that respect for the achievements of Papuan culture stood or fell with one's attitude to ceremonial and the aesthetic value of art, music, dance, oral literature Furthermore, none of these forms of artistic expression was compre-

One of two Orokolo masks used during the *hevehe* cycle described by Williams in *Drama of Orokolo*. Although these masks are as a general rule destroyed after the ceremony, two of the *eharo* reached the Pitt-Rivers Museum after Dr. Beatrice Blackwood visited Williams at Orokolo. *Eharo*, like the other Orokolo masks, are constructed of cane with a covering of bark-cloth. Typically, they bear on their heads realistic effigies of all manner of totemic creatures, or *aualari*. Above: a fish *aualari*. Reference: *Drama of Orokolo*, Chapter XVIII. (©Pitt-Rivers Museum)

Eharo representing a mythological character. Reference: *Drama of Orokolo*, Chapters XVIII, XX. (© Pitt-Rivers Museum.)

hensible except in the framework of the Papuan systems of thought
and mythology.

In these circumstances, he was embarrassed by certain aspects of
the newly dominant British functionalist school in anthropology.
While he admired Malinowski's work, he could not accept the
theory (Malinowski 1926) according to which mythology was
reduced to the function of providing a 'charter'—a pseudo-logical
post hoc justification—for institutions. As early as 1929 Williams
published an analysis of some myths from the Morehead District[10]
and concluded plaintively:

Can anything in their present-day function help us to understand what
gave rise to those curious episodes in Kuramangu mythology of which I
have given a few samples in this paper? It is obvious that mythology helps
to explain rain-making; but does rain-making help to explain mythology?

The 'magic of impersonation' provided Williams with an instance
he could use as a partial rebuttal of the functionalist view of mythology. He readily granted that certain passages in the myths served
as charters for certain Elema voyaging practices: stages of canoe
construction, the taboo on sexual intercourse, food avoidances, the
use of lime to drive away the *hevehe*, the canoe decorations, the
traditional cargo that was carried.

His criticism took two main forms. First, he drew attention to
passages in the myths in which the actors certainly did not follow
current Elema custom; if the myths were mere charters, why were
such passages included? But his main point was that, in order to
make magic by impersonation effective, the captains must use the
myths in their entirety as psychological models, and such models
differ for and within each clan, so that captains are to some extent
free to choose among a number of available models. The idea that
the myths were made up to justify and explain the captain's behaviour lacks plausibility. The captain is clearly an actor using an
existing scenario (though no doubt the scenario is modified over
time). The argument is even stronger as Williams is dealing with a
very recent institution; demonstrably, the myth existed before the
bevaia voyages began. Moreover, Williams showed in *Drama of
Orokolo* that the same myths were utilised in the older mask ceremonies which the *bevaia* voyages served to replace (and this theory of
replacement, at least, was very respectably functionalist). Finally, he
shows clearly, both in 'Trading Voyages' and in *Drama of Orokolo*,
that Elema actors use the sacred names not to appeal for help but to
establish their identity with the hero.

It is in the latter work that the 'magic of impersonation' is most
fully developed. The relation between the ancestor who provides the

scenario and the actor who impersonates him is not, however, quite the same for canoe captains and for *hevehe* masks. In the case of the masks there is a clear relation of similarity between the mask and the spirit it represents. Admittedly, one can never be sure what spirits look like; as Williams fitly remarks elsewhere, they are 'like nothing on earth' except 'gigantic bull-roarers'. The Elema, however, spare no effort to make the masks look like what they think the spirit to be. One may say that the mask is a metaphor for the spirit, and that in that sense they are similar.

The captain, on the other hand, looks like an ordinary man, not a spirit. He may blacken his face and wear a very special sprig of feathers in his hair but these represent no more than a very few attributes that used to belong to the ancestor when he was human, rather than to the ancestor as a spirit, i.e. as *hevehe* mask. The captain, like any actor, tries to 'feel' his way into the part, e.g. by imagining, as he sails along, that he wants to pluck the sprig of feathers from Iviri's head, just as his hero did. By blackening his face and wearing these feathers, he is establishing contact with the ancestor who is otherwise dissimilar. Basically, the magic of the voyages is probably not metaphorical but metonymic.

2. Bull-Roarers are not like Masks but Masks are like Bull-Roarers

While 'Bull-Roarers in the Papuan Gulf' is, for the most part, Williams' most elegant essay, is has a rather absurd conclusion. The historical background appears to be that the Vailala Madness on the Gulf Coast (for which see Chapters V and VI of the present volume) had created a good deal of alarm among the whites. After this movement died down, various ceremonial activities were resumed or started along the coast, though the great masked dances, the *hevehe* cycle was never taken up by any group that had previously abandoned it. It appears that bull-roarer initiations, far less onerous than mask ceremonies, were resumed in their traditional form, rather than as part of any millennial cult. Williams personally welcomed this, as he thought the cult was a form of ceremonial life well adapted to the conditions of that time. On the other hand, missionaries and servants of the administration painted a garish picture of what was happening. Whether Williams was successful in stopping proposed measures to suppress the cult I do not know, but to my knowledge no ordinances against it were ever promulgated.

In 'Bull-Roarers', Williams sets himself the objective of studying 'the relation between' the Elema people and 'their bull-roarer'. He understands the term 'relation' in two senses, which he distinguishes explicitly as functional and psychological. Much of the essay is occupied with a systematic survey of functional relations, largely in the manner advocated by Malinowski, i.e. by showing how the institution of the bull-roarer cult served a number of familial, legal, political, magico-religious and even economic purposes.

The term 'psychological' is not so clearly defined. Williams often used it to cover a range of questions that would have been excluded by the functionalists. The term puzzled Elkin, in his generous obituary essay (1943), where he made a useful list of the concepts Williams developed under the rubric of 'psychological'. Returning to these concepts thirty years later, it is easier to see a pattern in them.

In 'Bull-Roarers', two specific and detailed investigations occur which seem to fall within this 'psychological' rubric, namely those related to the position of women and those related to mythology. Both investigations are profound and highly original; both have implications which even today are not fully understood. Rather than labelling them theoretically, let us look at the questions at issue.

With regard to the mythology of the bull-roarer, there appear to be four main questions raised in the 'Bull-Roarer' essay, though some of these are developed more fully in Williams' other writings. These are the questions of totemic clans, of totemic classification, of the various modes of 'magic of impersonation', and of the relation of society to mythology.

Williams noted, in all the (always patrilineal) Papuan societies he studied, an element which, with much hesitation, he described as 'totemism'. The term referred to a practice on the part of patrilineal descent groups of various sizes to identify themselves spiritually with some natural species, plant or animal, or indeed almost any percept or concept derived from nature. At the time when Williams wrote, such relationships were considered to be 'totemic' only when they included specific features such as exogamy of the group, food avoidances (of the totem plant or animal), the notion that the 'totem' was an ancestor, a sense of awe felt by the group towards the totem, etc. Such specific features were largely absent from the *social group/natural species* relationship in Papua. Williams drew attention to the seeming anomaly in an early essay 'Plant Emblems among the Orokaiva' (1925), pointing out that these emblems certainly represented a relationship between an exogamous group and a species sometimes regarded as the group's ancestor, but that the avoidances and the religious respect were largely absent. Instead of this, the emblems were found to perform other functions, all rather minor. Williams concluded his paper by suggesting that the difference between these emblems and what were then called 'totems' was only superficial.

Williams found groups with the same characteristics among the Purari (the *larava* and the 'river clans'), in the Morehead district (*tuarar*, *yuvi*, sections), among the Koiari (*idi*) and among the Kutubu (*amindoba*).[11] Among the Elema, he found that the 'totemic' groups (*aualari*) were even more deviant from the accepted model in that they did not really regard the totem as their ancestor and they had no explicitly stated clan exogamy rule. He also found that some of these tribes had two types of patrilineal groups, namely some that were totemic and others that were not. Of the non-totemic type of clan, Williams drew a general picture rather similar to Barnes' (1962) model of patrilineal groups in the New Guinea Highlands. He showed that this type of clan was apt to change its name and allegiance in cases of migration, formation of new alliances and other political exigencies. On the other hand, the 'totemic' groups transmitted their membership much more in the manner of orthodox descent groups. This generalisation applies very well to the two types of Elema group, of which *bira'ipa* resembles the Highland type as pictured by Barnes, and the *aualari* is 'totemic'.

Williams was well aware that the kind of 'totemic' relation he discovered between social groups, individuals and natural species among the Papuans was inconsistent with the explanations of 'totemism' available at the time.

Essentially Williams' explanation was a folk-model he learnt from the Elema. Just as that tribe is subdivided into ten *aualari*, so the natural world is subdivided into ten categories according to some geographical and cosmological scheme Williams never fully reconstructed. [12] Though both the social and the natural world are subdivided more finely, it seems that any member of an *aualari* can set up a special relationship with any species allocated to the natural category corresponding to that *aualari*. The basis of such a relationship is individual magical knowledge. The species is supposed to have been created as the result of metamorphosis of a mythical hero; and the magic consists basically of knowing and being able to impersonate that hero. According to Williams' informants (1940: 137-8) it seems as though in the beginning there was a finite set of story folk who engendered and were present in the species of the natural world (by metamorphosis) and who made possible man's control over the natural world (by impersonation). Though each *aualari* claims to have its distinctive set of tales, Williams points out that these sets are variants of the same tales, Thus the Elema have a fiction that each *aualari* has its own logos, but in fact they all have the same logos.

It ought to be noted that this Elema totemism is not at all the same as the type Williams described for the Orokaiva, Koiari and Kutubu. Among the latter, the emblem was regarded as an ancestor and used, for instance, as an identity token. Among the Elema,

Williams emphasises that it was not an ancestor and that, far from
being an identity token, it was available merely as a *potential* model
for impersonation by those belonging to the same *aualari* as the
mythological hero (and the natural species).[13]

From this standpoint it becomes clear why Williams dismissed
as 'a matter of no great consequence' such questions as: what the
bull-roarer represents, what its ultimate meaning is, what is the
reality behind it. The individual bull-roarer or mask, as such, has
no clear meaning at all. Williams did not take the step of explicitly
stating that if the individual bull-roarer or mask has no ulterior
meaning, the same cannot be said of the total bundle of bull-roarers
or the total procession of masks which, of course, reproduce the
world order organised as *aualari* system. Williams makes it clear,
however, that neither bull-roarer nor mask ever occurs in practice
except as part of such a totality. We are thus faced with an ambigu-
ity in that Williams did not explicitly take the theoretical step that
would have made his 'psychology' into structural analysis (in the
Lévi-Straussian sense [14]), but that he placed himself in a position
where no other theory now known to anthropology could have
solved the problems he raised.

In 'Bull-Roarers', he rejected not only purely phenomenological
explanations (search for 'ultimate' meanings) but also functionalist
ones (though the myths contain 'charters' for customs, these are no
more than 'so much colouring or stuffing'). On the other hand, if
we adopt a basically structuralist attitude, many of the other points
Williams made about the bull-roarers fall into place remarkably well.

In that case, we may regard both the masks and the bull-roarers
as mediating devices between the social and natural levels of the
aualari system. Williams noted several similarities between them:
both are occasions for feasts and initiations; both play an important
part in the exchanges between nephews and maternal uncles;
both are regarded with awe. Both have more or less secret names
which belong to mythological heroes, often controllers of vital resources. By offering feasts to these heroes, men seek to earn their
benevolence. Both have the same shape: masks are larger replicas
of the named, decorated and painted bull-roarers.

The main difference between bull-roarer and mask noted by
Williams is that the former are permanently in the cult-house while
the latter are only temporary visitors, destroyed as soon as they have
been used for one festival. It is by virtue of this that Elema call the
bull-roarer the mask's elder brother. Another difference is that only
the bull-roarers are appealed to in prayers. This difference is
greatly clarified in an important later discussion Williams devoted
to bull-roarers (1940: 200-7). It appears that the opening ceremony

of the bull-roarer rite, i.e. the splitting of the coconut, occurs in identical manner at the inauguration of the *hevehe* mask cycle. The essential act in both cases is a sacrifice of food to the bull-roarers, evidently regarded as the spirits on whose support success in both enterprises depends. In order to make this sacrifice successful, the officiant depends on the familiar Elema device of the magic of impersonation (and Williams gives instances of the heroes or rather heroines appealed to on such occasions). We thus notice a difference in ritual sequence between masks and bull-roarers. To perform the mask ceremony, the sequence is: (1) impersonating the heroine who can feed the bull-roarers; (2) making an effective sacrifice to the bull-roarers; (3) constructing a mask which can be used to impersonate a mythological hero. The bull-roarer ceremony is identical, but the last phase is missing: the sacrifice is expected to restore the benevolence of the controllers of the species represented in the bundle of bull-roarers. The masks are thus a device to establish, from time to time, a relationship between man and nature more potent than the regular one with the bull-roarers. It is thus entirely credible that, as Williams suggested, the masks are fashioned after the model of the bull-roarers, because they transmit the same message in far more emphatic manner; but if masks are metaphoric bull-roarers, this relation is non-reciprocal, because no appeal to the powers of the natural order could be made without the bull-roarers, nor could the masks be constructed without them, whereas the bull-roarers do not require the masks to be efficacious in ordinary circumstances. The points I am making here are not explicitly developed by Williams, but clearly implied.

One small problem remains, namely, that the bull-roarers are not only objects of worship but also musical instruments, and that the act of sounding them is a form of impersonation. It might therefore seem at first sight as though the sharp distinction I posited between objects of worship and objects of impersonation does not really hold among the Elema. Williams emphasises, however, that the Elema adopt the unusual device of distinguishing without exception between the painted, decorated, named bull-roarers which are worshipped but never sounded and other instruments always unnamed, usually also undecorated and known as 'wild' or 'bush' bull-roarers, which are for music.

The former are therefore artefacts representing and concentrating in themselves the power of a natural species, much in the way of the *churinga* of the Australian Aborigines.[15] The musical instruments are smaller replicas of these, which may be called metaphoric representations of the bull-roarers that contain the power. These smaller specimens do not have the same permanence; though they are not ritually destroyed after use, like the masks, they may be accidentally destroyed without magical danger. They are thus symbolically on the same level of significance as the masks, whereas the named bull-roarers stand apart as mere models both for the smaller sounding replicas and for the larger masks. The systemic relations between the various mediating devices of the Elema are thus fully consistent with one another.

Even more interesting, but also more complex, are Williams' insights into the message system of the bull-roarer. He recognised that if such male cults exclude the women physically from seeing the bull-roarers, the women are still deeply involved in them both as actors and as symbolic objects. Thus, as part of his analysis of the 'psychology' of the bull-roarer, Williams distinguished between the 'meaning' of the cult to the uninitiated and to the initiated, adding some comments on the way the initiated interpret the cult to the uninitiated and vice versa. It is an example of his intuitively structuralist attitude that he treats each of these components of the total bull-roarer message system as containing relevant information and that he views the totality of this message system rather than any part of it as the Elema folk-explanation of the institution. It must not be forgotten that the myths explaining the origin of the bull-roarer, of which Williams summarises several versions, are not concealed from the women. The women also know the stories of the mythological heroes who are metamorphosed into, and control natural species. The idea that such spirits may inhabit the bull-roarer would also not be entirely alien to them. The secrecy rule seems to apply only to the appearance and the names of the objects and the source of the sound they make.

The story the women are told—that bull-roarers are snakes or crocodiles—is plausible not only because the word *hevehe* has all these meanings, but also because the myths suggest that story. It may well be symbolically true; it is a lie only if understood literally. When the women ask the newly initiated boys: 'Did the crocodile bite you?' the question is symbolically apposite even though literally inappropriate. Similarly the boys' answer 'No, he only dunged on us', is an instance of an apparent falsehood which could be symbolically apposite if the ashes covering them could be metaphorically described as 'crocodile dung'. I would assume such metaphor would be appropriate in the Elema language.

A structural analysis of this message system, even if it is possible from the available data, falls outside the scope of this essay. If such an analysis were attempted, it would need to start from the fact, not examined so far, that bull-roarer initiation is accompanied by an exchange whereby the nephew gives a pig to his maternal uncle and receives ornaments (crocodile dung?) in exchange. It is clear from Williams' ethnography that the nephew inherits the role of exchange partner from his father, so that the exchange system is basically affinal. A structural analysis should therefore answer the basic question: how is the bull-roarer cult related to an exchange system where the wife-giver always presents ornaments, and the wife-taker pigs? [16]

Williams' interest in the 'psychological' — in addition to the 'functional' — aspect of culture would seem, on the evidence of the 'Bull-Roarer' essay, to have led him to analyses which are intuitively structuralist. We shall meet this tendancy again when we look below at his work on kinship and marriage, and at certain aspects of 'Natives of Lake Kutubu'. The chief interest of Williams' analyses, however, does not lie in their structuralist tendency, but in clarifying issues that have remained a little cloudy even in quite recent ethnographies, especially as to the role of ritual secrets and false-hoods. Basically, Williams was most wary of making suggestions for which the empirical basis was dubious, and when he did so, he gave the reader careful warning. He was aware of the symbolic richness and complexity of the cultures he studied; and of the practical usefulness of providing interpretations of symbolism, so that persons having dealings with the Elema would see some meaning in the creative aspects of their culture.

3. *Sex Affiliation*

Many good descriptions of Melanesian systems of kinship and marriage are available today. The reader notices a remarkable diversity in the rules reported for different tribes; yet he may sense that somehow — it is not easy to see just in what way — there is a close family resemblance between these systems. It is as though a restaurant has a most varied menu, but if one looks closely, one sees that the chef uses only a few ingredients and few methods of cooking.

It is only recently that anthropologists began to inquire seriously what these few ingredients and structuring principles are in the kinship and marriage systems of Papua New Guinea.[17] Williams anticipated these recent studies to some extent on the basis of his personal detailed knowledge of several Papuan societies. In one point, he advanced beyond recent published comparative studies, namely in his analysis of a frequent ingredient of Melanesian systems, known today as patrilateral cross-cousin marriage. We find this analysis in his paper on Sex Affiliation (1932), reprinted in this volume.

In order to indicate the range of Williams' comparative perspective, let us briefly recall his contributions to this field of anthropology, especially in relation to moiety systems, sister exchange and the significance of intercultural and intracultural variations in the size of the marriage universe. In 'Natives of the Purari Delta' (1924), Williams' first monograph, he discovered forms of organisation ranging over that entire district, where previously no organisation above the level of the village had been suspected. These swamp-dwellers had large villages, subdivided into hamlet-sized cult-house (*ravi*) communities. Each *ravi* had a number of alcoves, allotted to exogamous lineages called *larava*. Williams found that each *larava* was associated with a wickerwork mask kept in a secret compartment at the back of the cult house. These masks (*aiaimunu*) contained the key to the Purari 'system'.

The *aiaimunu* were associated with (*a*) a particular river in the district; (*b*) an animal species living in that river; (*c*) a spirit communicating between the mask and the river; (*d*) a particular individual of the above-mentioned species, distinguished by special markings and living in an identifiable haunt in the river, which was the embodiment of the *aiaimunu*'s spirit in the river.

Williams found that the same *larava* names recurred in different *ravi* in the district; these were 'namesake' *ravi* who owed each other hospitality. Far more significant was the bond uniting *larava* whose *aiaimunu* shared the same river. All such *larava* (whether their names were the same or different) were believed to have a common ancestor. Williams termed them 'river clans' — in fact, they are dispersed patrilineal clans of which the *larava* were segments. One of the few attributes of these river clans Williams was able to discover were their sunset names: names of different shades of red supposedly characteristic of sunset above each of these rivers. These are likewise the names of the compass directions, each of which evidently belongs to one of the clans. Finally, these sunset names are the names of styles of face painting appropriate to each of the clans in question.

The river clans are divided into moieties which are exogamous and which, at least in Ukiravi village, occupy opposite sides of every *ravi*. These two sides have separate competitive or exchange roles in certain ceremonies. Each moiety has its own markings in face painting, and distinctive carved roof poles which project forward from the front of the *ravi*. Williams was careful to inquire whether moiety attachment could really be correlated with the place each *larava* occupied in its *ravi*. He found exceptions, but explained these by migration patterns: migrants tended to retain their own river names but to join the weaker faction in any new village they went to, whether this faction belonged to their moiety or not.[18] But Williams did not think this irregularity was basic. The important question for him was why the two sides of the cult house had become associated at all with the various other moiety symbols just mentioned:

Where we find a dual division in the Purari Delta it is not necessary to go to the beginning of things to explain it. It is rather the result of a habit of mind with the people; perhaps merely the outcome of a very deep-seated tendency—something resembling the spirit of competition. (1924:103).

Williams resumes the study of dual organisation in patrilineal societies in *Papuans of the Trans-Fly*. In this study of the tribes of the Morehead District, the clan system is basically similar to that of the Purari Delta. Williams was even more careful with local variations. He distinguishes between several levels of organisation:
(1) a local clan system, not integrated with larger social units and surviving in local totem groups (*yuvi, tuarar*);
(2) a system which divided some larger tribes such as the Keraki into three 'sections' — this system was being borrowed by surrounding tribes who were still basically organised according to the old system;
(3) a system of moieties, of which the local clan groups were segments — in order to reconstitute the three sections into moieties for purposes of marriage regulation, the two smaller sections were mostly opposed to the largest one.
    This study of dual organisation shows the lengths to which the Keraki went to force a dual organisation upon a situation which originally was not dualistic. Williams pointed out that the smallest of the sections was gradually being driven out of existence, in any case, by 'a social process which we may call the absorption of local section minorities'.
    The Keraki had a remarkable system of sister exchange which further added to Williams' store of data on dual organisation. He had already described sister exchange in his Orokaiva monograph, but for the Orokaiva this was just one mode of making a valid marriage contract. The same is true for the Koiari. The Orokaiva idealise sister exchange marriage, as being the most perfect form, and so, one presumes, do the Koiari. It is, however, impossible in practice to make this form genuinely universal, for obvious demographic reasons. Yet this is what the Keraki managed to do by the unusual device of sister purchase. If a boy did not have a sister he could exchange for a wife, his family bought him a sister, who lived with the family for a few years and was then exchanged for the boy's wife-to-be. As with all sister-exchange, the relation between the brothers-in-law was a close and valuable partnership. Obtaining

a wife by purchase or abduction or any other means was legally impossible. The system differed from the Purari Delta system in that in the latter first-degree cross-cousins were prohibited partners, whereas among the Keraki of course they had to be permitted for the sake of the logic of the system. Williams reports, however, that in practice marriage between true first-degree cross-cousins was very rare.

Williams recognised the theoretical importance of the system of sister purchase, which led him to one of his most interesting pieces of structuralist reasoning (1936: 166-9). Why is it necessary to buy a sister so that this sister can be given away? It seems, said Williams, that in order to marry, a man must be *in a position to make exchanges*. 'It is as if exchange was idealised, made an end in itself.'

Williams compared this procedure to food exchanges in the Morehead District, where most often the objects exchanged are identical and to the temporary exchange of wives at a feast, where the initiative is with the hosts who take pleasure in giving their women to the guests. He argued that all this is a way of cementing relations between groups.

This, then, is the suggested explanation of exogamy. The girls are *reserved for exchange*. If the first must be kept for this purpose, then it follows that they must not marry within the group...We may consider (exogamy) as a negative regulation: 'Thou shalt not marry in'; or as a positive: 'Thou shalt marry out' (which of course carries the negative in its train). In this thesis I have chosen to lay the stress on the positive side.

Although Williams had no difficulty in having this argument accepted as part of a thesis at the University of Oxford, it met with unfavourable treatment at the hands of Ian Hogbin (1936) when the thesis appeared in print. The exogamy theory was very interesting, suggested Hogbin, but not supported by empirical evidence. One wonders why Hogbin thought it necessary to make this criticism, for Williams does not suggest anywhere that his theory of exogamy is demonstrated, or even demonstrable, by empirical evidence. The procedure of sister purchase, as well as other aspects of Keraki exchange, are not easily explained by a functional theory, and indeed the same is true for dual organisation in general. All Williams did was to sketch a theory that might possibly account for such phenomena.

Though he did not discuss this theory again, we find signs in 'Natives of Lake Kutubu' that he continued to think about it. For in that ethnography we find a brief suggestion that there are two types of exogamy, namely those with positive marriage rules — such as in a moiety system[19] — and those which have only negative rules. The Delta and Morehead systems, as described by Williams, had positive rules, and the Kutubu only negative rules. The Orokaiva had two valid ways of making a marriage contract, one way that involved sister exchange (a positive rule), and another way (by purchase) for which there were only negative rules. Williams made a point of commenting that the theory of exogamy he proposed was equally applicable to both types of exogamy system, for both types of rule 'may in certain circumstances draw large groups into closer association'.

We note that Williams was sketching here a theory of marriage containing the two modalities known today as direct immediate exchange and complex exchange. Williams was also interested in systems of intermediate type which today we would call (elementary) generalised exchange, and especially in the modality known as patrilateral cross-cousin marriage. He described it in two forms, which we may describe here as 'general' and 'specialised'. In its general form,[20] Williams called it marriage exchange between 'reciprocating pairs of groups'. He noted it in the Morehead district and among the Elema; it was expressed in a rule that a woman should marry in the place where her mother was born. In a patrilineal, virilocal society this is effectively a patrilateral (classificatory) cross-cousin marriage rule. It is usual for a village to have a good number of partner villages with which the relationship of 'reciprocating pairs of groups' is maintained.

It is not infrequent to find, as among the Orokaiva (and, incidentally, the Koiari), that sister exchange occurs at the same time as the type of marriage I have just described. In that case, there are two possibilities for male egos (and of course female egos). When a girl returns to 'her mother's village', she marries her mother's brother's son, and the man marries his father's sister's daughter. Anthropology, being a male-dominated discipline, has called this patrilateral cross-cousin marriage, a term that will not long escape the attention of the Women's Liberation Movement.[21] However, under the provisions of sister exchange, the girl's brother would marry his mother's brother's daughter, i.e. he would marry a 'matrilateral cross-cousin'. There are thus two distinct preferential marriage rules, involving two categories of preferential partners. The ideal choice, for a man is thought to be sister exchange. In addition, under the rules of 'reciprocating pairs of groups', a man normally has a number of potential wives from debtor villages, among whom he may choose and upon whom he would have a claim. If he is adventurous, he may go further afield and set up a marriage link with a new village.

To the extent that the arrangement of 'reciprocating pairs of groups' operates without sister exchange, the brother and sister will have a different marital destination. It is this difference in marital destinations that gives rise to the special form of patrilateral cross-cousin marriage that intrigued Williams. Basically, this specialised form, which we may call the Koiari type of marriage, amounts to a strengthening of the bond between reciprocal pairs by institutional safeguards which reinforce the duty and the reward of a girl's return to her mother's village. Thus the Koiari affiliate the girl to the mother's clan, as Williams says, though this does not really make the system less basically patrilineal.

I am inclined to set aside Williams' speculation (Chapter 3 of this volume) that 'the idea of sex affiliation might be a very primitive one, preceding the idea of rigid descent in either one line or the other and the development of the clan system'. The rules of viri-locality, exogamy in the paternal line and several special rules reported by Williams make this extremely unlikely. In the Koiari case, we have merely an especially strong bilineal emphasis, expressed by the rule that a girl becomes heiress to her mother's land; but the basic patrilineal rule of inheritance prevails if she does not marry by the preferential rule that returns her to her mother's village upon marriage. Williams is careful to state that she is not affiliated to her mother's clan if the father's group desires her to marry uxorilocally. This implies a commitment that she and her husband will be given a sufficiency of land in her father's village.

Towards the end of his life, after some experts had questioned the accuracy of his report, Williams went to study the Keveri, where he expected to find another case of 'sex affiliation'. He was able to report (1944-5) that also among the Keveri 'males are affiliated to their father's group and females to the mother's' (ibid., p. 97). Unlike the Koiari, the Keveri had a rule forbidding a girl to marry into her mother's group.

But she is said still to belong to the latter group because she is primarily *at its disposal* in marriage. Marriage is preferably by exchange of girls (with purchase by native wealth as a substitute method); and it is maintained that the *wavae* or maternal uncle, properly has first claim. That is to say his right to exchange the girl on behalf of his son (i.e. her cross-cousin) takes precedence over the father's right to exchange her on behalf of *his* son (i.e. her brother)....The ideal method is for the girl to go and live under the guardianship of her maternal uncle and to be married "from his house" (1944-5: 98).

After marriage a man was expected to make periodic presents of pigs and garden produce to his wife's relatives—her parents, her *wavae* and her brothers; and these gifts were concomitant of every feast where pigs were slaughtered (ibid. : 99).

Unfortunately, Williams says nothing about the system of inheritance among the Keveri, but as the girl was forbidden to marry in her mother's village, she could not usefully inherit her mother's land. We find here again the key characteristic of patrilateral cross-cousin marriage, namely that the marital destination of brother and sister are radically different. It is this characteristic that sets it apart from moiety exogamy, as Williams clearly recognised. Furthermore, it is a mild device for widening the marriage universe, while at the same time providing much of the security and sentimental attachment of a moiety system. Williams' essay about the Koiari is important as a demonstration that one cannot reasonably, as some recent scholars have done, class patrilateral cross-cousin marriage under the general heading of direct exchange.

Williams' concept of sex affiliation is extremely useful as it is likely that traces of it can be found in many Papua New Guinean societies with patrilateral cross-cousin marriage. I have given an instance of such traces in my study of the Orokaiva. If Williams was wrong in supposing that such a system might precede, in an evolutionary sense, the development of unilineal systems, he was right in seeing that, by instituting that brother and sister have a different marital destination, the Koiari took a step of great potential importance for anthropological theory. It is certainly a crucial step away from a moiety system in which both brother and sister are bound to marry into the opposite moiety. The Koiari and Keveri systems make sense only as first hesitant steps towards generalised exchange. Without using the term patrilateral cross-cousin marriage, Williams contributed greatly to our understanding of this system by seeing, better than many subsequent students of this institution, what its essential features are; and his analysis supports the argument presented by Levi-Strauss, in *Les structures elementaires de la parenté*, where patrilateral cross-cousin marriage is treated as a modality of generalised exchange.[22]

4. *Disease as a Main Source of Intellectual Interest*
In the preceding sections of this introductory essay, we have seen in detail a number of instances of the kind of contributions for which F. E. Williams ought to be remembered, and in each instance we found the same kind of positive and negative characteristics: a raising of questions for which the theories of the time had no answers, always supported with data these theories could not explain: Williams' inability to develop an adequate general theory that might have solved them; the inability of later anthropologists to dispose fully of any of them. The 'magic of impersonation', for instance, is a phenomenon for which neither Turner's theory of

ritual (1969) nor Lévi-Strauss' method· of myth analysis fully provides. Adequate study of the 'magic of impersonation' (of which the *hevehe* mask ceremony is the supreme example) requires an analysis of aesthetic values, an 'ethno-aesthetics' which has so far been neglected by anthropologists. Williams' study of totemic phenomena opens up unfamiliar problems with regard to the classification of the 'logical operators' that are used to connect the social and 'natural' levels. In the present study I have kept to the familiar classification *metaphoric/metonymic*, but this is an oversimplification as the processes involved are numerous and very complex. Williams' inquiry into the meaning of the bull-roarer as a system of messages by all the actors involved, simple though its principle is, goes beyond most common practice in the study of ritual. Perhaps it would be wiser to follow Lévi-Strauss (1971) and call this kind of material 'implicit mythology'. In any case, it must include data on ritual secrecy and ritual falsehood, which somehow — like so many of Williams' interests — happens to be a neglected area in anthropology. Finally, with regard to sex affiliation, which may be regarded as the dynamic aspect of patrilateral cross-cousin marriage, we observe again that, even though Lévi-Strauss was impressed with Williams' concept, its possibilities have never been fully explored.

It is hard for any reader of Williams to believe that this flair for spotting difficult neglected areas is the product of an unstated master-theory. On the other hand, it is hard to believe in a series of pure accidents. The reader notices the question *'what does it mean?'* running as a steady refrain through most of Williams' work. The explanation he is seeking by this question goes beyond function or utility, beyond culture history, beyond the 'fictions' and 'fabrications' of the folk system. It also probably goes beyond semiotics and beyond structuralism. (I don't think Williams would feel that a structural analysis of the bull-roarer material would fully satisfy his kind of search.)

We might therefore assume that Williams' intellectual search— and no reader can doubt it was stubborn and unremitting—was deeply influenced by the intellectual preoccupations of his Papuan teachers. I fully agree with the drift of K. O. L. Burridge's recent book *Encountering Aborigines*, in which he argues that the history of anthropology is a history of questions asked by westerners and related to western intellectual preoccupations. One might well argue that even those anthropologists who collect folk-explanations and folk-philosophies are pursuing western preoccupations, inasmuch as they write up their findings in the context of western scientific debate. Williams, however, spent his twenty active years almost entirely in the field or near it. He communicated principally with

Australian administrators who, imperceptibly, were deeply influenced in their thought by the Papuan cultures around them. If there is one common factor in the special areas I listed earlier in this section of my essay, it is that each of these areas would, in my opinion, be of the deepest intellectual interest to Papuans. I am not referring to my own comments on these areas, in which I tried to relate them to familiar anthropological discourse, but to the way they were pondered by Williams himself.

In this sense the last of Williams' major works, 'Natives of Lake Kutubu', is perhaps the most Papuan of them all.[23] It is at the same time a masterly ethnographic presentation, which sums up many of the insights Williams gathered as he moved from one tribe to another, comparing, and developing his concepts with experience. At the same time it raises at least the usual number of awkward and unanswered anthropological questions. I shall give a few examples, very briefly, of ethnographic items, theoretical puzzles and Papuan presuppositions, all from this book.

(1) *Name taboos*. The author rejects all the usual reasons that are given to account for these taboos, on convincing evidence from Kutubu data. He concludes that we must forever remain as ignorant of these reasons 'as are the women who plug their ears and veil their faces'. The problem is not, of course, semiotic; as we know very well, a name taboo signifies a respect relationship. The problem is that we cannot say anything that applies to every one of these respect relationships except that they are marked by a name taboo. Anthropologists are beginning to become interested in that type of question,[24] largely under the influence of Wittgenstein. But the same question would preoccupy any philosophically-inclined Papuan.

(2) *Wrongs*. After summarising the types of wrong acts recognised in Kutubu society, Williams finds that any act by *alter* that *ego* regards as an affront is thereby defined as a wrong. This is not totally subjective as *ego*'s opinions are founded on a code and *ego*'s interpretation of that code is presumably rational, given *ego*'s position and interests. But the Kutubu have no way of ruling that *ego* is wrong in his definition of *alter*'s act as a wrong. What *alter* must pay for is essentially the injury to *ego*'s feelings. The claim is pressed by *ego*'s 'sympathy group', which normally accepts *ego*'s declaration of injury. The 'sympathy group' is something of an anthropological mystery. In the way that Williams explains it, it seems to be identifiable only when one such group is involved in conflict with another. Thus the sympathy group resembles the name taboo in that one can say nothing that is true for all members of such a group except that, in case of conflict, they side with *ego*.[25] Williams does not describe it as 'segmentary opposition', and all Papua New Guinea evidence

points to the fluidity of such groupings. Why do the members of such a group share each other's sufferings so readily? Universal explanations about 'bonding' will not do, as some characteristics, such as the 'sympathetic sanction' (see esp. *Orokaiva Society*), may be peculiar to Papua New Guinea. This again is a question no Papuan moral philosopher could ignore.

(3) *The Meaning of Ceremonies.* In many parts of Papua New Guinea we find drum dances, pig festivals, men's cults and magic of impersonation, but Kutubu are peculiar in that they put all such ceremonial exclusively in the service of the curing of disease. Thus curing rituals are far more elaborate than those Williams saw elsewhere, whereas Kutubu ceremonial life was otherwise austere. How do we account for these special preoccupations of the Kutubu; and how do we explain the great variability in the 'function' and 'meaning' of the ubiquitous Papuan forms of grand ceremonial? Williams dismisses the idea that the Kutubu obsession with curing rituals might be due to demographic factors, as he did not find an unusually high incidence of morbidity. He notes only that for Kutubu 'disease is a main source of intellectual interest'.

He seems to suggest that such an 'intellectual interest' would suffice to enlist drum dances, pig festivals, etc., in the exclusive service of healing rituals. Although he does not explore the theoretical implications of this view, it is highly interesting that Williams assigns no meaning to these rituals *in themselves* but only in the context of a cognitive system.[26]

A significant indication of Williams' deepening involvement with Papuan thought is that his presentation of this system is confined to a collection of Kutubu tales and myths (Part V of the monograph) which indeed explain, as clearly as any Kutubu could do so, why and how disease became a main source of intellectual interest. Williams had collected myths in all the places where he did fieldwork, but never allowed them, to the same extent, to speak for themselves. He obviously realised, and was able to communicate, their literary excellence. He also seems to imply that Kutubu curing rites have no 'meaning' beyond what is said in the myths. The search for 'meaning' is thus placed outside the scientific sphere for much the same reasons as are given by Sperber.[27]

It would be impossible and inappropriate to call attention in this essay to all the excellences of 'Natives of Lake Kutubu', but two of its analyses are worthy of special mention. In the analysis of the *usi* ritual (treatment of sago sickness) Williams recounts that, according to informants, the cure was not really due to the dramatic performance of extracting the hostile spirits—which he witnessed—but to the gifts of pig meat, by which the disaffected guests were reconciled to their hosts. But if this were so, what then was the meaning of the extractive treatment? In other words: what was the bridging mechanism between the magico-religious and social levels of action? Williams' answer was: when the pig was killed, its blood was poured over the stones used for the extractive treatment: hence the ritual of social reconciliation became a prerequisite of the reenactment of the *usi* myth, by which the cure was supposed to be effected. It seems a small point, but it is by attention to such questions that Williams must be regarded as a master in the reconstruction of traditional Papuan reasoning.

I would also mention Williams' exemplary interpretation of the arrowhead cult, in which he established that the mythological hero of the cult did not reside in the arrowhead, as most people would have carelessly supposed, but in an apparently unimportant object, a *kawa* stalk, of which the only overt significance is that members of the cult bite it during the ceremony. But this was the plant that grew out of the hero's grave, and thus the species (extremely rare in the district, and utterly lacking in utility) into which he became metamorphosed.

Williams made two interesting observations. The first was that the *kawa* plant is of high sacral importance in parts of Melanesia where it is prevalent and used for the making of beer, etc., and that the Kutubu revere and bite it in total ignorance of its biochemical properties—a case where meaning has become totally divorced from function, just like mushroom cults in areas where the mushrooms are not hallucigenic but are symbolically treated as though they were.[28]

The second observation is that the cult used two kinds of symbol. One was the sacred species of the cult hero and therefore logically necessary for the transmission of the hero's power; and the other was a kind of general symbol, like the arrowhead, which signified that the cult was performed with the object of success in hunting. Another general cult symbol was the axe, signifying the further object of success in manual labour. The distinction between such types of symbol is useful in the analysis of the 'language' of ritual.

These few examples illustrate the elusiveness of the merits of Williams' mature ethnographies. Often one cannot say more about them than that they are models of ethnographic and analytical skill, showing an uncommon knowledge of the mode of reasoning of the tribe under study. It is easier to learn from such work than to generalise about it. I have shown that such very close familiarity does not only produce 'good ethnography' but also raises some of the most refractory theoretical questions. The special merit of the questions raised by this process of dialogue with Papuan thinkers rather than western academics is that they are immediately relevant to Papuan thought and to the cultural traditions of Papua New Guinea. There is no reason why anthropology should continue, as Burridge has aptly shown it has done in the past, to pursue only those questions which arise out of basic contradictions in western cultures. There are other questions, equally universal, but for which we must depend on Papuan teachers if we wish to understand them. Williams' questions are often of this kind.

5. *Love and the Aeroplane*

I have not so far troubled to comment on deficiencies in Williams' work, but have been concerned mainly to draw attention to what is still relevant, leaving to the reader the relatively simple task of ignoring what is outdated. This procedure would not be appropriate in dealing with the two papers on the Vailala millennial movement, as Williams shared the attitudes of the Australian administration which detested all such movements, and unless I express dissent, it might be assumed that I agree with such attitudes.

There is much in these essays (Chapters V and VI) that I find objectionable. The practical measures Williams recommends for dealing with the cult were too unpleasant even for the Lieutenant-Governor to accept. The charges of charlatanism Williams makes against the cult leaders conflict strangely with his own far more enlightened writings on Papuan magic—he recognised very well the role which pretence (by officiants and audience) plays in such rituals. In one case where he imputes charlatanism, the Papuans discovered and punished it. In another case, the reenactment of the resurrection of Jesus, it is hard to see where the imposture lies. How did Williams expect the Elema to interpret the resurrection? They believed in it, but in the same way as they believed in other magic. They tried to reenact it in the way they were used to reenacting miracles. Did Williams think the Elema should have believed the resurrection *literally*?

It is also unfortunate that in his analysis of ritual, Williams keeps on using absurd, even semi-literate terms such as *automaniac*. The cult leaders, in a state of divine or spirit possession, made involuntary movements which communicated themselves to their audience. In Williams' day this phenomenon was known as 'automatism', applying to the involuntary movement not only of persons but also of objects, as in spiritualistic seances or in divinatory rites very well described in some of Williams' other works. The noun *automaniac* is incorrectly formed from *automatism*.

Why, in spite of such irritating flaws, should we still reprint these two essays? First, they are indispensable as primary documents.

There are hardly any accounts of millennial cults actually in progress, written by observers of Williams' quality. Secondly, Williams' deep knowledge of the Elema enabled him to understand aspects of their millennial cult which eluded the great majority of the theorists who wrote about such movements afterwards.

Insofar as Williams had a theory about the movement, it was functionalist. He rightly compared it with the traditional ceremonial life of the Elema, drawing especially on the villages Karama and Koaru, which were giving up the movement and returning to traditional ceremonies at the time of Williams' first fieldwork. Thus he related the mortuary feasts, which seemed to him the 'really fundamental fact' about the movement, to the *sevese* ceremony which at Karama and Koaru happened also to be a mortuary rite (the parallel would not have fitted Orokolo). One might regard the *ahea uvi* of the cult as a counterpart of Elema men's houses, the 'automaniacs' as a counterpart of masked dances, while the flagpoles resembled some elaborate traditional divination devices. The rules of conduct demanded of cultists resembled those of traditional initiation in the manner in which they were enunciated, and largely in content. Such evidence indicated that the Vailala madness was a replacement of the traditional ceremonies the whites were suppressing without providing a satisfactory substitute. The Lieutenant-Governor, commenting on Williams' paper, did not like this conclusion, even though based on the latest in the 'science of anthropology'. He thought Christianity was a satisfactory substitute.[29]

Williams was unaware of the political dimensions of the Vailala movement and attached little importance to the economic dimension. He did not see that it called into question the colonial relationships then prevailing, nor did Williams himself ever question their basic beneficence. If he advanced significantly beyond a functionalist view of the Vailala movement, it was in a direction somewhat similar to Burridge.[30] It was the general atmosphere of dream and revelation that impressed him—like Burridge—most deeply, especially in the later of the two essays. While the strange happenings of the movement resemble those the Elema traditionally experience after a death, the portents are of European origin—the spirits wear boots and appear as European dogs or torches. It is a time of miracles, resembling what Burridge describes as a time of myth-dream. Williams' description of this situation is especially vivid, as he was there when it happened.

Williams believed, like Burridge, that the core of such a movement consists of a myth which provides a kind of cognitive model for the movement. On the nature of this cognitive base Williams' analysis follows a direction somewhat different from Burridge's, and in my view it is perhaps more interesting. Burridge presents as the basic myth of the Mambu cults and old tale about sibling rivalry which was reinterpreted and modified slightly to provide an ideology of equivalence. Burridge shows with classic skill that this ideology informed the activities of a succession of cults. Williams, in contrast, describes his visit to the leader of the movement who had allegedly received secret papers from heaven. The leader denied the story, but showed Williams two documents: a novel called *Love and the Aeroplane* with a vivid cover, and a Lifebuoy soap advertisement depicting a field hospital. Williams suggested in his first report that these two documents—one may call them graphic or visual myths— represented 'the origin of the Vailala madness', in other words, the equivalent of Burridge's 'primal myth' in *Mambu*. In his second report (Chapter VI of this book), Williams' belief in the key role of these documents was confirmed in the light of many new facts.

In this Vailala case, the leader did indeed receive messages, no matter by what means they came, and his revelation took the form of a decoding of these messages. In their decoded form, the messages became the rationale for the movement's teachings and cult acti- vities. Even though Williams was hardly able to obtain a full record of the leader's act of decoding, he obtained enough to show that it involved an assumption that every detail in the two pictures had significance and constituted part of the message. Scattered through- out Williams' two papers are numerous instances of details of the pictures that were thus utilised. The essential point to retain is that these pictures were of European origin and had no meaning at all to the Elema until the leader revealed it.

In contrast, Burridge's basic myth was well-known in his district before the movement started; it was only the new meaning and some light changes of detail that were revealed. While for the Elema the mystery lay in the nature of the Europeans, and the aim was magically to impersonate them, for Mambu the problem was to set up a relation of equivalence with them. The key part of the sacral text was the supposed dialogue between the two brothers which stated the equivalence ideology.

Basically the difference between Williams' and Burridge's data is a difference of about one generation. While the Elema of Williams' day were still producing myth and gave to the two graphic docu- ments the highly specific logic of myth, Burridge's prophet was basically not a myth-maker but an ideological user of myth. Most of what the brothers did was of no interest to him; the other characters in the older versions fade into the background; only the dialogue between the brothers and the notion of cargo remain. Burridge managed splendidly with the data he could get, but by the time he reached the field, the real age of myth in Melanesia was passing away: his 'basic myth' is on the verge of turning into modern ideology.

The point of this comparison is to throw into relief the anthropological importance of Williams' material, marred though his report was by administrative prejudice. He had the merit of getting to the core of the problem of Melanesian millennial movements at a time when the Papuans were still creating real myths and when anthropologists generally understood this aspect of culture too little to know how to collect the relevant data.

This long essay has been little more than a journey through the works of F. E. Williams; on the way, like a tourist guide, I have pointed out what I thought worth looking at. At no point have I claimed that he provided us with a coherent theory, and in his 'Creed', which makes up the final chapter of this book, we shall not find it. Williams did not basically question the Christian faith, the capitalist system or the justice of Australia's control of New Guinea. His attack on functionalism was remarkably forceful and well-directed for that time. He attacked the Australian administration, equally forcefully, because he regarded it as incompatible 'with the principle of freedom to set about deliberately working for conformity' between the values of Papua New Guinea and white Australia.

In spite of these challenges, Professor Elkin (in the obituary essay referred to above, footnote 3) was right in calling Williams a 'modified functionalist' in the sense that when Williams could not provide a functionalist explanation for his data, he did not relate them to any other systematic body of theory. He never ceased to rely to some extent on his early influences in anthropology, such as Marett, Haddon and McDougall. When, in his mature years, he looked about for a new theoretical framework, it was indeed modifications of functionalism rather than alternatives that he was looking for.

As an indication of the framework he sought, Williams put forward two analogies—the rubbish heap and the 'tooglies' (cf. Chapter 7 of this volume). One may ask: how does Williams give theoretical significance to the many orderly cognitive patterns which, after great toil, his own ethnographic analysis established? The answer is that he did not fully appreciate their theoretical significance himself.

In his first analogy the rubbish heap contains the whole of culture; yet he is careful to point out that he regards culture not as devoid of system but as being only partly a system. Partly what sort of system?

Williams comes closest to presenting true 'systems' in his short
papers (the ones reprinted in this volume; 'Plant Emblems Among
the Orokaiva', 'Rainmaking on the River Morehead') and in the
last two monographs, *Drama of Orokolo* and 'Natives of Lake Kutubu'.
These systems are never of a 'whole culture' but are of particular
complexes which caught his special attention because of the logical
system he discerned in them. Broadly, they are systems not only in a
functionalist sense but also in a structuralist sense—i.e. they are
coherent in logic as well as in their fields of action. In *Drama of
Orokolo*, Williams seems to be mainly concerned with structure in a
syntagmatic sense: a passage in the ritual cycle is classified as not
'part of the system' if for historical reasons Williams believes that
the passage could be omitted without making it impossible for the
producers and actors to complete their cycle. Williams feels that if
one can do without a certain passage, it is not an integral part of the
system but an 'accretion'. In 'Natives of Lake Kutubu' he is more
concerned with the paradigmatic aspect of systems, e.g. the intellectual activity which produced the highly elaborate healing rituals.
Hence, any elaboration that could be historically regarded as an
accretion would still, from Williams' viewpoint, be regarded as an
integral part of the system as it would be a product of the same
intellectual activity.

Nonetheless, Williams preferred to think of culture as a rubbish
heap—a disorderly heap of material brought together by historical
accident—and of system or order as something that might take
place here and there in that heap. In his second analogy, the
'*tooglies*' do not constitute the whole contents of a house, but only
part of them, and the 'superfluous part' at that. They are kept because
they 'might come in handy some day'—they are 'survivals'. Unlike
the functionalists, Williams acknowledges their existence as part of
culture, but only as a residual category in an otherwise functional
model of the universe.

He never comes close to suggesting that such '*tooglies*' might be
the basic building blocks of cultural systems, as Levi-Strauss did
later in his concept of *bricolage*[31]. Such a presupposition may at
times be implicit in Williams' analyses, especially in 'Natives of
Lake Kutubu', but they are not in his theoretical discussions.

If we survey the theoretical issues raised by Williams and examined in the present essay, we note that some of them have indeed
become part of 'structuralist' anthropology, e.g. his interest in the
logic of totemism, in total message systems, in exchange and
exogamy, in patrilateral cross-cousin marriage, in ritual symbols,
and in the unravelling of the hidden structural opposition between
sea and bush in *Drama of Orokolo*.

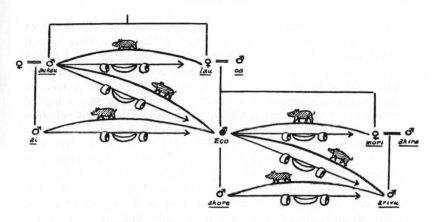

Diagram showing Circulation of Shell Ornaments and Return Presents of Pig. (F. E. Williams, *Drama of Orokolo*, p. 6.)

Williams' explorations in ethno-aesthetics (in *Drama of Orokolo*) and in decoding the graphic myths used by cargo cult leaders have an affinity with structuralism, as it is developing at the present time, and with kindred approaches[32]. Unfortunately not many anthropologists are able to combine a detailed interest in aesthetic expression with an adequate grasp of cultural context; and it is only recently that we have acquired theoretical understanding of the logic and strategy of the use of symbolism which make an aesthetic anthropology possible. Certainly, Williams will need to be studied as a pioneer in this field.

Some of his preoccupations, however, lie within the purview not of the structural traditions but rather of the Wittgensteinian school (the discussions on meaning, on name taboos, etc.) or of psychological anthropology (the discussions on bonding, and on the sympathetic sanction). I have already suggested that if we wish to see a system in all these apparently divergent preoccupations, it lies not in some academic school of western anthropology but in Papuan philosophy itself, as this was to an appreciable extent the university in which Williams' mature thought was formed. As such his work ought to prove inspiring to Papuans and New Guineans who choose anthropology as their academic discipline, and who wish to build on the tradition of their own thinkers in formulating and analysing anthropological problems. I hope to have shown that such problems, far from being incarcerated in a 'folk-system' and thus lacking objectivity, have a direct relevance to the anthropological theory now being developed in the rest of the world.

Prof. Elkin, in his obituary essay, mentions two memorable aspects of Williams' role in anthropology: first, as a 'laboratory specialist who spent many years in a laboratory of Papuan societies, in which he continually increased his efficiency; and secondly he quotes a remark Williams made on his work on *hevehe* masks: 'My main object has been to do it justice in description in the hope that the reader will come to admire it.'

Dr. Elkin evidently did not think there was a contradiction between these two preoccupations. I agree with him, but we may well ask what kind of laboratory it was that yielded expressions of appreciation of the arts as one of its chief products. This is a question which we cannot answer, but can perhaps illustrate from an analogy, taken from Williams' work:

Plagued by a regular alternation of heavy floods and a parched dry season, the Morehead tribes highly valued their rain-making magicians. They had elaborate secret laboratories, which were visited and minutely described by Williams (1929). Here the rain-maker used his paraphernalia to imitate the rain, the clouds, the thunder. He uttered spells invoking the principal deities of Morehead mythology. The rainmaker's laboratory is a kind of microcosm, representing the whole of creation, as wrought by the Originator Kambel. It thus, as Williams says, takes on a definitely religious character. The rain-maker believes that magic is being made simultaneously in his laboratory and, as the result of his appeal, by the moon-god Sikara Wambuwambu, Kambel's son, in heaven.

Undoubtedly Williams was a meticulous scientist, who helped to lay the foundations of Papuan ethnography. But in addition he was—and should be highly valued as—a rain-maker.

REFERENCES

1. I wish to thank the Canada Council for supporting my research with a leave fellowship and the library of the Royal Anthropological Society in London which provided bibliographical guidance.
2. *Orokaiva Magic*, 1928; *Orokaiva Society*, 1930; *Papuans of the Trans-Fly*, 1936; *Drama of Orokolo*, 1940. All four were reprinted in 1969. Full references are given in the bibliography at the end of the book.
3. 'F. E. Williams—Government Anthropologist, Papua', in *Oceania* XIV: 91-103 (1943).
4. See pages 45-47 below.
4a. This is: Territory of Papua, *Anthropology Report*, No. 8, included in the collection published as *Orokaiva Magic*, 1928.
5. Totoima wore detachable pigs' tusks when hunting. Williams records some myths about him in *Orokaiva Society*. The present author has analysed this figure in detail (Schwimmer 1973-1974 a and b).

Totoima is a great culture hero of both the Orokaiva and Binandere tribes.

6. In its final, celebrated form, this theory was stated in *The Golden Boughs* 3rd edition (1915), Vol. 11, pp. 304 foll.

7. F. de Saussure, *Cours de linguistique generale*, 1916

8. See esp. Schwimmer 1973, Chapter 7.

9. See this volume, P.

10. 'Rain-making on the River Morehead', 1929. The mythological and ritual information given in this important paper was greatly revised and strengthened with new field information, and included in *Papuans of the Trans-Fly*, Chapters XVI and XVII. Regrettably, the description of the laboratories was dropped. The relationship between the rites and the myths never became completely clear.

11. For Elema, see *Drama of Orokolo*; for Morehead, see *Papuans of the Trans-Fly;* for Orokaiva, see *Orokaiva Society* and Schwimmer 1973, Chapter 10, and 1975; for Purari, see 'Natives of the Purari Delta' (Williams, 1924); for Kutubu and Koiari, see Chapters III and IV of this volume.

12. Williams had much trouble finding a name for such groupings (viz. 1940:42), but surely they are clans. Perhaps we should distinguish between socio-political clans ('Type I) and totemic clans (Type II). The names of the clans are given on p. 72, footnote 17.

13. While the member of an *aualari* has a choice of many heroes he may impersonate, in totemism of the Orokaiva type, the individual has only a limited number of plant emblem-ancestors. No genealogical connections between individual and ancestor are ever traced. Orokaiva establish distant kin relationships by plant emblem rather than genealogy. For Orokaiva see Williams 1925 and 1930, Schwimmer 1973; for Kutubu and Koiari see the present volume, Chapters 2 and 3.

14. The argument is developed in *Le totémisme aujourd'hui*.

15. I refer in particular to Durkheim's interpretation of the *churinga* in *Les formes elementaires de la vie religieuse*, and to Lévi-Strauss' comments in *La pensée sauvage*.

16. The most famous system where two types of valuables are exchanged in this manner is the Trobriand kula system (Malinowski 1920, 1922) where in any partnership A—B, A always receives one type of valuable from B and always gives the other type of valuable in return. Over the whole of the *kula* ring, this results in the arm bands always travelling in one direction and the necklaces in the other. In terms of marriage exchange, such a system would be equivalent to generalised exchange. Unlike *kula* exchange, the Elema system limits such generalised exchange of valuables to two generations, after which a gift in the opposite direction terminates the relationship. As for the symbolism of the bull-roarer cult, it is tempting to see the bull-roarer as a feminine and the snake-crocodile as a male sex symbol, as the myths seem to suggest. A proper analysis, however, would be much more complex.

17. See Pouwer 1965 for the concept of structuring principles and their use in comparison of Papua New Guinea societies; Strathern and

Strathern 1969 for an excellent comparative model of Highlands marriage systems; and a paper by Rosman and Rubel, still unpublished, comparing the forms of dual organisation in different Papua New Guinean societies, and relating this type of system to a second type which has only negative marriage rules and therefore a complex form of marriage.

18. This kind of analysis of Papua New Guinean societies, in which it is held that migration is a continual process and a key factor in determining community structure, was developed into a general theory by Watson in his paper on society as organised flow (1970). Williams provides another instance in *Papuans of the Trans-Fly*.

19. In *Papuans of the Trans-Fly*, Williams attempts to account for the wide-ranging moiety system of that district by processes such as migration and extension. It is hard to see how Williams' general theory of exogamy can be reconciled with any extensionist hypothesis (cf. Buchler and Selby 1967.)

20. Several descriptions of the general form have appeared in the last few years, especially in relation to Highlands societies. The Maring (cf. Rappaport 1967 : 129) refer to the system as 'returning the planting material. Variants of it are found among the Manga, the Daribi, the Iatmul, the Chimbu (Glasse and Meggitt 1969). Though Williams did not note it among the Orokaiva, I found very clear evidence of it in my restudy (Schwimmer 1973).

21. A footnote to 'Sex Affiliation' records that Brenda Seligman, who read the paper before publication (1932), spoke a word of protest about Williams' predilection for the male ego and was offered a gallant red herring which sufficed for those days.

22. See the discussions on patrilateral cross-cousin marriage and on complex systems in Melanesia, in the second edition (1967). The Koiari case is discussed on pp. 534-5.

23. Reprinted in its entirety as Chapter 4 of the present volume. It appeared previously in *Oceania* (1940-2) and as Oceania Monograph No. 6.

24. See Needham 1971, Sperber 1974.

25. Discussions on this topic occur in *Orokaiva Society*, *Papuans of the Trans-Fly*, as well as in 'Natives of Lake Kutubu'. Williams also summed up his theory in 'Group Sentiment and Primitive Justice' (*American Anthropologist* (1940), vol. 43, pp. 523-39). This article appears, in abridged form, in 'Natives of Lake Kutubu'.

26. Several recent studies in the anthropology of art (e.g. by Forge and Newton) have shown to what extent New Guineans will borrow designs from other New Guinean cultures, retaining the form but changing the meaning. Williams found that this happened also with rituals. It thus becomes impossible to tell, from the form of rituals like pig festivals, what their meaning might be.

27. In *Le symbolisme en général*, Sperber reduces the semiotic aspect of culture to ideology or strategy, used in the pursuit of ulterior purposes, especially for coping with basic contradictions in the culture. I imagine that

Sperber depends on structural analysis in discovering just what are the basic contradictions expressed in a text, but he regards the stating of such contradictions—by a member of the culture or by an observers as an ideological act. Sperber's view of meaning appears influenced by Wittgenstein.

28. On mushrooms, see C. Lévi-Strauss, *Anthropologie Structurale Deux*, Chapter XII.

29. See J. H. P. (Sir Hubert) Murray, 'Comments', printed as a prefatory note to 'The Vailala Madness and the Destruction of Native Ceremonies in the Gulf Division', Territory of Papua, Anthropology Report No. 4 (1923).

30. See K. O. L. Burridge, *Mambu: a Melanesian Millennium*, 1960; *New Heaven, New Earth*, 1969; *Tangu Traditions* 1969.

31. In *La pensée sauvage*, 1962.

32. See recent work by Forge and Munn; Schwimmer 1974 Cf. also Oppitz's paper (1974) on the graphic myth of Shangri-la.

PART II

I

TRADING VOYAGES FROM THE GULF OF PAPUA[1]

Growth of the Bevaia Trade

The Lakatoi

Readers of the *Melanesians of British New Guinea* will be familiar with the *lakatoi*. Their expedition, or *hiri*, which Captain Barton described in a chapter of Dr. Seligmann's book,[2] is the most important event in the social life of the Motu, and one is glad to say that each year sees its repetition. The Motu live in what is known as the "dry belt" of Papua. It is a hard country with scanty rainfall. But the women are potters, and the men are sailors; and each year the *lakatoi* set forth on a voyage of some two hundred miles, bearing a cargo of pots which are to be traded for sago. The outward voyage takes place usually in September, at the end of the south-east trade wind season. The return should be made towards the end of the north-west monsoon season, *i.e.* before April, when the *lakatoi*, greatly enlarged by the addition of new dugouts, bring home many tons of sago to tide over the period of scarcity.

The *lakatoi*, a unique vessel, which is really a large raft of dugout canoes, and which carries the famous crab-claw sail, has been fully described in Captain Barton's chapter. There also will be found an account of the organization among the principals, the stages of construction, the sailing, the sojourn in the west, and finally the return, together with the attendant magical and ceremonial usages. I do not propose to spend time over these; readers must refer to the original source if they wish to make a detailed comparison with the subject of the present paper.

This subject is the trading voyages in the contrary direction, from west to east; and I shall confine myself mainly to the trade from the western end of the Gulf Division, between Kerema and the River Aivei. Most of my information comes from Orokolo, Arihava and Vailala, *i.e.* from the villages of the so-called Elema people.

The first part of the paper will deal with the rise and development of this trade, as illustrating the voluntary adoption of an important custom from a neighbouring people. The second and third parts

48

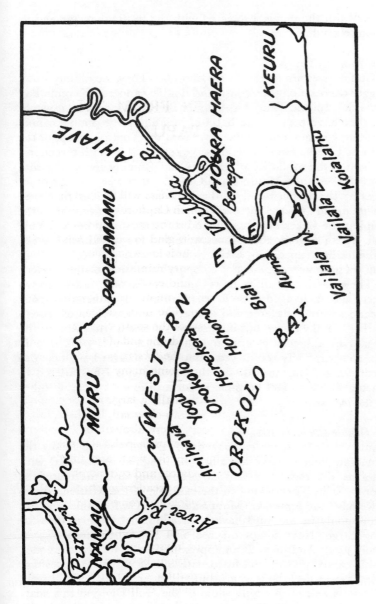

Map showing Territory of Western Elema and Adjacent Tribes.
Scale: 1 in.=4 miles. (F. E. Williams, *Drama of Orokolo*, P. 2.)

will deal with the magic associated with the trading voyage and its relation to myth.

Early Trading Voyages

The Gulf natives are no sailors by tradition. They use mainly small outrigger canoes along the coast, and double canoes in Kerema Bay and the delta of the Tauri-Lakekamu.[3] But from long ago, it would seem, they have been in the habit of building large double canoes for trading voyages along the coast. From the Toaripi group, at the eastern end of the Gulf coast, these vessels plied in both directions, and there is the authority of Holmes and Romilly for saying that they used to visit the Motu.[4] From Orokolo, however, and the other villages at the western end of the Gulf coast, it seems that they travelled mainly toward the east: they commonly went as far as the Toaripi at the Lakekamu mouth, and sometimes even beyond Yule Island. These large double canoes were and are called *haruka-iroki*, and the trading expedition, *hahi*.

The trade, however, was not comparable to that of the modern *hiri*. They carried mainly bows and arrows and native-grown tobacco, and exchanged these for shell ornaments rather than pots. The canoes were built large and strong, not with the idea of accommodating a bulky cargo, but in order to withstand what was for the Gulf natives a specially long and dangerous journey. It is only within comparatively recent years that these natives have taken to exporting sago, and accordingly the trading vessel has altered in character. It has in fact become, under a different name, no other than the *lakatoi*.

From Double Canoe to Bevaia

It is interesting from the technological point of view to follow the intermediate changes. We have first the original *haruka-iroki*, with paddles as the regular means of propulsion, and mats used as temporary sails. Then owing to the example of the Mission whale-boat we have the *para-iroki* (Motu *bala*=oar). Craft of this kind are still commonly in use, and have been adopted by the traders for loading cargo. Next comes the use of a permanent mast (*auvia*) and sail (*yara*). And then, as an approximation to the *lakatoi* model, a double canoe, masted and fitted with bulwarks, *piri* (Motu *biri*= nipa leaf), and deck houses, *uvi*, but still adapted for oars as well. I saw two vessels of this type while in the Gulf Division this year. Finally, we come to the out-and-out *lakatoi*, or what is technically a pretty exact copy of it.

This imitation *lakatoi* is called *bevaia*. I do not know what the word signifies, but it is the traditional name for the vessels which the Gulf natives used to sight every year when the Motu, or as they were called, the Derai-Haera, arrived about September. It is often smaller: I saw none with more than three dugouts, whereas the Motuan *lakatoi* often sail with four or five[5]; and in many cases as yet it is not so well put together. The names of the parts differ, the Gulf natives apparently retaining many of those that they formerly used in the construction of their own *haruka-iroki*; but the *lakatoi* pattern is followed very closely, even to the ornamental finish of the cane lashings.

There are, however, some significant differences in the preparations for and conduct of the expedition. I cannot find that there is any ceremonious manner of making public a man's intention of organizing an expedition and securing collaborators; nor is there any organization to compare with that of *baditauna, doritauna, udiha,* "mast captain" and "sail captain," such as we see on the Motu *lakatoi.* The spectacular trials in which the village girls dance on the fore platforms of the Motu *lakatoi* are not seen in the Gulf *bevaia*; but on the other hand married women, who are not permitted on the *lakatoi*, often travel as passengers. The magic, which will be our main concern here, is in some respects similar, or superficially so; but it is expressly denied that the *bevaia* magic, or *maho*, is derived from Motuan sources; indeed informants have said that they would be afraid to dabble with foreign magic. It is probably true that in all essentials the magic used for the fully-fledged *bevaia* is the same as the early voyagers used for the *haruka-iroki*.

Recent Expansion

Within the last few years there has been a rapid expansion of *bevaia* enterprise at the western end of the Gulf coast. The large village of Vailala, situated at the mouth of the Vailala River, claims to have been making *bevaia* for the last ten years and more, but I doubt whether they have ever previously reached the pitch of enthusiasm which has caused them in this last season (i.e., the end of 1931 and the beginning of 1932) to send out twelve *bevaia* and one large *haruka-iroki*. Beyond Vailala the first experiments were made only in the previous season, 1930-31, when three were equipped. But during last season, while I was in the neighbourhood, three were fitted out at Orokolo and four at the neighbouring village of Arihava.

The season the native himself gives for adopting the *lakatoi* model is that it saves time and labour. It is in fact questionable whether it does either, since he takes such an unconscionable time in the building of his *bevaia*. What he means is that, once away, he does not have to labour at the oar or the paddle. He can sit back and watch the wind do all the work.

It is not surprising that despite proverbial conservatism he should come to copy technical improvements when he sees examples so constantly before him; what does surprise, perhaps, is that he should have hesitated so long, and that having once made up his mind to build *bevaia* he should have begun building them with such a rush. There are two fairly obvious reasons. One is that of the tax. This may drive him afield to seek money, and it should be noted that the purpose of the *hahi* expedition is not so much to collect pots (the *lakatoi* from the east bring enough of them) as to seek shell ornaments, trade goods and money. The other reason is found in the after effects of the Vailala Madness, that startling religious movement which, temporarily in some parts, and (it may be) permanently in others, involved the destruction of the ceremonies.[6] This reason applies especially to Vailala itself, which remains strangely obdurate against a revival of the old customs, though the surrounding villages have been gradually taking them up again. A number of informants at Vailala spoke with enthusiasm of the present state of affairs. Formerly they were always busy in preparation for some ceremony or festival; now they have ample time for enterprises of a more profitable nature—at least commercially. As one man literally put it, it was their "one thought" nowadays to make money. Others did not lay so much stress on the money as on the actual *bevaia*. Previously they were *peraia*, "glad" with *hevehe*, *kovave*, and so on (*i.e.* the really fine mask ceremonies of the Gulf); now they were *peraia* with their *bevaia*. And it is a truly surprising thing to see this thriving village continually at work in shaping the enormous dugouts, in lashing them together, in building the superstructures, and in rigging the masts, all with meticulous attention to detail, or engaged in the making of sago, collecting betel, or the manufacture of dyed sago-leaf skirts for cargo. Nowadays, indeed, Vailala is more a port of native trade than any Motu village. Its inhabitants have discovered, unassisted, a substitute for the interest of the old ceremonies: they are quite mad on *bevaia*.

Setbacks and their Causes
But as we have observed the Gulf natives have no real tradition of seamanship. They are still learning the trade; and so far they are making heavy work of it. Their frequent failures have been due in part to ill construction. Whereas the Motu have had generations of practice, the Gulf natives are new to the game. Not infrequently one may see the Motu visitors helping in or even supervising the construction of a *bevaia*; but the independent product may lack the finish in lashing and caulking which in such a craft is essential to seaworthiness. A second cause of ill-success is sheer overloading. Even the experienced Motu sailors are sometimes guilty of this

mistake; but among the local experimenters it seems almost invariable. One after another of those *bevaia* that I saw settled down at its moorings after the loading; some did so more than once. And when it appears loaded to the very limit an enthusiastic and too numerous crew swarms aboard, completely regardless of human avoirdupois. One party deliberately left behind their stone anchor; they actually sailed anchorless rather than jettison a few bundles of sago or expel any of a crew of thirtysix. A third and more potent reason is that of delaying the start overlong. By April the winds are uncertain, and a south-east wind may spring up. But again and again, despite a full recognition of the danger, native dilatoriness has been responsible for disaster.

Even if it sails in good time, however, when the weather is usually calm, the *bevaia* may be overtaken by the tremendous northwest squalls that sometimes descend by night. Altogether the expedition is attended by many risks; and these combined with the sheer inexperience of the sailors have brought about a regular train of disasters, so that we may well be astonished at the perseverance of this new school of merchant adventurers. Vailala has apparently gained its experience. Of the seven *bevaia* that had sailed from Vailala before April last season, only two came to grief: one of them was wrecked on the Vailala bar; of the other the crew and passengers were rescued at night by the Government yacht in a gale off Port Moresby, the *bevaia* being abandoned. But of the seven which were fitted out at so much pains in Orokolo and Arihava only one got away successfully, and I cannot say whether she ever completed her voyage; three sank at their moorings and never sailed; two were driven ashore and broken, and the seventh was abandoned at sea on the very day of her sailing.

Bevaia Magic

The Sea Hevehe

Over and above the natural terrors of the sea there is one which is definitely regarded by the native as personal and, one may say, supernatural. It is that of the sea *hevehe*.[7] Here we reach an important religious belief, to which in the present paper I can only refer briefly. As against the *apa hevehe* or drum *hevehe* which appears in the magnificent mask ceremony, and the *be'ure hevehe*[8], *i.e.* ground *hevehe* or bull-roarers, there are the *ma hevehe* or sea *hevehe*. They are sometimes called *hevehe-havahu* or real *hevehe* because they enter into the complex of the drum *hevehe* ceremony, the latter being of course only masks or representations, whereas the former are supposed really to exist in the sea. They are identified usually with enormous fishes; not species, but individuals of limited number. Some few are identified with submerged rocks, floating logs, and so on. They have personal names and haunt different parts of the coast or the rivers. They are sometimes alleged to be seen near or above the surface, and it is said that they may rise to drag down a canoe. Many canoes and even cutters have been destroyed in this way on the Aivei bar.

The last of the previous mentioned losses is worth pausing over in this connection. After long preparations the *bevaia*, of which two men, Arepe and Tahia, were the *bevaia haera*, or principals, made a good start in the morning from Orokolo. There was very little wind and by late afternoon they had gone no further than Koialahu, just past the Vailala mouth, where they anchored. Although a light breeze now sprang up from the south the *bevaia* was apparently quite safe at anchor for the night; but Arepe and Tahia, after some argument among the crew, decided that she should put back to the Vailala for shelter. Such decisions are not necessarily made by the *bevaia haera*, though in this case the blame was subsequently laid on them. Incidentally, on entering the river she happened to strike a floating log, but without suffering any actual harm. Now, however, a changing tide prevailed against the wind, and she was borne some distance out to sea. The fact that she was actually moving against the wind seems to have baffled the sailors. Someone started the alarm that she had encountered a *hevehe* in the shape of the floating log and was being carried off. It was told how the *bevaia* jolted backwards and forwards unaccountably, so that the men almost lost their balance. Coconuts and betel were thrown overboard in the traditional way as an offering or bribe to the *hevehe;* but it was observed with horror that, instead of dispersing, the floating nuts kept clustered about the vessel—a sure sign that a sea *hevehe* had it in its power. Darkness was falling and some water was coming in, as to some extent it always does; but, convinced that they were supernaturally overtaken, the crew abandoned bailing. They climbed on to the deck houses and up the rigging, where torches were waved and conch shells blown, until village canoes and the Mission whale-boat put out to the rescue of the terrified mariners. Then the new *bevaia*, a comparatively sound one, was abandoned with a full load; and next morning at Orokolo we watched her drifting past under her crab-claw sail towards the Purari Delta. She subsequently became a total wreck with the loss of all her cargo. One or two canoes had ventured out to her as she passed, but no one had dared go aboard, for the coconuts and betel still clung around, and the water in her vicinity was seen to be bubbling and boiling. An Orokolo man, recently returned from a visit to the Delta, had brought a report that certain fisherman had seen the *hevehe* Laurei

Mairau, a mythical individual half snake and half man, bearing towards the east; and it was now generally believed that it was he who had seized the *bevaia*.

The Bevaia Haera

So far I have dealt mainly with the practical side of the *hahi* expedition; but we have seen that the sailor thinks he has obstacles to contend with which demand more than merely practical measures. Indeed, the whole success of the expedition is conditioned by the use of the appropriate magic. I do not mean to imply that the sailor discounts the practical aspects of his task. He is quite ready with explanations in material terms to account for disasters: it may be a case of faulty lashing, or of the use of an old dugout which would not stand the strain of the heavy seas. And while he believes that magical control of the winds is to some extent possible, he nevertheless accepts them as part of nature against which one does not contend out of season. Just as the rain and thunder maker does not perform his magic in the fair weather of the north-west, so the wind magician does not attempt to lay the winds for the *bevaia* at the height of the south-east.[9]

The magic or *maho* for the *bevaia* belongs to the man whom I have already referred to as the principal or *bevaia haera*, *i.e.* simply the *bevaia* man.[10] He it is who initiates and organizes the expedition of the particular *bevaia;* and he would not think of undertaking such a task unless he were in possession of the necessary *maho*. The *bevaia haera* of the Gulf corresponds fairly closely to the *baditauna* of the Motu *lakatoi*. Not infrequently two principals will join in fitting out a single *bevaia* (in one case that I observed there were three); and each of these individuals is referred to as *bevaia haera*.

The *bevaia haera* will bear his part in the work of building together with the other men who have agreed to make the voyage. When it is complete each will put on his load of sago, which he has made, probably with the assistance of his wife, in that part of the vessel which has been allotted him by general agreement. The trading away of this sago (and the other commodities such as grass skirts, bows and arrows, etc.) is an individual matter: there is no attempt at organizing the sales or allotting the profits, and the *bevaia haera* does not receive any recompense from the members of the crew for his responsibility and expert knowledge.

That expert knowledge, as we have seen, is of magic. The *bevaia haera* is not necessarily naval architect or captain, though as an experienced voyager he commonly figures as both. His business is to know the magic and carry it out, and thereby to "make the *bevaia* go fast and escape rough weather."

He is responsible for certain observances at various stages from the very beginning of the enterprise, *e.g.* at felling the tree to make the dugout, at the commencement of lashing, at the commencement of loading, at the final embarkation, and during the voyage. I do not pretend to have anything like a complete account of his actions, but what I have gathered is sufficient to show the general nature of *bevaia maho*. We may begin with the personal taboos which the *bevaia haera* undergoes, and then follow him in the performance of some of these successive rites.

Taboos

He must avoid certain kinds of food: all meat; all fish, with the exception of *piria* and *avaha*; coconuts; rice; and sago cooked with any of the before-mentioned. His ordinary fare is plain boiled sago *mahea* (*ma-ahea*, literally, not water), and bananas, to which may be added the European luxuries of tea, sugar and biscuits. Taro is eaten by some *bevaia haera* and avoided by others.

The reason invariably given for these food taboos is that they ensure lightness in the *bevaia haera*, and thus indirectly in the *bevaia*, Whereas among the European foods rice is regarded as heavy, tea, sugar and biscuits are excepted for the express reason that they are light. (The fish *piria* and *avaha*, two varieties of mullet, are permitted as food because of their reputation for exceptional speed in the water.) The idea of fasting to ensure lightness is in evidence elsewhere, *e.g.* in preparation for the *apa hevehe* ceremony, when the young men who are to wear the masks submit to similar taboos for a month and more before the final ceremony in order that they may be able to dance well in these enormously top-heavy structures.[11] But although in these connections the object of fasting is claimed to be lightness, it would appear elsewhere to be a preliminary condition for magical performance at large, where lightness is not always particularly in point: in sorcery and weather magic, for instance. Thus one rain and thunder maker, after revealing some of his secrets to me, observed that it was a good thing he had eaten that morning, for had he been fasting the things he had told me would have brought on an untimely thunderstorm.

Besides fasting, the *bevaia haera* must abstain from sexual intercourse himself and even from indirect association with it. While the *bevaia* is building, his food must be cooked by his wife alone, and he must accept it from her hand: another woman would not be expected to have observed the taboo. The members of the crew at large are not under the same restriction; but it is claimed that any man who had had intercourse would absent himself from the work of building for a while.

The object of this taboo once more is to ensure lightness: it is expressly stated that intercourse would make the *bevaia haera* heavy, and through him, the *bevaia*. The same idea is seen in connection with the mask ceremonies. A youth who had to run in a *kovave*[12] would be sluggish in his movements if he had indulged and if, knowing that he was innocent himself, he found the mask heavy and unwieldy, he would accuse a previous wearer of having broken the taboo. Further evidence of this belief is found in the myths. When Bitawabu, for instance, visits the girl Aviara, he flies from the Aivei to Yule Island in a *ruru*, *i.e.* an artificial structure or model, representing a bird. He refuses an invitation to sleep with her, for in the morning he must mount his *ruru* again and fly home: he fears, as he explains, the heaviness that would result from intercourse. A precisely similar episode occurs in another myth when the youth Iviki wearing a *ruru* that represents the bird of that name rejects the offer of the girl Boro. His younger brother Kowoko, however, is less cautious; he yields to the charms of the younger sister, Mavu, and donning his *ruru* next morning finds that he can rise only to the lower branches of a bread-fruit tree, where he proves an easy mark for the arrow.[13]

The *bevaia haera* is subject to another restriction: he must not wash. For this I have heard no native explanation; but it is a familiar notion that washing dispels magical power, and if may be connected with the supposed importance of heat in magic which, as I shall now show, is not absent from this culture of the Gulf.

The Chewing of Ginger, etc.

Besides observing the above-mentioned taboos the *bevaia haera* must from time to time chew *upi* and *apiapi*, two kinds of ginger root, of which he carries a supply in a small woven bag (*hivi*) about his neck In addition to these he chews various barks such as *meouri* (cinnamon) and *herevari* and *paiha* (both unidentified). These and others all share the characteristic of heat; *i.e.* they are hot to the taste. (I should add that most of the herbs used for this purpose are also strongly scented, which appears to be from the magical viewpoint an equally important characteristic.) One reason given for chewing ginger and these hot barks was to "harden the stomach" of the fasting *bevaia haera*; but more usually it is explained that they make him hot, and thus ready for magic-making. In the same way sorcerers chew certain barks and leaves to make themselves hot; the sap of a creeper, specially "hot, like curry" is applied to the pointing stick; and prior to one rite of divination the young men chew a plant called *paidava* with the same stated intention. A magician has explained to me that before commencing operations he gets himself as hot as possible; puts the leaves of *oe, puo* and *laitohe* under his mat; and then lies down close to the fire. He makes pretence of being ill to give colour to this action, but his real purpose is to make himself hot for magic. Finally it was definitely stated in connection with the secrecy of magic that a man would lose his *maho ahea* (magic heat) if he communicated his private knowledge to others: he would become *bevehere* (cold) and powerless.

Felling the Canoe Tree

The fasting and other taboos, as well as the chewing of ginger, etc., commence with the first episode of the *bevaia* enterprise, viz. the felling of the chosen canoe-tree. It is for the *bevaia haera* himself to strike the first blow, and as he does so he spits ginger and *paiha* on the axe, and mutters, or thinks of, a secret name for the tree and for himself. It is in the use of these names that the essence of *maho* consists and I shall refer to it at greater length presently. I do not believe he ever gives audible utterance to them: informants have constantly said that the magician merely thinks the names, or at most frames the words under his breath. It is certain that he would not utter them aloud, for that would be to make his secret public. Nor can I find that there is any set formula to go through. I have witnessed some of the rites in which magic names were used, but there has never been any noticeable pause, nor have I observed the principal engaged in uttering what could be called a spell. I think it may be said that spells, in so far as they exist, must be of a very rudimentary nature, and that they are thought rather than spoken.

Having struck his few blows at the tree the *bevaia haera* leaves the work of felling it to the other men; but before leaving he gathers the chips he has himself struck off, stows them in a bag and keeps them until the voyage of his *bevaia* is brought to an end. It is explained that he must not leave them lying on the ground to become soggy in the rain, or the hull of his canoe will become equally soggy.

Lashing

He has a further rite to perform when the dugouts have been fashioned complete. He in person must begin the work of lashing, and when he ties the first of the series of *kwari-haro*, or cross-beams by which the dugouts are held together, he binds in a parcel of secret medicines. I was quite unable to get any further information on this subject, though it evidently represents a regular duty of the *bevaia haera*. When there are two *bevaia haera* or more, only one of them, it is said, will bind in his medicines, for those of two might not correspond, and then the effect would be to make the *bevaia* labour or go awry.

Loading

While the construction proceeds the *bevaia haera* sleeps close to or even aboard his vessel, ostensibly to guard it from sorcerers or suspicious characters; and when after a good many weeks it is completed, he must begin the loading by himself putting aboard the first bundle of sago. Here again he makes use of some secret name or other, according to the *maho* he possesses. It is some secret synonym for sago connected with the particular myth which underlies his *maho*. His bundle is decorated with streamers and maybe symbolic ornaments, and is hung up in front of the *uvi* or deck house in which he spends most of his time on board.

By now the canoe is, or should be, completely ready. It is fully rigged and the stays are fluttering with *hapa*, sago branches with finely frayed leaflets. Ornaments of more significance hang from the rigging, light models of fish, or of *pipi* the flying fish, or of birds that have some mythical association with the sailing of *bevaia* such as that of *iriri* or *arariori*, with a pair of decorated betel nuts fastened under its wings.

The first bundle has been put aboard by the *bevaia haera* at dawn, and thereafter the loading goes on apace. By afternoon all has been stowed away and a feast is in progress.[14]

The Ivaiva[15]

I am assured that an *ivaiva* or ceremonial offering is made at this stage. In the only case where I was an actual observer the *ivaiva* was certainly not made, but I have been told of it often enough to believe that it is a usual practice. It is, at any rate, a common feature of Elema ceremonies. Before certain feasts a half-coconut vessel is filled from the pots of stew, as yet untouched, and passed round the objects (sometimes people) in connection with which the *ivaiva* and feast are being made. Thus it may be passed round the *hevehe* or *kovave* masks, or round the posts of the men's house (*eravo*). Then it is cast on to the ground and the feast proceeds. In this case, according to various informants, the half-coconut is carried on to the *bevaia*, passed round the mast and rigging, and then with its contents thrown away in the customary manner. It is very difficult to get at the native theory of this rite. One good informant said that the food was being offered to the spirits of the dead, who would be angry and damn the expedition if they did not receive it. It was never suggested that this was a preliminary act of placation of the sea *hevehe*, although, as we have seen, they may be placated by offerings of food when they are actually met. I feel fairly convinced that, if the native has any object of placation in mind, it is rather vaguely the *bevaia* itself. (A similar feast and *ivaiva* are made at the final dismantling of the *bevaia* on its return, the object then being more definitely the sail, which is put away in the *eravo* for safe keeping till the next expedition.)

Embarkation

While the feast is going forward the *bevaia haera* and his closer associates, *i.e.* the joint organizers of the expedition and the steersmen, who are to some extent in his magical confidence, are decorating themselves in the closed *eravo*. Their mode of decoration itself is determined by the particular *maho* that is being used. When they are ready the temporary door of the *eravo* suddenly bursts open and the *bevaia haera* emerges, perhaps blackened with charcoal and with strips of fresh nipa leaf from neck and limbs. In the case where I was a witness he was accompanied by half a dozen colleagues similarly dressed. All uttered shrill bird cries, "*kekekeke—!*" waved their arms as if flying, and thus danced down toward the *bevaia*. The women started wailing—for the real moment of departure was at hand—and all rose to follow. The *bevaia* being moored close against the river bank the *bevaia haera* and his associates had simply to leap aboard. Had it been any distance out they would have been hoisted from the shore, for on no account must their "toe-nails get wet"; and once there they continued their leaping and dancing and blew clouds of chewed ginger and spittle into every part of the vessel. All who are intending to sail crowd aboard after them, save one or two who have to run back to the village on errands of their own. Then it is found that the stock of soft-wood plugs used to stop leaks has been forgotten—someone runs off for these. One old man is shouting that this is a breach of the proper routine; that once aboard, all should stay aboard for the present. But amid the babel he is disregarded and finally he turns his back abruptly, tosses his hands loosely in the air, and walks off as if he for one did not care what happened to their *bevaia*. Now the strays have returned, the steersmen cluster at the stern with their great oars, and the *bevaia* is pushed off. A great cheer is raised, and with her master still frantically dancing and her model birds swaying realistically aloft she moves downstream to anchor for the night against an early start next morning.

At the actual getaway the scene is much the same. The bar is crossed on a rising tide; many have assembled at the river mouth to see her go. There is the *bevaia haera*—or as he is sometimes called at this stage the *bevaia laho* (*laho*=seagull)—dancing with arms outstretched, waving a switch of cassowary plumes and spitting ginger. The younger men push the *bevaia* out over the shallow bar, the crab-claw sail goes up, and she is away on her doubtful journey.

On the Voyage

On the high seas the *bevaia haera* remains very much in charge of his ship, though not necessarily as captain, and certainly not as steersman. He handles no sheets or oars and it is stated as a general rule that he gives no instructions to the crew. It is to the *bevaia* that he gives instructions: "My child, go fast; my crew are getting tired." He must never sleep while under way, only at anchor. Opinions were freely expressed by some of the crew that the loss of Arape and Tahia's *bevaia* recounted above was due to their negligence: they had slept on the shelter of the *uvi* instead of watching and dancing.

One of the functions of the *bevaia haera* is to raise the favourable winds and to lay the unfavourable. The switch that we saw him waving as his *bevaia* was crossing the bar is used for this purpose. It sweeps back the south-east wind and beckons the westerlies. How it does so in itself is not explained; indeed, as a piece of the most elementary and spontaneous kind of magic, this action in the native view calls for no explanation. The same kind of switch is seen frequently in use at large dances, when it may be waved solemnly to and fro, as a party of guests is entering a village; both guests and hosts use the cassowary switch (*hore*) in this way, ostensibly to dispel the magic which may emanate from the opposite party. The *hore* is simply a magician's wand.

But apart from these motions the *bevaia haera* has a far more potent means of controlling the winds. Once again it is in the use of secret names derived from the myths. One man for instance will use those of Oveai and Kairai, another that of Berare Kiwai, or Divea and Lauvea, and so on. My information about these wind-names is very incomplete, but there is a large number of them, and by using more than he should a wind magician (and the *bevaia haera* is always such to some extent) could cover the sky with clouds and call up a tempest. In fact, the thing could be easily overdone.

I have spoken of the sea *hevehe* as a source of danger, but it does not seem that the *bevaia haera* has this danger constantly in mind: his duty is to know how to placate them if they happen to threaten. He should know the names of the individual *hevehe* and be able to reel them off[16]; for the *hevehe*, which does not usually show itself, will not respond to the act of conciliation until it hears its own name.

The method of dealing with the *hevehe* may be that of conciliation, when an offering of sago, coconuts and betel is cast into the sea, as

we saw in the case of Arape and Tahia's *bevaia*; or attempts may be
made to scare it off, when the *bevaia haera* spits chewed ginger and
scented bark on to his hands, mixes the spittle with lime, and throws
it into the water. The lime will temporarily blind the monster, as
it did in one of the myths to which I shall presently refer and the
smell of the barks will drive it away.

A regular business of the *bevaia haera*, however, is to burn his
leaves and barks (generally *heheva* or *pairava*) on the potsherd vessel
within the *bevaia*. This potsherd (*heaia*) corresponds to the Motuan
keikei and the place of burning, *i.e* within the hulls of the dugouts
on either side, is the same, yet Elema informants insist that it is an
ancient practice and not copied from the Motu; and a precisely
similar procedure is followed on other occasions where there is no
question of a Motuan prototype; *e.g.* in the fumigation of bows and
arrows and of the anthropomorphic plaques, *kaiavuru* in the *eravo*,
preparatory to a pig-hunt. The barks and roots used in both cases
are characterized by a strong odour. The cinnamon (*meouri*) is often
used, and a root called *ivuru* is a stock ingredient. The latter gives
off a sweet and remarkably pungent scent.

Different reasons are offered. It has been suggested more than
once that this scent enters the water and scares away the *hevehe*,
just as that of the chewed bark thrown into the water, as above-
mentioned. Others see in the nature of some of the barks used a
property of lightness magically transferred to the *bevaia*. Thus *meouri*,
hevoko and *kerevari* are strangely elusive trees: if a man comes on
one of them in the bush and wishes to cut it down he must not
leave it in order to fetch his axe. When he returned it would have
disappeared. The only thing to do is to stay by the tree and call for
someone else to bring the axe. Again, one of the trees mentioned,
hevoko, is used by runners in the *kovave* masks: a fragment of bark on
the tongue will bear them along so that their feet hardly touch the
ground. But the third reason suggested is the commonest; fumigation
with the strong-smelling smoke of the bark is meant to humour
the *bevaia*, to please or flatter it, or as the equivalent in Motuan
(*hanamoa*) says literally, to "make it good." This is the explanation
offered for the practice of fumigating the weapons before a hunt.

The above-mentioned ingredients in the *heaia* crucible are said
to be all common knowledge; but different *bevaia haera* have secret
ingredients of their own which belong especially to the particular
maho they are using. Only one man, Epe, whose *bevaia* was named
"Hedi Houvu," even consented to reveal such a secret medicine to
me, and the doubt remains in my mind whether he was sincere.
It was the large glossy red seed *hepahepa*, about the size of a florin,
which will split or explode in the fire, the two halves flying in
different directions. At the sound of each explosion the crew would

give their cheer, "*Uah!*" and Epe would stamp his foot and say, "*Hedi haravara, Houvu haravara!*"—"Run Hedi, Run Houvu!"

The Return

I will not attempt to follow the *bevaia* any further in detail on its voyage. If successful it will reach the Motuan villages, dispose of what sago it can at each of them, and on its return voyage collect the price in shell ornaments, trade, or money. When it reaches home it may be welcomed with great enthusiasm by the women, but on the other hand there may be no noticeable demonstration. It is quickly dismantled. The sail is set up in the village to dry out, and then folded up and stowed away in the *eravo*. This is said to be the occasion of a feast and an *ivaiva*, the object of which is said to be the sail itself. It is addressed (or nominally so) in such words as these: "Now we wrap you up and send you to the *eravo*. If the men are strong they will set you up again; if they are weak, you will stay there."

Myth in Relation to Bevaia Magic

I have attempted to show that magic of some kind or another accompanies all stages of the construction, equipment, and sailing of the *bevaia*, and that in some phases rites of placation are in evidence. But so far I have not come to the heart of the magic of the *bevaia haera*.

The Use of Mythical Names

One of the first things that strike us in our dealings with him is his secretiveness: he is reluctant to pass on his magic knowledge lest it lose its power. And we find that even the names of the *bevaia* themselves are often kept secret. Informants will try to put one off with the stereotyped Motuan names, Oalabada, Kevaubada, etc., of which there are only a few. But it soon transpires that each *bevaia* is known as one of a much longer series of local names, and that each such name forms part of what might be called a magical complex. Such complexes are theoretically of limited number, but there is a good deal of interfusion and, with some *bevaia haera*, a tendency to eclecticism, so that the system is not entirely cut-and-dried. Any one complex will be known to a number of men, and anyone who possessed it would be, as far as magical qualifications go, competent to organize a *hahi*. The magic is commonly passed on from father to son; but in some cases a man may for personal reasons cut his son off in favour of another; and at any rate it is rather freely bought and sold. A *bevaia haera* who has failed with one complex may discard it and buy another for his next venture.

The leading feature of each magical complex is the assumption, or application, of certain secret names. These names belong to certain myths. The myths of the Elema are numerous and long-winded. The greater part of each myth is public; but nearly all of them, I think, contain esoteric passages which have a magical value. These in open narration are always omitted, and one can too often detect by the sidelong glances of an informant and the garbled nature of his story that he has reached and is endeavouring to steer clear of such a passage. The legend or myth is called generally *lauu* or *oharo*; if it contains secret passages of magical value then it is called *maho-oharo*; or it might be more correct to limit this latter name to the actual passages of this kind.

The myths are respectively associated in a broad sense with some one or other of the ten totemic clans of the Elema.[17] And they tell of the exploits and particularly the wide travels of various individuals in some sense belonging to the clans. Not a few of these myths deal with long voyages with a successful issue, and thus they provide exemplars for the modern voyagers. The names of the *bevaia* themselves and those used in magic at the successive stages of the whole enterprise are names which appear in these myths.

The myths provide magic not only for *bevaia*, of course, but for all sorts of other undertakings, whether of love, or war, or rain-making, or fishing, or whatever else. The magician must know the relevant parts of the appropriate myths; above all, he must have at his command the secret and potent names. The generalization, as framed by one informant, stands thus: magic to be effective must employ the names of long-ago people, born in the beginning. I shall give some examples in abbreviated form of the myths that have a bearing on *bevaia maho*.

The Myth of Evarapo's Journey to Lavau[18]

Evarapo, a man of the Hurava, or western clan, lives on the Aivei River with his younger brother Iriri. So far he has been unable to win a wife for himself, but one day he receives a visit from two young men, Lere and Pove, in the form of birds; and these visitors recommend him to try for their sister Aviara, who lives at Lavau, or Yule Island. They volunteer to carry a decorated betel nut from him to the girl as a form of proposal.

Evarapo, under instruction from Lere and Pove, now sends his younger brother Iriri as an envoy or go-between; and to provide for his passage to so distant a part makes him a *ruru*, or model, of a bird in which to travel. Iriri, in his *ruru*, after resting at certain places on the way, finally reaches Aviara, bearing a duplicate message-nut. He rejects her offer to sleep with him as we have already seen, because sexual intercourse would make him heavy and so endanger the success of his return flight (another version of the story, however, has it that he does not wish to usurp the privilege of his elder brother). Having delivered his message and ascertained that the girl is willing to marry Evarapo, he returns, carrying a small load of *taitu* and earthenware pots in his *ruru*, to prove that he has actually been to Lavao. He has informed Aviara that she will eventually be called for in a large canoe made from a *meouri* tree.

Evarapo now sets to work to make the canoe and the story gives details of its construction, and of the launching, when Evarapo, with body blackened and bedecked with strips of nipa leaf (the typical decoration of the Hurava, or Delta, men) dances on the canoe platform. In due course he reaches Yule Island and elopes with Aviara. Her father, Oa Laia (elsewhere called Oa Birukapu and Oa Idiva) learning of her elopement, gives chase. He enters the water and becomes a *hevehe* in the form of a huge fish. At Motu he stops and procures a house, which he carries on his back through the water, apparently to make his appearance more terrifying to the fugitives. He causes a storm to arise, and the canoe, "Meouri," is threatened with destruction. But Evarapo throws lime into the water, the *hevehe* Oa Laia is for the time being blinded, and thus Evarapo manages to escape and bring his bride safely home. The myth goes on much further. Oa Laia follows the fugitives to the Aivei and comes ashore after them, where, lying in hiding, he later devours, inadvertently, the son of Evarapo and Aviara, named Birau Upumake. But the subsequent episodes of his destruction and the return of his bones to the east do not seem relevant to the *bevaia maho*.

This myth makes it sufficiently plain why the *bevaia* should be in some cases called "Meouri," and in others "Iriri." It does not seem quite so reasonable that other *bevaia* should be called "Meouri-Oa Laia," though Oa Laia, travelling through the water with the house on his back, might be something for any *bevaia* to emulate. It gives precedents for the stages of construction, the taboo on sexual intercourse, and the use of a model bird as decoration with carved betel nuts fastened under its wings. It also accounts for the conventional decoration of the *bevaia haera* of Meouri or Iriri, which is that of the Hurava man, and for his imitation of a bird. The whole myth might be made to square with a voyage to Lavau for pots, and in his magic the *bevaia haera* is recalling the details of that early venture.

The Myth of Eau's Arakaita

Another of the *maho-oharo* used in *bevaia* magic is that of Harai and Eau. Harai (identified with the morning star) comes from Kauri, the east, or more particularly from the upper Biaru River. Walking along a rattan cane, which he throws from one tree top to the other, he makes a long journey toward the west, and at the end of it finds the woman Eau (a kind of nipa palm) beyond the river Aivei. He marries her and she bears a son, but Harai decides to return to Kauri. He has a large single dugout made, *i.e.* a canoe of the Delta type, called *arakaita*, and after fasting and decorating himself he loads this with sago and embarks with his wife and child. On the way they encounter bad weather, but Eau cries out *"Harai, arave Orovuvira."* The word Orovu indicates a mythical place of great beauty in the west, since overwhelmed by mud, and Eau's cry may mean, "Harai, my husband in Orovu." Since Harai comes originally from Kauri, the east, this does not seem an entirely satisfactory explanation, but at any rate the canoe passes safely through and reaches its destination. Some *bevaia*, especially those sent out by men of the Kauri clan, are called "Eau-ve-arakaita" (Eau's dugout), or "Orovuvira." I have no details of the *maho* used in connection with them.

The Myth of Aori and Iviri

Another *maho oharo* is associated especially with the Auma clan. It tells how Aori, who lived at Auma point, went to the Kemera River to bring home as his bride the woman Iviri. Iviri is the name of a hill on the Kerema River, but in the story she is wholly human except that she was born with a *love*, or sprig of feathers growing in her hair. He first goes in quest of her in a *ruru*, representing the little bird *aori*, and having found her he plucks out this *love*, tells her he will call for her later in a canoe, and then flies home to make his preparations. The canoe completed and given the name "Heava," he travels again to the Kerema River and in due course returns home with his bride. They are pursued by her parents, who enter the water and become sea *hevehe*, but eventually are left behind.

Later on, when the fugitives are camped at Bie (the Bluff) a local woman, Kikiriapu, takes all the ornaments from the sleeping Iviri, and before daylight induces Aori to set off again, posing as his bride. There is much more to the story: Aori reaches home before discovering his mistake, but after many adventures Iviri, who has followed along shore, succeeds in reuniting herself with him and displacing Kikiriapu. These episodes, however, do not as far as I know have any bearing on the *maho*.

The *bevaia haera* who told me this story made it quite plain that when he set forth on his *bevaia*, which was named "Heava," he was impersonating Aori himself. He wears the costume which Aori is supposed to have worn, with a blackened face (and in a way prematurely) the same kind of *love* in his hair which Aori plucked from

Iviri's head. As he boards the *bevaia* he thinks, as he puts it, to himself, "I want to pluck the *love* from Iviri's head." He dances on the platform and extends his arms like Aori's wings. Another man, master of a *bevaia* of the same name, "Heava," told the above story in a somewhat different form. The hero was a man, Baiaiapo, who sent the bird Aori as messenger to Iviri before actually going himself. In this case the *bevaia haera* said that in loading and embarking he pretended to be Baiaiapo: "My name is Baiaiapo," he says under his breath; and, to the canoe, "Keep your eyes on Nabo and Horoi" (two mountains behind Kerema, where Iviri lived).

The name Heava was said by this last informant to be a synonym for *ova*, a kind of mangrove. The dugout is always, I believe, actually made from a softwood tree called *ihohea*, and my informant, who made no secret of the name "Heava," was very reluctant to reveal the intermediate name "Ova," whispering it in my ear as a great favour. It would appear that it is this latter name that has the magical power. He also said that in loading he applied the name "Kikiriapu," that of the usurping bride, to the sago, though he was unable or unwilling to make the connection plain. Another informant told me subsequently that I had been deceived, and suggested that the name "Kikiriapu," as that of an ill-deserving and ill-fated woman, was used only in malicious magic, *i.e.* in the endeavour to ruin the sago and the enterprise of a rival *bevaia haera*.

The Myth of Hedi Houvu

The Kaia, or sky, clan may use the name "Hedi Houvu" for their *bevaia*. The myth, which I give very briefly, relates how two men Oveai and Kairai were rescued by the girls Kawaka and Pupuvari from the continual attacks of their enemies. *Kawaka* is some kind of boring insect which I could not identify; *pupuvari* is the carpenter bee. They bored into a *laura* and an *aravea* tree till they were hollow and then told their people to hide themselves inside; this done, they bored a little further till the trees fell into the river, when they were bound together as a *haruka iroki* which was called "Hedi Houvu," and eventually made off to the Motu coast.

Hedi and *houvu* stand respectively for the trees *laura* and *aravea*, the latter names being, as before, the specially secret ones, which are applied in magic to the softwood *ihohea*. *Oveai* and *kairai* are secret names for the north-west wind *avara*. The names "Kawaka" and "Pupuvari" are assumed by the *bevaia haera* himself as he begins the felling of the tree, and with his axe he pretends, instead of chopping (*haiakive*), to be boring (*parerekive*) in the manner of these two insects. Here, however, as elsewhere, it was denied that any set spell was used.

The Myth of Aroae

As a last example I shall refer to the myth of the Baiu clan, which has an old-established legendary connection with the Motu *lakatoi*. It is claimed that the man Baiu made the first expedition to the Motu coast, accompanied by another canoe of the Kaia clan. He had married his daughter Aroae to Lavai, of the Vailala River, and she had borne a son. But the child died, and when later Baiu set out on his expedition and was anchored at Kearu for the night, Aroae stole up and put the dead child on board. Next day Baiu's canoe sank, and he had to transfer his belongings to that of the Kaia clan. This proceeded down the coast, but at every stop there was Aroae, who had preceded them along the beach under cover of night. The people did not recognize her, but because of what they thought her resemblance to the real Aroae at home they gave her presents of bows and arrows, the regular cargo of the early trading canoes. By the time they reached the Motu coast their stock was exhausted; but Aroae had preceded them again, and there they finally settled together. This, according to the myth, was prior to any other settlement on that coast. Aroae herself discovered how to make pots and subsequently Baiu and his people made expeditions in real *lakatoi* to the west. They were the first to do so; in fact they were the veritable Derai Haera, or Motu.[19]

The Baiu *bevaia* is called "Aroae"; though as in some other cases the connection does not seem entirely logical. Indeed, the narrator of the above legend had abandoned it owing to the failure of a previous expedition, and instead bought the Harava magic, and with it the name "Meouri." However, the myth recalls what is supposed to be the earliest trading voyage and indicates the method of trading, viz. by leaving parcels of bows and arrows at various places of anchorage and collecting pots on the return.

In this and the other myths referred to there is no doubt a good deal of *maho* that was not revealed to me. The only piece of magic that my informant would consent to tell me in this connection was of a malicious nature. To sink a rival's *bevaia* it was only necessary to wrap up a parcel of leaves (what they were he would not say) and place it secretly on board, calling it as he did so "Lavai-Kaki." That means "Lavai's namesake," and the parcel represents the dead child of Lavai and Aroae, which the latter placed on her father's *bevaia*.

The Magic of Impersonation

The foregoing treatment of myth in relation to *bevaia maho* is all rather fragmentary, but it is enough to show the importance of mythical associations, particularly of mythical names in Elema magic, and further to suggest the connecting link, or the way in which the name gives power.

When a man thus employs a name to help him in his purpose we might at first sight be inclined to think he was actually calling on the bearer of the name for help. I am not at present prepared to state that such an idea is entirely absent from Elema culture, but it does not represent the construction which the magician himself here places upon his action. As a number of definite cases show, he is rather applying the mythical names to himself or to this or that feature of his undertaking. In short, he is himself impersonating a mythical character, or identifying some feature of his undertaking with a corresponding feature of a mythical undertaking which reached a successful close. He apparently feels more confident of success himself by pretending to be the great man of the long-ago and by making his present undertaking, so to speak, a reproduction of the great man's exploit. Such pretence or impersonation is helped out by details of costume and action and by such extras as that of the model bird fixed in the rigging.

The same general method, and with it the same explanation, is applicable to other phases of magic as well as to *bevaia maho*. When a man goes a-wooing, for instance, he will, if he knows it, employ the name "Marai," a highly secret synonym for the moon (*papare*). In the myth the moon, as a person, is peculiarly attractive to women; and for the time being the lover actually impersonates him. He does not whisper to himself, "Marai, help me to win this woman," but he thinks, without even whispering, "I am Marai himself, and I will get her."

Again, Kivavia Orokiki Akore became infallibly successful at shooting fish with the bow and arrow; this was because two men, Berari Kapipi and Kiwai Kapipi, had informed him in a dream that they would come to him as decorated arrows and that he should use them on his fishing. In due course Kivavia picked up two floating arrows on the river and used them with the success they had promised. A man who knew this *maho oharo* told me that when he went fish shooting he pretended to be Kivavia himself, and as he took down his arrows he addressed them or thought of them as "Berari Kapipi" and "Kiwai Kapipi."

I could give more instances from magic devoted to other purposes, but these will be enough to indicate the common use of what we might call the magic of impersonation.

The essential equipment of the magician is, of course, a knowledge of the relevant parts of the myths, but special stress is laid on the secret names. It remains somewhat obscure why the secret name should be more potent than the public name. It may be that the special reliance on the former has its rise in the magician's own secretiveness: he is very jealous in guarding his own magic, and fearful lest it be communicated to others. The ostensible reason is that magic made public loses its power; but we may suspect that the real reason is the fear of losing a prerogative and a private source of influence. The magicians then stick close to their several secrets so that they alone may have the advantage of them; and this secretiveness itself may give rise to the general belief that magic drawn from secret sources is the most potent. But the argument may be that the secret name is more real or intimate, and that the knowledge of it brings the magician into closer relation with the mythical character, thus making the impersonation easier and more effective. This, however, is a subject which I did not sufficiently explore.

It is not by any means implied that this magic of impersonation covers the whole ground of *bevaia maho*, but that it is the dominant feature of that *maho* in so far as it is dependent on myths. Even within this more limited field it is difficult to see how it can explain the use of some names, as *e.g.* those used in raising the winds. In Elema myths the great majority of characters can be identified with, or in a manner represent some creature or natural object; and in this way certain names are interpreted as synonyms for the winds. It may be that in using them the magician is actually calling up the winds. Once more, I missed the opportunity of looking particularly into this matter, and will not venture to speak with any finality until I have seen more of Elema culture.[20] But in the cases where informants could make their meaning plain it appeared with sufficient definiteness that they were acting on another principle, viz. the one I have attempted to formulate under the name of magic of impersonation. They were themselves impersonating characters from the myths and seeking to re-enact the successes which those mythical characters had achieved.

REFERENCES

1. (Originally published in *Oceania*, vol. 3, 1932-3, pp. 139-66. E. S.).
2. C. G. Seligman, *Melanesians of British New Guinea*, 1910, Chapter VIII. (This edition reproduces all Williams' footnotes. The only alterations made in these footnotes occur where Williams refers to a paper reprinted in this edition, and gives page numbers referring to the original edition. In such cases, I altered the page numbers. I also clarified references to books and articles. Thus, in the above footnote, Williams did not give the year of publication of Seligman's book (1910), but I added it, and

give full details in the bibliography at the end of this volume. Finally, I corrected spellings, see Footnote 8 below.

As well as Williams' original footnotes, this edition carries a minimum of additional footnotes by myself, always marked by my initials. The main purpose of such notes is to draw the reader's attention to certain developments in Williams' researches. Some passages in these papers raise questions reopened, even resolved in Williams' later works. If the reader wishes to understand the subject matter of such passages, he will have to consult the references I added in my footnotes.

Numbering of the footnotes in Chapters 1-3, 5-7 had to be modified partly to allow for the editor's additions, partly to achieve a uniform and clear style throughout the book. Footnotes have been numbered consecutively in each chapter. E. S.)

3. Very large outrigger canoes are used between Kerema and the Lakekamu for fishing with seine nets.
4. *Melanesians of British New Guinea,* 118 sq.
5. The Motu *lakatoi* are reconstructed in the Gulf or Delta and return with as many as ten or twelve dugouts.
6. (See Chapters 5 and 6 of the present volume. F. S.)
7. *Hevehe* is the pronunciation at the western end of the Gulf Division of the more familiar *sevese*. (See *Drama of Orokolo*, Chapter IX, and Chapters 2 and 5 of this volume. E. S.)
8. (The original text reads *beura*, but we find the word spelt consistently as *be'ure* in *Drama of Orokolo*. Where such conflicts in spelling occur, I have always adopted the spelling of *Drama of Orokolo*, as Williams was far more meticulous about spellings of Elema words in this work than in the earlier ones. Although Williams never learnt the Elema language he did record many Elema words and phrases, using the same kind of orthography as the functional school of anthropology, especially after his visit to England. With regard to his use of the Orokaiva language, which I was able to check personally, occasional errors may be noted, but the Orokaiva data were collected very early in his career. E. S.)
9. In the Gulf Division the rainy season is that of the south-east (the Southern Hemisphere winter) and the dry season is that of the north-west (summer). In the "dry belt" where the Motu live it is precisely the opposite.
10. At Vailala I heard the terms *oropa haera* and *aireke haera* (fore man and aft man) which may indicate a tendency towards the organisation *baditauna, doritauna* etc. of the Motu. Other terms in use are *bevaia oa,* literally father of the *bevaia;* and *iroki-aue-haera,* an expression which means canoe-tail-man, and refers to the responsibility for steering with the great oar at the stern. This no doubt harks back to earlier times, for it is nowadays part of the *iroki-aue-haera's* duty to handle the steering oars of the *bevaia.*
11. (See *Drama of Orokolo*, Chapter XIX. E. S.)
12. (See *Drama of Orokolo*, Chapter XXIII. E. S.)
13. (Williams refers to myths not quoted in the present paper, but in

Drama of Orokolo (pp. 135-7 and 179-81, and pp. 83-4 below) he points out that each *aualari* had its own body of mythology; the stories of the different *aualari* are very similar, though variations occur in the names of the characters. For a discussion, see Part II of the introduction to this book. E. S.)

14. In the case where I made definite enquiry the feast was a mutual one between two sections of a small village which had joined in fitting out a *bevaia*. In the ordinary case it is provided by the *bevaia haera* and those associated with him in the enterprise to all the outsiders who have helped in the work of building.

15. (For a fuller analysis of the *ivaiva*, see *Drama of Orokolo*, Chapter XIV. E. S)

16. The practice of naming the *hevehe* in succession is seen at one of the final stages of the *apa hevehe* ceremony, when the remnants of the masks are cast into the sea for the sea, or real, *hevehe*. (See Chapter XXIV of *Drama of Orokolo*. E. S.)

17. *Kaia*—Sky; *Ahea*—Sea; *Hurava*—West; *Purari*—River Purari; *Miri*—Beach; *Baiu*—? (Aivei Mouth); *Auma*—Auma Point (the *ma-hevehe* at the Vailala River mouth); *Vailala*—River Vailala; *Nabo*—Nabo Mountains; *Kauri*—East. (For a fuller discussion see *Drama of Orokolo*, Chapter II. The word "Month" for "Mouth" in the text is an obvious misprint. E. S.)

18. (For this myth, see *Drama of Orokolo*, Chapter X. I have changed the spelling of the hero's name from Evarapu in the original, to Evarapo, for reasons set out in footnote 8, above. E.S.)

19. Another version of the story has it that Aroae preceded the canoe as far as Kerepuna at the mouth of the Kemp Welch, where she remained, her father receiving payment for her in armshells and pots.

20. In the meantime I should say that I have found nothing at the western end of the Gulf Division to endorse Holmes' statement that "Prior to setting out on this journey, Avaralaru, the god of the north-west wind, has to be conciliated. To this end, the village sorcerer is engaged at a good fee to intercede with Avaralaru and the god of the sea, that they may give to the voyagers a safe journey and bring them back safely to their village and friends. Two old men, who are considered to be sacred during the voyage, are especially commissioned to accompany those expeditions, that they may use their influence in appealing to the gods of the winds and the sea to refrain from bringing any calamity upon the party." (Holmes 1902 quoted in Barton 1910: 119. E.S.)

2

BULL-ROARERS IN THE PAPUAN GULF[1]

Part I

Introductory Questions of Scope and Method

A bull-roarer is a bull-roarer wherever we find it—a wooden slat of characteristic shape which, being swung in circles by a string attached to one end of it, revolves rapidly on its longer axis and so produces a characteristic noise. This definition might do fairly well for all varieties (though we should perhaps extend it to include some that have turned silent), and an article on the bull-roarer itself might thus end where it began. But the *cult* of the bull-roarer is a thing of infinite variety. It is indeed to be expected that within the limits of any wide area the cult will be found to follow somewhat the same lines wherever we choose to examine it. But every case will present significant differences because it will be bound up with the local culture to which it belongs, and every such local culture differs on innumerable points from the one next door to it. If in this article I deal with the bull-roarer cult as it is (or, in some parts, was) to be found along the western coast of the Gulf Division of Papua, i.e. among the so-called Elema people, I shall be treading ground that seems in part familiar. But the relation of the cult to the particular culture and to the particular people themselves must be a new subject wherever we take it up.

It is not the purpose of this article to trace the Gulf Division bull-roarer to its cultural provenance; much less to discover its origin. The answer to the latter question is so completely lost in the mists of antiquity that no one, at least no serious anthropologist, would waste his time in looking for it. The former question might indeed admit of an answer provided we limited the object of our search to the more or less immediate provenance. But even this is a very elusive and perplexing problem, and it remains more than questionable whether its solution is of any real importance. We should not know much more about the bull-roarer cult in the Gulf Division even if we did succeed in tracing it reliably to a source, or intermediate source, in some other part of Papua or of the world. For two reasons then, first that the evidence is so confused and conflicting that such inquiries seldom reach more than a doubtful conclusion,

73

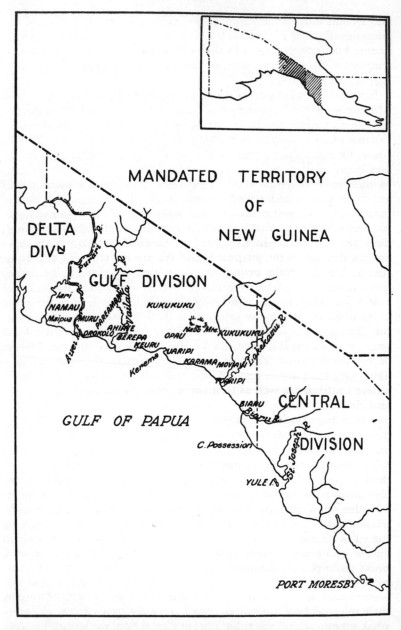

Map showing Gulf Division of Papua. Scale: 1 in.=40 miles. (F. E. Williams,
Drama of Orokolo, facing p. xxvi.)

and second that the conclusion itself, whatever its validity, is of no great significance, I intend to leave this question on one side. Indeed, having burnt one's fingers in this sort of investigation before, one is tempted to forswear any further dabbling in the kind of anthropology which it represents.

Nor do I intend to pursue the comparative method. It is a question whether we should appreciate the significance of the bull-roarer to the Elema natives any better for knowing what it means, or meant, to some other people among whom we happen to find it. If we discover, for instance, that the bull-roarer is elsewhere represented as swallowing and disgorging the initiate, we may indeed be helped to interpret some ritual detail in the light of a survival, but we shall not be helped to understand the real significance of the bull-roarer to the Elema themselves, among whom no such idea at present exists. No one would deny that comparative studies of the kind indicated have great academic interest, and a charm of their own; but they are not directly to the purpose here.[2] We are not studying the bull-roarer, but a certain people among whom it exists: to be more precise, the relations between that people and their bull-roarer.

We shall therefore be concerned with the Elema bull-roarer cult as it survives at present, or as it was in the near and reasonably well-recollected past, or as (in some parts) it is fighting for its existence under changing social conditions. If incidentally I recount a number of legends about its origin, it is not with the idea of throwing any light on that insoluble problem, but rather to illustrate the modern native's attitude as well as to make a point on the relation of myth and ritual.

If we limit ourselves to the field which I have defined it seems that there are two general lines of inquiry which may be profitably followed. I would not venture to assert that they are wholly separable, though a more uncompromising, perhaps more exact, logic than I possess or care to apply might insist on differentiating absolutely between them. At all events, in the first place we have to consider what part the bull-roarer cult plays in the culture as a whole; in what way the bull-roarer is dependent on other parts of the culture, and in what way again those other parts are dependent on the bull-roarer; where and how, in short, it finds its place and bears its part in the cultural system of the Elema tribes. In the second place we have to consider what may be generally called the mental attitude of the people towards their bull-roarer; what are their relevant beliefs, motives, and sentiments; and, above all, with what emotional satisfactions it provides them. It is obvious that these two lines of inquiry will sometimes cross one another and will sometimes pursue an identical course. The first, however, which I

take to represent the functional method in its chaster mood, is predominantly sociological; the latter is largely, and quite frankly,
psychological; so that there is at least a general distinction between
them.

I do not propose to limit myself either to one or to the other of
these methods. One who holds a position connected with native
welfare, need make no excuse for keeping the practical application of
anthropology in mind while he endeavours to follow it as a pure
science; and it seems to me that the main problem of applied
anthropology is that of *evaluating* native custom. For this purpose
both sociological and psychological considerations are important—
not necessarily of equal importance, for I think that the latter, viz.
the sentiments, the motives, the emotional attitudes of the native
towards the matter in debate weigh more heavily in the scale than
do its more strictly functional associations. But both methods may,
I believe, assist us in forming a judgement on the value of any factor
in a culture; and accordingly I do not limit myself to either in
treating of the subject in hand.

Distribution

The so-called Elema people occupy the coast of the Gulf Division
from the eastern edge of the Purari Delta to Cape Possession. They
are divided into a number of local and dialectal units which we may
call tribes, but for which it is quite impossible to give any generally
and consistently recognized names. I shall therefore mark them off
simply by enumerating the main villages of each. Beginning from
the west they are—

1. Orokolo, Arihava, Vailala.
2. Muru (in Arihava hinterland).
3. Iori, Berepa, Keakea.
4. Keuru.
5. Uaripi, Mei, Kerema.
6. Opau (in Uaripi hinterland).
7. Karama, Silo, Wamai, Koaru.
8. Motumotu.
9. Moviavi (in Motumotu hinterland).
10. Lese, Biaru, Yokea.

These tribal groups will be referred to in each case by the name of
the first village mentioned.

The bull-roarer cult formerly belonged to all these tribal groups;
though, as we should expect, it was not wholly uniform throughout
them. My own work has been done mainly among the first group,
that of Orokolo, Arihava and Vailala (where, as it happens, the

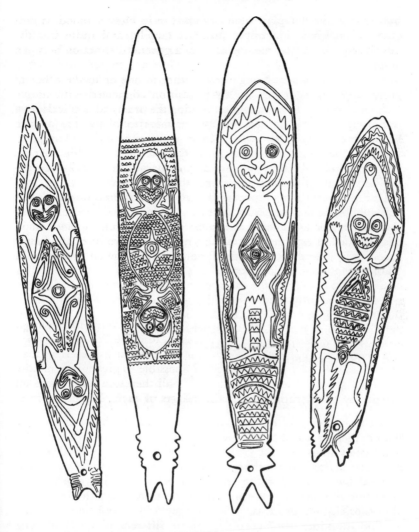

Orokolo Bull-Roarers. Traced from rubbings. Longest 24¼ ins.
(F. E. Williams, *Drama of Orokolo*, p. 167.)

bull-roarer did not play such an important role as among some others). But I have had opportunities for studying the people fairly intensively, though for somewhat shorter periods, as far as Kerema and beyond; and we shall observe some new and important features in the cult as found among these central tribes. Further east, in group 7 (Karama) there are again substantial differences, though I cannot pretend to have made an adequate study of them. In the last groups towards the east, where the influence of the mission has been more strongly felt over a long period, the cult is largely a thing of the past. The present article will deal principally with the tribes from Kerema westward, and among these will concern itself especially with the first-named, that of Orokolo.

One most interesting aspect of the whole inquiry is the struggle for existence of the bull-roarer against various influences during the past sixteen years or so. In some tribes the cult has died out; in others it has persisted as vigorously as ever. Within the same tribe one village has wilfully thrown it away while another has kept it. When the Vailala Madness, which very nearly made a clean sweep of the coast, was at its height, the majority of villages cast away their bull-roarers. Apparently they were to be silenced for ever. But, to make things more interesting, there have been within the last few years definite signs of revival. Of this, which has a practical as well as a theoretical import, I shall have something more to say towards the end of the present article.[3]

General Names of the Bull-Roarer

Apart from the personal names which attach to individual bull-roarers there is a rather wide variety of general names in use, and this variety illustrates the common habit of bandying words about from one culture to another. Words sometimes seem to pass over cultural boundaries (or the transition belts in which one culture fades into another) more easily than the things, whether material objects or customs or ideas, to which they originally belong; so that we find the same word cropping up in different places with very different meanings.

Thus one of the common generic names for the bull-roarer in the Orokolo Group (No. 1) is *kaiavuru*. This, I feel confident, is simply the Orokolo rendering of the Purari Delta word *kaiemunu* or *kaiaimunu*, which is there applied ordinarily to the large wicker-work monster kept in the interior of the men's house or *ravi*[4]. In the Orokolo group it is applied equally, or more often, to the small carved coconut "charm" used by sorcerers, which has no ritual connection either with the bull-roarer or the *kaiemunu*, though it happens to resemble the latter in shape, being like a tiny miniature made in another material. But this diversity of meanings for one and the same word is best exemplified in the name *hevehe* (more specific-ally *be'ure hevehe*) by which, at the Orokolo end, the bull-roarer is most commonly known.[5] We shall pass on to consider this word *hevehe* in detail, after noting the other names in use along the coast.

Among the central groups (Nos. 5 and 6) the name (over and above *hevehe* or *be'ure hevehe*) is *rubu*, a word which if repeated rapidly gives a good imitation of the sound of the bull-roarer in action. Further east the ordinary name is *tiparu*, or less often, *bukari*. This latter word usually means "chief," but as the "chief" has a close con-nection with the bull-roarer the name is applied to the instrument itself (unless indeed it is the other way about, the name *bukari* having first signified bull-roarer and been transferred to the man who controls it). This subject of the *bukari* will occupy our attention later on. In the meantime I propose to spend some time on the word *hevehe* which is worth discussing as one of the most significant in Elema anthropology.

The Word Hevehe

Hevehe, which in the east becomes *sevese* or *semese*, is a word common to all the dialects of the Gulf Division coast. Holmes translates it as "warriors,"[6] a meaning which no doubt it possessed in the Toaripi or Motumotu dialect, but which I feel confident is a derivative one. This meaning is not recognized at the Orokolo end of the coast.

Again at the Motumotu end the name *hevehe* (or *sevese*) is given to the carved wooden figures which, as possibly ancestral effigies, were placated with offerings and whose aid was invoked for the hunt or the fighting expedition.

In the languages of the western half, *hevehe* may stand for certain monsters of the deep, marine or fluvial. Such are called more specifically *ma-hevehe*, or "water-*hevehe*." They are huge sharks, dugongs, etc., more or less fabulous creatures, sea-serpents, levia-thans. They are represented in an imposing ceremony which is still frequently to be seen, or rather heard, between Kerema and Orokolo. A great crowd of men gather silently on the beach under cover of darkness, and then proceed towards the *eravo* or men's house, creat-ing by various means an unearthly uproar. They enter the *eravo* and after a pause return in the same manner down the beach. The hullabaloo dies away in the distance and finally ends in silence as the *ma-hevehe*, having thus paid a visit to the village, returns to its element.

Again the word *hevehe* is applied to those singular, elongated masks sometimes 20 feet or more in height, which form such a notable feature of the material culture—as well as the decorative art—of the Elema people. These are called, to distinguish them, *apa-hevehe* or "drum-*hevehe*" because each of them, as worn by a man, carries and beats a drum.

Next we come to the bull-roarer itself, which is specifically the *be'ure* or "ground" *hevehe* (from *bea-ure*: inside, or under, the ground). Why it should be given this qualification has never become really clear to me: no native informant, at any rate, has been able to give me a satisfactory explanation.

Lastly, and perhaps here we have touched rock-bottom, *hevehe*, in the language of the Keuru and Opau groups (Nos. 4 and 6) is the ordinary generic name for "snake."

It must be understood that the word *hevehe* without any qualification is used for any and all of these things. If a man is speaking of the masks, he calls them *hevehe*, not *apa-hevehe*; if of the sea monster then *hevehe* not *ma-hevehe*; if of the bull-roarer, again simply *hevehe*; and so on. It is cerainly perplexing, but by no means uncommon, for one and the same word to be used with a number of widely different meanings.

It is pretty well impossible to be sure of origins, but just here I propose to indulge the passion which, despite my protestations on a previous page, I share in secret with many anthropologists of the Functional persuasion. It is hardly necessary to say that what follows is no more than a conjectural sequence. But, retracing the steps taken in the foregoing paragraph, I suggest that the meaning "snake" is probably an original one. For the snake is a familiar creature—all too familiar—and it is hardly likely to be named after any of the other things known as *hevehe*; not nearly so likely, at any rate, as that one of them should be named after it.

Next, going backwards, we come to the bull-roarer. The fact that it is called a "ground-*hevehe*" might fall into line with the derivation I suggest, though this explanation has never been put forward by an informant. There is however the very significant fact that the bull-roarers are often represented to the women and uninitiated as "snakes." This is not always the case; sometimes they are lizards or crocodiles; and more often simply undefined creatures known only by their unearthly voices. But I have recorded the snake interpretation more often than the others; and it is significant that in the Keuru group (No. 4), where the snake is called *hevehe*, that was the only interpretation given. There the women are al-legedly bluffed into believing that the bull-roarers, i.e. the creatures which they do not see but only hear, are snakes; and that the men in the *eravo* make them howl by poking their tails with a stick.

We next come to *hevehe* (or *apa-hevehe*) as the name of the tall mask. Why this mask and the ceremony which belongs to it should bear the same name as the bull-roarer is a puzzle that seems to call for inspiration rather than sober comparison for its solution, since the two cults in their present form are (as far as any elements in one and the same culture can be) mutually independent. Of the *apa-hevehe* ceremony, a tremendous affair in itself, I shall write at much greater length elsewhere. The origin of mask ceremonies—if that concerned us—would have to be sought far beyond the bounds of the Gulf Division. But the local name of this particular mask ceremony may admit of a local explanation, and this is where the inspiration comes in. The reader is asked to consider the strange shape of the *hevehe* masks as shown on plate V. They are long, narrow, flat, spatulate, or compressed-ovoid. They are not recognized as resembling anything by the native himself; they are *sui generis*. One might find something to support the surmise that they were once meant to resemble fish. But I think a better surmise is that they were once meant to resemble bull-roarers. One might at first glance say that they were like nothing on earth. But it will not be denied that they are is shape at any rate gigantic bull-roarers, painted and befeathered, and set upon masked figures who carry them out of the secret *eravo* into the open. This interpre-tation has no backing in native ideology. The most I can quote is the saying that the bull-roarer is the "elder brother" of the *apa-hevehe*: it is thought to be of earlier origin. No native has ever pointed to the resemblance between the two things, nor have I ever referred my hypothesis to a native for criticism or support. It is merely put forward here as a conjecture. The reader may form his own judgement of its plausibility and, all said and done, neither he nor I need care a hang whether it is right or wrong. But my suggestion is that these masks are called *hevehe* because they were once huge walking bull-roarers.

Next we come to the *hevehe* as sea- or river-monster. The great *apa-hevehe* ceremony which we have been discussing is both a complex and (from evidence which I cannot here review) a composite affair. It has (at any rate at the western end of the Gulf Division, where I have mainly studied it) incorporated the *ma-hevehe*, or water-*hevehe*. The ceremony of impersonating the sea monster by a crowd of men is repeatedly carried out in connection with the making of the *apa-hevehe* masks within the *eravo*; and when the latter finally emerge it is said that they are the "children" of the sea-*hevehe* which in their previous visits they have left behind them. It may be that the name for the sea monster derives from their association with the *hevehe* in the *eravo*, or else that the word *hevehe* has come to stand for monster or supernatural creature in a general sense.

Lastly there is the meaning of *hevehe* as "warrior." At the western end of the coast, as we have seen, this is simply unknown; but a distinction is there sometimes drawn between the *hevehe-haera* (the *hevehe* men) and the *avai*, or old men. The former are the able-bodied, those who work and hunt and fight, as against those (in Orokolo society a most powerful and important class) who sit down and eat, being waited on by their more active juniors. One seldom hears mention of this distinction however, and I do not think we should be wrong in regarding it as an echo of the real distinction which is found further down the coast. At Uaripi (No. 5) the expression *sevese-karu* (*sevese* men) was sometimes used instead of the more general *mai-karu* (arm-men, or workers) to indicate the class opposed to the *bukari* or chiefs. Now it was the function of the *mai-karu* to swing the bull-roarers in response to the summons of the *bukari* to do so; and it seems plausible that the name *mai-karu* or *sevese-karu*, was given them because they did the actual work of swinging. It was said further that the *sevese-karu* were the fighters, the *bukari* possessing a special function as peacemakers. I suggest then that the *sevese* men as warriors may have derived their name from the circumstance that they swung the *sevese* or bull-roarer. At any rate it seems improbable that "warriors" can be, as implied by Holmes, the fundamental meaning of the word.[7]

The foregoing may pass as an example of that fanciful kind of reconstruction which for so many anthropologists (myself included) constitutes a pleasurable exercise. Not for one moment would I bank upon its validity; nor, granted it has any, would I be certain of its value. While it does seem to me probable that the original meaning of *hevehe* is nothing more than "snake," the attempt to trace its application to all these other, widely differing, things must be merely conjectural; and one doubts whether it serves directly any useful purpose.

The mere fact of this multiplicity of meanings has been, however, worthy of attention. For it seems to me to illustrate very well how an element of culture (and a word, a name, is as truly an element of culture as a method of fishing or a burial rite) may pass over from one place, or from one set of circumstances, to another, and in doing so may leave its old meaning behind it and pick up a new one. It illustrates the piecemeal, haphazard manner in which cultures build themselves up, and the strange conglomeration in which this process results.

Myths of the Bull-Roarer

We may now return to the particular kind of *hevehe* with which we are concerned, viz. the *be' ure-hevehe* or bull-roarer, and consider first of all its place in the Elema myths. We shall find here an even more perplexing variety in native belief. Even if we confine ourselves to one group, e.g. that of Orokolo, Arihava and Vailala (No. 1) which speaks one dialect and possesses a highly homogeneous culture, we shall find, not one myth of the bull-roarer, but a number, more or less intermixed but plainly independent.

It will help us to account for this multiplicity of myths if we remember that the whole Elema people, and each major group within it, is divided on lines of patrilineal descent, into a number of totemic sections,[8] and that each of these sections possesses its own elaborate system of mythology with which its long list of totem species and its magic, black or white, are intimately connected. Unfortunately, however, we find, wherever we turn, that this neat theoretical division is in practice over-run, distorted, and confused. A man of the Kaia, or Sky section, may give you one myth and will tell it to you in secret, with elaborate precautions lest he be over-heard. A man of the Ahea, or Sea, section will give you another in the same manner; and a man of the Kauri, or East, section will give you a third. But while each of the ten sections possesses a body of myth which it can call its own and lays claim to its own mythical personalities, there is no small amount of cribbing and overlapping.

Another general point in regard to the myths should be noted. The knowledge of them is very unevenly spread throughout the people. They are closely connected with magic, and this magic is owned and handed on by one individual to another in private. A knowledge of the relevant myth, and particularly of the secret names of the mythical characters, is the essence of the magician's power, so that it is no matter for surprise that the myths themselves should be in some large degree secret. There is no individual at Orokolo who knows more than a fraction of the whole mass of myths which, unequally distributed and partly secret as they are, exist in the village at large; and only a relatively few well-informed men who know in any detail the myths of their own section within the village.

In view of these two points, first that, even within a highly homogeneous culture represented by a single village, there are a number of separate myths relating to the origin of the bull-roarer, and secondly, that the knowledge of them is so unevenly distributed among individuals, we should find it impossible to establish any close correlation between the myth of the bull-roarer and its ritual. For in contrast to the multiplicity of the myths, their confusion, and their sectional or (in certain details) even private nature, we find that the ritual of the bull-roarer is strikingly simple, and is one and the same for all lineal sections and communities within the village.

The myths are often very long stories, and if one were to record the variants heard from different informants there would be no end to this dissertation. They are recorded here as mere abstracts.

(1) A sky-man name Hare (the sun) made models of a man and woman in the sand at Popo[9] (behind the present village of Arihava). Later he looked down and spoke to the models, whereupon they rose as real human beings. The two mated and the woman gave birth to a bull-roarer. It was a thing of mere bones, without flesh, and when it cried it made a noise like a bull-roarer, not like a baby. Hare came again and told them it was a *hevehe*. They were to hide it away and initiate their subsequently born children. Next the woman produced a *kovave* mask;[10] then an *apa-hevehe*; and finally a human child, who was initiated to these things.

(2) The Haive people lived on the middle Vailala River. Their three leaders were the *hevehe* or bull-roarers named Aihaipo, Hurava and Evoa. They led their people on a migration to Muru, burrowing underground. A Muru man who was out hunting saw the trees overturned and the ground churned up as they approached. He drew near and saw the string "tails" (i.e. the strings by which the *hevehe* are swung). He seized them and pulled the bull-roarer men to the surface and they lived with him at Muru and told him how to initiate the Muru people.

(3) An old woman, Orohahape, lived alone with her daughter, Miriuku-vari, on the beach at Popo. The waves cast up a dry coconut which took root and grew into a tree. The ripe nuts fell from this and split open and a number of boys emerged. The old woman made friends with them, and eventually with another man Herevakore, who lived on the coast some distance towards the east. Then the old woman went down into a hole in the ground, to what is spoken of as her "other village," and thence brought up a bull-roarer, to which the boys were initiated, the stranger Herevakore standing as their maternal uncle.

(4) Two women, Mori and Ape, lived at the Purari mouth. They had a *maia* tree, two branches of which used to rub together in the wind, making a noise like a shell trumpet. This tree they called their *hevehe*, and they would heap up food at the butt of it as

an offering. Now two men from Auma, who used to live on nothing but wild fruit, were drawn to the spot by the sound, and discovering this pile of food by the *maia* tree they secretly helped themselves. Then they made real bull-roarers on their own account (how they discovered them is not told) and sounded them in the bush. The women heard them and called them *merava-hurava*, i.e. "wild" or "bush" *hurava*, thinking they were the children of their own *hevehe*. The men now discovered themselves to the women, seized them, married them, and begot children by them. These children were in due course initiated.

(5) A man from the west named Bitavabu travelled by canoe to Yule Island and from there eloped with a girl named Aviara. Her father, Oa Laia, pursued them in the form of a sea monster, and coming to land about Orokolo lay hidden in the trees by the beach. The girl in due course bore a son who used to play with other little boys on the beach until Oa Laia, who had lain in wait for, and swallowed many of the other little boys by intention, now swallowed his grandson by mistake. The mother discovered the child's fate and the villagers tried to kill Oa Laia. All efforts failed until the help of two men from the Delta country was enlisted. These two discovered a vulnerable spot on Oa Laia's body and killed him. In his belly was found the bull-roarer.

(6) The bull-roarer was a man who slept in the *eravo* and used to call out with a bull-roarer's voice. Once a woman wanted some fire, so disguising herself as a man she went up into the *eravo* to procure it (a thing which of course no woman is allowed to do). But she was seen and questioned. To placate the offended bull-roarer man the people offered him all sorts of food, but he refused it. Only when they killed and offered up the woman herself was he appeased. The woman's husband was very angry. He piled up wood about the *eravo* and burnt it, and the spirit of the bull-roarer man, who was destroyed in the fire, went into a *pira* tree. Later on a man was told in a dream to fashion a bull-roarer in the present form from the wood of this tree, and thus the bull-roarer was invented.

(7) The bull-roarer (*rubu*) was originally like a crocodile and came from the Cupola (the hill overlooking Kerema Bay). It came along the ground, making the bull-roarer's noise as it did so and entered the *eravo*. Here, as in the previous story, a woman entered to obtain fire during the absence of the villagers, and this set the *rubu* howling. When the villagers returned, they discovered the cause of the *rubu's* anger and finally appeased it by putting the woman inside its open mouth. Having swallowed her the *rubu* left the *eravo* and went down into a stream as a crocodile. It was caught and killed and its entrails thrown away. Two women fishing subse-

quently came upon these entrails and found in them the bull-roarer. The women found they could sound it and conspired to frighten and impose upon the men by means of it. But finally the men captured it from them and thereafter it became a secret known only to the males.

One or more of the above myths, with variants,[11] are to be heard, here there and everywhere, between Arihava and Kerema; though the ordinary informant, if he knows one at all, will probably know no more than one in any detail. The first four were recorded from the closely adjacent villages of Arihava and Orokolo. As for the fifth, my memory tells me that that also belongs there; for the story of Oa Laia itself is one of their most important myths, though I do not find in my notes any verification for the actual discovery of the bull-roarer in his entrails.[12] Even without the assistance of this fifth, however, it will be seen that a small homogeneous group, such as Orokolo and Arihava together constitute, can have a number of alternative myths relating to one and the same subject. There is no question here of myth and ritual being in any sense equally balanced. There is a decided superfluity of myth.

The Bull-Roarer as Material Object

The Elema bull-roarer is usually distinguished by a "mouth" which is reminiscent of the "fish-mouth" of the Elema drum. Otherwise it conforms to the usual type. Those which are intended for actual use are made of palm or some kind of hardwood and are mostly undecorated. Others, usually larger, are made of softer wood and are often ornamented with incised patterns, either stylized decorative forms, or anthropomorphic, or showing crocodile or lizard motives. Many are painted all over with red ochre. They vary greatly in size, from about 9 inches upwards. The largest I have seen (at Muru) measured 3 ft. 2 in. in length and 5½ inches in breadth; another (at Uaripi) was 2 ft. 2 in. by 7 inches.

As so often elsewhere a distinction is drawn between major and minor bull-roarers. The latter, *hevehe-titaika* (i.e. little bull-roarers) or *merava-hurava* ("wild" or "bush" *hurava*), are actually sounded. The former, which are not nearly so numerous, and often of obviously greater age, are merely displayed within the *eravo* at the ceremony. These latter are known by personal names, though in no single case have I found a native to give a certain explanation of the name's meaning. The major *hevehe* belong to large kinship groups within the *eravo*; the minor are owned individually, each boy receiving one at his initiation. All, both major and minor, are kept in a large parcel of palm spathe or coconut fibre in one of the *larava,* or alcoves, of the *eravo.* They are under the care of a curator (Orokolo: *kwalaivira haera*) who alone is supposed to open the parcel. He is not necessarily the chief of the *eravo.*

Pretexts for Initiation

Initiations to the bull-roarer, which may be conducted at any time of the year, are often very small-scale affairs, the candidates numbering no more than two or three. An Elema village may comprise upwards of a thousand inhabitants, but it is divided into *eravo* communities which constitute very well defined units within it, and it is usual for such an *eravo,* acting by itself, to undertake the responsibilities (which are mainly those of providing food) for initiating its own boys. An individual will put forward the suggestion; several others will agree to collaborate with him; and the undertaking is launched, with full certainty of the *eravo's* co-operation.

There are two main considerations—boys and pigs. The motive for carrying out an initiation ceremony is always said to be the same, and we may accept it, I think, pretty well at its face value; certain boys have reached the proper age, and their fathers, or those who stand in an equivalent position towards them, think it desirable that they should be introduced to the secret. But the other consideration is of no less importance; the father must possess a pig. Indeed the possession of an animal of the right age and proportions is often the real reason for setting the ceremony in motion. A man who owns such a pig feels that he must make use of it. Not only does it give him an opportunity for the kind of self-display which is so dear to the native heart, but it is the public-spirited thing to do; and this, the initiation of his son, is one of the many ways of doing it that lie open to him. It is certain that the individual who first suggests carrying out the ceremony has got a pig which will enable him to play his part, and his fellow *eravo* members welcome the suggestion because it implies a feast and all its associated pleasures, which are far from being merely gustatory. I have recorded for instance that in a certain *eravo* a number of men had jogged the chief into taking action; it was a long time they said, since the last feast. Sometimes, no doubt, it is true that the feast is the real thing, and the bull-roarer an excuse for it.

It is possible to unearth some esoteric meaning in the bull-roarer, but I may state with all possible emphasis my own view that mundane, secular interests are uppermost in the minds of most of those implicated in the ceremony; and to overlook or under-estimate these in the search for magico-religious implications represents a grave omission, a kind of anthropological error to which too many students have been prone. One thing is certain, that while the bull-roarers in their magico-religious character are felt to exercise some influence over the prosperity of the community at large, it is not with the express idea of promoting that prosperity that the particular ceremony is undertaken.

Most boys in the Orokolo group are "initiated" twice at least. On the first occasion they may be so small as to be nursed throughout it in the arms of an adult. It is recognized that they are too young to appreciate the meaning of the ceremony and no attempt is made to draw their attention to the bull-roarers themselves. I could not elicit from informants any reason for this preliminary initiation: they do not seem at the present time to entertain the idea that it confers any benefit on the child, though from the formulae used in the ceremony it may perhaps be taken that this is implied.[13] A more practical reason however, and one which commends itself more to me personally, is that the father may have pigs to spare and may seize upon the occasion to dispose of one. By so doing he ingratiates himself with the community at large and at the same time finds opportunity to make another of those presents to his brother-in-law (the child's maternal uncle) which form an essential feature of the relations between affines. For this brother-in-law is the actual recipient of the pig.

Some boys have been initiated as many as four times—those, it is explained, whose fathers have many pigs. But twice is usually enough. Some years after his childhood initiation the lad is shown the secret again, being now of an age to take notice and understand it. And this occasion is marked by the presentation of a badge in the simple form of a sprig of *dracaena*. Henceforward he may wear a *dracaena* leaf in his armlet to show that he has seen and understood the bull-roarer. It is one of those ornaments which cannot be worn till the right has been bought at the price of a pig. If his father is rich enough he will provide another pig later on, and on behalf of his son purchase the right to wear *dracaena* leaves in both armlets.

Women never see the bull-roarer—or are supposed never to see it—but some of them in their youth undergo a form of initiation. Whereas the boys are shown and presented with actual bull-roarers within the *eravo*, the girl candidates are merely led up to the barrier without passing it, and furthermore their eyes are bandaged. Like the boys they receive gifts from their maternal uncles as well as the right to wear *dracaena* in their armlets, but the real secret is kept from them. Such privileged girls—if the privilege amounts to anything—are girls without brothers. It is said significantly that a man who has no sons may initiate a daughter. It is as if he looks for a pretext to give a pig to the *eravo* at large and his brother-in-law in particular, being of course repaid very handsomely by the latter with shell ornaments.

The ceremony of initiation is practically the sole occasion, as far as I know, for sounding the bull-roarer at the Orokolo end of the Gulf Division coast.[14] Among the central groups (Nos. 5-7) we find it used for other purposes, viz. when the *bukari* or chief causes it to be sounded, e.g. to restore his dignity or preserve the peace. Of these functions of the bull-roarer I shall speak later on; in the meantime restricting the inquiry to the western end of the coast I shall describe the ceremony of initiation.

Kinship Obligations

In the typical case a father arranges (which means that he provides the pig) for the initiation of his son; and the father's brother-in-law, i.e. the boy's mother's brother, or *aukau*, gives him the bull-roarer. If the boy happens to be an orphan, the deceased father's place is taken by some responsible relative such as a paternal uncle or an elder brother; and if the mother happens to be without a true brother, then the latter's place is taken by one of her classificatory kinsmen. There is always an individual who, whether he is the mother's true brother or not, assumes permanently the role of *aukau* towards the child, his *arivu*.

There exists between these two a lifelong bond of amity characterized by the exchange of gifts and the performance, by the *aukau*, of certain ceremonial duties. It grows out of the relationship between a man and his wife's brother, who on the birth of the child becomes its *aukau*. In the early stages of the child's life it is naturally the father (*oa*) who bears the active, responsible part on his behalf. When he reaches adult years he acts for himself. When, in the course of events his *aukau* dies, the relationship continues with the son of the *aukau*, i.e. the *ai*.

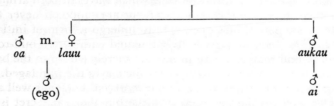

Father, *oa*; Mother, *lauu*; mother's brother, *aukau*; sister's son, *arivu*; mother's brother's son and father's sister's son, *ai* (reciprocal).

The gifts from the *arivu* (or his father or other representative) usually take the form of pigs (dogs, fowls, and other food are also given). The return presents from the *aukau* are typically ornaments comprehended by the term *eharu*. These, which constitute the condensed wealth of the Elema native, are dog's teeth, crescent pearl-shells, armshells, shell disk frontlets and so on. Besides these the *aukau* gives to his *arivu* a succession of more utilitarian gifts, but still in a very formal manner—his first bow, his first drum, his first string bag, etc. And he must play the leading part in the various rites which the *arivu* passes through from his childhood upwards. Without attempting to enter more fully into the relationship between *arivu* and *aukau*, I may state my considered opinion here that the giving of the gifts is by far the most important consideration in it. The importance in native eyes of maintaining this exchange can hardly be overemphasized. What a man receives as *arivu* or *ai* he will have to give away to someone else as *aukau* or *ai*. A very high value is attached to these ornaments and the interest shown in them is intense.[15]

The initiation to the bull-roarer, and the presentation to the initiate of an actual bull-roarer as well as a number of ornaments, is one of this succession of duties which the *aukau* performs in return for a succession of pigs.

"Waking Up" the Bull-Roarers

The *aukau*, having received due notice of the ceremony, makes a new bull-roarer for his nephew. He paints it red and may carve it if he is good at carving. The string of such a presentation *hevehe* is a short one bound with several score dog's teeth and decorated with a few tufts of cuscus fur. It is known as the *hevehe-aue*, or "tail," and itself constitutes a costly gift. The new bull-roarers are left hanging in the *eravo* for all to see.

Meanwhile the food has been brought together by the candidates' fathers and the patrilineal kinsmen who help them, and on the day preceding the actual initiation (sometimes the morning of the same day) there occurs the ceremony of "waking up" (*hurapakive*) the *hevehe*. A few pots of stew (*papaa*) have been prepared, together with a dish of *poi-koru*, or sago balls,[16] and the curator has placed the parcel of bull-roarers ready in one of the two front *larava* where a number of older men are gathered. Now one of the initiates' fathers brings in a dry coconut and places it on the floor before the bundle of bull-roarers, while the curator, without opening the parcel fully, extracts one which he has previously provided with a string and a small peg as handle. He now retires further towards the rear of the *eravo*. Those present, who may number about a dozen (for it is a small affair, without guests), have hitherto been chatting and laughing. Now, as the *poi koru* are brought into the *eravo* and set down before the bundle of *hevehe*, they suddenly become silent. The *eravo* chief holds the dry coconut poised in one hand, with an axe ready in the other. The curator swings the bull-roarer noiselessly for a moment till he has taken the measure of the space available. Then, appealing to all present to utter a good loud *yakea*, or united hoot, at the right moment, he suddenly stamps his foot and accelerates the swing. As he does so the *eravo* chief splits the coconut with one well-directed blow of his axe, the men utter a spirited *yakea*, and the bull-roarer begins to roar. The *hevehe* have woken up.

The string is necessarily short and the bull-roarer is a fairly large one, so that its voice is of the low, almost growling kind, unlike the high pitched notes of the smaller instruments which are later on to be sounded in the open. The curator, with more stamping of his foot, continues to swing for several minutes until the pots of *papaa* are brought into the *eravo* and placed beside the *poi koru* and the bull-roarers. Then he lays down the instrument he is swinging, opens the parcel, and extracts a number of major importance, which he lays side by side on the floor. Having done this he takes out one of the sago balls, crumbles it in his hands and allows the fragments to fall upon the bull-roarers. Conversation now recommences; the *papaa* is ladled out into smaller dishes by the *eravo* chief; and everyone sets to. The ceremony of "waking up" is over.

All this is done with an air of some solemnity, though in an easy-going, comfortable manner: a ceremony so many times enacted has acquired something of a routine nature. We need not suppose that the participants are keenly alive to its meaning any more than Christian worshippers are alive to the meaning of the psalms which they gabble in church. Indeed we may suppose they are much less so. For most psalm-singers, if interrupted and asked to explain what they were singing, would be in a very fair position to do so; whereas the ordinary native, if faced with a similar poser in regard to the ritual of the bull-roarer, would be, to say the least, in serious ideological straits.

I have watched a man named Abiara in action at such a ceremony to see if he were uttering any kind of formula (hearing is out of the question); and I thought I detected a movement of his lips as he was opening the package of bull-roarers. But like nearly all formulae among the Elema people the words are "thought" rather than spoken, and it is to be presumed that during a ceremony or an act of private magic they are used in a very sketchy manner. In fact it is doubtful whether they could be said to constitute a formula at all, since no stress is laid on the necessity of sticking closely to a set form of words.

The following which was communicated by Abiara after the ceremony was certainly not pronounced by him, even under his breath, during its course. He began by giving me, in a whisper, the secret names of two most ancient bull-roarers, "Oro Uravu" and "Karo Uravu." These names he had received from his predecessor in office, a man Maii who died recently, as the very essence of his ritual duty. They were actually secret from the other men of the *eravo*, and Abiara confided them to me as a great favour. He would have told me what the names stood for if he had known; but I am sure he was quite honest in saying he did not.[17]

After revealing these two names he did not care to repeat them, but used the phrase *haera orahouka*—"two men"—as a harmless, euphemistic substitute.

> *Haera orahouka, aipekive poi, larive; ekaka, larive; ape-larive.*
> You two men, I place here sago, eat it; fish, eat it;
> with your mouths eat it.
> *Akore hekai, larive eavakive.*
> The small boys see you eat.
> *Hihiri kau, mekakure, heaha kau.*
> Be not angry, be well disposed, be not evil.
> *Eapapo laikive, ikivere laikive.*
> Make them big, make them good-tempered.
> *Haera orahouka, laikive obohae eavakive.*
> You two men, make them see with their eyes.
> *Haera orahouka, eapoi avarikive.*
> You two men, food we give.
> *Maia eapapo laikive, heaha kau, heroi iveve.*
> Make (their?) bodies big; be not evil, be compassionate.
> *Haera orahouka eavakive ira, poi; aukuvei larive; aaipekive.*
> You two men see the pig, the sago;
> eat them up; I put them here.
> *Eavakive hoavakive, epavakive, aipekive, earive.*
> See I swing, I stand up, I put down, eat.

Even if Abiara does not actually utter these words they represent, by his own account, what he means. Here, then, there is obviously no play-acting. We are facing a new aspect of the *hevehe*. Abiara is making a serious appeal to a thing of power.

The Ceremony of Initiation

Having been thus aroused the *hevehe* will be heard from time to time calling hungrily for food; and as the women respond by carrying up pots of stew which are handed into the interior of the building, the same noises may be heard again as expressions of ravenous delight. With the onset of darkness the *hevehe* issue into the open; and then, as well as the deep-voiced monsters of the *eravo*, may be heard the *merava hurava*, or *hevehe titaika*, smaller instruments which are swung by long strings attached to rods as handles. When a number of bull-roarers are sounding together there is a perfect babel of queer noises ranging from deep murmurs to ear-splitting shrieks, for each has the quality of rising and falling that belongs to a siren whistle. It is the young men of course who indulge in this form of larking about the village. The women and uninitiated children take very good care to remain inside the houses.

The following day is that of the initiation.[18] The pigs are killed, singed, carved and cooked; and a considerable portion of the meat is prepared in the form of sizable junks, for presentation by the *arivu* initiates to their *aukau*. The door of the *eravo* has been closed and only men of years and importance pass the barrier. They spend the day in a manner which the native finds eminently to his taste, sitting with their guests on the floor, chewing betel (of which several bunches have been provided by the initiates' fathers) smoking, talking, and sometimes dozing. Every now and again the bull-roarer's voice is heard (by daytime only within the *eravo*) and more dishes of food are handed in. It is a very easy-going sociable day. These older men do not look forward with any excitement to the actual ceremony of initiation. It is merely an episode, a little piece of routine which for them has long since lost its thrill. But meantime they are enjoying themselves, and there will soon be the presentation of gifts, which is an absorbing spectacle even to those who are not implicated.

At about 4 p.m. the young initiates are ready for their ordeal, and a very light one it proves to be, whatever they may have been expecting. They have been cleaned up and their faces and bodies smeared with a few decorative streaks of red ochre. Each wears a baldric of green areca nuts and pepper fruit threaded on a string, and each carries in his hand a *hapa*, i.e. a young coconut frond with the tender leaflets frayed out so as to hang in the form of a deep fringe. To this *hapa* are attached more areca nuts and pepper fruit as well as half a dozen junks of pork. Thus arrayed and equipped they are led up by their fathers or guardians to the barrier at the *eravo* door. It is removed and they enter to learn the bull-roarer's secret.[19]

Two men armed with light switches of coconut midrib lie in wait for them inside, one on either side of the door-way, and as the boys enter they receive a harmless stroke on the back. This ritual beating is so unimportant that it is often omitted, and it is so light that I doubt whether the initiate, in the excitement of the moment, even feels it. For a crowd of men are elbowing through the entrance and the narrow space within is almost filled. The initiates stand in the centre and their *aukau* now come forward to make the presentation.

The Giving of Gifts

Each *aukau* takes the *hapa* from his *arivu's* hand and divests him of his green baldric. (The pork, the betel-nut, and the pepper fruit are the maternal uncle's perquisites.) He takes the new *hevehe*, with its "tail" of dog's teeth, which he has made ready for the occasion and hangs it over his *arivu's* shoulder. Then, fidgeting with a string bag which he wears under his arm he proceeds to the most important business of the day. He produces from it one after another the fine ornaments which, as maternal uncle, he is to give to his sister's child.

He places the broad shell circles (*huaiea*) on the boy's arms: he hangs the pearl-shell crescents (*huave*) about his neck; and binds upon his forehead the handsome frontlets of overlapping shell disks known as *apakoro*. I have known a lad receives as many as eleven *huaiea*, as well as other expensive ornaments; and it is an amusing sight to see the smallest initiates, sometimes, infants in arms, fairly loaded with ornaments many times too large for them. Sometimes the infant takes it well, though of course without the slightest inkling of what is going forward. But sometimes, frightened by the throng, he bawls and kicks with all his might. I have seen an *aukau*, after vainly trying to tie some pearl-shells round an infant's neck, succeed finally in inducing it to clutch an ornament in its hand. But the child, becoming conscious of what it held, dashed it to the ground with every sign of infantile anger and to the great amusement of all present. The *aukau* gave up in despair and handed all the ornaments to the child's father, who was in any case due to take charge of them.

I really believe that to an initiate who has reached years of understanding the receipt of the presents is perhaps of greater moment than the revelation of the secret. For while we may reasonably doubt whether the bull-roarer is a secret at all to an intelligent youngster, there is no question of the reality and importance of the ornaments. I remember well a rather affecting incident in connection with one initiation. There were only three little brothers as candidates—a child in arms, a boy of about four years, and one of about six. The *aukau* of the last mentioned happened to be absent on indentured labour. It was said, before the ceremony, that one of his kinsmen might come forward to take his place; but in the event none did so. When the three small brothers entered the *eravo* the two younger received their presents. The baby howled and buried his face in his father's breast; he was too young to care for them. The second child stood solemnly while his uncle tied three pearl-shells round his neck and placed an armshell on each arm, telling him to clench his fists to prevent their falling off. Then there was a pause, of which everyone, I think, felt the awkwardness. No one had appeared to bedeck the eldest child of six. After a moment's silence the little boy took the initiative: he turned on his heel and fled out of their midst in tears. Thereupon the tension was relaxed, and the presentations being over, all sat down to eat. When sometime later I left the *eravo* to go home I saw the little boy of six leaning alone and disconsolate against a coconut tree. I told him I would be his *aukau* in a small way, and that if he visited my camp on the morrow I would make him a present of a looking-glass. When early next morning I opened my eyes from slumber, the first thing I saw was my little *arivu* squatting silently beside my bed and waiting for his looking-glass.

The Maternal Uncle's Harangue

As he is investing his nephew with the ornaments the *aukau* takes the opportunity of giving him a public talking-to.[20] While the words, of praise or blame, are directed towards the initiate, they refer more often than not to his adult relatives, the sister and the in-laws of the officiating *aukau*, and as they are uttered in a loud voice they amount to a public pronouncement. This is a privileged occasion: the initiate himself must make no answer, nor have I ever heard any from the relatives concerned. They must take their medicine in silence. The following are samples which I have actually heard.

One man, as he ties the pearl-shells on the boy's neck simply and loudly announces that his mother is a "strong worker" and always helps him (the *aukau*, or in other words, her brother) when he wants it. Another speaking to an older initiate cries out, "You are a bad boy. Like your elder brother—lazy! You never work for me at all, but I give you many ornaments. If you work hard for me I'll give you some more. If not—finish."

Another: "Your father and mother have been saying nasty things about the size of the ornaments, we (i.e. I and my wife) have given you. We are ashamed.' (Not that he admits the gifts are deficient in size: he means that he is offended and embarrassed.) "If they help us at our work we will give you some more. If not, then these are the last."

Another, a man of the Hurava, or "West," section addressing his female *arivu* who has just been "initiated," blindfold and with a cloth over her head:[21] "Everyone says I am a Kaimari man." (This is by way of repeating a joke against himself. He is really a man of importance in Auma, but because he is Hurava he has been said to belong to a village in the Purari Delta, where wealth is not so much in evidence.) "Well," says he as he produces the armshells from his bag, "I am a Kaimari man, but I have plenty of ornaments." Then turning to the girl, "If I want to make sago can you do it?" The girl, who at this stage has had her eyes unbound, remains silent. "Yes," he shouts, as he ties two beautiful *apakoro* upon the girl's forehead, "You are just like your elder sister. When I ask her to make sago she always has something else to do." Meanwhile, though noticeably trembling with the excitement of speaking in public, the *aukau* is really in a fine humour; he is obviously popular and as he scolds his *ariku* his face is wreathed in benevolent smiles.

The End of the Ceremony

The ceremony of initiation is now over. It is probably 5 o'clock in the afternoon or later, and the hosts and guests sit down to eat; then the party breaks up, the *aukau* bearing away to their own homes the gifts of pork and other food which they have received. Meanwhile the initiates have handed the ornaments over to their fathers. They do not continue to wear them, though they are entitled to flaunt a sprig of *dracaena* in their armlets. The boys simply disperse. They have received no special instruction regarding the *hevehe*, nor do they undergo any subsequent rite of purification.

During the night the bull-roarers may be sounded on and off; but the enthusiasm has departed. Next day at a small feast within the *eravo* the curator wraps them up in their package again where they remain until the next initiation. I find I have not recorded at Orokolo any form of words uttered on this occasion, but if there is any, it may be something like the following recorded at Uaripi (group No. 5). "Do not let snakes and crocodiles bite our women and children. Don't let our children fall out of coconut trees. We have fed you well and given you pigs. When we call on you again, cry out for us."

Part 2

Meaning of the Bull-Roarer to the Uninitiated

When we approach the question of what the bull-roarer really means to the Elema natives we find, as must be the case wherever we deal with a secret cult, that the question resolves itself into two: what does the *hevehe* mean to those who are out of the secret, and what to those who are in it. To employ the technical terms, what are its exoteric and what its esoteric meanings?

I fear I am not in a position to answer either with any degree of confidence. As for the first no female informants would dare discuss the matter, and it remains a question how much they know of it. One can say with certainty that they remove themselves very effectively from sight when the bull-roarers are in action in the open. But that is not to say that they may not, on occasion, peep through the cracks of the houses. As a matter of probability it can hardly be credited that a practice which has been going on for generations and with such careless methods of concealment should have reminded a sheer mystery to one-half of the population. And beyond this there is some positive evidence that the bull-roarer, as such, is actually known to the women. A communicative friend of mine related how once, when he was philandering with a married woman in the bush, they heard the sound of the *hevehe*. "Aren't you frightened of that?" he asked; and received the answer, in the confidence of a *tête-à-tête*, "Go on, I know all about it. It is piece of wood."[22] But apart from such isolated evidence a little there is the fact that during the Vailala Madness the bull-roarer, along with other secret cults of the Gulf coast, was deliberately exposed to the women. When it was resumed the women must accordingly have known about it, yet they very readily fell back into the old position of what may be called a fictitious ignorance.

Both males and females combine however in maintaining the form of secrecy, and there are various fantastic explanations allegedly offered to the uninitiated sex. The *hevehe* are sometimes represented at Orokolo as snakes or lizards of various sizes, from *obo*, the great carpet snake, downwards: at Muru (No. 2) and Keuru (No. 4) they were represented again as snakes. The lizard simile is common at Orokolo side by side with that of the snake, the special variety named being *bea hurava*, a lizard with a red belly. At Mei (No. 5) and Opau (No. 6) the *hevehe* were represented as crocodiles; at Karama (No. 7) a number of alternatives were given

—lizards, parrots, crocodiles, fish and snakes. But in general there is no too clear picture of the *hevehe*: they are merely awful creatures that occasionally visit the *eravo* when they are hungry, that roar and howl, and finally leave when they are satisfied. Sometimes it is given out that they come up from the ground, whence probably the specific name, *be'ure hevehe*.[23] I have never heard the fiction that they swallow and evacuate or disgorge the initiate, though there is to be seen at Opau and Mei an interesting detail in the ceremony which may be a survival of the *Verschlingungsmotiv*. When the initiates enter the *eravo* to see the bull-roarer and receive their gifts, a mess of ashes, dirt and stew is plastered on their bodies. When later they return and are asked by their supposedly anxious mothers, "Did the crocodile bite you?" they answer, "No, he only dunged on us."

To what extent the women and children are imposed upon by these fabrications I cannot presume to say. I gather from male informants that they do not discuss the matter with their womenfolk, because the womenfolk never ask for information. It is not necessary therefore to concert any set pretence: the *hevehe* are just *hevehe*, and the women are supposed to be left wondering. But I think it likely (though this is only a surmise) that they may at times enter into the spirit of the thing sufficiently to let themselves imagine there really are some strange creatures in the *eravo*, just as the European child may conjure life into the inanimate characters of a story or a game. At some later date I hope to be able to obtain some real information on this matter.

Esoteric Meaning of the Bull-Roarer

To answer the further question of what the bull-roarer really means to the initiated is no easier. We have seen how, at the ceremony of "waking up," the *hevehe* are given offerings of food in the form of sago sprinkled upon them and pots of stew placed before them, and how at the same time the curator makes them an address. And these things, it should be noted, are done with some solemnity and in the privacy of the *eravo*. Whatever may be the truth regarding the pots of food which are brought up by the women during the ensuing day, this preliminary offering is no part of the general bluffing of the uninitiated; and this argues that the initiated males entertain towards the bull-roarers some sentiments of greater weight than would attach to a mere plaything.

One might expect the associated myths to throw some light on the question of how the *hevehe* were really regarded. But we have seen that even within one group the myths are many and various, one being known to one section of the people and another to another; while some men remain practically ignorant of them all. In the face of the uniformity of the ritual it cannot be said that any one of the myths corresponds with it—if indeed myth ever does correspond with ritual, or ritual with myth. There can be no doubt, however, that the myths are taken seriously and largely believed; so that to those who know them they may represent what are really thought to be the bull-roarer's antecedents. The reader is referred back to the pages on which they are summarized for what enlightenment he may find.

In this connection, however, it should be incidentally noted that where the myth enters into detail about the initiation of the boys, such information obviously gives us no help; for it is simply added as so much colouring or stuffing by the narrator. Where we hear that the women (in myth 4) used to heap up food at the butt of the sounding tree and that they used sago balls (rather an unusual form of cooking) similar to those broken over the *hevehe* at the "waking up" ceremony, we may suspect that this is merely another dash of colouring. And when we read (in myth 3) how a coconut opened on the beach and liberated a number of boys we must beware of seizing upon this episode as an explanation of the ritual splitting of the coconut when the *hevehe* are "woken up." Indeed we may be pretty sure that it has nothing to do with it. I am not for a moment attempting to deny either that myth can throw light on ritual, or vice versa; but am merely asserting that, while in any particular case they may have more or less in common, they may still be very largely independent.

But there is another, and more promising track which we may follow in quest of the real meaning of the bull-roarer. It is that of the personal names by which the more important specimens are known.[24] As with the *kovave* and *apa-hevehe* masks and the carved and painted wooden plaques (*hohao*)[25] which adorn the interior of the *eravo*, each has its identity. The name is usually found to belong to some character in the myths, one who was in the beginning a human character, or at any rate endowed with human powers of thought and speech though possibly taking the form of bird, animal, fish, tree or other natural phenomenon. That character is now believed to live immortally in the bush, the river, or the sea, having, in many cases, been transformed at the end of its mythical term into some natural object or creature. It is now regarded as inseparable from such a thing of nature, but still has its existence as an individual personality. The Elema universe is thronged with such spiritual beings; though I should add, for fear of giving a wrong impression, that to the Elema native, as an ordinary human being, they remain in the background of attention. The *kovave*, the *apa-hevehe*, the *hohao*, are usually named, then, after these mythical characters, sometimes after the leaders in those dramatic times, sometimes after mere supernumeraries whose place in the vast tangle of Elema mythology it is difficult to find.

The personal names of the bull-roarers seem to belong to this latter class. I have not met with any that went by the great mythical names of Epe, Kivavia, Kaiva, Evarapu, Iko, Kauaru, Hiraki, etc. In the majority of cases where interpretation is possible they are the names of some vegetable species—Oro-uravu and Karo-uravu (from *oro* and *karo* trees), Yapo and Merove-yapo (two kinds of cane), Tape (a *dracaena*), Ova-ouku (log of the *ova* tree), Para (mangrove), Ohavo and Kirive (trees), hevehe-miro (a kind of palm). But this is not invariable. I have noted such names as Kerara (green parrot) Hita (some small bird), Ope (a hawk), Herivo (one of the megapods), Kavo (a bat), and Hauu and Koro (two river fish).

Each such natural species belongs to one or other of the ten sections of the Elema people,[26] in the sense that it belongs to their mythology. It would be wrong, in fact absurd, to say that the whole of nature is thus divided by the Orokolo native into ten sections; but a very large number of species are allotted to this section or that because of their mythical association with it. And this association is through the medium of the individual personality, whatever form it may have taken, who played some part in the section's mythical history, and who now, though in a sense identified with the species, continues to live a separate personal life.

These spiritual personalities are believed to influence the lives of the present day people, especially in the bush, where they mainly reside: so that they are petitioned to prosper hunting, sago making, gardening, etc., and to guard the people from danger. In the guise of *kovave* and *apa-hevehe* they are brought temporarily into the village, entertained, and sent back; while in the more permanent form of the *hohao* they are placated from time to time in the *eravo*. I think that the bull-roarers fall into line with these others, as impersonations of these mythical characters who live on to the present day and whose favour is sought by occasional acts of placation.

It is worth noting that the nervous curator who told me how he addressed the two bull-roarers, "Oro-uravu" and "Karo-uravu," but would mention their names aloud no more than once, spoke of them subsequently as "two men." The mythical characters were human in their intelligence and conduct, whatever form they took; but I refrain from falling back on the facile interpretation of the bull-roarers as "ancestors." It is possible that they may represent ancestors in other cultures; even conceivable that they may have once represented ancestors in the culture of the Elema. But that question, of their original meaning, does not concern us. It seems to me quite certain that they do not represent real ancestors to the native of to-day.

After so much time spent in trying to show what the bull-roarer means in an ideological sense to the Elema native, it may seem that the conclusion is expressed in very vague terms. Such terms however are entirely in keeping with the vagueness of the native's own ideas on the subject. I have never had from any informant a clear or intelligible statement of what the bull-roarer represented, of any reality that stood behind it. To the ordinary native it certainly possesses some significance over and above that of a musical toy or a thing with which he scares his womenfolk; but it is beyond his powers to express in set terms what that significance is; and with some men—perhaps a considerable majority—it may be taken, I believe, that the ulterior meaning of the bull-roarer, about which their knowledge is so indefinite is really a matter of no great consequence.

Sentimental and Emotional Attitudes

This brings us to an aspect of our subject which is of far greater importance than the merely intellectual conception of the *hevehe*; and that is the place which it holds in the native's emotions and sentiments.

First regarding the bull-roarer itself we find that it is treated with a very considerable amount of respect. When the young men are swinging the *merava hurava* in the village it is true they handle them as roughly as they please. With a ten foot string attached to a pliant rod of about the same length the bull-roarers are rotated in shrieking circles, and the bystander likes to have near him the shelter of a coconut palm in case they should fly loose. When this happens, as it not infrequently does, the swinger merely retrieves his bull-roarer and busies himself with mending the string. If the instrument is broken no great concern is shown. It is the business of the moment to make as much noise as possible, and the young men vie with one another in a game which requires some skill. But these are the smaller nameless bull-roarers. The larger ones are, as far as I know, never sounded, nor are they ever as much as shown in the open. At an initiation ceremony they are hung up in the *eravo*. When the ceremony is over they are restored to their package. It is true that the interior of the most orderly *eravo* is inclined to be ramshackle, and the package of bull-roarers may appear to be thrust neglectfully into a corner. But that is merely the Elema manner. The package is under a strong tabu. No one of course would ordinarily wish to open it, but it is plain that no one, except the curator himself or someone privileged by age and chiefly position, would dare to do so. And this is not simply through fear of the curator's sorcery, which might be applied as a punishment for interference with his prerogative: a man is to some real extent, I believe, afraid of the bull-roarers themselves. Some are potentially more dangerous than others; and most dangerous of all, according to certain Orokolo informants, is one named "Aihiapo" which they claimed to be the very original. It is kept safely wrapped up at Muru. And a man with a baby child would not dare to touch it: his child would be struck dumb.

It was at Muru that I saw the finest, and apparently the oldest specimens. Here the principal ones were kept, not in a package, but on a hearth-platform in the *eravo*. One, named "Hevehe Pairapo," was supposed to have dated from before the first coming of the bull-roarer to Muru. For "Hevehe Pairapo" and "Kwaeva" were the two bull-roarers who, in the *eravo* of the Hopoa Kearu people, had devoured the woman as a sacrifice for her own sin of intrusion (cf. myths Nos. 6 and 7), and had then migrated to Muru, moving crookedly along the ground, like snakes, and leaving in their track the bed of Kiravi Creek (cf. myth No. 2). It is no wonder then, that the Muru people treasured this relic. It was not one of the largest, nor was the carving anything but indifferent: but it was in good condition and bore a beautiful polish which bespoke much handling. I was struck at the time by the pride which the people showed in this specimen, and the almost affectionate way in which the chief man stroked and polished it. One could not say that all older bull-roarers are treated with such obvious pride and tenderness; but it is quite safe to say that they are all highly treasured by their communities.

We have seen that the *hevehe* are placated by offerings, and the forms of address (pp. 91-2 and 98), whether actually spoken or not, show that the attitude towards them at the more solemn moments of the initiation ceremony is really one of prayer. They are asked to give their favour and protection to the initiates. It is not indeed to be supposed that this frame of mind is a dominant one. I think anthropologists have sometimes imputed far too much to the religious side of the native's life and thought, as if he were almost obsessed with religion. But we must fight shy of the opposite extreme.

The bull-roarer has a religious value which we cannot afford to ignore.

The attitude towards the *hevehe* itself fades, as it were, into the attitude towards the ceremonies and social doings which belong to it. At the Orokolo end of the coast, as we saw, initiation provides the only occasion for sounding the bull-roarers. But this is perhaps the favourite among Orokolo ceremonies; at any rate it is the most frequent. No great preparation is needed as with *kovave* and (much more so) with *apa-hevehe*. Given the boys and the pigs and the uncles a bull-roarer initiation can take place anywhere at short notice. And apart from the esoteric functions which we have discussed it has justifications of another kind. A crowd of people are brought together, the visitors (mainly the *aukau* and their relatives) coming from other *eravo*; there is conversation, tobacco, betelchewing, and the imposing display of great junks of raw pig-flesh on a platform; at every house the women are cooking food and conversing with the visitors of their own sex, and when the proceedings are over the pots of stew are brought forward and set in a long row for display before they are distributed; finally there is the episode, in native eyes both important and absorbing, in which the *aukau* make presents to their *arivu* and at the same time speak their minds for all to hear. The ceremony of the bull-roarer, then, has all the attractions which belong to the native feast; and they are very considerable attractions. We must accord it due measure of what may be called convivial or festive value and we must recognize that it gives scope to the individual and to the small group concerned to display their wealth, generosity, and public spirit.

Over and above this it shares with *kovave* and *apa-hevehe* the partial character of a game; in short there is some fun about it. Perhaps to the older participants this aspect is not so much in evidence; they have played the game too often. But the younger men still enjoy hoaxing the women and children. At Opau, whenever a pot of stew was bought up to the *eravo* by a woman and handed in, the bull-roarer roared suddenly and briefly and the pot was immediately handed out to the woman, empty. The contents had really been capsized into another, larger, pot kept inside the *eravo* for the purpose; but the woman was given to understand that the *hevehe* had swallowed the offering in one noisy gulp. The men like their joke about the crocodile's excrement on the initiate's bodies; and they like to pretend that they make the snakes howl by tickling their tails with a stick. And above all they like to create the fearful noise of swinging the bull-roarer and to show off their skill in doing it. All this represents what we may call the lighter side of the *hevehe*. But it is far from being the least significant side. In fact I am inclined to regard the recreational function of the bull-roarer as more important than any other.

The Women's Attitude

In discussing the emotional and sentimental attitudes of the native towards the *hevehe* we must not forget those of the women. I confess that I here have comparatively little to go upon, for, as we have observed, the women always refuse to discuss the thing, or else feign complete ignorance of it.

Whenever the bull-roarer is out the women make themselves scarce, either hiding in their houses or taking to the bush. But it does not as a rule appear unexpectedly, or inconveniently. The men are dependent on the women for various things, in particular for cooking their meals: so that it would not pay them to drive the cooks from their work at the wrong time, nor to keep them long away.

The women, then, usually receive notice, and as far as I have observed they take the whole thing very well. I have seen them on the afternoon of an initiation ceremony herded out of the village at about half past three. They went off *en masse* and in high good humour, a little distance into the bush. We could still hear them laughing and chattering when the bull-roarers came out; and when, in about 15 minutes, all was over, they returned as noisily as they had gone and resumed their cooking for the feast which was to end the day. At times perhaps the presence of the bull-roarer may be an inconvenience to the women or even an infliction upon them; but, speaking for the western half of the coast, I should say from general observation that they do not resent it.

To show how anxious they are to avoid an open revelation of the *hevehe* I may quote an incident of which I heard not long ago at Auma. It appears that a former missionary was preaching to a congregation largely composed of women and girls, whose minds he wished to disabuse of a groundless fear. Intending therefore to drive home his point by practical illustration, to show them in fact what the *hevehe* really was, he produced one from his pulpit-desk and swung it before their eyes. The result must have filled him with astonishment. For the female part of his congregation rose panic-stricken to its feet and in one wild scramble fled the church.

Such an instantaneous response points to some direct fear of the bull-roarer itself. The fact that it is merely a piece of wood does not make it harmless in the eyes of the women: it is a fact with which they are probably acquainted already. We know well that many obviously inanimate and harmless objects are filled with life and power in native imagination, and, as we have seen, even the initiated males can regard the bull-roarer as a thing intrinsically dangerous. How much more may the women fear such an object, when they are never supposed to see it, much less to handle it! I think we should be justified in saying, then, that the women fear the bull-roarer itself, not only in its imagined form as a monster that hides in the *eravo* or goes roaring about the village by night, but in its purely material form as a piece of wood.

But there is another and very powerful cause of fear, and that is the threat of sorcery. The *hevehe* is ostensibly guarded as a secret by the males. The women must not pry into it, and they are made to understand that prying will be punished by sorcery. The effect of this standing threat—although for the most part it remains a tacit one—is to make the women avoid all possible appearance of knowing the secret. When the Samoan teacher at Vailala, with the laudable though somewhat mistaken intention of breaking down the *hevehe*, tried recently to instruct his female adherents about it, they would not stay to hear him. They were afraid of sorcery as a penalty for knowing what they should not know. No doubt those who stampeded from the church would have argued the same way if they had taken time to think.

We may accept it as certain that no woman under these circumstances allows herself to be caught showing curiosity. It is quite often said, however, that the death of women and girls is due to sorcery inflicted as a punishment; the theory being that once a woman has gained knowledge of the secret, she must be put out of the way for fear she should spread it among others of her sex. When during the Vailala Madness the bull-roarers were exposed at Arihava while they remained secret in the conservative Orokolo next door, many women of the latter village were supposed to have learned everything in their visits to the former, and to have been talking and laughing over the secret in their homes. Then it was that they began to die off: the old men of Orokolo were taking their revenge. I do not suppose that this is anything but a picturesque way of expressing a belief in the existence of this sanction. If certain women or girls did die in Orokolo at the time their deaths would be ascribed to the sorcerer, and this, viz. punishment for prying, would be one of the motives which would suggest itself to minds which, whenever a death occurs must look for someone to blame. It is clear that the secret of the bull-roarer is generally believed, both by men and women, to be guarded by the sanction of sorcery.

As far as the western tribes are concerned, however, ignorance of the bull-roarer, enforced as it is under the tacit threat of sorcery, does not constitute an imposition upon the women. They are content to hew wood, fetch water, cook meals, and carry loads, and they do not resent these things as impositions. They work hard at times, but so also do the men, and both sexes have abundant leisure. If the men have somewhat more leisure than the women, I am sure the latter never think of feeling sore about it. They know their position and as far as I can see they are content with it. Maybe in the future we shall hope and expect to see some relative improvement in that position; but if we attempt to alter it too suddenly we may probably count on some opposition from the very people we are trying to benefit. The whole thing is governed by a rigid sense of propriety. Just as a woman never hankers after entering the *eravo*, and never aspires to wear a *kovave* mask, so she never seeks admission to the secret of the bull-roarer. In Elema society there are things that belong to the men alone; and an Elema woman would no more think of intruding than would a lady on a railway station of pushing her way into the "Gentlemen Only." The threat of sorcery is really no more necessary to keep out the one than is a policeman to keep out the other.

That the women, or the population at large, among the western tribes, should suffer particularly from sorcery as a result of the bull-roarer cult seems to me unlikely. But it has been maintained by the Rev. M. Nixon of the L.M.S. at Yokea that where the cult is active at his end of the coast, it is bound up with sorcery and, for this and other reasons, constitutes a real infliction upon the women. This brings us to another aspect of the bull-roarer with which we must deal at sufficient length before attempting to sum up on the cult as a whole.

Politico-Legal Aspect of the Bull-Roarer: the Bukari

Mr. Nixon refers especially to the village of Karama (No. 7). Here the bull-roarer, apart from the ceremony of initiation, which takes place from time to time in the ordinary way, is often employed in what may be called—if the phrase is not too high-sounding—a politico-legal capacity. These extra functions belong also to the Uaripi (No. 5) and the Opau (No. 6) groups, but I have found no trace of them further westward. I have accordingly made no mention of them hitherto for fear of confusing the picture of the cult as it exists among the Orokolo group, which I know best. The functions which we shall now consider are well exemplified in the Uaripi group, and most of the information I can give about them comes from there. But such inquiries as I have made further to the east indicate that what follows would apply very closely to Karama.

In both these tribal groups (i.e. Nos. 5 and 7) each clan[27] (typically speaking) possesses its own individual major bull-roarer known by a personal name.[28] Connected with each such bull-roarer are two functionaries, or bodies of functionaries—the *bukari* and the *mai-karu*. The *bukari* belongs to the clan in question. He is really an individual and is typically the chief of it; but his kinsmen of the clan are also called *bukari* in relation to their bull-roarer. The *mai-karu* almost always belongs to a different clan; his kinsmen are also called the *mai-karu* of the bull-roarer. Thus in respect of any bull-roarer, one clan will constitute its *bukari* (under a principal *bukari*, or "chief"), and another its *mai-karu* (likewise under a principal *mai-karu*).

Those who are *bukari* in respect of one bull-roarer may be *mai-karu* in respect of another. The tabulation of a few examples will make this clear.

These all belong to the village of Uaripi where I made a list (which is possibly incomplete) of nine major bull-roarers with their respective *bukari* and *mai-karu* as above.

Uaripi

Bull-Roarer	Bukari			Mai-Karu
"Birarubu" ...	(Principal)	MARAI	...	YAVURE.
	(Clan)	Mareavo	...	Kasa.
	(Eravo name)	Avaroa Ravi	...	Sarea Ravi
"Oroharuavu"		AIFA..	...	MARASI.
		Leikopi	...	Lavai'ipi.
		Avaroa Ravi	...	Murua Ravi.
"Poiavi" ...		PAE..	...	AIFA.
		Beraripi	...	Leikopi.
		Meouri Ravi	...	Avaroa Ravi.
"Foavu" ...		MAIE	...	HOARA.
		Aisasu	...	Buasa.
		Kauri Ravi	...	Pori Ravi.

The same organization exists at Karama where I have listed twelve, each with its *bukari* clan and its leading *bukari*, or chief, and each with its clan of *mai-karu*.[29]

When there is occasion for calling up the bull-roarer it is the *bukari* who does so. He is in a sense in control of it. But he does not concern himself with the actual swinging. This is for the *mai-karu*, the "worker." Whenever he calls up his bull-roarer the *bukari* must be in a position to give a pig to the *mai-karu*; and the *mai-karu* in return must give shell ornaments to the *bukari*. All this recalls the relation between a man and his brother-in-law, i.e. the *aukau* of his son; and there is some evidence to suggest that the set organization above described has developed out of this relation between affines. This however need not concern us: we can take the organization as it stands.

Now *bukari* is commonly translated as "chief," but it does not signify ordinary secular chieftainship. The *eravo*-chief in the Uaripi group is called *lahio* or *papuvita*; at Karama, *migiosora*. The *bukari* are in point of fact often *eravo* chiefs, but this is not necessarily so; and certainly some true *eravo* chiefs are not *bukari*. I think the *bukari* should be looked upon as specifically "bull-roarer chiefs," a view which is strengthened by the facts that their functions concern the bull-roarer, and that the word *bukari* itself may be used as a synonym for the more ordinary term *rubu*. In the Uaripi group I heard the human *bukari* referred to as *rubu-papa*, "father of the bull-roarer."

In times past (perhaps a good deal more than at present) the *bukari* were men of power and importance. They were to be distinguished by the habit of carrying a string bag (*aroa*) and a gourd lime-pot (*arofae*). It was not as if these were their monopoly, but worn by the *bukari* they were both conspicuous and sacred. Nor have these symbols lost their significance at the present day. If a *bukari* tear his string bag, or if he smash his *arofae*, even by accident, there is trouble in store for someone. These are signals for the *mai-karu*. He brings forth the bull-roarer of which the *bukari* is the "father" and he himself the curator, and sounds it. The rest of the proceedings follow automatically: the *bukari* kills a pig for the *mai-karu*; the *mai-karu* gives a number of ornaments to the *bukari*; and the third person, on whose account the bull-roarer was aroused must provide a pig for the *eravo*. The tearing of the bag or the smashing of the lime-pot are forms usually dispensed with. It is sufficient for the *bukari* to call upon his *mai-karu*, and the action is set up. We shall appreciate the significance of this use of the bull-roarer if we consider a number of instances in which it has been thus sounded.

Punitive Functions

In not a few of them it seems to be called up in order to maintain or restore the prestige of the *bukari*.

Thus Berare (*bukari* of the bull-roarer "Laurei" in the village of Mei) quarrelled with a man Auri for sleeping in the place usually occupied by himself in the *eravo*. Berare called on the *mai-karu*,

Puka, to sound "Laurei." The exchange of gifts—pig for ornaments —took place between these two, and the offender, Auri, had to provide a feast.

Again Berare quarrelled with a man, Lai, for selling certain masks to the magistrate at Kerema and (allegedly) keeping the price for himself. Berare called on the *mai-karu*, killed a pig and received ornaments. Lai also had to kill a pig.

Marai (*bukari* of "Birarubu") was arguing with another man when the latter dashed a stick into the fire and, presumably by accident, caused some ashes to fall on his opponent. Marai's son intervened and abused the offender. Finally the bull-roarer was sounded and all three paid pigs, the *bukari* of course receiving ornaments from the *mai-karu*.

Karave, another *bukari*, happened to be driven into the sea by some mischievous young men parading the beach in *harisu* masks.[30] His *mai-karu* named Dyamu observed this and on his own initiative sounded the bull-roarer. The *harisu* wearers happened to belong to Dyamu's *eravo* (hence his perturbation) and they assisted him in providing ornaments for the pig which Karave killed.

Berare, above mentioned, was once displeased with his wife because she had not prepared lime for him (by burning shells). When she herself asked him for some for chewing with betel he lost his temper and smashed his sacred lime-pot. Both he and his wife supplied pigs.

Uru the *bukari* of the bull-roarer "Obo" once scolded his wife for failing to cook his breakfast. Asked what she had ready she answered, "I just sit down nothing," whereupon she was chastised. The bull-roarer was sounded and Uru provided a pig.

In the last-mentioned case it seems as if the *bukari* calls up the bull-roarer and pays the pig in a mood of repentance, though it should be remembered that he receives his ornaments from the *mai-karu* as a matter of course and so stands to lose nothing. It is said, however, that he may call up a bull-roarer to banish his own feeling of shame. Thus Hiviature, son of Marai, the *bukari* of "Birarubu," seduced a betrothed girl in the absence of her young man. There was a magisterial case and Hiviature was advised to make good the payments already made on the other's behalf and marry the girl himself. This was done as the best way out of the difficulty. But the *bukari* called up the bull-roarer "to put an end to his and his son's shame." Hiviature in this case supplied the pig himself, and as eldest son of the *bukari* received the ornaments from the *mai-karu*.

The foregoing instances show how the bull-roarer may be called up in cases where the *bukari* is directly concerned as a party. But they may also be called up in cases where the quarrel is between others and the *bukari* is only an intervener.

For instance a man, Beraseikya, is found quarrelling with his wife. Their small son has thrown sand into the cooking-pot whereupon the mother has beaten him, and the father, a thorough partisan, has begun to beat the mother. The *bukari* intervenes, but the father's blood is up. He takes no notice, and, to make matters worse, lands an unlucky blow on the *bukari's* body. The bull-roarer sounds, and the offender pays a pig. (It must be understood that this is apart from the payment of a pig by the *bukari* himself whenever he summons the bull-roarer. The pig-ornament exchange between *bukari* and *mai-karu* takes place as a matter of routine in all these instances.)

A *bukari's* wife is quarrelling with another woman over a broken pot. The *bukari* calls on his bull-roarer, and both women pay pigs.

Fereapo is wrangling with his son over some bread-fruit which the latter has appropriated. The *bukari* comes between them. Being disregarded he smashes his lime-pot as a signal; the bull-roarers sound; and in due course both father and son pay pigs.

Erevu and his younger brother fall out and fight with fists, the latter having refused to accompany the former on a trip up the river. When they do not desist upon the intervention of the *bukari*, he tears his string bag,[31] which leads to the sounding of the bull-roarers, and both men pay pigs.

It should be noted that, whereas the pig which is in every case supplied by the *bukari* goes to the *mai-karu* in especial, and is paid for in ornaments, those which are supplied by the offending parties go for the consumption of all the men participating, and are not paid for in ornaments. In this way it is seen that a breach of the peace, particularly when it involves an affront to the *bukari*, may be punished through the mechanism of the bull-roarer.

This boresome list of cases will give some idea of the uses to which the bull-roarer may be put by the *bukari*. He can, indeed, summon it at will, and upon very slight pretext. It is said that he sometimes does so "because he wants ornaments"; or again because he has plenty of pigs and thus makes an opportunity of expending one; or when he has lost and found a big pig (a thing which happens often enough) and therefore calls on the bull-roarer for fear he may lose it again for good. A big pig is not killed and eaten without some fuss, whether of a ceremonial nature or in the interests of some social obligation; and the bull-roarer is no doubt sometimes made an excuse here, just as we saw that it was at the Orokolo end,[32] for the more vital concern of providing a feast.

Apart from this sort of motive, however, we have seen that the bull-roarer is often called up to assert, or to restore, the *bukari's* prestige. His person and his accoutrements—the string bag and the lime-pot—are sacred. Even a small accident, such as a stumble as he descends from his house veranda, may afford a pretext for the bull-roarer ceremony; and if he is affronted he can always secure reparation by this means. The old-time prestige of the *bukari* may be gauged from a description given by some informants at Opau. There, it appears, he stood forth before the village at the end of the ceremony and was publicly proclaimed. On his shoulder he carried the string bag (distended by means of a length of cane bent into a half circle), and upon this were affixed the ornaments which he had received, inside the *eravo*, from the *mai-karu*. (The women were not supposed to know whence these ornaments came: presumably they viewed them as gifts from the bull-roarer, or *rubu*, in its supernatural character, gifts made in return for the pig which the *bukari* had given it.) Thus arrayed he was presented to the assembled people by certain old men, powerful in magic. They declared that he was a chief in his village, that his person was inviolable, that his voice was always to be hearkened to, and so forth. If he intervened in a quarrel the participants must stop, lest he smash his lime-pot and cause the bull-roarers to sound, when those who were at fault would have to pay pigs. And if they failed to do so, then they would die at the hands of the sorcerers. These sorcerers themselves placed a tabu, as it were, upon the *bukari*. This picture is probably somewhat overdrawn: such pomp and formality seems out of keeping with Elema methods. But it shows well enough that the *bukari* was supposed to be held in high respect. He was *haera bikari*, a "high man."

It is his function as peacemaker that interests us most. If he found two people disagreeing he could tell them to stop, and recognizing his voice alone they would do so; or, it is said, he could quell a disturbance by holding aloft his string bag and lime-pot, the sight of which would be enough; or he might cry, "Are you not afraid of these?" adding significantly, "I have plenty of pigs," by which he meant that he could readily fulfil the qualification for calling up the bull-roarers. If they still disregarded him, then, peaceful negotiations being at an end, he could tear his bag or break his pot and scatter the lime among them.

It is plain from the account given of the old-fashioned *bukari* that sorcery can be recognized as an ultimate sanction of his power. But I have asked on more than one occasion why a man, who perhaps thought himself to be on the right side in a quarrel, should be willing to sacrifice his pig merely because the bull-roarer sounded; and informants have been at a loss for an answer. Uaripi informants and I know one another well enough to make it unlikely that they were purposely hiding this factor; the explanation is, I believe, that it was not present in their thoughts. A man who was thus called on by the *bukari* would hardly hesitate to comply. It is the usual thing, and public opinion would demand it of him.

Furthermore there is the magico-religious sanction. We have seen that the bull-roarer does possess a significance of this kind even to the initiated; and we may suppose that it carries far more weight with the uninitiated. The theory of the bull-roarer in its punitive aspect has never been explicitly stated to me—perhaps it has largely faded out of present-day recognition; but it appears so obvious that one may venture to state it. When the *bukari* has been offended he may call up the monster itself. The monster is a thing of terror, capable of harming the whole community. It remains in the village until it has been placated with a pig, that is to say, until the offence has been wiped out. I have no doubt that a fear of the bull-roarer itself, as some undefined being with capabilities for evil, has some effect as a sanction for obedience to the *bukari*.

But behind these two, the sanction of public opinion and the magico-religious sanction, undoubtedly stands that of sorcery. This is what we should inevitably expect; for sorcery, or rather the unspoken threat of it, stands in the background as a formidable defender of all manner of rules and customs, good and bad. While however the use of the bull-roarer in a punitive capacity is to some extent dependent on sorcery, it should be kept in mind that sorcery is by no means dependent on the bull-roarer. It can, on the contrary, be used at any time or place; it has no need of the bull-roarer as a medium.

Summing-up on the Functions of the Bull-Roarer

I shall now attempt to sum up on the functions of the bull-roarer cult. It is not possible, of course, to lay a finger on one in particular and say, "This is what the bull-roarer does for society." Nor it is possible to enumerate them all; for in the extreme sense of Functionalism they are innumerable. I shall merely draw attention to some that are more or less outstanding.

Initiation to the bull-roarer forms one in a series of social steps normally taken by every male. It is commonly the first of them, and the first initiation often takes place at a very early age. It does not mean anything to the child at the time, but as he grows a little older he comes to feel a certain self-importance and security because of it—at least we may deduce as much from the fact that boys who for any reason have not passed through may be laughed at by those of their age-mates who have. Obviously it cannot be said of the cult among the Elema that initiation marks the entrance of the boys into manhood; but it is nevertheless an early stage of the male's ascent in social status.

As a male secret society the bull-roarer cult falls into its place (along with *kovave*, *apa-hevehe*, and the *eravo*, or men's house, itself), in that very marked dichotomy between the lives of the sexes. It is one of the means of keeping the women in what the men consider, and the women themselves agree, to be their proper place.

The performance of the ceremony is one of the occasions for those feasts and for gatherings which play a role of such importance in all Papuan societies, and which apart from their intrinsic attractions provide a means of drawing people together and extending the circle of goodwill. It also gives occasion for the interchange and circulation of wealth in the form of shell ornaments, of which one must see something at close quarters to appreciate its significance. Again the initiation represents one of those transactions between affines and between maternal uncle and nephew which constitute an essential part of social relations

On the magico-religious side—which should be neither over-nor under-estimated—the cult provides one of the means of maintaining relations with the world of spiritual beings, the mythical characters who live on from the primeval past and can influence for good or ill the lives of the present-day Elema.

Lastly, though these functions belong to the central tribes and not to those on the west—we have seen that the cult can fulfil a political function in that it is made to guard the prestige of certain powerful individuals who may be called chiefs; and a legal one, in that it can be invoked to prevent strife and punish offenders.

The above are predominantly sociological functions. We may now—employing the rough-and-ready distinction drawn on pp. 75–6 pass on to note the psychological values attaching to the cult. As for the bull-roarers themselves, we have seen that, despite a fear felt by both initiated and uninitiated, they are treated with something like reverence and are the objects of real attachment. And further, while secular motives are uppermost in the performance of the ceremony, and while the inner meaning of it may be but vaguely understood, the attitude towards the bull-roarer at certain times is one of prayer, and the ceremony is in part an act of placation. This being so we may assume that the native goes on his way with a shade more of confidence after he has performed it.

I feel inclined, however, to attach more importance to the mundane aspect of the cult. We have dwelt on its festive and convivial character; and on the opportunities it affords for self-display, whether individual or corporate, as well as for the virtues of generosity and public spirit. And last, but by no means least, we must recognize its value as a recreation. The native likes his bull-roarer and he enjoys bringing it out.

Abolition and Restoration

It is highly interesting in this connection to recall the fact that during the "Vailala Madness" of 1919-20 the bull-roarers, together with the paraphernalia of the other secret cults, were along most of the coast wilfully exposed and thrown away or burnt.[33] The bull-roarer cult was ostensibly discarded for good and all. Some few villages indeed, notably Orokolo, refused to be overcome by the new movement, and these remained throughout strongholds of the old culture. But Arihava, about two miles west of Orokolo, and Auma and Vailala, about eight miles east of it, were completely converted. They "threw away" not only the bull-roarer but *kovave*, drum-*hevehe* and sea-*hevehe*. They pulled down all their old *eravo* and rebuilt them on new lines; they discontinued the seclusion of boys; they discarded the most picturesque features of marriage and mourning ritual; and made many more changes, down to clipping their hair short and foregoing the use of drums and feathers.

Despite all these changes the villages of Arihava and Vailala (they are very considerable, the former with more than 1,000 inhabitants) continued to thrive not less mightily than the conservative village of Orokolo between them. Their culture was undoubtedly changed and, I think, seriously impoverished. But it was far from being wrecked. It was the same culture with a difference.

Consideration of such facts as these has led me to form the opinion that the functionalist conception of culture may be carried too far. But of this subject I hope to write at greater length elsewhere. The thing that concerns us here is that in Arihava and Vailala there has been a distinct revival of certain elements in the old culture within recent years. About 1930 a man named Epe organized a return of the bull-roarer in Arihava. He had the approval and co-operation of practically the whole village. Pigs, dogs, and fowls were provided in plenty, and a great band of visiting *aukau* (from Orokolo and other conservative places inland) passed from one end of the village to Epe's *eravo* at the other, beating drums, blowing shell trumpets and whirling bull-roarers, while the women, to whom the bull-roarer for the last ten years had been no secret but allegedly a jest, hid themselves again in their houses or fled into the bush.

The bull-roarer has reappeared in other villages where the cult was formerly thrown away, and we may ask why it is that people who were content for ten years or more to do without it should take it up again. The answer is not, I think, that it fills a really essential part in the culture, as if it were something that must come back of necessity. If this were the case, the same could be said of the much more significant *apa-hevehe*. But both Arihava and Vailala are at present, 16 years after its destruction, resolute against the revival of that ceremony. The answer is rather that they like the bull-roarer and want it back. That it to say—if these words "like" and "want" are thought to be too plain, or not to go deep enough—the emotional and sentimental attitude towards the ceremony may count more than its functional associations with the other elements of the culture. *Apa-hevehe* they would also, no doubt, have restored (and they may still do so); but again and again I have heard the same excuse, and considering the greatness of the undertaking and the character and circumstances of the Elema native, I have no hesitation in believing it: *apa-hevehe* means too much work. The bull-roarer on the other hand is easy. They can have the sort of fun they like at the cost of little trouble. They could get on without it; but they prefer to have it. In the relations between the Elema natives and the bull-roarer cult the main factor for us to bear in mind is that they like it.

The Problem for Mission and Government

We come finally to the problem which the bull-roarer presents to Mission and Government. The anthropologist who wishes to help in such problems should devote himself as keenly to discovering the abuses and maladjustments in any primitive society as to pointing out its excellences; and he who fails to discover some of the former is either very simple or very biassed. I fear, though, that some of the more enthusiastic exponents of cultural anthropology have been so much in love with the subject of their study, viz. primitive culture, as to be hardly able to see anything wrong with it. In the application of anthropology we must, I think, be prepared to dispense with the idea of a culture as a fully integrated and working whole which is worthy of preservation intact and in its own right. We must be prepared to make abstractions and consider separate elements on their merits, in the confidence that, owing to the plasticity, the adaptability, the living character, of culture, we shall not necessarily destroy it utterly if we see fit to alter it.[34]

The particular question at issue here is whether the bull-roarer cult in the Gulf Division should be suppressed. While personally prepared to advocate the suppression of some things, I should not hesitate to say, on the results of my own studies, that the bull-roarer in the Gulf Division is not one of them. Indeed the question would hardly have occurred. But a series of charges have been laid against the cult by the Rev. Nixon, and he is able to show, what we should expect, that it possesses some features that are undesirable.

Mr. Nixon's objections fall under two main heads, first that the bull-roarer is an infliction on the women, and second that it is bound up with sorcery.

As for the first of these contentions, Mr. Nixon should be better qualified than I to interpret the women's views; but it should be borne in mind that his informants must be mainly of a class that has already come under mission influence and is possibly prejudiced. He writes, "I know from conversation with the women that they loathe it"; and he compares it to the "arrow that flieth by day, the pestilence that walketh in darkness." These are stronger words than I should have thought necessary, at any rate for the western part of the Gulf Division coast. There, as I have pointed out, the women take the bull-roarer as a matter of course and I have seen nothing to suggest that they are living under a reign of terror. They know when they have to make themselves scarce. The bull-roarer is first sounded inside the *eravo*, and while this continues the women go about their ordinary business. They may even come right up to the *eravo* with a dish of food while the *hevehe* is roaring within and they don't turn a hair in doing so. When at night it roars about the village the women simply keep to their houses. And when finally it appears in the open by day, they have been fully fore-warned to get out of the road. Nor does the bull-roarer remain long in the village. I have indeed known more than a week to elapse at Uaripi between the "waking up" and the final feast, but during that time the village life went on as usual, for throughout the day the bull-roarer remained inside the *eravo*. It is simply inconceivable that a large village group like Uaripi would allow its life to be disorganized because one *eravo* chose to bring out its bull-roarers; and the men of the *eravo* are too well acquainted with their own interests to keep their women-folk a long time from necessary tasks.

The above probably represents the ordinary procedure. But one can have too much of a good thing in native life just as in our own. Speaking of Karama, Mr. Nixon says, that *tiparu*, or the bull-roarer, is sounded "on an average two or three times each month." And Patrol Officer Rutledge, writing at the same time, says that at its last appearance at Karama it actually remained for a month. This is indeed a state of affairs! If neither has made a mistake it would appear Karama might be perpetually under the reign of the *tiparu*. If this is the case I cannot but believe that the disorganization and terrorism attributed to the bull-roarer cult have been much exaggerated. It would be intolerable not only to the women but to the men.

Assuming, however, as is perhaps reasonable, that the *tiparu* does appear too much in Karama and thereby causes discomfort, inconvenience, or undue fear to the women, then it is to this extent an abuse. The cure for it, if such a cure is really required, is to curtail the number of appearances of the *tiparu* or the duration of its stay in the village: or to introduce some regulation which would prevent the sounding of bull-roarers by day in the village except for one brief period which would satisfy ceremonial requirements. If the conditions which I have studied along the rest of the coast prevailed at Karama I do not think the women there would have very much to complain of.

Let us turn now to the second of the main charges laid against the cult, viz. that it is bound up with sorcery. We have seen that sorcery stands in the background as a sanction to prevent the uninitiated from intruding into the secret and to enforce the authority of the *bukari*. I do not believe we need be greatly concerned about the former of these two,[35] because the matter is in the hands of the women themselves, and they see to it that they do not butt in. Nor do I see any reason why they should be encouraged to butt in. As I have pointed out Elema society reserves a great deal for the males to the exclusion of the females. This may not accord with modern ideas of women's emancipation, but it is the time-honoured Elema fashion in which the Elema women acquiesce. If we really feel bound to mend it I think we should defer the experiment for a long time— say a century, or until we see our own women as Freemasons.

As a sanction for the power of the *bukari* sorcery might indeed be employed for unjust ends. It so happens that none of the cases I have myself collected are of a kind that show the *bukari* in an evil light though the possibility is obviously there. It should be remembered, however, that the *bukari* must himself supply a pig, which is some deterrent against a capricious use of his power; and further that the whole transaction is of a very public kind, so that the victimization of individuals would have to stand the light of general criticism.

There is no doubt that the bull-roarer cult, like *kovave* and *apahevehe*, are generally thought by the natives themselves to be productive of sorcery. But I believe that the native is for the most part construing as an actual fact or happening, what is in reality only a tacit possibility. In short I believe that the association of sorcery in its overt, harmful form, with the bull-roarer is in popular estimation wholly exaggerated.

Sorcery may be employed for worthy objects, and a defence may rightly be made for it. But I adhere to my opinion that by and large it is a very great evil, and that the best service the missionary can do the natives is to educate them out of their belief in it. It does not seem clear, however, that he would do much towards this end by exposing the secret of the bull-roarer. Nor could the Government do much by suppressing its cult. For sorcery, alas, would continue to flourish in the Gulf Division even if the bull-roarer were blotted out of existence.

If, in the meantime, undue victimization of individuals is reported or complained of, then the cases can be dealt with by the magistrates on their merits. Many abuses are possible under institutions which may be otherwise beneficial and highly valued by society. The course most likely to meet with the approval of the society concerned is, not to abolish the institution, but to check the abuse of it.

There is one final question. While it is all too obvious that sorcery could continue apart from the bull-roarer, can we hope that the bull-roarer would continue apart from sorcery? It is really not a practical question, for, however far the observance of the cult may extend into the future, we may be pretty sure that sorcery, a thing much harder to kill, will outlast it. But it has, I hope, been made clear that sorcery is not the sole sanction for respecting the secret of the bull-roarer and the authority of the *bukari*. The supernatural or magico-religious sanction has some force; and over and above this there is the heavy weight of public opinion. This last may be correlated with the individual's sense of propriety. He tends to do what society approves and to refrain from what it condemns. I suggest that it is this primarily which causes both the initiated and the uninitiated to conform to the rules of the bull-roarer; so that we can proceed with our educational campaign against the belief in sorcery and continue to take Government action against its overt use in particular cases, without feeling that we are thereby making the survival of the cult impossible.

In the meantime one may venture to suggest a modification of the missionary's attitude towards the cult—and I refer specially to the native mission teacher, who tends notoriously to be over-zealous and to lose his sense of proportion. My suggestion is that he should be encouraged to view and treat the bull-roarer with a touch of humour; to cease regarding it as something utterly wicked and dreadful; to desist from his endeavours (which are in questionable taste) to expose the secret; and if ever he finds it necessary to mention the subject, to wink as he does so. I have a shrewd idea the women might learn to wink back at him.

REFERENCES

1. (Unabridged text of Territory of Papua, *Anthropology Report* No. 17, published under the same title by the Government Printer, Port Moresby, in 1936. Listed as Williams 1936b in the bibliography. E.S.)
2. An admirable example of this method is F. Speiser's treatment of the bull-roarer in *Uber Initiationen in Australien und Neu-Guinea*, Emil Berkhausen & Cie., Basel, 1929; also P. Wirz's *Beitrage zur Ethnographie des Papua Golfes*, B. G. Teubner, 1934.
3. (See also Chapters 5 and 6 of the present collection. E. S.)
4. *See* the writer's 'Natives of the Purari Delta', Government Printer, Port Moresby, Papua, 1924.
5. Other names in use at Orokolo are *hevoa*, for which I have no explanation; *hevoa botobobo*, the latter word being an obvious onomatopoeia; *haravea hakaia*, a figurative expression meaning 'slivers of the *haravea* tree; and, more commonly than any of these, *hurava*. *Hurava* means 'west' (the name reappears as that of the village of Urama in the Era river delta). But it cannot be seized upon as evidence that the bull-roarer came to Orokolo from the west. There is, incidentally, more evidence that it came from the east. But the question will not be discussed here. (Williams devoted a polemical note to it under the title 'The Kaiamunu-Ebina-Gi cult in Papua', cf. Williams 1939c. The theory of western origin was held by Wirz, cf. Wirz 1937. The original text of "Bull-Roarers in the Papuan Gulf" gives the name *beure hevehe;* I changed this into *be'ure hevehe* for reasons given in Chapter 1, footnote 8. E. S.)
6. *In Primitive New Guinea*, Seeley, Service & Co., 1924, pp. 129, 194. (The question of the word hevehe is taken up again by Williams in *Drama of Orokolo*, Chapter 11. E. S.)
7. The meaning of 'warrior' for *hevehe* (or here *sevese*) which appears to belong to the eastern groups (Nos. 8-10) might be connected with the carved wooden effigies which are there known by the same name. These appear to represent mythical ancestors, who among other exploits, distinguished themselves in fighting; so that they came to be appealed to by raiders before an expedition. Why the name should apply to these effigies, or more generally to 'warriors' remains, however, wholly unclear.
8. Among the western half of the coast these number definitely ten. (See Chapter 1, footnote 17, where Williams describes them by the term 'totemic clans'. In Part II of my introduction I have accepted that term as the closest to contemporary usage. In *Drama of Orokolo* Williams calls them '*aualari* groups', as he recognises a difference between the *aualari* and the standard socio-political clan. I would advise against use

of the term '*aualari* group' as this would place Elema kinship outside
the sphere of comparative analysis. E. S.)

9. Popo is now some miles inland. The nature of the country makes it
   plain that the coast has made to the southward in recent times.

10. The *kovave* mask differs from the *apa-hevehe* and their two cults are quite
    independent. *Kovave* are smaller and usually conical in shape. Their
    wearers may pursue and beat women and children whereas the *apa-
    hevehe* dance with them. Holmes has described the *kovave* cult (op. cit.
    pp. 121, 178). I should say that I have never heard the bull-roarer used
    or even mentioned in connection with the *kovave*; and that I am quite
    unable to agree with Holmes' interpretation of Kovave, (apparently a
    personal deity) as 'god of the mountains'. The *kovave* are innumerable
    and represent minor spirits who dwell mostly in the bush. (See page 109
    below. Williams discusses *kovave* in more detail in *Drama of Orokolo*,
    Chapter VII. E. S.)

11. Holmes gives a myth of the bull-roarer on op. cit. pp. 189-91. It has a
    good deal in common with No 5 above, though with considerable
    differences which are noteworthy as showing the variability of the myths.

12. (In a detailed version of the tale of Oa Birukapu in *Drama of Orokolo*,
    pp. 172-9, Williams records the bull-roarer was found in the entrails.
    Williams treats the names Oa Laia and Oa Birukapu as interchange-
    able. E. S.)

13. The words of the formula on page 92 below, as well as the act of
    laying the bull-roarer on the initiate's shoulder, seem to accord well
    with Speiser's thesis (1929) that the bull-roarer is a *Krafttrager* and
    initiation a *Kraftübertragung*. I cannot however make capital of this
    thesis here, despite its plausibility, because no informant ever advanced
    this motive for initiating the boys. If it exists at all in the society we are
    discussing it is in the far background of the native's mind.

14. I have only heard it sounded on one occasion for another purpose.
    That was in the course of an *apa-hevehe* ceremony, which is a vastly
    greater affair, extending in its various stages over a number of years.
    When the masks were ready to be feathered a bull-roarer was sounded
    in the village for a moment before they were brought out of the *eravo*.
    At the sound of it the women all took their departure and this made it
    possible to carry the *apa-hevehe* masks (which they must not yet see)
    out into the open where there was room to work. (A fuller account of
    the use of the bull-roarer in the *hevehe* cycle is given in *Drama of Orokolo*,
    pages 164-8, 200-7. E. S.)

15. (A full discussion of *aukau—arivu* exchanges and of Elema kinship
    generally is given in *Drama of Orokolo*, Chapters II, xviii-xx, pp. 220-2,
    237-40 *et passim*. E. S.)

16. These are of roast sago, about the size of cricket balls. The sago is said
    always to be prepared in this form for this particular feast.

17. *Oro* is a kind of tree which happens to appear in the name Orokolo
    'leaf of the *oro* tree'. In one version of Myth No. 4 above it was an *oro*
    tree which gave out the noise by the rubbing together of the two
    branches. Abiara was apparently unaware of this circumstance. *Karo*
    is another kind of tree which grows by the beach.

18. In all cases which I have seen, the initiation took place on the day following the waking up. There may sometimes be some delay, however.

19. At an initiation which I saw at Arihava the bull-roarers were sounded in the open as the initiates were brought up, the women having been of course cleared out of the village first. That is to say the boys saw the bull-roarer in action before they entered the *eravo*. On the other two occasions when I attended initiations at the Orokolo end of the coast they saw it for the first time inside the building.

20. The same sort of pronouncements are made on the other occasions when the *aukau* performs a ceremonial office and gives formal gifts to his *arivu*.

21. The presentation, in the case of boys, occurs inside the *eravo*. The *hevehe*, with its *aue* or tail of dog's teeth, having been laid for a moment on their shoulders, is taken away before they emerge. In the rare case where the initiate is a girl she is invested with the ornaments outside the *eravo;* and of course she receives no *hevehe*.

22. Mr. Nixon, L. M. S. Missionary at Muru, informs me that at Karama a woman is sometimes accosted privately in the bush and shown a bull-roarer. The man who thus tricks her will demand her sexual compliance on pain of informing against her as one who has seen the forbidden thing. I have recorded a similar method of seduction in the case of *kovave* though never in that of the bull-roarer. It is improbable that this is often put into practice, but where a woman has been placed in possession of the secret she very probably passes it on to some others of her own sex.

23. There is a sort of harmless millipede called in the Orokolo language, *be'ure hevehe*. It is found in shallow pools in the bush after rain, being supposed to have come up out of the ground (*bea*). This is not expressly associated with the bull-roarer. The word *hevehe* is literally "worm", and is to be identified with the word *hevehe*—snake in the Opau and Keuru languages. The Orokolo word for snake is *ekaroa*.

24. The smaller, "utility", bull-roarers are unnamed.

25. (The text reads *ohau*; the spelling *hohao* appears throughout in *Drama of Orokolo*. See Chapter 1, footnote 8. E. S.)

26. There is some amount of overlapping.

27. The large sections (see page 83 and footnote 8 above) are subdivided into much more numerous subsections, and these again into local representative groups. It is to these that the name clan is here given. An *eravo* usually contains two and often more of these clans. (It is more usual today to refer to such 'local representative groups' as 'local clan segments'; and to the 'subsections' as 'sub-clans'. For the composition of an *eravo* group see *Drama of Orokolo*, Chapters I-II. E. S.)

28. This personal name refers to the bull-roarer as a being invoked by the clan in question. Each clan of course employs any number of bull-roarers in the material sense. These are nameless. Or it may be that they all go by the one name, that of the major bull-roarer. When they sound it is the voice of this bull-roarer, "Obo", "Foavu", or whatever it may be called. I cannot say whether there is in every case a real bull-roarer in existence representing the ideal clan bull-roarer, but I

think it is doubtful. Several of the Karama "Bull-roarers" depart entirely from the usual pattern, being bamboo pipes or whistles. These at any rate could not have a long life.

The usual generic name of the bull-roarer at Uaripi is *rubu;* at Karama, *tiparu*, a word which includes the bamboo variants.

29. I found that a list made in 1932 corresponded exactly with one made when I stayed in the village nine years previously. The names are: (1) Sefo, (2) Fivo'ivo, (3) Araro, (4) Arakakeapo, (5) Kaiovo, (6) Soi, (7) Irukuavu, (8) Love, (9) Marukwa, (10) Eara, (11) Karara, (12) Lavapo. Of these all are true bull-roarers except Nos 1, 3, 5, 10, 11. No. 1 consists of a small bamboo tube open at both ends placed in a larger tube which is half filled with water. The player blows on the edge of the smaller tube, raising or lowering the larger tube as he does so. By this means he can produce slurring intervals as horrible as those of a "Swanee-whistle".

Another (which it is I have not recorded) consisted of a pair of bamboo tubes, of different length, each closed at the end. Two players are required and they play alternately—*do me do me do me*, etc.

30. These correspond to *kovave* at Orokolo. (See footnote 10 above. E. S.)

31. When the lime-pot or string bag is destroyed it is the business of the *mai-karu* to supply a new one together with the ornaments.

32. I have also recorded (at Karama and Moviavi) that the bull-roarer (*tiparu*) may be summoned by the *bukari* when he wants some work done, e.g. making a house or a fence. He supplies a feast so that the helpers are rewarded in the usual way. Further, at Moviavi, it appeared that the *tiparu* was sounded on the death of the *bukari*. I am unable at the moment to verify these as occasions for the ceremony in the Uaripi group.

33. (See Chapters 5 and 6 of this volume. E. S.).

34. *See* the writer's *Blending of Cultures* (Wellcome Essay): Government Printer, Port Moresby, 1935.

35. As for the point already mentioned in footnote No. 22, viz. that a man may show the bull-roarer privately to a woman in order to frighten her into submitting to sexual intercourse, I can hardly believe that this is anything but a very rare occurrence. It possibly falls under the head of those "customs" which natives are fond of quoting as such when they really rest on no more than one or two notorious cases in the past. At any rate one is entitled to question the "custom" on grounds of probability. If a man shows the bull-roarer to a woman, he has himself committed an offence against the secret society, and one which is punishable by sorcery. How then would he venture to tell on her, or even admit to his fellows that he had secured a woman's favours in this way? If it is implied that he would punish her refusal by his own private sorcery, why should he trouble to show her the bull-roarer? He could threaten her with sorcery without doing this.

However, Mr. Nixon writes that two such cases were reported to him (whether they were recent or not I cannot say); and if this trick is actually put into practice it is obviously an abuse.

3

SEX AFFILIATION AND ITS
IMPLICATION[1]

Part I

Introductory

The present paper discusses a form of social classification which may be referred to provisionally as sex affiliation. The essence of it is that male children are classed with their father's group and female children with their mother's. I shall first endeavour to give an account, in its more or less relevant aspects, of the social organization of the people among whom this sex affiliation is practised; after that we may discuss the practice itself in greater detail and consider its implications.

I am not in a position to define the distribution of sex affiliation in Papua. It may prove to be wider than is at present thought. But I have met with it myself only among the Koiari-speaking people of the central division, and I am not aware that it has been reported from any other district in the territory.

The Koiari[2] country extends from the immediate hinterland of Port Moresby and the neighbouring Motu villages to the main range and even beyond it. Its inhabitants sometimes divide themselves according to their environment into three groups. They speak of (1) the Grasslanders or *Isu-bia;* (2) the Forest-men or *Idutu-bia;* (3) the Mountaineers or *Mavota.* The first of these divisions occupies the rolling plains near the coast, where savannah alternates with wide stretches of lalang grass. Leaving the grasslands one passes—almost at a stride, for the transition is so abrupt—into the rain forest which clothes the foothills. Finally, crossing a boundary which is less clearly defined, one leaves the home of the *Idutu-bia* and enters the rugged country occupied by the Mountaineers, *Mavota.*

It was among the intermediate division of forest-men, or, as we might better call them hillmen, that most of the data for the present paper were collected; and among these hillmen I shall refer especially to the inhabitants of what is roughly called the Sogeri district.[3] The same social structure, with the special character of sex affiliation, is said to exist among the mountaineers, and this statement has been verified by various witnesses whom I have met. But except for a

short trip in the Uberi district I have not checked the information
by personal enquiries on the spot. Among the grasslanders the data
are somewhat conflicting, and it becomes evident that there is here
a strong tendency toward a purely patrilineal condition such as that
of the Koitapu,[4] the Koiari-speaking people who nowadays dwell
on the coast.

Ethnographical

The Koiari have continued to speak a Papuan language,[5] but
racially they are mixed to no small extent with the Melanesians.
The population is scanty—a mere fraction of what the land might
support—and the standard of culture is comparatively low and poor.
The small villages are situated on minor hill-tops or spurs. Seven or
eight houses (sometimes fewer), built on the edge of the slope so that
their back piles must be much longer than their front ones, face
inward and surround a clean patch of red clay. The centre may be
occupied by a *varo*, or what remains of it, *i.e.* a degenerate form of
the coastal *dubu*. Further in the mountains this gives place to the *naga*,
the high platform on which food has been stacked and pigs slaughtered for a bygone feast. On the hillsides, sometimes at a surprisingly
great distance, may be seen the gardens, principally of yams, which
form the staple diet. Game is plentiful enough, especially in the
grasslands, but the Koiari are very definitely gardeners and quite
dependent on the soil. Being a scanty population in a comparatively
fertile, forest-covered country, they continually clear and burn off
fresh patches of bush and abandon them after cultivation. Fire is
made by the "saw" method. Their weapons are the spear and the
club. Their decorative arts are best exemplified by the poker-work
ornamentation of bamboo pipes and by the patterned bags of netted
string, stained in various colours.

Their dead are exposed in inaccessible rock clefts. They do not go
in special fear of the ghosts (*hua*) of their dead, and do nothing to
conciliate them; but they recognize local spirits (*dirava*) which
inhabit great trees in the forest and are placated by formal offerings.
The bull-roarer is not known, and there is no seclusion of youths
or girls.

The coastal people are afraid of the Koiari, and give them a great
reputation for sorcery of the particular kind which is usually called
vada in Papua. The sorcerers are supposed to confront their victim
in a place of solitude, to strike him senseless and actually to disem-
bowel him; next to piece him together and send him back to his
village, where he is doomed to die without being able to recollect
who assaulted him.

The Koiari resisted the early whites with great bravery and

tenacity. Partly in consequence, no doubt, they have been called treacherous and bloodthirsty, and native murder cases have certainly been relatively common in their district. On the other hand they are given a good character by employers as honest labourers and pleasant men to work with. A further point in this rather mixed reputation is that of their suspicion and secretiveness in their own homes. I was warned before going among the Koiari that I should find them hard nuts to crack, and my own experience has done nothing to prove the contrary.

However, during several short trips in 1929, 1930 and 1931 I found two subjects of special interest, one that of their primitive rock-paintings and carvings, the other the unusual form of social organization which forms the subject of this paper.

The Rule of Sex Affiliation

When paying a short visit to any part of the territory I take the opportunity of filling in a technological survey form, mainly dealing with points of material culture. One of the facts to be ascertained is the mode of descent, whether patrilineal or matrilineal. This, of course, is usually settled very easily. Having discovered the mode of social groupings one takes a number of concrete cases of families, and it will be found that all the children pass as a rule into one group, whether that of the father or that of the mother.

When, however, I approached this matter in the usual way at Sogeri I found the male children classed with their father's group, and the female with their mother's. The following are typical cases. (The group-names are in brackets.)

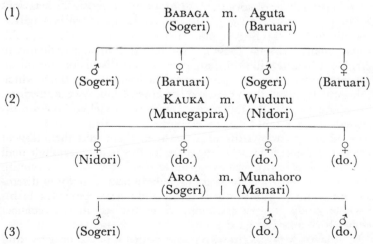

(1)
                  BABAGA m. Aguta
                  (Sogeri)   (Baruari)

     ♂   ♀   ♂   ♀
  (Sogeri)   (Baruari)   (Sogeri)   (Baruari)

(2)
                  KAUKA m. Wuduru
               (Munegapira) (Nidori)

     ♀   ♀   ♀   ♀
  (Nidori)   (do.)   (do.)   (do.)

                  AROA m. Munahoro
                  (Sogeri) (Manari)

      ♂   ♂   ♂
(3) (Sogeri)   (do.)   (do.)

As these instances show, there is no question of making a fair division between the two groups; even when all the children are of one sex no exception is ordinarily allowed.

The Nature of the Groups

Such is the stated rule, and it seems hardly reconcilable with the main rules of descent as we know them. It should be our business therefore to discover what the rule amounts to in effect; and the first question is that of the nature of the group.

As we have seen, the Koiari are roughly divided into grasslanders (*Isu-bia*), forest-men or hillmen (*Idutu-bia*), and mountaineers (*Mavota*). These are general divisions which do not concern us here: they are based primarily on differences of environment, though they involve also differences of language and certain other cultural factors. There is no definite social cohesion within the environmental division.

But these main divisions are split up into a number of small groups with definite names, and the member of such a group is well aware of its identity. The *Idutu-bia*, whom we shall be mainly discussing, are thus divided into the following groups:—

Sogeri (proper)	Manari	Adori
Munegapira	Yaritari	Umudori
Nidori	Borebere	Senari
Baruari	Korohi	Mofiri
Haveri	Maiari Bareri	

The list is probably not complete; at any rate, it makes no mention of certain previously existing groups which have been disrupted since the occupation of the Sogeri plateau by plantations. Having sold their land many years ago these groups have split up and settled with others. Occasionally still their names crop up in discussion.

It is sometimes more difficult to draw the line between the hillmen and the grasslanders,[6] than between the kind of country they respectively inhabit; e.g. Taburi, Nadeka, Dauri and Ekiri, although they are called *Isu-bia*, might be included in the Sogeri district, and I have discovered no essential difference between them and the hillmen except that of dialect. Many of the notes for this paper were collected among these four last-mentioned groups.

The names listed above belong to groups of people, not to villages. It is true that the population is so sparse and the groups so small that one whole group is very commonly concentrated in one village, possibly with one or two garden settlements in the neighbouring hills. But the village (*yaga*) has its own name, which is not to be identified with that of the group. The life of the village is more or less limited, and the country abounds with abandoned sites of villages in which groups have been settled in the past; but the group itself and its name survive these changes.

The nearest approach to a generic name for "group" in the sense in which that word is here used may be found perhaps in the native word *uhea*. *Uhea* was not actually given me as a generic term; nevertheless at feasts, when the guests arrive at different times and more or less according to their groups, a man will speak of *datuhea*— "My group," or say to another, "Here comes *atuhea!*"—"Your group." It is obvious, however, that *uhea* is not strictly synonymous with our word "group," since it appears in such compounds as *dadimuhea*, "my nephews and nieces," or *daghoghohea*, "my younger brothers," both spoken of *en bloc*. There is no such clearly defined concept as that of the Motu and Koitapu *iduhu* of the coast. The group as we find it is not a compact, cut-and-dried section of society, and I can only conclude that there is no real generic term in the vernacular to describe it. I shall continue for the present, therefore, to use the most non-committal word, viz., group. For those who are beyond the pale of the group I have only heard the phrase *yaga gaita bia*, "people of another village."

The word "clan" would not, I believe, be applicable. In the first place the group is not exogamous. In actual fact the large majority of marriages take place outside the group, but the opposite cases are not few enough to be dismissed as exceptions to a strict rule, and I have even noted some cases where the intra-group outnumbered the extra-group marriages. Furthermore, I have been confidently assured that young people may marry within the group if they wish. In short there is not even theoretical exogamy in the Sogeri district.

The Plant Emblem, Idi

Secondly there is no true totemism. Since, however, we are endeavouring to form an idea of the nature of the group we must not pass over an institution which certainly has something in common with totemism. It is that of the *idi*, literally "the Tree," for which may be suggested the name plant emblem.[7]

By way of example the Haveri group has *wofunia*, a kind of banana; Manari has *wurewure*, a grass; Yaritari has *mahai*, also a kind of grass; Baruari has *otiara*, a red-leaved ornamental shrub. In some instances the group name reappears in the name of its *idi*: Nidori, *e.g.* has *nidoridubu*, a kind of lily; Wanoari has *wanoa-gagari*, the creeper called "Dutchman's Pipe"; and Korohi has *korohi-dubu* (unidentified).

But there is no little vagueness regarding the plant emblems, and the plain fact is that many a man is quite unable to name his *idi* if you ask him. It is only after thrashing the matter out in full discussion that a group of informants are prepared to give definite answers, and then the doubt remains whether their answers are reliable. Some groups, it would appear, have alternative *idi*, for different informants on different occasions have given names which failed to agree, while in other instances two plants were named as alternatives at one and the same time, *e.g. waha* and *urema* for Taburi, *alai* and *bemu* (as well as *korohi-dubu*) for Korohi. The existence of such alternatives may point to minor groups, but on such points I was unable to obtain any satisfaction. The people seem both ignorant and indifferent regarding their *idi*.

The main function of the plant emblem is that of a mark of identity. A sprig might be left on the track to show that one of the owners of the *idi* had passed; or if a Wanoari man, for instance, saw a fine bunch of bananas he might take it and leave behind a piece of *wanoa-gagari* as a sort of receipt. When the owner of the bananas in due course saw this he would realize that the man who took them belonged to the Wanoari group and would know whence to expect a return. Since informants were so often not only uncertain as to their own *idi* but quite ignorant of those of other groups, it follows that the practice of leaving a mark of identity as a receipt could not easily extend beyond a single group. However, this use of the *idi* as a mark of identity was amply verified.

Another use of the *idi* is for the feast rack. Pyramidal structures called *taru-idi* are erected as means of displaying food and as alternatives to the more solid *varo* and *naga*. When the *idi* happens to be of a sufficiently substantial kind it may be used for the poles of the *taru-idi* or the posts of the *naga*.

Only one other function of the *idi* has come to my notice. For purposes of divination the corpse is examined after death, and any scrap of bark or dirt found upon it is taken away and buried. The spot where this is buried is marked, and if any particular *idi* should spring up there it will indicate the group of the sorcerer who was responsible for the death.

It may be added that no sacredness attaches to the plant emblem. If it be of an edible nature it may be eaten by those of the group to which it belongs as well as by everyone else. If it be practically useful in some other way, it may be used by all. The Taburi group has two *idi*: *waha*, a tuber, and *virima*, a kind of tree. They eat the one and adze out floor-boards for their houses from the other. Lastly I have never heard that the *idi* was regarded in any sense as ancestor.

If men are often uncertain of their *idi* or ignorant of it, women are still more so. When questioning a group of women on the matter I have seen them look despairingly at one another and wait for male

prompting before they will commit themselves. The unmarried girl
will probably give her *idi* as that of her mother, as we might expect.
But a married woman in her husband's village will sometimes say
that she belongs to her father's group and name his *idi* instead of her
mother's. One such married woman said that she belonged to her
mother's group, but gave her father's *idi* as her own. These are only
further evidences of the confusion regarding the plant emblem, and
they reveal its unimportance. When the matter has been thoroughly
discussed it is invariably agreed that the girl belongs to her mother's
group and that in consequence she possesses her mother's *idi*.

Local Character of the Groups

The majority of the group-names appear to be of local origin, being
derived in most cases from the hills (*numu*) of the district.

> Sogeri from Sogenumu or Hogenumu, near Yaritari.
> Bemuri from Bemu, in the Astrolabe range.
> Haveri from Havenumu or Favenumu, near Javareri.
> Taburi from Tabunumu.
> Nidori from Nidonumu.
> Dauri from Daunumu, in Koitaki plantation.
> Ediri from Ekinumu.
> Ienari from Icna, a certain stream.
> Yaritari from Yaritari-bei, a spur near present situation of
>   the group.

Tradition points to a migration from the east into the Sogeri
district, viz., from the direction of Yovi and Seramina; and there is
little doubt that there has been such a movement. It is seen that
some of the local names do not correspond with the present habitat
of the groups to which they belong: Sogenumu, *e.g.* is near Yaritari
to the east, and Favenumu near Javareri, also to the east. Nevertheless the fact that the group-names, as far as they can be explained,
seem all to be of a local character may well point to the assumption
that the groups themselves are primarily local. At present each
group owns its particular territory, defined by boundaries (*tamagava*)
which usually take the form of streams. Land ownership pertains to
the group, though we find here and there a tendency for the group
territory to be split up nominally among family groups. It is not,
however, divided among individuals: a man may clear and make a
garden wherever he pleases in his group land. Informants are usually
ready to say who will take over their land when they die, but the
examination of a number of cases has convinced me that there is no
definite system of bequest. The land continues to belong to the
group, while they live on it. If any person who by birth has a

nominal claim to the land goes to live in some distant part, then his claim eventually lapses. The same holds good when the group itself migrates. The movements of the various groups cannot be traced in detail. When, as is sometimes the case, their names refer to places at some distance from their present homes, this may well give a clue to their respective provenances, but it does not indicate that they have any claims of ownership over the original land. Each group is closely bound up with the land it occupies at present.

There is little doubt, I think, that the groups have always been local in character. The fact that they have in some cases drifted away from the regions whence they got their names and in which they presumably came into being as groups does not prevent us from still regarding them as local. This is undoubtedly what they are, for, as we shall see, membership of the group is decided ultimately and in theory by residence; its members in fact are those who live on and cultivate its land. Since then there is no exogamy, and since the rules governing membership are not to be reconciled with those of clan-descent, it seems unavoidable to reject the word "clan" and to refer to the unit as a *local group*. It must be understood then that "group" in this paper means "the local group."[8]

Membership of the Group

As stated above, the rule governing membership of the group is that the male child belongs to that of his father and the female to that of her mother. Marriage is with very few exceptions patrilocal, so that the male child belongs to the group in which it is born, whereas the female, nominally at least, does not.

I have recorded only three instances in which a male child was classed with the mother's group. One remains without explanation; but in the two others it appears that the men in question, having lost both father and mother as children, were for some reason brought up among the mother's people rather than those of the father. Now each is referred to as belonging to his mother's group; and one of them, a man of perhaps 35 years, classes his son in the same way.

A number of cases show that an individual may be absorbed into a group to which neither his father nor his mother belonged. Among the Korohi people, for example, are two adult males who were originally Nidori. One of them stated that he had been brought up among the Korohi since his childhood, and therefore now reckoned himself as one of that group. The other gave the same explanation, and it was recalled that his father, a Nidori man, had taken refuge with the Korohi after a tribal raid and had remained with them. The sons of these two men are now counted without hesitation as

Korohi. Similar cases have arisen from the dispersal of certain groups, due partly to the sale of their lands to white settlers in the Sogeri district and partly to the ravages of epidemics. A man, *e.g.* of the defunct Wakari group, which occupied what is now Koitaki estate, settled and married among the Munegapira. The name Wakari is now hardly more than a memory, and this man is called Munegapira. Another man, one of the now scattered Dauri group (who speak an *Isu-bia* dialect) had also settled among the Munegapira. His son is now referred to a Munegapira, having, a informants explained, been brought up on the Munegapira language. It seems therefore that to be born and reared among any particular group suffices to make one a member of it; in fact that the social groups of this district have a local rather than a lineal constitution.

When we come to consider the case of the female child, who should be classed with her mother's group, we again find a few exceptions. These will be considered fully later on; they will be found to throw a valuable light on the problem before us. In the meantime we may note the important fact that the affiliation of the female with her mother's group usually goes back no further than one generation. In the ordinary case, informants will state that a daughter belongs to her mother's group; but the mother will say that *she* belongs to *her* mother's group, and this may prove to be quite a different one. If the classing of the daughter with the group of her mother were a matter of true descent, then a girl would belong to the group of her mother, grandmother, great-grandmother, etc. But obviously we are not dealing with descent of female children in the female line. The fact is that the girl is classed with her mother's father's group, or, what is the same thing, with the group of her maternal uncle. Beyond that the antecedents of the mother in the female line are not counted. Unless there happen to be some elderly informants present with good memories, the group of the grandmother is probably forgotten altogether.

A concrete instance will show how far this sex affiliation goes and where it lapses:

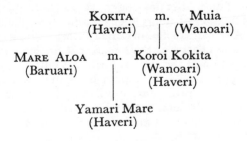

The girl Yamari was classed, not of course, with her father's group, Baruari, but with that of her mother. She was referred to as Haveri, and she spoke of her mother as Haveri. But Koroi Kokita herself declares that she is Wanoari, because that was her mother's group; and everyone is ready to back her up in this. If we were dealing with true descent in the female line we should find both Koroi and Yamari to be Wanoari. Since this is not so it appears that the affiliation of the female with the mother's group is not part of the hard-and-fast regulation of descent. It is something much less permanent, lasting not the lifetime of a people, but only the lifetime of an individual.

It should be noted that a husband speaks of his wife as belonging to the group of her father and brothers rather than to that of her mother. Very often, particularly when she hails from some distant part, he will be quite ignorant of what her mother's group actually is. In the concrete instance given above Mare Aloa would on the spur of the moment speak of his wife as a Haveri woman, though he would be quite ready to admit that she was also, or in strictness, Wanoari. It is certainly more usual, however, for the husband to speak of his wife's group as that in which she was domiciled before he married her; and this group is normally that of her father and brothers.

Domicile and Control of Children

Since marriage is patrilocal, children in the normal instance are brought up in the village of their father. Naturally, however, they will see something of their mother's village also, for, unless it happen to be very distant, the married couple are accustomed to make gardens on the wife's ground as well as the husband's.

During their childhood, sons and daughters are the responsibility of their parents, and the free and easy control of the children belongs to them. While the father lives, he, not the *waiuki* (maternal uncle), is responsible for keeping them, the girls no less than the boys. When, however, the father dies leaving a young family, we see some practical application of the rule of sex affiliation. Then, while the male children remain in the deceased father's village, the females may become the charge of their maternal uncles and he thence-forward brought up in the mother's original village. This at least is the stated rule, and sufficient cases are brought forward to show that it is a fairly common procedure. But it is by no means a strict rule; individual cases are decided by the wishes of individuals, and the rule is, perhaps, more honoured in the breach than in the observance.

When the orphan (*gori*, m. or f.) is old enough to have a will of her own she usually remains in her father's village.

Until her marriage, then, the girl is domiciled in her father's village provided he is still living, and to all practical purposes she is a member of his group despite her nominal affiliation with that of her mother. We may, I think, leave the question of group descent out of the discussion. It has already been found that the groups are local rather than lineal, and that the individual belongs to the group by virtue of living in its midst and sharing its social and economic life. Except in the cases of some orphans, the *maiogho*, or unmarried girl, belongs in this sense to her father's group. When she marries — and this is a point of some significance—she virtually transfers her allegiance to the group of her husband. How then, it may very well be asked, does the group of the mother come into it? We shall have to examine the social organization of the Koiari a good deal further before, in the second part of this paper, an attempt is made to answer that question.

To continue in the meantime, the *waiuki* does not possess any special authority over the children, either male or female, except in so far as he sometimes becomes responsible for rearing an orphan girl. I once suggested by way of hypothesis that father and maternal uncle might each want possession of the girl, and asked who would prevail. Characteristically, my informants found it difficult to deal with a hypothetical case, and they could not imagine such a direct contest of will or authority; they declared that one would say to the other, "Ah no, you take her if you want to!" But when I pressed the point they finally agreed that the father would have his way. The fact is, of course, that the maternal uncle never takes the girl from the father; the real authority lies with the latter. Fathers and mothers may smack their children, though assuredly they do so very rarely; I am told that a maternal uncle would never do such a thing. He would be too "belly-sore" or compassionate. Again, if the father were angry the child might run for temporary refuge and consolation to its maternal uncle. In fine, it appears that maternal uncles are very fond of their nephews and nieces, but it is obvious to the observer that the father's affection for his children and his sense of responsibility for them are altogether stronger.

When he is old enough to work effectively, the youth will do service from time to time in his maternal uncle's garden, at fencing, etc.; and it is after such a period of work, when he has tested the lad's diligence and skill, that the maternal uncle is supposed to offer him his daughter in marriage.

Among the *Isu-bia* (though not, as far as I could discover, among the hillmen) the young men after a dance are accustomed to make ceremonial presents to their maternal uncles. These take the form of a strip of cane, called *konama*, which they have worn about their waists during the dancing, hung with fragments of coconut, betel, pig-fat, and tobacco. On similar occasions girls wear over their backs the patterned string bags called *yago*, stuffed full of yellow betel nuts, and these also are given to the maternal uncle. It is explained that since a man has given his sister to another in marriage it is fitting that her children should remember him.[9]

Relationship Terms

The terms of relationship are shown in the following list:

Relation	Man speaking	Woman speaking
1. f.f.; m.f.; f.m.; m.m.; sn.ch.; d. ch.; br. (class) ch.	*ivahike*	*ivahike*
2. f.; f.br. (class); m. sis. (class) h.	*baba*	*baba*
3. m.; m. sis. (class); f. br. (class). wf.	*inei*	*inei*
4. m. br.; f. sis. h.	*waiuki*	*waiuki*
5. f. sis; m. br. w.	*yayaika*	*yayaika*
6. br.; f. br. sn.; m. sis. sn.; (senior to speaker)	*danane*	*danane*
7. sis.; f. br.d.; m. sis.d.; (senior to speaker)	*datate*	*datate*
8. br. or sis.; f. br. ch.; m. sis. ch.; (junior to speaker)	*daghoghe*	*daghoghe*
9. m. br. ch.; f. sis. ch.	*nubagha*	*nubagha*
10. son (own)	*damoi*	*damoi*
11. daughter (own)	*damai*	*damai*
12. br. (class) ch.; m. br. d. ch.; f. sis. d. ch.	*damoi, damai*	*dadime*
13. w. sis. ch.	*damoi, damai*	
14. sis. (class) ch.; m. br. sn.ch; f. sis. sn. ch.	*dadime*	*damoi, damai*
15. h. br. ch.	—	*damoi, damai*
16. wife	*damabare*	—
17. husband	—	*damobore*
18. w. f.; w. m.	*daware*	—
19. d. h.	*daware*	*daware*
20. sn. w.	*dawarutane*	*dawarutane*
21. h.f.; h.m.	—	*dawarutane*
22. w. br.	*hiba*	—
23. sis. h.	*hiba*	*dataname*
24. w. sis	*dataname*	—
25. h. br.	—	*dataname*
26. br. w.	*dataname*	*da'ene*
27. h. sis.	—	*da'ene*
28. w. sis. h.	*abere*	—

An important collective term should be noted:—

	Man speaking	Woman speaking
Brothers (class) senior or junior	—	*dakahide*
Sisters (class) senior or junior	*dakahide*	—

The possessive form has been given in almost all cases, with *da*, "my," prefixed. Thus *moi*="son"; *damoi*="my son." The words *ivahike, baba, inei, waiuki, yayaika, nubagha* and *hiba* are heard more often without the possessive prefix, being thus used as genuine terms of address. When the prefix is used they appear as *davahike, damame, danine, daghaiumi, dayaye, danubai* and *dahibagi*.

There are some collective terms, formed mostly by the use of the word *uhea* (*see* p. 127), senior brothers (class) are *dananuhea*; junior brothers *daghoghohea*; children (class) *daghamohea*; nephews and nieces, *dadimuhea*. As already stated the general term *dakahide* is used reciprocally by men for their classificatory sisters and by women for their classificatory brothers.[10]

The relationships have been arranged so as to draw attention to the difference in connotation in some cases between the man's and the woman's use of the same term. The most striking instance is that of *damoi* and *damai*, son and daughter. Both men and women use these terms for their own children; but the man extends them to his classificatory brothers' children, and the woman to her classificatory sisters' children. This is a common phenomenon, but none the less striking. Together with the converse rule (by which men call their sisters' children, and women their brothers' children, *dadime*, or nephews and nieces instead of classificatory sons and daughters), it calls for some explanation other than as a mere formal convention that the sexes should use different terms for certain identical relatives. Such an explanation will be attempted later (*see* p. 156).

The reciprocal terms used between parents-in-law and the spouse of son or daughter are *daware* and *dawarutane*. They are used respectively as indicated below.

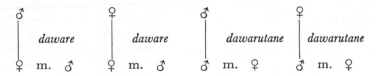

The same two terms are said to be used between the maternal uncle and the paternal aunt on the one side, and the spouse of the *dadime* on the other. The husband of the female *dadime* is *daware*, the wife of the male *dadime* is *dawarutane*, both terms being reciprocal. Informants were consistent on this point, though one may doubt whether the relationship term is actually employed for such distant relatives.

Hiba is a term used only between men; *da'ene* only between women. The latter was said to mean *nubagha* (women speaking of woman).

There is no parallel on the female side for *abere*, the reciprocal term used by the husbands of two sisters. I could discover no functional relationship between the men who call one another *abere*.

The words for brother and sister, viz., *danane*, *datate* and *daghoghe* are sometimes heard instead of *nubagha* for the cross-cousin. A man may say that so-and-so is *daghoghe* when he is his mother's brother's son, or father's sister's son; but he will admit that he is also, or properly, *nubagha*. Such a use of the word "brother" to describe a cross-cousin is not met with, of course, in taking down genealogies. But it is common enough in everyday use. It happens that I have observed it usually among members of the same community, though I would not say that it is always so restricted. There is certainly, however, a tendency to refer to all of one's generation in the village as "brothers and sisters."

It should be noted that these terms are used in the classificatory sense. The *waiuki*, *e.g.* are the mother's own brothers and the other men of her father's group, whom she calls brothers; *hiba* are the wife's own brothers and her father's brother's sons; *nubagha* are not only the true children of the mother's brother and the father's sister, but the children of all those whom the mother would call brother and the father call sister. The extent of these categories is sometimes rather disconcerting to the ethnographer. Although as proper terms of relationship they should technically be limited to true kindred, it is certainly a fact that they are often applied to people with whom the speaker is quite unable to trace his relationship. This is very noticeably the case with the *nubagha*.

There is, however, no mere lumping together of all the relatives, who are classed under one term. The native is perfectly sensible of nearness and distance of relationship. Although a number of men may be *waiuki* to the speaker, it is his mother's own brother who is his real *waiuki*; similarly, it is his wife's own brother who is his *hiba* in especial; and he distinguishes his own brothers from his parallel cousins, his first cross-cousin from more distant cross-cousins, etc., by the word *maite*, "real." The word *gaita*, "other" or "different," is used to mark off the remoter relatives. Thus, *danane maite*, "my own elder brother"; *danane gaita*, "my classificatory elder brother," etc.

Personal Names

Patronymic Surnames

Every child has two personal names; its own distinctive name, and that of its father. A catalogue of ancestors –unusually long—given by the principal man of the Taburi group will serve as an example; Kuana Wafuru; Erisu Kuana; Numu Erisu; Yana Numu; Magara Yana; Yofia Magara; Daube Yofia. The last mentioned was my informant.

The girl is named in precisely the same way, her second name being that of her father, not her mother's. (It is interesting to note, incidentally, that many, if not all, personal names may be used for either male or female.)[11]

Occasionally the mother's name may be used for surname instead of the father's, and this is the case with boys as much as with girls. Sometimes both surnames are well known and used without preference. The use of the mother's name as surname may arise from the circumstance that the mother is better known in a certain district than the father; when, for instance, a woman marries into a distant group, her children are sometimes known to her own relations by her name, rather than that of her husband. But another quite plausible reason has been given more than once: if the father's name does not run euphoniously with the personal name, then the mother's may be substituted. Gomara, the son of Borakape and Inoa, is known as Gomara Inoa because "Gomara Borakape" would be *gorogoroa*, "crooked" or "awkward." It should be added that the occasional use of the mother's name for the surname does not imply that the boy is classed with the mother's group.

This use of the father's name as surname for both sexes is sufficient to show that there is a strong tendency for both to reckon descent in the male line.

Name Avoidances

The names of certain relatives by marriage are tabooed. A man may not utter the names of his *daware* (*waru*); *hiba*; or *dataname*; a woman those of her *daware* or *dataname*. There is no taboo on the use by a woman of her *da'ene*'s name; and none for either sex on the name of the *dawarutane*. It is thus to be noted that a woman may address her parents-in-law by name, but a man may not do the same to his. To both man and woman the name of the daughter's husband is taboo; the name of the son's wife may be uttered.

The native knows no reason for these name avoidances. It is sufficient that their use would be in some manner offensive to the person concerned. But it is evidently not a serious matter. When a lapse occurs, the guilty one will turn aside his head and bite the back of his forefinger with an expression of consternation mingled with amusement on his face. He has dropped a rather harmless brick. To utter one of these forbidden names, however, brings bad luck. When a man misses a pig with his spear, his companions will say, "Ah, you must have used your brother-in-law's name!" There is no actual avoidance of the society of relations by marriage.

Marriage

Courtship

Marriage is usually preceded by a period of courtship, during which the girl receives night visits (*woto*) from her lover in her father's house. Before this can commence, the lover will have received some sign of favour, such as a fragment of tobacco slipped into his hand during the dance. Small lovers' presents known as *komuni* and consisting of tobacco, betel, armlets, etc., pass between them, and they are, so to speak, engaged. If, during the period of courtship, one or the other of the parties grows tired or is supplanted by a rival, the affair comes to an end. Otherwise it will conclude in marriage. We need not suppose that love-making of this kind is innocent, although informants often protest it is. When it leads to premature conception, it is said that the young man always marries the girl and avoids the shame (*mati*) of default.

In the usual event, when the pair have made up their minds to marry, the suitor will make some present to the girl's parents. He may hang up a cuscus or wallaby on their house verandah. If they accept the gift it is a sign of acquiescence. The boy will come openly to help in their gardens for a few days. At the end of what purports to be a time of probation, he will remain to a meal in their house. The girl shares tobacco and betel with him, and they eat together; then he stays the night with her in the house. After several more days of work in the gardens of the parents, he will take his bride home to his own village.

I am told that there is something in the nature of a wedding feast. It is not quite clear when this occurs, but it is a comparatively small affair and unconnected with the subsequent feast made at the time of payment. At this wedding feast the piles of food are laid out and taken by the more prominent guests as their names are called, but the last of them is reserved for the daughter, *i.e.* the bride. Her father will say, "These are the yams for you and your husband," and this is the only dowry she receives.

More often, it is said, the girl goes to her lover's house without any such preliminaries. It is still necessary for him to secure the goodwill of her parents, and he goes about it again by making a gift. If they do not care to accept it they may follow their daughter to his house, upbraid him as a thief, and try to get her back. But I do not hear of any case where they have not finally acquiesced.

An early sequel to the union is the payment for the bride (either in goods or by the giving of a girl in exchange). This will be discussed presently.

I think that Koiari marriages are usually preceded by mutual attraction and courtship. It is at least true that girls are not driven into matrimony against their will; and even when a brother wishes to give his sister in exchange for a girl he has already married, it is only with the free consent of the sister in question that the transaction can be completed. On the whole, since girls commonly take the initiative in courtship, and since they are acknowledged to be fickle and hard to please during its course, we should be right in concluding that they show a good deal of independence. It should be observed that the normal marriage is between young men and young women of approximately the same age. Girls do not marry very young; in fact, I have been struck by the number of young women, some of them attractive, who for reasons entirely their own have avoided the lure of matrimony.

Marriage and Kin

It is frequently affirmed that girls may marry where they please— into the group of their father, or into that of their mother, or into any other. As informants will tell you with a kind of tolerant amusement, there is no saying what a girl will do; if she sees a boy who takes her fancy she will go anywhere. In practice, then, there is at present no strict positive regulation of marriage. As we shall see, however, there is such a regulation in theory.

Marriages within the local group are common enough, but nevertheless they represent on the whole a rather small minority of cases. Such marriages may be between *dakahide* (classificatory brothers and sisters), but this is not necessarily the case with all intra-group marriages. Although, as we have seen, there is a tendency for all of the same generation within a group to refer to one another loosely as "brothers and sisters," it turns out that some stand to others in the relation of *nubagha* rather than that of *danane*, *daghoghe*, etc. Indeed, such a situation arises inevitably from any marriage between *dakahide* in the group: the husband and the wife's brother, who were formerly "brothers," now become *hiba*; and to the offspring the mother's brother is both *baba* (paternal uncle or "father") and *waiuki* (maternal uncle); while his children they will call both *danane,* etc., and *nubagha.* Intra-group marriages may therefore prove to be between *nubagha.*

Informants have not been very consistent in naming the relations between whom marriage is permitted, some being much more liberal in their views than others. These free-thinkers have said that a man might marry *nubagha, dakahide, dadime,* and *damai.* Others cited a case where a man had married a woman whom he called *inei* (mother) but they were unable to trace the relationship definitely.

Among the hillmen proper I was unable to discover a single case in which a man had married a girl whom he called *damai;* and nearly all informants agreed in saying that such a union was forbidden. It was among the Nadeka and Taburi groups of the *Isu-bia* (Grasslanders) that I met the only cases I have recorded; they numbered four out of nineteen in which the previous relation of husband and wife was known.

Of these last-mentioned nineteen marriages, two others had been between a man and his *dadime;* but among the hillmen proper I could obtain news of only two such marriages altogether. One was actually with the daughter of the step-sister,

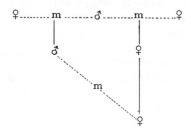

and this was condemned outright as bad. The other, represented as follows,

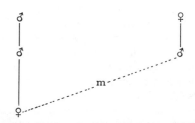

was regarded as rather an amusing episode and evidently as rather an improper one also. The bride and bridegroom belonged to the same village, and the woman was referred to as the man's "daughter" as well as his *dadime*. Informants were unable to take up any other cases of marriage with the *dadime*, and some declared outright that it was not a proper thing. It must be very rare, and we shall probably be right in regarding it (as well as marriage with the *damai*) as against customary law.

Marriages between *dakahide* are not so uncommon. One well-known instance, that between a man Wuiena and his first parallel cousin Oua Nanuka of Sogeri,

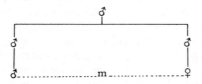

was referred to more than once with disapproval, not unmixed with that sort of sly amusement we take in a not-very-serious scandal. Neither the principals in the marriage nor their fellow villagers show anything like shame over the transaction.[12]

Two instances, precisely similar to one another, showed the marriage between children of step-brothers, both belonging to the same group.

These were condoned as between *dakahide*, who were "a little bit different." The same excuse was made for a marriage of the following type (the fathers of the couple belonging to the same group):

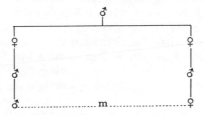

Such unions are spoken of as *uyawia*, "little bit good," *i.e.* "not altogether good but good enough." Marriages between *dakahide*, however, are relatively rare. They certainly cannot be regarded as having genuine social approval, for if one asks a youth (or a girl) whether he will marry his *dakahide*, he will reply with an emphatic "No!" accompanied by mild but unmistakable signs of aversion.

It remains, therefore, that there is only one class of relatives with whom marriage may be properly contracted, viz., the *nubagha*; and investigation proves that *nubagha* marriages are in an overwhelming majority. Now the term *nubagha* is, as we have seen, a very wide one, embracing cross-cousins in every degree. Owing to the absence in present practice of positive marriage regulations and the consequent freedom to marry in any quarter, a man is likely to have *nubagha* in a number of different groups. When he wishes to marry, therefore, he is not likely to have any difficulty in finding a girl who stands, at least nominally, in the right relation to him. If you ask a man what was his wife's relation to him before marriage he will nearly always answer *nubagha*. Quite often, however, when you try to elicit the genealogical connection he finds himself unable to trace it; and I am convinced that in many instances the relation is a fictitious one. It may even prove to be definitely false; the bridegroom in a marriage of the following type,

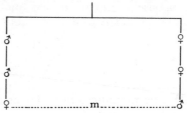

said that his bride was *nubagha* to him, whereas to judge from the pedigree given she technically stood to him in the relation of *daghoghe*, "younger sister" (*i.e.* she was one of his *dakahide*). Some men who have married girls from more or less distant parts confess that they do not know what relationship formerly existed between them; they make no bones about it and are honest enough to abjure the pretence that the girls were their *nubagha*. One man, a Nidori native, who had met and married a girl from the Korohi group, confided to me that she, in making the characteristic advances, had informed him that she was his *nubagha dogodogoa*—"*nubagha* little bit," *i.e.* small degree but sufficient for a match. While then it is evident that some men contract marriages with girls other than their *nubagha*, it is equally evident from the general consistency of their replies that the marriage should be with the *nubagha*. As one

informant put it, the best marriages are between *nubagha*; but if
youths and maidens are attracted by one another, then they will
marry, no matter what their relation. It is probably not too much
to say that these other marriages are exceptions, and that the
original marriage law is that a man should marry only his *nubagha*.[13]

Marriage with the first cross-cousin, either mother's brother's or
father's sister's child, is permitted. The following concrete case
shows an exchange between two cross-cousins :

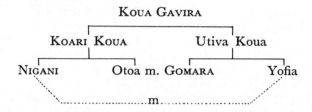

It is constantly stated that there is no rule against the matings of
first cross-cousins of either kind. Indeed, as will presently be shown,
there are some grounds for believing that such unions represented
the original ideal. Nevertheless, they are not very common, and
sometimes we come upon traces of a prejudice against them. This
prejudice is apparently based upon economic grounds; as we have
already seen, some informants have used the argument that to
marry the first cross-cousin is to sacrifice one's claim to a share in the
payment for her.[14] The prejudice, in so far as it exists, does not
seem to reflect any intrinsic objection to the marriage of near kin.

Exchange and Purchase

We have discussed the preliminaries to marriage and the question
of marriage and kinship. There remains the important economic
question, viz., that of squaring up after the marriage, of compensat-
ing the family and group to which the girl belonged.

A woman or girl is attached to the group as much by economic as
by sentimental ties. She is a potential child-bearer, and she plays an
important part in producing food and preparing it. When a girl
marries she becomes, for all practical purposes, a member of her
husband's group and family. Together with her husband she may
return to cultivate a plot in the village of her childhood, but henceforward she spends most of her time and does most of her work
among her husband's people.

Compensation is made either by giving another girl in exchange,
or by payment in valuables. The former transaction is called

damuna, the word signifying "pay back" or "equivalent payment". It could be well enough applied to the payment in valuables for the bride, but this may be referred to more specifically as *tohe*, the word for native ornaments in general, because these ornaments figure largely in what may be called the bride-price. A native therefore obtains his bride either by *damuna*—"exchange," or by *tohe*—"valuables." The contrast is sometimes expressed merely by the expressions *damuna*—"exchange" and *damuna vehite*—"without exchange."

In exchange the girls are normally, though not invariably, true sisters of the two men concerned. It is not necessary that the two marriages should take place simultaneously. There appears to be nothing like a celebration in connection with marriage, much less a joint celebration of two marriages. In a straightforward case that came to my notice a man Gudu, from Naduri in the mountains, had married a Taburi girl named Borakape about one year before the second marriage could be negotiated and the exchange rendered complete. [15]

Exchange marriage is always, I believe, accompanied by formal payment and repayment of native valuables (and nowadays money). The two groups are at pains to see that they give and receive exact equivalents. Various relatives of the bridegroom will contribute pig-tusks, armshells, and so on; and when the amount is handed over it will be distributed among the relatives of the bride. But these latter bear in mind that they will presently have to make return payment, so that any man who accepts any item must be in a position to pay back its equivalent. The main receiver and distributor will in fact make sure that he gives away the articles only to such as are in a good way to pay their debts. He will ask, "Have you an armshell?" "Yes." "Then take this armshell." When the time comes the recipient will furnish another armshell as contribution to the return payment. (Since this all seems rather fruitless I suggested that a man might keep and eventually hand back the same armshell. But my informants were very much amused at the idea.) If, as nowadays it sometimes does, money forms a part of the formal payment accompanying exchange, the same return, detail for detail and pound for pound, is demanded.

When, as very often happens, a man has no sister to offer in exchange, he buys his wife outright. The prices are variable. One man named two pigs and £3 5s., together with a quantity of vegetable food and smoked wallaby; another, five knives, some native grass skirts, some calico cloth, a pearl-shell ornament and one pig; a third (fresh from European employment) £5, a table cloth, a native mat, six calicoes, a boar's tusk, and five wooden dishes.

I am assured that in these cases of direct purchase there is no obligation on the part of the bride's people to make any return present. This seems entirely reasonable, since they have exchanged the person of the bride for the price received. Yet it is not unusual for them to make a very substantial return; and at any rate for an indefinite period after the marriage there will be reciprocal feasts given by the husband and his people to the wife's brother and his people and *vice versa*, *i.e.* presents of food passing between the two *hiba*. It is said that a man must keep on good terms with his relations-in-law.

The question of the original return by the bride's people in cases of outright purchase proves to be quite a thorny one. The final solution is, I think, definitely, that no such return is obligatory; and yet various informants have actually maintained that the return is no less than exactly equivalent to the original payment. Various explanations have been offered: the return payment anticipates any dissatisfaction or "rowing" on the part of the husband's people; or again it absolves the bride's people from the responsibility for replacing the bride with another girl if the former dies; or, generally speaking, the husband's people would be "wild" and the bride's people "ashamed" if such a return gift were not made.

In one or two cases I have discovered that the return of an equal amount in what was ostensibly a case of outright purchase really assumed the subsequent giving of a girl; that is to say, they were not genuine cases of purchase but really of exchange deferred; and it is possible that all these apparently illogical transactions are explicable on the assumption of a contemplated exchange of girls. It may be also remarked that, as natives are so vain of their resources in wealth and food, there is no question on which they are more inclined to draw the long bow, or to give false information with a grandiose thoughtlessness for the truth.

Attention should be drawn to the argument above mentioned that the return of the full equivalent of the bride-price relieved the bride's people of the necessity of substituting another girl if she died. This explanation was offered on only one occasion, and I think it may be dismissed as a piece of sheer sophistry. No instance could be furnished of such substitute for a deceased bride, and in response to many enquiries as to the practice of the sororate I have always received firm and consistent denials. Indeed it has been said that if the bridegroom demanded another girl the parents would answer, "No fear, you killed one girl, you are not going to get another !" It should be noted that the levirate also, even in the widest sense, is not recognized. The widow does sometimes marry another man of the husband's group and village, but she is in no way bound to do so.

If still young, she commonly chooses to go back to the village of her parents, and she may remarry when and where she pleases. Even when, as in the normal or ideal case, she has married into the group of her *waiuki*, that group has no rightful claim upon her as a widow.

Nowadays at any rate it would appear that marriage is much more commonly by purchase than by exchange. Yet when I raised this question an old and trusted informant confidently answered that exchange was the usual fashion. When we tested the matter by examining 24 cases of marriage on the spot and found that 17 had been by purchase and only 7 by exchange, he affirmed that exchange was in his day much commoner than it is now. Even to-day, when purchase marriages are so much more numerous than exchange marriages, informants have declared that the latter form, when feasible, is to be preferred. The reason given is that a girl's parents are thereby assured of help and attention in their old age; they will at least have a daughter-in-law when they lose a daughter. Should their daughter be bought outright, then their son might fail to produce a wife later and so they would be stranded. This is the only argument I have heard for preferring exchange marriage to marriage by purchase. It is noteworthy that, although it represents the standpoint of the parents, it was advanced by a young bachelor. We may be right in viewing exchange marriage as the ideal Sogeri form, and in assuming that the alternative, viz., purchase is a later development which, whatever the reason, has supplanted the original in popularity.

The Recipient of the Bride-Price

Now in the case of marriage by purchase we may enquire who is the proper recipient of the bride-price. This is a matter of some importance in regard to the problem of sex affiliation, but it is unexpectedly involved. The evidence would at first appear to be flatly contradictory. Some informants have declared that the bride's father is the proper recipient; others, with equal assurance, that it is her *waiuki*. There is agreement on the point that both paternal and maternal relatives usually share in the distribution; but some have it that the father's people retain the major part of the goods and give the remainder to the mother's people; others put the thing *vice versa*. It is probable that informants are here thinking of particular instances and rather thoughtlessly converting them into generalizations. From all the evidence I collected, however, it becomes evident that while the main recipient is sometimes the *waiuki* it is far more frequently the father.

One of my earlier notes (taken at Borebere, where it was hoped that the girls would marry in their own group) recorded the native

ruling that "if they marry into the father's people the *waiuki* takes
the pay; if they marry into the *waiuki's* people the father takes the
pay; if they marry into some other people the father takes the pay
and gives some to the *waiuki*". It appeared later, however, that the
girl never marries into her father's people in the narrow sense. Even
when she marries into her father's local group, as happens often
enough, it is not, of course, into her father's immediate family; and
it never happens that the *waiuki* takes the pay to the exclusion of the
father. In cases of intra-group marriage the family of the bridegroom pays the family of the bride, who share with the *waiuki*.

In the other clauses the original note is substantially correct.
When a girl marries her first cross-cousin (true *waiuki*'s son) it would
be absurd to give the pay as well as the girl to the *waiuki*'s family.
As one informant put it, such a marriage "closes the way" to payment to the *waiuki*. The payment is then made to the girl's father
alone.

In the usual marriage, which is neither into the father's group nor
into the immediate family of the *waiuki*, the payment is made to the
father, who shares more or less equally with the true *waiuki*.

The outstanding fact is that both the father and the *waiuki* have a
claim to the girl (the latter, of course, on behalf of his son). If she
happens to marry into the *waiuki*'s actual family then they have the
girl herself and cannot demand any pay; but if she marries elsewhere
then the claim of the *waiuki* must be compensated by payment. This
claim is a very real one, so much so that some groups, as we have
seen, gave the rule that the *waiuki* was the principal, and the father
only the secondary, recipient.[16] Another point may be recalled to
illustrate this claim. It should be understood, of course, that the
sons of the *waiuki* share with their father, and more than one set of
informants have pronounced against marriage between first cross-
cousins for the reason, which seems to be an odd one and not entirely
logical, that the *nubagha* by marrying the girl would lose his share in
the bride-price.

It is apparent that in respect of payment or squaring up, marriage
is primarily a transaction between families rather than local groups.
Various members of the local group of the bride-groom may assist
him in payment, and on the other hand, that payment will be
distributed among various members of the bride's father's group
and that of her *waiuki*. But it is for the man himself and his immediate
relatives to get the payment together, and it is to the true father (and
brothers) of the bride and to her true *waiuki* (and true *nubagha*) that
the payment is made: classificatory relatives of the father and
maternal uncle only share in it by virtue of the generosity of these
individuals.

Property and Inheritance

Man and wife are said to be joint owners of their dwelling and their pigs. Other property they hold separately, according as the various items pertain to the one sex or the other. Thus, men own pig-nets, weapons and dogs, and a variety of ornaments (dogs' teeth, shell frontlets, a dance or fighting ornament held in the teeth and called *mimisa*, and feather headdresses, etc.) which are commonly worn by males only. Women, on the other hand, have their own kinds of ornaments, their pots, dishes, and water-vessels, their string, their grass skirts and their bark-cloth blankets. All these they hold and bequeath as individuals. Moreover, some of the objects previously mentioned as normally pertaining to males may be owned by their wives independently, and this is often the case with European articles like billy-cans and trade knives. Thus one woman, thanks to a generous present from her son on his return from indenture, could give a much longer list of personal property than could her husband.

The rule of inheritance with regard to such personal property is that a man bequeaths to his sons and a woman to her daughters. With regard to land the position is not so clear. We have already seen that the land (despite a tendency to divide it amongst family groups) is owned by the local group rather than individually by its members; and that while it is commonly stated that the child will live upon and cultivate its parent's land, this does not mean individual inheritance. At any rate land inheritance (if we may use the expression) is dependent upon the child remaining a member of the local land-owning group.

But while endeavouring to follow up the subject of land-inheritance I have again and again met with the statement that the son receives his father's land and the daughter her mother's. This cannot be taken as a genuine regulation, for men, enumerating the areas to which they have a claim, will sometimes give those that belong to their mother's as well as those that belong to their father's people; they will professedly bequeath to daughters as well as sons; and even when they name their sons as successors they also say that their daughters "can have the land too if they please."

Nevertheless, even if it is constantly broken or disregarded, the rule is stated persistently enough, and occasionally it may be definitely observed. The Sogeri group, who sold their land to the Itiki Rubber Plantation, have now settled on lands that belonged formerly to the Manari and Baruari groups, but which have been left unoccupied by them. (This is an entirely friendly transaction, without payment; as informants say, there is more than enough land for everyone, and this no doubt accounts for the laxity of the land-laws.) Nowadays the Sogeri gardens are made mostly on the old Manari ground; the Baruari area is said to belong in particular to the Baruari woman Aguta, the wife of Babaga, the chief man of Sogeri; she is named as the *biagua*, or owner, of it. Now whereas Babaga's sons and the other males of the group will inherit the other lands, informants stated explicitly that the Baruari area would be left to Aguta's two daughters; and at present it is Aguta and her two daughters who make gardens on it.

But should these daughters marry at a distance, then, my informants declared, they would *ipso facto* abandon their claim to the land, and it would be taken over by their brothers and the other males of the group. We have seen that when an individual leaves his group permanently and goes to live at a distance, his claim to part-ownership of the old land is eventually neglected and forgotten; and it is made clear that this happens very commonly in regard to a girl's claim on her mother's land. After her marriage, most of her gardening will be done on the land of her husband, and if she cultivates another plot it is usually on the land from which she came as a girl, viz., her father's. Her mother's land she may never see again. Its evident therefore that the supposed rule that daughters receive their mother's land will not work out as genuine inheritance in the female line.

When informants say "mother's land" they mean the land of that group to which the girl's mother belonged as a girl herself. The girl does not actually inherit this land; and yet under ideal conditions it is just the land she will eventually live on and cultivate. The ideal conditions are those of her marriage into the group of her mother's brothers.

Part II

Recapitulation

After the foregoing more or less general sketch of Koiari social organization, we may now examine more closely the particular feature of it which I have called sex affiliation. We have yet to discover and define in what sense the female offspring belong to the mother's group rather than to the father's. After that we may briefly discuss the implications of this rule.

It may be as well to recapitulate the more strictly relevant features of the organization. We have found that the principal social units are non-exogamic and non-totemic; they are best described as local groups, of which the membership is ultimately decided by residence and by participation in group life. We cannot speak of clans and and clan-descent. Within the family and the local group, however, descent is virtually patrilineal. With males this is quite obvious: there is a system of patronymic surnames and the male offspring normally and almost invariably belong to the father's group. Incidentally, property is inherited by sons from their fathers.

With female offspring the position is not so clear. They likewise use patronymic surnames; they are normally brought up by their fathers; and in some connections they are spoken of as belonging to their father's group. Evidently there is a strong tendency towards patrilineal descent with females as with males. Nevertheless, they are constantly said to belong to their mother's group. Inheritance is also normally from mother to daughter in respect of paraphernalia and nominally in respect of land.

When we examine the statement that the daughter belongs to her mother's group, however, we find that it holds good for only one generation back; and it really means that she belongs to the group of her mother's father and brothers, or to use the usual expression, to the group of her maternal uncle. Her mother by the same rule may be found to belong to quite a different group. This is therefore no case of the true descent of females in the mother's line, and I have ventured to adopt, instead of "descent," the term "affiliation."

We have also found that, although girls marry much as they please, the proper marriage is with the *nubagha*, *i.e.* the cross-cousin in any degree. Marriage may be with the first or true cross-cousin, either mother's brother's child or father's sister's child, but it is usually with a *nubagha* further removed. Exchange and purchase are both practised as forms of marriage, but there is some evidence that the former is regarded as the ideal. The maternal uncle (*waiuki*) has a claim over the girl on behalf of the son, her true *nubagha*. If the latter does not marry her, then he is entitled to a share, with the *waiuki*, in the bride-price by way of compensation.

The Native Explanation of Sex Affiliation

Now when we ask a native why the girl belongs to her mother's group and the boy to his father's he will answer that the thing is obvious; the former has the sex characters of the female, the latter of the male. If we ask what it *means*, or what it amounts to in effect, he will say that the girl, when she marries, must go back to the place her mother came from. These two explanations have been repeated again and again. I have never heard any reference in this connection to the obvious sex division of labour; nor again to the nominal inheritance rule of son from father and daughter from mother,

though informants have sometimes laid emphasis on the assumption that the girl will go back to use the *land* of her mother. As
a rule, however, native explanations may be summed up under
these two points: (1) the girl-child has the sex characters of her
mother, and (2) she is destined in marriage to go to the place of
her mother.

(1) The first is certainly a very obvious means of classification,
hardly requiring any explanation out of native theories of genetics.
It is fully recognized that the male plays a part in fecundation and
contributes something to the make-up of the child. It is thought
that repeated acts of coitus are required. Some informants have
maintained that the child's body is made up of semen; others that it
is compounded of the father's semen and the mother's blood; and
one suggested that the offspring would be male or female according
as one or the other component predominated. I heard no other
explanation of the mystery of the child's sex, and I clould not
discover whether any kind of magic were used to influence it during
pregnancy. The plain fact of sex is accepted as determining whether
the child is to be affiliated to its father's or its mother's group; as one
informant put it, "I have my father's body and so I belong to my
father's group; my sister has her mother's and so belongs to hers."
From its sheer obviousness this classification might well enough
represent a very elementary or primitive idea.[17]

The Functional Significance of Sex Affiliation

(2) It is the practical application of the idea, however, its functional
significance, that interests us most. The girl belongs to her mother's
group in a practical sense because she is destined to live there as an
adult; she is to be the wife of one of its members. This is expressed
by such phrases as "She must go back to her mother's place," or
"her mother's land"; or "She must go straight along the path her
mother came by." (The custom already noted of rearing an orphan
girl in her mother's village is not commonly cited in explanation
of sex affiliation; at any rate it should hardly be spoken of as a custom
but rather as a permissible practice.)

Although this explanation was given again and again it was not
till I was confronted by some exceptions to the rule of sex affiliation
that I fully realized its significance. In the Borebere group, when
I visited it, there was a predominance of young females, though the
population had for one reason or another been much depleted. The
principal man of the group, one Bore, had married a Veburi woman;
he stoutly maintained, however, that his two daughters by her, as
well as his two sons, belonged to the Borebere group. Another man,
Babaga, who had married a Maiari woman had five unmarried

daughters. Bore, who evidently ruled the roost in Borebere and could speak for all, declared that these also were Borebere and not Maiari, a decision in which Babaga fully acquiesced. Now these men and the others present were fully aware, they professed, of the ordinary rule that daughters were classed with their mother's group.[18] But Bore had made up his mind that his own daughters and those of Babaga at any rate were Borebere. And he gave this explanation: they were to remain, even when married, in their father's village. That is to say, he would require their husbands to forgo the regular custom of patrilocal marriage, and to come and settle in the village of their wives. His reason was that he wished the population of his group to be built up again. He admitted that it might be impossible to carry out his wish since so much depended on the will of the young women; but since he was a man of undoubted influence and personality he might well have his way.

I came across a parallel case among the Wberi group. The chief man of these scattered people, who was also the village constable, had recently formed a small village on a good site. He had no daughters himself, but his brother had two, the offspring of a Moroka woman. The village constable and his brother, who seemed to be overborne by him, declared that these girls were Wberi rather than Moroka. I did not succeed in getting an explanation from him, but as a matter of fact one of the daughters in question does continue to live in her father's village though married—one of the very rare exceptions to patrilocal conditions that I have met with. It is also worth recording in regard to the other daughter that her father remarked, in quite a different connection, that he wanted her to remain in the village to look after him, since he was an old widower. It should be emphasized that these also were regarded as exceptional cases: the brothers of the two women did not hesitate in their father's absence to class them as Moroka, thus following the rule of sex affiliation.

These cases show that, since the daughter may be in exceptional cases affiliated to the father's group because of her prospective residence in it as a married woman, there should be no difficulty in accepting the explanation given in the normal case, viz., that the girl is affiliated to the mother's group because she is destined to marry there.

We have seen the wide popularity of marriage with the *nubagha*. It amounts to more than preferential mating, for it is generally conceded that the *nubagha* is the only proper mate. Further, while the term *nubagha* is very liberally interpreted, it is sufficiently clear that it is among the *nubagha* in the actual group of her mother's brother that the girl should make the ideal marriage. For this we have the constantly reiterated statement, and also the fact that the mother's brother and his sons (if she does not marry one of the latter) claim a share in the bride-price as an alternative.

Whether the ideal marriage was ever considered to be with the first cross-cousin can only be decided by inference. It may well have been the case, however, since marriage, as we have noted, seems in its economic aspect to be a transaction between family groups rather than between the larger units I have called local groups; and the claim to part payment belongs first to the true *waiuki* and *nubagha* rather than to the group at large. The very argument which is used sometimes against the marriage of first cross-cousins, viz., that the *nubagha*-husband would thereby sacrifice his claim to a share in the bride-price, might be turned to show that he was nominally entitled to the girl herself. Moreover, it is said that when a youth goes, as he ordinarily does, to help in the garden of his maternal uncle, the latter keeps an eye on him as a prospective son-in-law. If his work is up to the mark, the maternal uncle says, "My daughter is yours." The young man either accepts what would thus appear to be his right, or if he wishes to evade it, says, "No, let her marry someone else and give me a share in the bride-price instead of her." That such candid offers and refusals take place in actual fact may be considered very doubtful, but they would appear to represent the theory that the ideal, or "first choice" marriage should be between first cross-cousins, and that other unions are a substitute for them.[19]

But leaving this point aside for the moment, I think it has been sufficiently demonstrated that the functional meaning of the affiliation of the girl to her mother's group is that she is nominally destined to belong to it in marriage. Having passed her childhood with her father, she should spend the greater part of her useful life as wife, mother and food-producer in the village of her maternal uncle. We need not consider the highly frequent exceptions in present-day marriages. The above is the rule as it is given and the explanation.

The Implications of Sex Affiliation

Reciprocating Pairs

By the rule of sex affiliation when a woman born in one group (A) marries into another group (B) her daughter should go back to the original group (A) to marry; their daughters again should go back to (B), and so on. That is to say, (A) and (B) constitute a pair bound permanently together by a succession of unions.

There seems still to be some trace of such pairing of groups; Haveri and Manari, Nidori and Munegapira, Nadeka and Ienari, for instance, might be respectively paired off together, for they still intermarry to some extent. But such alliances between groups would necessarily be disrupted by the actual freedom of marrying out in all directions.

It is not necessary to suppose, however, that any one of the present-day local groups was ever solely attached by such marriage ties to any one other local group. It might form alliances with a number of groups at the same time; but once begun, then according to strict rule the process of sending each generation of daughters back and forth would continue. It is as if, when a girl married, her brothers should say, "Remember your girl children belong to us. You and your husband will keep them while they are young, but when they are of an age to marry they must come back to us. They are to marry the young men of our group."

So far it has been shown that according to the rule of sex affiliation certain females of one group would in each generation marry into another group with which the former had the sort of marriage alliance we have envisaged. Now marriage by exchange is still common in the Sogeri district; there is some evidence that it is preferred when feasible to marriage by purchase, and that in the past it was commoner than it is now. We need only assume one exchange between two groups and, if the rule of sex affiliation is strictly carried out, those two groups would thenceforward be committed to perpetual interchange of girls. They would constitute, as far as marriage was concerned, a *reciprocating pair*.

Group (A), as I have already implied, is not of necessity bound solely to group (B); it may have formed a marriage alliance with group (C) and a number of others as well. (A) and (B), (A) and (C), etc., are then reciprocating pairs. In any generation certain girls of (A) should marry into (B), and certain into (C), because their mothers came from those groups. At the same time, certain girls from (B) and (C) must marry into (A) because their mothers came from that group, and so on. This organization of society into a system or multiplicity of reciprocating pairs is, I think, the logical outcome of sex affiliation combined with marriage by exchange. Nowadays, it is true, marriage rules are lax and marriages almost indiscriminate. Yet the nominal rules remain: the girl should marry her *nubagha*, and he should be a *nubagha* in her mother's group.

We have noted that at the present day marriage in its economic aspect is a transaction between family groups rather than between local groups. The responsibility for payment and the right to participation are more or less diffused through the local group of which the family groups are respectively members. If this has always been so, then the reciprocating pairs would be constituted originally by family groups, which might in course of time develop or merge with others into the larger local groups. Although nowadays we find a tendency to avoid the first cross-cousin in favour of a *nubagha* somewhat further removed, it would appear that in theory a man is actually entitled to his first cross-cousin; and this may be taken to imply that the reciprocating pair consisted originally of two family groups.

The constitution of the groups, however, is not of any great importance. The general hypothesis remains, viz., that as a result of sex affiliation and exchange-marriage, society would form a system of units arranged in reciprocating pairs. The units would presumably be small ones, viz., small village communities not unlike those that constitute the present-day Koiari population.

Relationship Terms and Residence

Let us see how such a hypothetical system would square with the relationship terms. It seems reasonable to suppose that when under the classificatory system a number of relatives are referred to by one and the same term, they should have something in common to justify it. There are the obvious factors of sex, generation and age (seniority and juniority), but under a system of reciprocating pairs of small units such as I have assumed to be at the basis of Sogeri society, it could be argued that the classificatory term is largely accounted for by *residence*.

It is important to recognize that certain terms are first used by the speaker when he is a child; others only come into use when he has reached something like marriageable age or is himself married. In the list of terms (p. 134) numbers 1–9 are those used first in childhood (with the exception of *ivahike, i.e.* grandchild); the remainder are terms used normally by adults (though, of course, a child could use the terms for brother's wife, brother's son, etc., when brothers and sisters are widely separated in age).

Now to a child living in a small more or less isolated community, all the males of its father's generation would represent a class by themselves. They are the full-grown men whom he sees about him every day. His father is one of them and, of course, by far the most important, and the child extends the word *baba* to the other lesser fathers because they live and work together with his true father in the same small community. Similarly his *inei* are the women of his mother's generation who live in his community. They are like his mother; they constitute a class by themselves as the working women who garden, fetch wood and water, cook, and look after infants like himself, all within the bounds of his little world in especial, the small community in which he lives. But the child knows another little world, not quite so familiar as his own community, but much more so than all the others scattered about in the hills: it is the community of his mother's father and brothers, where his parents may take him from time to time for fairly long visits. This is of course the other community of the reciprocating pair. The child has one name, *waiuki*, for the males, and one, *yayaika*, for the females of the previous generation living in that community.

The children of his own generation in his own community form a distinct class to him. They are like his true brothers and sisters, his regular playmates, and he extends to them the term *danane*, *daghoghe*, etc. The children of the other community are a class apart, and he has one name for all of them, *nubagha*.

So far the brothers and sisters, having been brought up together in their father's household and being subject to the same social contacts, have used the same terms as one another for the various relatives in their own and the preceding generations. But now they marry; they assume the same status as the other married adults, and they beget or bear children of their own. At this stage normally they begin to use a whole series of new relationship terms—(1) for their relatives-in-law, and (2) for the generation of their children. But in marrying, the sister has parted from her brother; she has gone to live in "the other" unit, and it is now found that brother and sister no longer always use identical terms for the same relatives.

Both men and women call their own children (m. and f.) *damoi* and *damai*. But whereas a man applies these terms to his brother's children and not to those of his sister, a woman applies them to her sister's children and not to those of her brother. This, I suggest, is because the husband and wife, who call their own children *damoi* and *damai*, extend that name to all the other youngsters who live in their village community. The terms *damoi* and *damai* are equivalent to "my children and their village playmates." To the husband these are his brother's children; to the wife they are her sister's. The youngsters of the other village (from which the wife came) they both call *dadime*; these are the man's sister's children, and the woman's brother's children. By the fact of altering her residence for the sake of marriage, the woman has to adopt terms different from those used by her brother.

What I wish to suggest is that residence in one community may be one of the essential factors justifying a common relationship term for a number of people. This appears most strikingly in the case of the terms for the younger generation. The children of "my" village (m.s. or w.s.) are sons and daughters; those of "the other" village in the reciprocating pair are nephews and nieces. But it is possible to put the same interpretation on certain of the terms for relations-in-law. *Dawarutane* used by man and woman for the son's wife, and by woman only for the husband's parents, refers in each case to relatives in "my" village. *Daware*, used by a man for his wife's parents, and by man and woman for their daughter's husband, refers to relatives in "the other" village.[20] Similarly the term *dataname* (m.s. or w.s.) is applied to brothers-in-law and sisters-in-law in "my" village whereas the terms *hiba*, used by men, and *da'ene*, used by women, refer to the corresponding relatives in "the other" village.

It is probably impossible to discover the actual meanings or derivations of the relationship terms. It is my object here merely to demonstrate that their application to a number of people may, in part, result from the circumstance that those people reside in one or other of the two small communities which together constitute a reciprocating pair. It might be claimed at first sight that the relationship system of the Sogeri district implied the former existence of a Dual Organization, but there is no positive trace of such organization there; and I think the terms of relationship are fully in keeping with the system hypothesised, viz., a number of small communities which have fallen naturally into reciprocating pairs.

Cross-Cousin Marriage

I have spoken of the rule of sex affiliation as if it has led up to such a system. It is true that it may on the contrary have been evolved out of it as a sort of wisdom after the event, though if we assume this we abandon a feasible explanation of certain common phenomena of social organization.

Viewed, however, as a true cause, of which the system of reciprocating pairs is the natural result, it would account also for the practice of cross-cousin marriage. The daughter belongs to her mother's unit in the sense that she is expected to marry into it; and in view of the special claims of the *waiuki* it would seem that the unit may be in strict theory the family. Further, it should be recalled that among the people with whom we are dealing, marriages are nowadays normally between young men and women of approximately equal age; it is not necessary to assume that any preposterous unions between different generations were ever customary. The natural mate would, therefore, be the cross-cousin, and in a fully reciprocating pair this would be either the mother's brother's child or the father's sister's child. Such a marriage, however, can only be taken to represent the "first choice." We need not suppose that it was ever strictly enjoined. Nowadays, young people show a great deal of freedom in selecting their mates, and probably they were always allowed some latitude. A youth might not want his first cross-cousin, nor a girl hers; in that case they would take another cross-cousin, one to wit who offered the necessary sex attraction. Thus the rule is observed at least nominally, and the economic obligations are met by payment.

It is conceivable that the idea of sex affiliation might be a very primitive one, preceding the idea of rigid descent in either one line or the other and the development of the clan system. Moreover, such a conception might underlie the system described as bilateral descent. But until what I have called sex affiliation has been discovered and recorded among other peoples it would no doubt be unwise to claim too much for it as a clue in sociological theory.

REFERENCES

1. (Originally published in *Journal of the Royal Anthropological Institute*, vol. 62 [1932], pp. 51-81. E.S.)
2. The name Koiari belongs properly to one of the local groups of the grasslanders. It has been applied loosely to all who speak similar dialects right up to and beyond the central range.
3. Like Koiari, Sogeri is really the name of a local group only, but has been extended to a general neighbourhood. In this popular sense the the Sogeri district is included iń and forms only a small part of the Koiari country.
4. See Seligman, 1910, *Melanesians of British New Guinea*. (For a more recent study see Firth 1952. E.S.)
5. See S. H. Ray, 1929, pp. 65 ff. (For a more recent study of this language family see Dutton 1969. E.S.)
6. Groups of the grasslanders (*Isu-bia*): Taburi, Nadeka, Dauri Ekiri, Bemuri, Aghoberi, Wanoari, Magibiri, Monatori, Ghasiri, Omani, Derikoia, Yanari, Kerakadi, Ehara, Vaḍiri, Dabunari, Daghoda, Seme, Veburi, etc.
7. The *idi* of the Koiari evidently has something in common with the *heratu* or Plant Emblem of the Orokaiva, but the system is by no means so exact or thorough-going. *See* "Plant Emblems among the Orokaiva" (*Journ. Roy. Anthrop. Inst.*, vol. lv, 1925, July-Dec.) and *Orokaiva Society*, 1930, chap. VIII.
8. (The term "local group" seems confusing, as Williams shows—above—that the village and the group have distinct names and are designated by distinct terms. Williams' discussion on "Marriage and Kin"—below—casts doubt on his assertion that exogamy rules do not exist. The rules are often disregarded, but are not absent. My own impression is that the Koiari have rudimentary patrilineal clans, and that these determine totemic identification, kin terminology as well as—ideally—marriage. E.S.)
9. There is at present no ritual bestowal of the first perineal band in the Sogeri district, and the nasal septum and ear lobes of the child may be pierced, it is said, by any relative. There is no direct evidence that these were formerly ritual deformations or that the offices were performed by the maternal uncle.

10. There are terms for a number of generations of ancestors, but I found the greatest confusion regarding them. No two lists were quite the same; always some terms would be omitted or transposed. The following is, so to speak, a composite version in the Sogeri dialect:—

f	....	*baba.*
ff	....	*ivahike.*
fff	....	*davavore.*
ffff	....	*daidike.*
fffff	....	*dateteke.*
ffffff	....	*datigitia.*
fffffff	....	*dararave.*

The same terms are used for the sequence: mother, grandmother, etc. Sogeri natives as far as I know them cannot have much use for these terms, so that the confusion is not surprising. Feats of genealogical memory seldom go back as far as the *daidike*, great-great-grandfather.

11. Names are offered by *ihimeni*, "godparents," before the birth of the child. The term *ihimeni* is reciprocal. The senior makes the offer of his name together with a *yago*, or bag, for carrying the baby. Since the same names are used for male and female it does not matter what the sex of the child should turn out to be. Between senior and junior *ihimeni* there are mutual gifts and other attentions when the latter grows up. It is not necessary that the godparent should stand in any set relationship to the godchild.

12. A marriage between half-siblings occurred not long ago.

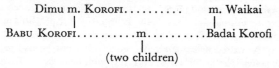

The husband, wife and children are still living. Informants were both ashamed and amused at the mention of this case. "What sort of body," one of them exclaimed, "had this Babu to cohabit with his own sister?"

13. If any further evidence is required, it may be pointed out that in the slightly different terminology of the *Isu-bia* (Taburi group) the term for brother's wife (m.s. or w.s.) is *di-nubaghe* (for *danubai*), the same word as is used for the cross-cousin.

14. It is interesting to note that one man used the same argument against marriage with the "sister." He would be "eating the pay for her."

15. His was probably a love match, though it is doubtful whether the same could be said of the marriage between his sister Gigina and Borakape's brother, Moio. However, Gigina had given her consent to equalize matters by marrying the young man Moio, who would appear to be some years her junior, and who still finds a good deal of difficulty in understanding her language. In such a case, viz., the second of a pair of exchange marriages, the bride may virtually have to go where she is told. In most others, as we have seen, she follows her own choice.

16. Taburi and Haveri groups were as strong in maintaining this rule as the others were in denying it.

17. (A similar theory, assigning to the female child a different genetic constitution from the male, exists also among the Orokaiva, viz., Schwimmer 1973, Chapter X. E.S.)

18. By way of verification I called upon one of the women who had married into the Borebere group. She had come from Maiari and had a little daughter. Having warned all present to let the woman make her own answer I asked what group her child belonged to. For a long time she was silent, petrified by shyness; but after looking despairingly for guidance to the men who sat around, she whispered the single word "Maiari."

19. I am indebted to Mrs. Seligman for pointing out what may appear an inconsistency. If the young man marries the daughter of his mother's brother, then the girl marries, not into the group of her mother's brother, but into that of her father's sister. It is only on the supposition of previous brother-sister exchange that the girl, under the above conditions, can be said to marry into her mother's group.

It will be made plain, however, that the hypothesis of reciprocating pairs does postulate marriage by exchange, and thus presupposes that by marrying her father's sister's son the girl is at the same time marrying into her mother's brother's group.

20. It has already been stated that the terms for the husand of the female *dadime* was given, when asked for, as *daware*, and that for the wife of the male *dadime* as *dawarutane*. These do not square with the explanation put forward. I do not place complete reliance on these terms, however, for I doubt whether the native is greatly interested in the wife of his *dadime* and whether the term of relation is ever applied. (The argument put forward in Part III of my introduction might account for the seeming terminological anomaly pointed out by Williams here. As ego's daughter is claimable by the male *dadime*, the latter's wife could logically be called *dawarutane*. As ego's son is not bound to marry the female *dadime*, the latter's husband may well be *daware*. Obviously if the female *dadime* marries ego's son, her husband would not be classified as an affine at all. The terminological difference here is strong evidence that the Koiari recognise a different marital destination for the brother and sister. E.S.)

PART III

4

NATIVES OF LAKE KUTUBU, PAPUA[1]

Part I

Introduction

The present report is the result of a short stay in the Lake Kutubu district when I was attached as a sort of supernumerary to the Police Camp. It had been arranged that I should be the first anthropologist to work in the then uncontrolled area, and the opportunity for getting there easily and inexpensively arrived when the seaplane was taking in the yearly stores. I reached Lake Kutubu on November 18, 1938, and left it for Port Moresby on May 7, 1939, having spent the greater part of the intervening time on the investigations which are embodied in the present report.

I should begin by expressing my appreciation of the help given me by both Mr. Champion and Mr. Adamson and of their sympathetic attitude. Between them they treated me virtually as a guest, and all practical arrangements of any consequence were made for me by them. At Mr. Champion's request I went up alone; but everything I required—accommodation, carriers, escort and staff—were provided on the spot. This meant some extra burden on the camp's resources, which had to be carefully husbanded; but it was a pleasant change for an ethnographer to have the practical side of a field trip looked after for him. I should say in addition that thanks to the company of the officers of the Police Camp this trip was the most pleasant of its kind I have ever made.

The time spent in the uncontrolled area was divided as follows: Nov. 18-Dec. 28, Lake Kutubu; Dec. 29-Jan. 19, Mubi River; Jan. 20-Jan. 31, Lake Kutubu; Feb. 1-Feb. 9, Augu Base Camp; Feb. 10-Mar. 27, Augu Village; Mar. 28-Apr. 14, trips to Ibi and Wela with Mr. Adamson; Apr. 15-Apr. 17, Augu Base Camp; Apr. 18-May 7, Lake Kutubu. To be exact this means that I spent ninety-three days studying the Kutubu natives (including those of the Mubi who are practically identical) on the spot. But during the six weeks spent at Augu village I had with me several reliable Kutubu men, and every day spent some time in checking over and amplifying my notes about the Lake people. Altogether it might be

161

said that my field work on the Kutubu people added up to about four months.

Communication was in pidgin Motuan. I make no apology for this. Considering the shortness of the time which I intended to devote to this region it seemed advisable to adopt the medium which offered itself. It proved remarkably effective. Mr. Adamson has succeeded in acquiring a working knowledge of the Kutubu language and uses it in speaking to the natives—a considerable achievement under the circumstances. But within three or four months I could not have expected to go very far in the study of the language; and I am fully convinced that had I attempted to work through Kutubuan the results of four months' work would have been a mere fraction of what they are in quantity and probably worse in quality. (Among the Grasslanders the situation was entirely different: no means of communication was available there, and I made it the principal object of my stay to discover one, viz. by learning the language from scratch. I cannot pretend, at the end of six weeks, to have been in a position to record anything but superficialities about them.)

My principal interpreters were the local armed constables, Girigi, Hameno, Kavarepa and Waipi. These were remarkably good boys, well disciplined and amenable. Although their hearts were in squad-drill, saluting and the handling of their ancient rifles (they carried no ammunition), they showed themselves very willing on the whole in the less romantic business of anthropology. The fourth boy, Waipi, though perhaps the best policeman, was a good way behind the rest in his knowledge of Motuan and I did not make much use of him. But the other three were very good interpreters, and when Mr. Champion placed them at my disposal during my stay at Augu I used them directly as informants. (I find it wholly unsatisfactory to use a man as interpreter and informant at the same time; but it is very useful to run through your notes again with your interpreters afterwards. I went right through my Kutubu material while at Augu with these men and one or two others, and they did a great deal to correct and amplify it.)

Girigi had profited by a visit to Port Moresby and a term at headquarters. It was probably this which gave him a higher sense of responsibility than the others. He was an agreeable person of a very gentle disposition. He had many recollections of Port Moresby, the most vivid being (as I gather) the personality of the sergeant's daughter, a very small girl who had given him much "strong talk." He also told how in retreating before a dog at the Police Head-quarters he had stepped on a china plate and smashed it; he had been afflicted with unendurable shame at this mishap, but the H.Q.O. had let him off because of his inexperience.

Hameno was a very temperamental youth of a rather more spirited and masculine type.

Kavarepa was the steadiest as an interpreter though a very negative character in himself. He wore a rather long-suffering air and seemed to grow more and more dispirited. Finally, when he had been at Augu for about ten days, Mr. Champion advised sending him home to the Lake for a holiday; and then we were astounded to hear that within about a week of his home-coming he had died. It is pathetic to record his own diagnosis of his illness. He explained that he had been in the habit of giving his weekly ration of matches to his brother in Wasemi rather than to his maternal uncle; and (since a supernatural sanction governs obligations towards the

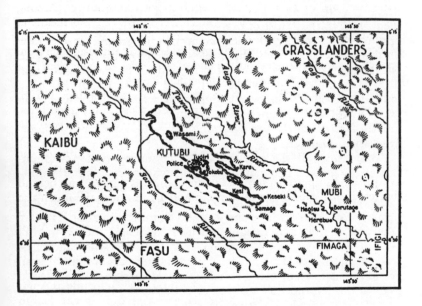

Lake Kutubu District

maternal uncle) it was his own tactlessness that had led to his break-down in health. Alternatively he recalled that while on the Mubi with me (about a month previously) he had had his hair cut. It was from that moment, he said, that he had felt unwell, the inference being that a Mubi man had secured some of his hair and made sorcery against him. On reaching home, I was later informed, he had undergone many of the treatments to which the Kutubu people pin so much faith, the maternal uncle participating and thereby clearing his name. When they proved of no avail the second explanation was accepted and it was assumed that he had died by Mubi sorcery.

These local armed constables had all begun by being the personal attendants of members of the regular force. The youths of the district like to attach themselves to admired individuals in the capacity of unpaid batmen, and at the barracks they pick up a knowledge of Police Motuan. There are a number of youths at the Lake who have become fairly proficient in this way, and among them a boy, Kaivira-Ka, who is amazingly so. I used him as an interpreter for some weeks and thought him, irrespective of race, one of the brightest boys I have ever had dealings with. But he was too young and irresponsible to be a complete success. He was fidgety to a degree; his alert young mind was distracted by every noise or movement, and in the midst of our sober enquiries he was perpetually fiddling with his knife, drawing pictures on the ground, or searching for lice in his belt. It was impossible to discipline him; he broke his engagements and turned up just as he wished, his face wreathed in disarming smiles. Finally, he just faded out and went off on a journey to Fasu without even asking for his wages. He received them with amiable nonchalance when I returned to Kutubu some three months later: a clever and charming boy—often most infuriating— aged about fourteen.

Considering all the circumstances the interpretation was unexpectedly good. The natives on the whole were quite willing informants, though on such a brief acquaintance one does not expect to go very deep. It is true that some of them grew tired of me—but that is the case everywhere and it would be most surprising if it were otherwise. I began by making much of Nekinagu, an old man of Wasemi who had met Champion and Adamson when they first reached the Lake. He was a very ingratiating person, but with an eye to the main chance and an acquisitive disposition. He possessed some authority and was much in evidence at the Police Camp. (It was, I understand, a native—whether a villager or one of the camp, I do not know—who gave the nickname "Nekinagu" to the dominant rooster of the Kutubu fowlyard.) But the human Nekinagu turned out to be of less importance, socially and intellectually, than had at first appeared, and we soon grew bored with one another. He gave an amusing demonstration of his feelings one day when I landed on the island of Wasemi. He was lying in the open, stretched on a mat, nursing a sore on his leg which he had burnt with a cooking-stone; but as soon as he saw me approaching he rose and hobbled off in the opposite direction shouting, "*tasitibu hasibu wae*," which means, "I refuse to talk."

Generally speaking, however, the natives showed the usual readiness to reveal and explain things about themselves—they do not resent enquiries (in fact they probably appreciate them) but only at times grow weary of the laborious methods which an ethnographer has so often to adopt. This obstacle to his progress is less serious when he is at work in a populous region in which he has many informants to choose from and does not have to pester the same people continually. From this point of view Lake Kutubu and the Mubi do not constitute a very favourable field of operations. On the other hand, I do not think my informants deliberately kept much from me. They are at least free from the inhibitions which missionary influence and a stricter mode of government will eventually lay upon them.

Subject to the limitations indicated above the present report will take the form of a conventional monograph. It should possess such theoretical value as can attach to a somewhat summary account of a single people, viz. as providing a specimen of human culture. But I do not suppose that it will have any great practical value, except perhaps in so far as it deals with a people who are making their very first contacts with civilization. While it must be admitted that the inhabitants of Lake Kutubu and their neighbours do not, relatively speaking, constitute a very important unit of humanity, they at least provide an example of the so-called primitive state, and it is as well to learn something about such people in such a condition before we set about altering them.

Lake Kutubu

Lake Kutubu is a narrow sheet of water about twelve miles long, running north-west and south-east. At the south-east end it is mostly hemmed in by precipitous hills; but towards the north-west the valley broadens out and the surrounding land is reasonably accessible. All is heavily forested and, where it is not actually lime-stone, appears to be good country.

Climate
The Police Camp is situated on a little promontory about half-way down the lake, and from the Assistant Resident Magistrate's house at the highest point of the clearing one enjoys a magnificent view. During my stay the weather was fine and the character of the lake was one of unfailing serenity. In the early forenoon, before the breeze sprang up, the white cumulus clouds and the dark shape of the mountains would be reflected in its waters as in a mirror; and the ruggedness of its surroundings seemed to enhance its

peacefulness. Away to the north-west the imposing contours of Mt. Champion (the Death Mountain of Hides's expedition) would dominate the scene until as the morning advanced they became lost in clouds. But while clouds would gather even on the nearby hills, Kutubu continued to bask beneath the sun. It would be safe to say that during my stay more than ninety per cent. of the forenoons, and most of the afternoons, consisted of glorious sunshine. It seemed possible to me—I do not know what a meteorologist would say— that the expanse of water in itself was responsible for a special share of clear weather. At any rate on May 7, when the plane came for me, the pilot located Kutubu directly beneath what seemed the one and only hole in a blanket of clouds; and when we left I had a splendid bird's-eye view of the lake so long as we continued to circle for height, and thereafter saw nothing but clouds beneath until we almost reached the coast. Altogether Kutubu is a delightful place to live in, and when Mr. Champion wrote, "we can promise you the finest view and climate of any station in Papua" I do not think he was overstating its claims.[2]

But even in the time of summer calms Kutubu can be somewhat moody. Sudden squalls will whip up its surface in the course of a few minutes and then travelling in the rather miserable dugouts of the district is both uncomfortable and dangerous. In the winter season the south-easter presumably sweeps the lake from end to end and I can imagine that it is then a far less agreeable place.

The natives recognize a series of seasons, which are no doubt well enough defined by nature but not so well established in the minds and memories of Kutubu informants. After an astonishing amount of argument and contradiction I venture to set them down as follows:

1. *Abari-hasi:* time of ripening of the red pandanus *abari*. Begins probably in November and runs on into the following season.

2. *Anumu-hasi:* time of ripening of *anumu* (the plant known as "New Guinea asparagus," Motuan *mimia*; an *Andropogon*). Begins probably about January and ends about March. The weather throughout is sunny and mild; the prevailing wind (*anumu-kuba*) is from "Wasemi to Tugiri," i.e. north-west.

3. *Waria-hasi:* time of fruiting of the *waria* trees. (These are the trees used for canoe dugouts. The fruit is a small inedible berry.) Begins in April. The weather continues sunny. The prevailing winds are from "Kesi to Tugiri," roughly south-east.

4. *Pango-hasi:* time of ripening of the *pango* fruit. This is not eaten by humans but used as a bait in the little traps (*pugunu*) for bandicoots (*fagena*) etc. This season is presumably about June. The weather is good and there is said to be "no wind."

5. *Me-hasi:* (lit. bush time) or *Sokainyu* (mist, drizzle). This is the winter season presumably beginning about July and lasting to, say, September. The weather is cold and rainy, clouds lie on the hill-tops continually and the forest is always drizzling. The various megapods, *tabura-hua, kai* and *ya-hua*, make their mounds and lay their eggs; and game is plentiful in the forest. (There is a belief that the animals come down from the sky in the clouds.)

Without living through a year at Kutubu it is impossible to be sure that the seasons are even named in their right order (some informants placed *Pango-hasi* after *Me-hasi*); and it is out of the question to date their beginnings and endings. The only point on which everyone seems quite sure is that *Anumu-hasi* occurs about the end of our year. The word itself is used for "year," just as we may speak of so many "summers." I was at Kutubu myself during the summer only, and am prepared to believe that later on in the year the weather may be dreary rather than pleasant.

The Legend of the Lake

The lake, to a layman's eye, looks as if it had been formed by some great disturbance of nature which has blocked up the lower end of the valley. So many streams run parallel along the flank of the central range in this region, all in a south-easterly direction and all at the bottom of prodigious valleys, that nature might easily have provided us with some more Lake Kutubus: they would have made a world of difference in a hopelessly inaccessible region. But no doubt we should be grateful for the existence of one, since it has at least made plane transport a possibility.

Against all my own sense of fitness the lake empties from its north-west end. At the south-east end, the ranges closing in on either side, it terminates in a swampy area, separated by a low divide from the Samaga River, which follows the course of the valley down to the Mubi. According to native legend it once extended further. The myths and legends which seem worth recording will be mostly collected at the end of this report, but I shall give at this stage one of the several versions I have heard of the origin of the lake.

In the earliest days there was no lake at all—only trees and mountains; and the population consisted solely of women. These women, who lived at Mt. Dagiribu (somewhere to the north-west of the present lake) hunted a great deal and caught animals in plenty, but there was no water, so that they naturally complained of thirst. Only their dog named Niyibe knew where the water was: he would slip away after the hunt and when he returned they would look at his wet muzzle with envious eyes. Finally one of them thought of tying a string to one of his legs, and by this means they were led to his secret source, a hole at the base of a huge ficus tree (*konyamo*). They saw him disappear in the hole and heard him lapping the water, and then they brought their axes, established a camp beside the tree, and set to work to cut it down. It took them two and a half days. But when the tree finally fell the water gushed out from the hole in such volume as to fill the whole valley. The women rushed for safety to the hill-sides and as they saw the water making down towards the south-east they made magic and chanted a song to stop its progress: *Ketewaio farefare, kaberemaio farefare, ira subiwaio farefare, ira kaka'agi farefare, kajukanogobio farefare, Afuma-imo farefare*, etc. These names are synonyms for paddles, fish-spears and canoes[3]; the word *farefare* apparently means "stop" or "stay"; and Afuma is the mountain where the waters were finally stemmed. Where Afuma actually stands I could not discover; but it is apparently some distance beyond the south-east end of the lake. In response to the women's spells the waters receded to their present boundary, though they have left a trace of their former extent in the large pool, Kutubu Kewaga at Fimaga, some miles to the south-east. But for this timely arrest of the flood all the canoes, paddles and fish-spears to which the Kutubuans attach so much value would have been swept away; yet, as Girigi the traveller observed, had it been otherwise the waters would have made their way straight down to "Kiko" (Kikori) and have reached to Port Moresby, when the steamer which so greatly impressed him would have been able to come right up to the lake.

A further notion (which corresponds very closely to one I heard in connection with the Wassi-Kussa in the Trans-Fly) enters the story as told by some informants, though not altogether consistently. It concerns the origin of the various inlets and islands of the lake and of neighbouring rivers. When the immense ficus tree was finally brought down, the ground was turned into water wherever the many trunks, branches and aerial roots touched it. The bulk fell on Lake Kutubu, but the spreading branches caused the inlets of Kara and Yokobu, while the islands in the lake were left just where there happened to be vacant spaces between them. The neighbouring rivers and creeks were caused by the far-flung branches, large and small, which broke off as the tree was falling.

It is worth telling what happened to the women. In one version they took taro plants and threw them into the lake, whereupon they turned into the water plants, *ketakai*, which now line its banks in many places. After that the women dived in themselves and became frogs. In another version they fled up the mountain sides and still remain there, having turned into *tirifa* palms. These beautiful trees are very numerous on the rocky cliffs near Yokobu. It is pointed out that their leaves represent the women's hair, and the flower-sprays their skimpy little skirts.

The Kuruka

I do not imagine the natives possess any religious feeling towards their lake as such. They are certainly fond of it, and probably proud of it. On the way home, when they catch a glimpse of its shining waters from some hill-top on the track, they give utterance to the usual expressions of satisfaction, and sometimes when they are paddling on the lake itself they ejaculate "*Ivu Kutubu!*" i.e. "Kutubu water!" as if it somehow aroused their admiration. They call it *Ivu-hua*, which should mean "Mother of Waters."

Nor does it seem to play any important part in their religion or mythology. Its supernatural inhabitants, to which the following paragraphs are devoted, are mere supernumeraries. It is difficult to give them any place in the religious and mythical scheme of things.

These supernatural beings are the *kuruka*. Informants will sometimes assure you that there is a numerous population of them, with sublacustrine houses, gardens, pigs and dogs. But in its more genuine form the belief in *kuruka* envisages a smaller, though still indefinite, number of individuals who bear personal names and inhabit specific parts of the lake. I have collected the names of only seven—Tabuame, Hewarira, Kesoka, Heakaia, Wagainyeria, Sobomia and Nabo. These have certain characters of their own. Tabuame, e.g., is a young man and lives at Kabugi, the romantic little grotto situated at "Cave Point." (I first heard of the *kuruka* here, when I jokingly threatened to leave Hameno behind in the cave because he was a little lazy with the paddle.) Hewarira is very big and old, with teeth like pig's tusks, and lives near the tiny isolated rocks beyond Kesi (a few jagged stones, just awash, which provide observation posts for gaunt fishing birds); and Kesoka is a man with a fair skin who may be heard beating his drum under water at the foot of Bebere, the bare cliff on which are exposed the skulls and bones of some long-ago Kutubuans. But there is no very clear idea of what the *kuruka* look like, and that for a very good reason: for if anyone sees one face to face it is because it has risen from the water to drag him down, and he does not live to record his impressions.

The only men I have ever heard of who, by way of exception, survived to tell of such a meeting was Hiwadobo of Tugiri. He was bringing home a newly-made dugout from the other side of the lake when a heavy squall sprang up, "a great wind which blew from all quarters." In a few moments the waves were running high, Hiwadobo's canoe was swamped and sank, and he was left swimming for

his life. His fellow villagers of Tugiri witnessed the disaster from the
shore and only one of them, the old man Eraga, who was my
informant, had the courage to go to his help. But he succeeded, and
Hiwadobo, much upset in more ways than one, was enabled to tell
the tale of an actual encounter with the *kuruka*. He had seen a
multitude of fishes in the waves, and among them what looked like a
gigantic lizard (*ivukobe*). This was the *kuruka* Tabuame. Eraga (who
had not seen the monster himself) pointed to the trunk of a bread-
fruit tree to show how big it was.

It may be this incident which accounts for the belief—I do not
know that it is a general one—that the *kuruka* are like snakes or
lizards when seen on the surface of the water. The universally
accepted notion, said to date from ancient times, is that when in
their natural element they take the form of human beings. They may
inhabit the rivers as well as the lake and they do nothing but harm
to real humans. Cases of drowning (I have recorded four fairly
recent ones) are invariably put down to seizure by *kuruka*. The most
pathetic was that of the old woman Kogoiubama who was diving
for prawns. She thrust her hand into a hole in a tree under water,
somehow got it caught, and did not come up again. Others had
seen her go under, and they dragged and dragged at her legs; but
when the old woman was brought to the surface she was dead. She
had been seized by the *kuruka* Nabo. In other cases the victim's
corpse has been recovered floating on the surface some days after
death: the assumption is that it has been down to the bottom of the
lake with the *kuruka* in the meantime, but from that region no one
comes back alive. The fact that some corpses appeared somewhat
damaged indicated that the *kuruka* had been gnawing at them.

I have no evidence that the supernatural creatures of the lake
are ever conciliated; and it may be surmised that they are very
seldom in the native's thoughts. Except for occasional squalls Lake
Kutubu is a very safe place, and while the native strongly dislikes
the idea of facing rough water in his dugout, he goes about his
ordinary voyaging without any sense of risk. The lake is free from
crocodiles, so the people are luckier than they know.

The Kutubu Group and its Neighbours

The Lake Population
The population of the lake is a small one, probably less than 400.
There are five villages, Wasemi, Tugiri, Yokobu, Kesi and Keseki.
A sixth, Kara, has disappeared since the first coming of Champion
and Adamson. It is now represented by two houses which are
obviously temporary, and its few inhabitants are dispersed. All five

of the existent villages are built on high ground. Two of them, Wasemi and Kesi, are on islands. The former is a large and comparatively fertile piece of ground at the north-west end of the lake. Much of its original timber has been felled with the steel axes which have become so plentiful, and this fact has doubled its attractiveness. When in years to come the darkness of the surrounding hills is similarly relieved by the pale green of grass and potato gardens, the lake will be even lovelier than now. At present, despite all that can be said for it, it is sometimes a shade gloomy.

Kesi is perched precariously on a tiny barren islet, the summit of a submerged pinnacle close to the southern shore. At this end of the lake it is admittedly hard to find even a small patch of level ground, but the reason alleged for this strange choice is one of defence. The Kesi people were driven out from Samaga, the swampy region at the south-east tip of the lake, and it is said that after wandering from one place to another they finally settled on this queer little island because it would never be taken by surprise. The three remaining villages are established on the shores of the lake with steep paths down to the water; and Kesi furthermore is approached only by a winding passage through the reeds, so narrow that a long dugout requires a great deal of manoeuvring to round the bends.

Allied Tribes

Closely allied to the Kutubu people are those of the Mubi River. These may be divided into three groups and called (1) the Mubi tribe, (2) the Fimaga tribe, and (3) the Ifigi tribe.

(1) The Mubi, as they are commonly called at Kutubu, occupy three villages on the upper part of the river, a few miles below the point where it emerges from underground. They are Hegisu, Borutage, and Herebu. The river hereabouts is some fifty yards wide. Its banks are amazingly fertile, with abundant sago-palms and magnificent clumps of bamboo. Breadfruit and other useful trees indicate that the ground has all been cultivated, and there are scores of little gardens and many brown-thatched garden-houses to be seen on either side as one paddles downstream. When I first embarked on the River Mubi, on a fine clear morning, I thought it presented one of the richest and most beautiful views I had ever seen in Papua—exuberant greens, blazing sunshine, and a blue sky with vast cumulus clouds.

We made a triumphal progress downstream, with all the gear in one outsize Mubi dugout, and escorted by a fleet of smaller canoes full of inquisitive natives. During the second half of our journey, however, the landscape was fairly blotted out by rain; even the river banks were hardly visible; and we made camp at Herebu in the midst of a deluge. It seemed as if it were only necessary to get away from Kutubu to run into rain. I think it has been the experience of others who have camped there that the Mubi is definitely better than Kutubu.

The Mubi population seems larger and more thriving than that of the lake and the men's houses are in conspicuously better repair. Those of Hegisu and Borutage stand on low ground close to the water's edge; that of Herebu on a hill overlooking a bend in the river. This is a good position, and the rear of the village is defended by a ditch and palisade. It seems that considerations of defence are also much in the minds of the Mubi natives.

(2) Fimaga has two villages, Fimaga and Damaiu, close together in a common clearing, and a third, Kenahabu, which I did not see. These are on hilly ground some miles from the Mubi River. I looked forward to visiting them several times while camped at Herebu, but one journey quite satisfied me because the number of leeches was beyond belief.

(3) The Ifigi group live further down the Mubi. Their villages were said to be Ifigi, Pugahugu, Eragahugu, Kuhu and Harebuio. I did not visit these. The people are evidently one with those of Kutubu, Mubi, and Fimaga, in a general sense, but they are apparently sometimes at enmity with them.

Kutubu and Mubi dialects are virtually identical; Fimaga somewhat different and Ifigi more so. It is probable that other groups further to the south-east, Foi and Kafa, will also be found to speak dialects of the same tongue.

Neighbouring Peoples

Apart from the abovementioned tribes which all speak dialects of one and the same language, we may briefly consider their neighbours, who speak various different languages and who are culturally distinct from them. These fall roughly into three groups: (i) those to the south-east, viz. Foi, Kafa, etc.; (ii) those to the south and south-west, viz. Fasu and Kaibu; (iii) those to the north-west and north, viz. the Augu and Wage people, or the "Grasslanders."

I have seen nothing of the first two, except as represented by a few random visitors to Kutubu; and among the third I spent only two months, which were mainly devoted to learning the rudiments of their language. I shall not therefore attempt to give any description of them here. (A brief superficial account of the Grasslanders has already been published in the *Annual Report*, 1938-39.) But it is worth summarizing the cultural influences on Kutubu which may be attributed to these several groups. Their relations with Kutubu seem to be on the whole peaceful. There is a good deal of visiting and trading and, in the case of (ii), a good deal of intermarriage.

(i) *Foi, etc.* These people represent the principal intermediate source of shells, which continually find their way up from the coast; and since shell is of such exaggerated value to the Kutubuans, this in itself makes the relationship important. From the direction of Foi comes also the *Usi* cult (a secret method of treating sickness which involves an initiation and much ceremonial) and the practices embodied in *Usanehabu* (which also have to do with the treatment of sickness). It is solely in connection with *Usanehabu* that the drum is beaten at Kutubu, so we shall possibly be right in assuming that the drum itself is an importation from the south-east.

(ii) *Fasu-Kaibu.* These people are in close touch with Kutubu and it will be found that many of them have actually settled on the lake. It is alleged by the natives themselves that the highly sacred *takorabu* plant, used in the ritual of *Piakagwabu*, has come to Kutubu from Kaibu; and it is quite possible that the *Piakagwabu* cult itself has come from that direction. The bull-roarer, which is plainly a new and only half-assimilated cult on the lake, is expressly stated to have come from Kaibu; while Fasu and Kaibu between them are responsible for two habits which have been making headway on the lake, viz. those of betel-chewing and cannibalism.

(iii) While communication with the Grasslanders seems very friendly and quite frequent it is difficult to say what actual contributions they have made to Kutubu culture. The Mubi (who are more in touch with these upper villages than are the Kutubu people) often wear the netted string apron; they have a sort of bamboo pan-pipe; and there is at Herebu the already mentioned defensive ditch and palisade. These things were all said to have been copied from the Wage Valley; but they are, of course, no more than cultural details. It may be that the rather ramshackle exposure-coffins of Kutubu are degenerate imitations of the well-made Grassland coffins; but that is no more than a guess. While I should be prepared to find that Kutubu and the Grasslands had much in common from the cultural viewpoint, there seems to be little in the former's culture which can be directly ascribed to Grassland influence.

Trade

Kutubu's contacts with its immediate outer world, a sparsely-peopled and rugged country, are mainly brought about by trade. In all the essentials of a simple life the population of the lake is self-supporting; but there are certain inessentials (from the utilitarian standpoint) which its people go to endless trouble to secure. The principal of these is shell—gold-lip, melo and cowrie. Apart from the pearl shells distributed from the Police Camp, which have rather flooded the local market, Kutubu was already supplied with this and the other kinds of shell before the camp existed. The question therefore arises how it ever got there.

The lake itself has little to offer in the way of commodities. It produces palmwood for bows, and an important kind of vegetable grease, locally called *tigaso*, which is used for anointing the hair and body. It also produces pigs and a certain quantity of tobacco. Yet it imports (in a modest way by merely individual transactions) stone celts, salt, arrows, string bags, tobacco, pigs and pearlshells from the north; and from the south, pearlshells, melo shells, cowries and (since the advent of Europeans in the Delta Division) steel knives and axes. The inference is plain: in trading Kutubu is an intermediary between the south and the north. In former days the principal *raison d'être* of the natives' trading enterprise was shell, and the principal source of shell is naturally the coast (though as we shall see, there is a remarkable, indeed mysterious, accumulation of it in the high valleys). When they travel north to obtain polished stone celts, vegetable salt, etc., it is partly to meet their own direct requirements, but partly also to obtain the means wherewith to barter for shell from the south. Other commodities are traded for the same indirect reason. Thus the Kutubuans grow their own tobacco; but they are ready to buy it (in parcels of dried leaf) as well as to sell it; and while at ordinary times they have plenty of pigs of their own, they often buy them from the north and sell them to the south—and probably vice versa, too, if it suits their purpose.

The pig is the second great consideration in the barter system. Small sucklings are carried remarkable distances (in a string bag under the arm) to be exchanged for a string of cowries or an axe; while at feasts the visitors come from far and near prepared to buy pieces of pig-meat for the price of a shell ornament. The relative scarcity of a meat diet gives the pig an extraordinarily high value. In a general sense it is impossible to say which takes precedence in native estimation—pig or pearlshell; but it is safe to say that a full-sized animal is the equivalent of a large quantity of shell, and even a tiny sucking pig will fetch a ten-foot string of cowries or a gold-lip of moderate size.

The third great consideration is the steel tool which at present has a very high value. This value cannot always maintain its high level in respect of exchange, for the market will evidently be glutted; but for the time being steel stands as high as pig or pearlshell. It is essentially these three which keep the trade of Kutubu in motion.

It is worth devoting a few paragraphs to the three most interesting of the trade commodities.

Salt. Packages of squashed spherical shape, neatly bound with strips of pandanus leaf, are often to be found in Kutubu men's-houses. They are of vegetable salt, about five 1bs. weight, brought from Augu or the Wage where they are purchased with cowries (*bari*). The stuff is dark grey and powdery with a salty flavour. European salt is very much sought after and would be a success as "trade" except for its weight.

Tigaso. This is the specialty of Kutubu for the northern trade. The tree from which it is obtained is said to grow plentifully in the south but not in the high valleys, where the grease is much in demand for anointing hair and body. The tree is a large one (I have no idea how to identify it, but its leaves are set fanwise and are blunted-spatulate in shape, and as much as 18 in. × 6 in. in size). A deep cavity is made in the trunk near the butt (I saw one about 3ft. × 2 ft. 6 in. × 2 ft. 6 in. deep) and its inner walls are from time to time chipped with an axe blade. The sap drains down and floats like thick oil in the rain-water which lies in the bottom of the hole. It is gathered in gourds (*ponobe*) for home use; but for export to the Grasslands may be stored in long bamboos. I was astonished to see (in a Mubi men's-house) some palmwood "pokers" (called *kamave*), measuring 27 ft. in length by about ¾ in. in diameter, which were used expressly for removing the internodes in bamboo *tigaso*-carriers. One of these long bamboos, about 3 in. in diameter, measured 24 ft. It would eventually go up to the Wage valley full of *tigaso* oil, carried by two or three men. It must be an extraordinarily clumsy burden; and I would hardly have believed such a thing could ever be got there had I not seen a similar specimen in the Wela Valley which had been brought from the Mubi.

The *tigaso* itself (also called *kabumame*) is a dirty brown oil with an unpleasant smell. It is smeared on the body, sometimes with an application of soot, and there is no denying that the naked savage, oiled to the very eyelids with this unlikely mixture, presents a really smart appearance. It is also said to be a specific against lice (*tabari*) for which purpose it is rubbed into the hair and the pubic apron (*kunagubu*). The natives of Kutubu and the Mubi were beyond compare the lousiest I have had to deal with in Papua. My informants and interpreters used to annoy me continually by searching for parasites in their hair, their beards, their belts, and their pubic aprons, and my unavoidable proximity filled me with apprehension. But I never interfered with the hunting, unpleasant as it was to see, for I could console myself with the reflection that for every kill there was one louse less.

Pearlshells. Crescents of gold-lip pearlshell are the most valuable of all ornaments at Kutubu and in the Grassland valleys, a fact which Mr. Champion took advantage of by laying in a large store of ready-cut pearlshells for "trade." At the lake itself pearlshell is often called *segere;* but I fancy this is a Fasu word. On the Mubi it is called *magami,* which is the ordinary Kutubu word for "thing" and probably the correct name at the lake also. (One is reminded of the fact that among the western Elema a shell ornament is called *eharu,* i.e. "thing," or the "thing of things.") The Grassland word is *momag.*

It has been noted that there seems to be a large stock of pearlshells in the inland valleys, and Kutubu natives declare that they obtain their shell from the north as well as from the south. They speak almost with awe of the fine specimens which belong to the Grasslanders, and the reason why they do not obtain more from that source is that they cost too much. I was told that it would be a matter of difficulty to see the good specimens, for they were kept carefully hidden away, and this proved to be the case. The Grasslanders do not wear their finest shells—at least on ordinary occasions—but keep them in the penetralia of their stuffy little houses. If they can be coaxed to show them, they will cautiously undo the voluminous wrappings and reveal shells of a size and weight that are quite astonishing. They are furnished with a finely woven band for the neck, reddened with ochre, and it so happens that the few such specimens I saw had all been broken across and carefully mended. They have the appearance of considerable age and are beyond comparison larger than any I saw in Kutubu. Furthermore, they are often rather different in shape, tending to a broad crescent rather than the narrow one which is favoured at Kutubu and further south. (I saw none however in the full round, as previously reported at Mt. Hagen.)

It would appear then that there is in the upland valleys a great reservoir of shell some of which is occasionally traded down towards the south. (It may be recalled that Mr. Austen once reported that natives on the Turama, I believe, declared that their best shells came from the direction of its source.) The mystery of how so much fine shell comes from so far inland remains unsolved. It is probable that it was all taken there originally from the coast, but this must presumably have been very many years ago, for nowadays the Kutubu people believe it actually belongs to the interior. The alternative suggestion that it is actually found in the limestone mountains has been ruled out by Dr. Glaessner, Palaeontologist to the Australasian Petroleum Co. Two legends accounting for the origin of pearlshell, the apple of the Kutubuan's eye, are given at the end of this report.

Provenance of Lake Population

It remains to say something, most inconclusively, of the provenance of the Kutubu people. It is a question, in my opinion, of small importance and I make no apology for my inability to answer it. Generally speaking it appears that the Kutubu people belong to the *Kulturkreis* of the Delta: their affinities are rather with the coast dwellers than with the inlanders, though, as I have suggested, they will no doubt be found to have much in common with the latter also when these have been studied.

I took no physical measurements, and it is very difficult to record any definite impression of the Kutubuans' appearance. They generally lack the extremer traits of the western Papuans, i.e. the "Jewish" noses and dark skin-colour, but I would not hesitate to put them in that class on the whole. At the same time, they show a considerable range of variety in skin-colour and facial features, and it seems likely that racially they are a mixed lot.

There would appear to be few marriages with the Grasslanders at present. I was told that some Grassland women had settled as wives at Wasemi: but within recent times no Kutubuan women have moved in the counter direction. Whether there was more intermarriage in the past I cannot say.

With the Kaibu and Fasu people on the south the case is different. Intermarriage is frequent and numbers of men as well as women from those tribes have actually settled on the lake. The Kaibu people are most strongly represented in Wasemi; the Fasu in Yokobu. The latter is in fact largely a Fasu village, and one of my interpreters, Girigi, complained that they often speak the Fasu language there, which he is unable to understand. The reason given for the migration of individuals from Fasu to Kutubu is that the latter provided more sago, bamboo, "cabbage," and fish.

Apart from these foreign elements the main population of the lake would itself appear to consist of immigrants from the Mubi a few miles to the east; in fact I have formed the opinion that it represents an offshoot, a western colony, of the large group, Mubi-Fimaga-Ifigi, etc., already spoken of. Individual immigrants still find their way to the lake, often as fugitives: they have quarrelled or been accused of sorcery, and their home villages have grown too hot to hold them. If questioned personally any such Mubi immigrant will usually declare that he came to Kutubu because of the fishing. Measured by the results commonly obtained this would seem to provide a very inadequate motive; though there is no denying that the Kutubu natives are much engrossed in fishing as a pastime. But apart from this (and its blessed freedom from leeches) Kutubu has no material advantages over the Mubi, which is in fact a much richer environment. One suspects that the main reason for migration, assuming it to have taken place, was one of security: movement of villages owing to small-scale warfare has been common, and, with all that water and their command of the means of transport, the people of the lake consider it a comparatively safe retreat.

Material Culture

Dress

Kutubu men commonly wear a pubic apron (*kunugabo*) of barkcloth. The netted string apron (*kou*), occasionally seen on the lake and more often on the Mubi, is a Grassland fashion.

The apron is suspended either from a series of plaited and knotted strings worn round the waist, or from a bark belt. The former (*hao*) are made by women: I make no attempt to describe the knots, which have some ornamental value until they are lost sight of under grease and body-dirt. The bark belt (*kakho* or *ka'o*) is unornamented. It may be as much as 6 in. wide. Strips of cane are sometimes fastened tightly round the *kakho* so as to cover it with a series of yellow bands, a neat and effective kind of ornament. I am assured that the cane is used when need arises for fire-making.

To cover his rear the Kutubuan sticks a branch of cordyline(*ko*) into his belt, hanging downwards. When he wishes to appear well dressed he will stick in another branch or two, pointing upright. The cordyline may be green or red, and when fresh they look very jaunty indeed. A substitute tail-piece, worn by those who possess it, is the *gu-ko*, a voluminous bunch of plaited strings reaching to below knee level.

Coils of plaited string (*hao*) similar to the waist-bands are sometimes worn over the shoulder, baldric-fashion.

Armlets (*ya-tava*) and garters (*en'doko*) worn below the knee are of fine cane strips, plaited. They are purely ornamental. A bracelet (*mumogu ya-tava*) of coarse can, twisted in several thick strands, and a necklet of the same kind are also said to be worn merely for ornament, though it seems probable that they must have had some significance as marks of mourning: at any rate they still have this significance when worn by women.

In full dress, e.g. for *kimisi*, i.e. journeying or visiting, when Kutubu men always make the most of their appearance, they wear some feather decorations in their hair (usually a fringe of cassowary plumes) and a flowing cloak of bark-cloth (*kosaka*). This last is inevitably rather dirty and crumpled, but it can be worn with quite an amount of dash. The usual function of the *kosaka*, however, is that of a sleeping robe or blanket. Every individual possesses one and uses it as such.

Despite the unpromising sound of this catalogue a Kutubu native can do himself up very well. The general effect is rather dingy and, when he has oiled himself and treated his whole body with soot, can be quite satanic; but his white shell-ornaments provide a very striking contrast and the red autumn-tinted leaves stuck in his armlets add a smart touch of colour.

The clothing of Kutubu women is only to be described as wretched, providing a faithful reflection of their general status. It is to be assumed that they possess their average share of good looks, but I have never beheld any race of women who were so indifferent to them. What beauty they possess is concealed beneath their ragged cowls of *kosaka* which hang, shapeless and untidy, from the crown of their heads to below their knees. Underneath they usually wear nothing but a very short fore-and-aft skirt of string; though they have another garment, the *fifayogo-kosaka*, consisting of a wide strip of bark-cloth covering chest and back, which is put on for festive occasions. Women often wear shell ornaments even if they do not own them; but one never catches more than a glimpse of them beneath the folds of their *kosaka*.

Hair

Men usually wear their hair in tags falling to the shoulders, sometimes matted together into thick lumps. There are no mops or wigs as among the Grasslanders. Boys clip their hair short. There is, as far as I can discover, no formal transition from short hair to long.

When a youth grows up he lets his hair grow as a matter of course; he greases it and it gradually assumes the tag form. Some older men also cut their hair short, and there is a modern tendency among the younger to follow the example of the armed constables at the Camp, at the undeniable sacrifice of good looks. But a fine growth of hair is admired and prized by those who are still interested in their sexual attractiveness. Certain medicines are used to promote it, among them a grass which is squeezed to a pulp, mixed with water, and applied as a sort of bright green hair-oil.

Beards are universal—at least they were until the armed constabulary set the fashion of the clean shave, still more to the detriment of the Kutubuans' manly appearance. A long beard, once again, is apparently a matter for pride. Nekinagu used to finger his affectionately. When once I suggested that he was not speaking the truth he answered that a man with a beard like his would never tell a lie; it was the longest in Kutubu!

Women always wear their hair short. They cut one another's and
their children's with bamboo knives.

Deformations

The piercing of the nasal septum seems to be universal among both
sexes. The reason given is the simple one that it makes possible the
wearing of a *saboro*, or "nose bamboo," when going on *kimisi*. The
operation is performed at the age of seven or eight and it is to be
noted that for once it is not the special business of the maternal
uncle; indeed I was assured that if he bored the hole the operation
would prove unduly painful. It may be done by anyone, as I was
told, "for a present of a fish or a rat." Ear-piercing evidently take
place later, and a good many never undergo this operation at all.
Some have a hole in one lobe and not the other. Some have holes in
the helix as well as the lobe. It is all a matter of free choice.

Some individuals have keloids on chest, arms, or legs. The scars
form no special pattern and once more they appear to be entirely
optional and without meaning. They are made by burning.

Ornaments

Headdresses are of modest dimensions and not very inspiring. They
seldom rise above fringes of brown or black cassowary feathers. The
red plumes of raggiana are fairly common, and single white tail
feathers of hornbill are often stuck into the hair, with the familiar
device (cutting away part of the quill on one side near the base) to
make them flutter. A rather distinctive head ornament is the bandea
of yellow and white cuscus fur.

The most popular and striking of Kutubu ornaments is the white
forehead-band called *sosere* (the name of the little shells used) or
ifamderubi (from *ifame*, "forehead"). This consists of a series of small
white shells sown in close parallel rows on a base of thin, leathery
material called *konemi kako*. (This material is the skin of a sort of
sheath, or bag, in which the *konemi* insect deposits its eggs. I never
succeeded in seeing one of the bags with the eggs in it nor could
I discover what a *konemi* was.) A peculiar feature of the forehead-
band is that a gap about $\frac{3}{4}$ in. wide, not covered by shells, is invariably
left in the middle. Precisely similar ornaments are used by the
Grasslanders, and there I saw once or twice a strange substitute for
the little shells, viz., discs of cassowary egg-shell ground down to
minute ovals with holes for threading. At Kutubu, and to a less
extent in the Grasslands, there has been a great rage for small white
beads (*igiari*) as trade. These are eventually sewn on to *koemi kako*.
They make a poor substitute for shells, but nearly everyone can now
afford an *ifamderubi*.

The commonest form of shell ornament is the *bari*, a medium-sized white cowrie. There must be thousands of these hoarded at the lake, strung together in strings called *kira*. Kutubu natives are, for Papuar expert arithmeticians, but there seems to be no regulation length for a string of *bari* or number for the shells it contains. A string, varying in length round about 3 ft., is spoken of as "one *bari*." When a man says that so many *bari* are included in a bride-price he means strings (properly *bari-kira*, not individual shells).

Plates of white *melo* shell (*faua*) are worn on the breast, often suspended by a string of *bari*. Together they make a very handsome ornament; and well illustrate the good taste of the conventional preference for white shell.

I do not think this preference extends to dead whiteness, however, though I believe I formerly suggested that this was the case. Far more valuable than *melo* are the gold-lip pearlshells (*magami* or *segere*), and, while it was declared by a number of informants that they liked the dead white ones as well as any, it nevertheless seems plain that they have an appreciative eye for the sheen. It is amusing to see how the native gloats over a fine specimen. Various factors enter into the evaluation: (1) size (the first consideration), (2) finish, (3) symmetrical shape (of surprisingly small moment), and (4) an incandescent sheen. The specimen is held at arm's length and viewed with intense seriousness. Then a finger is moistened under an armpit or drawn down the side of a nose, and with a touch of sweat or body-grease the surface of the shell is deliberately polished. Champion and Adamson have evolved the technique of touching up their trade shell with rifle-oil.

It is obvious that *magami* vary a great deal in value and so cannot be called "shell money." A good specimen incidentally is said to be worth more than a steel axe.

It seems that the Kutubu people (none of whom with the exception of Girigi has ever seen the sea) were in many cases actually ignorant of the natural origin of pearlshell. A group with whom I discussed the subject refused to commit themselves: all they would say was that they got it by hand, i.e. by trade, and mainly from the south-east. The large stocks brought as trade by the government have created an impression (not wholly consistent with other native theories as to their origin) that pearlshells actually derived in the first place from white men. On two occasions I noted down the following series of place names to indicate the trade route from the south-east: Kutubu-Fimaga-Kafa-Foi-Kewa-Sauwada. It was late, made clear to me that the last name on the list was no more than a local pronunciation of "*Taubada*,"[4] the "white men" from whom the shell was supposedly obtained.

The Men's House

The Kutubu village consists of one long men's house (*aa*) with a number of small women's houses ranged in a line along one side (rarely both) and facing it. The *aa* at Wasemi, the biggest on the lake, measured 213 ft. in length (including verandas of about 6 ft. in breadth at either end). Without having stepped them out I think those on the Mubi and at Fimaga were longer than this: they were certainly in better condition.

The house is set on numerous spindly piles, which vary in length because it is seldom built on flat ground. The floor might be said to be about 6 ft. above ground level, and at either end is reached by a very broad ladder of poles which is difficult of access for a friend, and would surely be impossible for an enemy.

The roof, which is thatched with palm leaves, falls rather steeply from a ridge-pole about 16 ft. above floor level, and is extended symmetrically at each end to form a projecting gable, cut away beneath. On either side it overhangs low walls of say 3 ft. 6 ins. height.

The only entrances are the doors in the front and rear of the building, each about 6 ft. by 3 ft., though the side walls sometimes have a few little holes through which cooked food may be passed in by the women. For purposes of decoration a series of light poles is affixed to the end wall, radiating towards the middle line over the door; and the edges of the projecting gable-roof are fringed with tassels of palm leaf. It is said that the villagers are proud of their *aa* when newly constructed; but it would be hard to imagine that they felt any pride in those which stand at Kutubu to-day. One and all are in a state of deplorable disrepair.

Since the only light from outside comes through the end doors, it is very difficult to see the interior of a well-built house. On the Mubi, indeed, I was driven to use a torch when I wished to examine the place at all thoroughly. In the Kutubu men's houses however the task is made fairly easy by the holes in the roof, walls and floor. Apropos of this general untidiness it is interesting to note that Kutubu villages seemed to suffer more neglect than those of Fimaga and the Mubi; and Mr. Champion tells me that when he first set eyes on them in 1936 the village sites, overgrown with weeds, were in a state far worse than at present. This seems in general keeping with the idea that the Mubi is a more thriving, go-ahead place than the lake.

The floor space of the *aa* (Fig. 1) is divided into a central passage, *iga* (about 12 ft. wide) and two lateral aisles each about 10 ft. wide, which contain the hearths and sleeping places. There are no central pillars: the roof is supported by a series of posts (*fugi*) arranged in

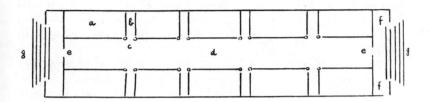

Fig. 1. Diagram of Men's House, *Aa*.
(*a*) Sleeping places. (*b*) Hearth, *kanema*. (*c*) Roof posts, *fugi*. (*d*) Central
passage, *iga*. (*e*) Doorway, *iga-koro*. (*f*) Verandah. (*g*) Steps.

pairs down each side of the *iga*. The central floor space is covered
with planks of palm-wood, set laterally; that of the sleeping places
with sheets of tough bark, or sometimes with further palm-wood
planks with a slightly concave bend.

The hearths (*kanema*), which are slung with rattan slightly below
the floor level, consist of frameworks filled with earth. Planks set
on edge protect them on either side, and above each is a two-storied
rack for firewood, etc. These hearths, each in line with a pair of
fugi, would appear to divide the interior on either side into a series
of alcoves; but these apparent alcoves seem to have neither name nor
significance. It is the place against the fire, at each end of the
"alcove," that is the recognized sleeping place of one or more
individuals. It may be worth noting that two light poles, bent and
lashed together so as to form a semi-circular arch, pass over the
"alcove," bearing against the roof. They are called *seriya* and I
imagine they serve some merely structural purpose.

The *aa* provides sleeping quarters for all males except the smallest
of little boys, who sleep with their mothers. The places next to the
hearths belong to individuals or small groups of two or three—a
man and his young sons, a pair of brothers, etc. They lie on pandanus mats and rest their heads, like Jacob, on a log of wood. The
fires smoulder throughout the day and towards evening blaze redly
amid clouds of smoke which fill the *aa* from end to end. Since its
occupants are sitting down they escape most of it, but it is almost
unendurable to the eyes of a European who ventures to walk through
the building at this hour. It struck me—though I never carried out
the idea—that the most comfortable means of progress would be on

hands and knees. It may be that the eyes of the Kutubuans are more or less inured to smoke and have ceased to smart. The fires serve for cooking, which is very simple, men or boys roasting their own sago or sweet potato as they want it; and they burn through the night while their owners sleep beside them enveloped in their bark-cloth cloaks.

The personal property of the Kutubu native amounts to very little. Some of his belongings (particularly his shell ornaments) he keeps hidden away in a corner of his wife's house; but the rest may be seen hanging on the hearth-racks or stuck in the wall or the thatch of the roof above his sleeping place. String bags (*ko*), bags of woven bark (*arera*), packages of bark-cloth—these contain his odds and ends. Axes of steel or stone, paddles, wooden bowls, bows and arrows, shields, conical fish-traps (see on the Mubi, not at Kutubu), bamboo tongs, pandanus mats, bark-cloth cloaks, packages of palm spathe containing feathers, drums carefully wrapped up in bark-cloth, and toys such as Jew's harps and spinning tops—these almost exhaust the list of things to be seen in the *aa*. In addition there are long bamboo *tigaso*-containers, packages of salt and tobacco, rows of tobacco leaves hung up near the roof-tree to dry in the smoke, and, tucked away in various convenient places, the numerous *kaminu* or quarterstaffs. Outside, over the door in the front wall, are ranged the skulls of pigs, a record of bygone feasts, and on either side the small skulls of various marsupials—cuscus, bandicoot and long-nosed echidna—which are kept as trophies of the chase. These are brown and shiny with smoke and certainly have a pleasing decorative effect. It is said that they are kept for three reasons: as house decoration (*aa-sanubu*); as trophies; and on the magical argument that to throw them away would spoil the hunter's luck. The most striking of the outdoor decorations of the *aa*, however, are the small plaques of bark painted so as almost to resemble heraldic shields, which are affixed here and there to the front wall. These are the *bodo* used in the *kwi-usanehabu* ceremony (see below). Several men's-houses on the Mubi had outsize examples of these, up to 2 ft. in height, set immediately above the doorway.

The building of an *aa* is a big undertaking for a small community and its completion involves some ceremonial. The people of Yokobu, where a new building was certainly overdue, declared that they were going to have one ready by the time I had returned from the Grasslands. But when, two months later, I did return, I found they had done precisely nothing, so can give no more than a brief hearsay enumeration of the proceedings.

The Kutubu people would appear to have used no drums in their, own indigenous dances (the drum probably came from the south-east together with the *Kwi-usane* cult which at present provides the sole occasion for its appearance). They used instead a kind of rattle, *gasoro* (a long pod with a number of loose shells inside it), and the dance and feast of this original kind was called *sorahabu* (distinguished from *usanehabu*, when the drums were beaten). There were apparently three justifications for a *sorahabu*: the capture of a bush pig; the launching of a particularly large canoe; and the completion of a men's-house. There were, normally, at least three such dances in connection with the last-mentioned: (1) when the floor boards (*tirifa*) were laid, (2) when the hearths (*kanema*) were installed, and (3) when the whole building was complete. The first two of these were minor occasions, only local guests being summoned, and only the flesh of wild animals being provided. But for the third there was a general tidying up of the site; many village pigs were slaughtered, and platforms were set up to expose the meat. For the men's house at Wasemi this *sorahabu* was attended by guests from all the lake villages, as well as from Fimaga, the Mubi, Fasu, Kaibu, and beyond Augu. The Grasslanders brought sucking pigs, salt and dogs' teeth; the others, cowrie, pearlshell, knives, axes, etc., and these goods were traded for lumps of pork. A big feast thus brought many people together and evidently developed into something of a market. The women thronged into the *aa* (they enter it only for dances and funerals) and sat as spectators while the men danced, holding an axe in one hand and shaking a seed-rattle with the other. In the morning the guests dispersed having been well fed in the meantime. I am assured incidentally that the Kutubu dance involves no special licentiousness. There is no custom of wife-lending on these occasions, and no slipping off of couples in the darkness. It is not to be imagined that the natives of this region are perfect in their sex morals, but it is worth noting once more that a native dance is not necessarily an orgy.

Probably the *aa* requires some architect's magic but I have heard of none except in connection with the finishing touch, viz. the fixing of a length of palm-wood called *aa-serere* under the ridge-pole. This is supervized by some old man who uses his magic on behalf of the whole *aa*-community. Its function seems not so much to secure the stability of the *aa* as to insure the general success of its members in those two quests to which Kutubu magic seems most often directed— hunting and the accumulation of shell valuables. In the former respect it is observed (as if it explained everything) that *serere*, the material used, is the kind of palm used for arrow points. As for the shell magic, it goes without such explanation. Shell, however, is an

obsession with the Kutubu people and it is said to be the magicians'
business to attract many visitors who will bring shell in their bags
to trade with.

Lesser Buildings

The woman's house (*kanya*) is a small edition of the men's house,
but with the peaked gable at the front end only. It stands on piles
and the ridge-pole is about 10 ft. above floor level. Its surroundings
are rubbish-strewn and overgrown with grass in which the young
pigs may be seen lurking towards evening when their mistresses
catch them and carry them up into the houses. The interior usually
has six hearths with sleeping places on either side for a man's wife,
his unmarried daughters, his brother's wife, son's wife, adopted
son's wife, etc. The woman's house may be entered by men and
they often spend some time there. I have never heard, however, of a
man sleeping in a *kanya*.

At some distance behind the row of *kanya* will be seen several
kasera, or women's retiring houses. They can only be described as
shanties. Women occupy them (1) during their monthly periods,
(2) during childbirth, and (3) for the first few days of their seclusion
as widows.

Much of the Kutubuan's working life is spent away from his
village in a country residence, either the *eh-aa* (garden house) or the
sabu-aa (hunting lodge). The former may be quite a well-made
house in pleasant surroundings. Both are characterized by a cross-
wall dividing the building into two parts, for males and females
respectively. For, even in the privacy of a family dwelling, males and
females must be separated while asleep.

Canoes

The canoe which is so essential to life on the lake as well as on the
Mubi is a plain dugout, somewhat roughly made. The timber is
waria, which grows plentifully in the district. The trees are owned
by individuals or families if they grow on old garden sites; but in
the bush they are available to anyone. The dugout is hewn on the
spot, often some miles from the water, and is dragged down by
rattan and lianas, many men and boys helping. There is said to be
no reward other than food given for assistance in hewing and hauling.
When the canoe is an especially big one, however, the owner will
give a feast at its launching and the *sorohabu* will be danced. This
represents a reward for those who have mustered to haul it down.

The canoes are mostly small, but the male paddler, who stands
upright, is a master of equipoise. They are slightly raised at the
prow, coming to a thick blunted point; at the stern they are rounded.

The function of the raised point is probably to enable it to breast the waves which are often pretty choppy and fill some natives with alarm.

Kutubu canoes no doubt meet well enough the demands made on them, but they certainly lack finish, and they are cut rather thick. I witnessed one interesting incident, the mending of a hole as big as a five-shilling piece cut accidentally through the bottom with the stone adze. At the water's edge, just before launching, a thin chip of wood was applied to the hole and a lump of resin (*ira kanaro*) held against the edges. This was melted with a hot stone, and, when this proved insufficient, with a glowing coal held in a bamboo tongs and blown upon by the operator. The job seemed to be a success, for the canoe was forthwith launched and the owner declared his faith in it.

Weapons

The bow is named *piaka* after the black palm from which it is made. The arrows (*pa'i*) are light, made of the usual cane shafts with plain points of palm wood. The only barbed points which I noted at the lake were importations from Fasu (among them were some with bone tips). Some arrows have bamboo blades.

The spear (*tabu*) is used in conjunction with the bow and arrows as a fighting weapon. A raiding party advancing in mock performance put the spearmen first; but so many more bows and arrows are to be seen that I imagine that they take precedence as fighting weapons. The *tabu* is light and without barbs. Some (*kigi-tabu*) are tipped with bone.

Two kinds of shield (*kunu*) are in use (Fig. 2). They are made of a strong bark. The spearman's shield has two or more sticks attached crosswise on the reverse side for support, with one vertical stick for a handle. Such shields vary in length from about 3 ft. 6 ins. to nearly 6 ft. They are square at the bottom and pointed at the top. The bowman's shield is a similar but smaller sheet of bark (about 2 ft. 6 ins. long) with a loop of cane behind to pass over the wearer's left shoulder.

Some palm-wood clubs (*poki*) are to be seen and a very few stone ones (*kanahai*). Those that I saw of the latter kind were inferior specimens of the "pineapple" type and were declared to be very old. It is evident that stone clubs are not made nowadays on the lake. One, which I bought, had a ridiculously long and clumsy handle and one cannot think it would be very useful as a weapon.

Much more important, though less deadly, are the *kaminu*, i.e. the quarterstaffs or fighting-sticks. These are strong poles some 8 ft. long which are kept handy in the men's house against a local or

Fig. 2

(a) Small shield (rear view). Length 3 ft. 6 in.

(b) Full-sized shield (front view). Length 5 ft. 10 in. Painted in red and white

(c) Bowman's shield (rear view). Length 2 ft. 6 in.

inter-village brawl. They are not weapons for killing expeditions but for the more or less innocuous melees which take place within the *aa* itself or on the cleared ground outside. Such conflicts are alleged to be fairly frequent, though I did not have the pleasure of seeing one. To show that serious casualties are deprecated, it is said to be the custom for some, as would-be peace-makers, to intervene between the combatants, holding their *kaminu* horizontally above their heads so as to ward off the blows from either side. This however is admitted to be highly dangerous in itself, and those who adopt the role of peacemaker are recommended to hold the *kaminu* between finger and thumb, with the fingers pointing upward rather than clenched; this to save the knuckles.

This brief list covers the Kutubuans' whole armament of war. Incidentally they do not possess cassowary-bone daggers. The implements which so much resemble them are designed for splitting the red pandanus fruit and dislodging its seeds.

Tools and Implements

Steel axes have, in a very brief period, almost entirely replaced those of stone. The latter, which, I understand, used to be carried habitually by almost every adult male (as they still are in the Grasslands) are now seen mostly in the men's house. Nevertheless the native does not part with his stone axe very readily; he still uses it in hollowing his canoe because of its convenient set. No doubt in course of time steel adze-blades will be made to fill this need also and the *gagebo* will become an antique.

The blades (*hibu*) are imported from the Grasslands. They are often very well made, with squared sides, i.e. oblong in section. They taper towards the butt end, where they are inserted in a tang (*kou*) consisting of two pieces of wood, appropriately shaped, which are tightly bound together with cane. The tang itself tapers towards the distal end. It is bound on to an elbow-shaped haft (*fia*) with cane, often criss-crossed in an attractive manner. It should be remarked, however, that the Kutubu axes are rough, utility implements. One does not see any specimens to compare with the beautifully shaped axes of the Grasslands: the cane binding is not of the same finely finished character, and there are none of the delicate pale green celts.

The tang can be turned in its socket of cane so that the tool may be used as an axe or adze. To attack a tree it is twisted slightly so as to give the blade a half-and-half, oblique set. A man does not make a "scarf" in chopping timber: he uses a downward stroke all the time, and with a good sharp stone makes pretty fair progress. The use of the steel axe, incidentally, takes some learning. Hejon, a youth of Augu, purchased one (for a piglet) while I was there. He was obviously proud of it, but the first day out cut himself between finger and thumb, and the second day between toe and great toe. The latter injury was quite a bad one which kept him at home and made him a good informant.

The imported stone blades are too valuable to use (when new) on sago bark, for it is so hard as to chip them. The substitute is a locally made hammer-stone, *toio* (Fimaga: *amaga taua*). This is a long pebble worked down by "pecking" towards a point at each end and then hafted in the same way as an ordinary celt. It thus constitutes a hammer, or very blunt sort of pick which is not likely to break and is no great loss if it does. I presume that the proper *gagebo* is used to cut through the bark when it has been more or less reduced to pulp. I was not successful in buying a hafted *toio* though I offered a mirror. It is an implement still very much in use. The sago scraper (*wasa*) is hafted in the same way, but the working edge is provided by a pebble, or piece of flinty stone, snapped off sharp.

Flint flakes are used for small tools, i.e. as knives, scrapers and awls. The flakes are struck off at random and suitable ones selected. They may be bound into small haftings of wood or bamboo; and I am told that as drills they may be fitted into arrow shafts which are rotated between the palms. The ordinary method of boring a hole, however, is by using a pointed flint in the hand as an awl. There is no attempt at secondary flaking of flint.

The only bone implements which I remember seeing, apart from spear points, are the pandanus-fruit splitter (*viribu*) and gouge (*fagebu*), both formed from cassowary bones. As mentioned already, the former resembles the well-known dagger, but comes to a chisel-end rather than a point. It is used for splitting the long red pandanus fruit (*abari*). The *fagebu*, a scoop-ended bone, is used to dislodge the red seeds after the fruit has been cooked in the hot-stone oven. The *viribu* however is often made to serve both purposes.

A wooden bowl (*kawaso*) is specially made for these pandanus seeds, which are mashed up with the fingers and reduced to a sort of bright-tomato-coloured porridge. This bowl (Fig. 3) may be well finished—almost surprisingly so, for the Kutubuans are not, generally speaking, careful workmen. It is sometimes 2 ft. in length, elliptoid in shape, and at one end has a sort of spout by which the thick red soup, which is the best part of the meal, may be poured out and shared round. The seeds remain in the bowl, to be taken in handfuls, sucked, and spat out. The *kawaso* often has a hole and a loop of string so that it can be hung up.

Water vessels are usually lengths of thick bamboo, though calabashes (*komuru*) are in common use. There is also a bucket (*winimabu*) of palm spathe bent into oblong shape and sewn (Fig. 4). There are no coconuts at Kutubu, and the one or two half coconut shells that I saw (importations from coastwards) were used especially in the ritual of the *Usi* cult, a further hint that the cult itself comes from the south-east.

Besides providing water vessels, *tigaso*-carriers, arrow points

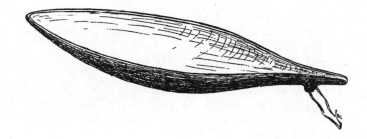

Fig. 3. Wooden food bowl (*kawaso*). Length 22 ins.

nose-pencils and small receptacles for odds and ends, bamboo is the material of the ordinary knife. The *oro-sabe* (bamboo knife) is often shaped down to a narrow handle with a broad blade. To sharpen it a man simply wrenches off a strip along the edge, using his teeth. Bamboo (a length bent double) also supplies the tongs, which are very necessary where cooking is mainly by means of hot stones.

A wooden bark-cloth beater (*wabuia*) with longitudinal grooves is made from pinewood. Bark-cloth beating is women's work (the men go so far as to beat out their aprons but not their large cloaks). The bark, which comes specially from a tree called *buru*, is hammered on a log. Having passed through a thick, blankety stage, it is finally beaten out to a broad sheet, perhaps as much as 5 ft. × 4 ft. This is gathered at one end so as to hang from the crown of the head as cloak or nightdress.

Fig. 4. Palm-spathe water-vessel (*winimabu*). Length 18 ins.

Fig. 5. Stone mortar (*duabo*) and pestle (*toio*). Diameter 7 ins. (approx.)

Stone Mortars

It remains to mention the stone mortars (*duamo*) of which at least four have been found in the neighbourhood of Kutubu, viz. at Yogobu, Tugiri, Kesiki and Fimaga. It so happens that three of the four are used for a specific purpose, viz. for pounding the medicines used in the *Usi* ritual, whence they may be called *usiakana*, or "medicine stones." It seems, however, perfectly clear that they were not expressly made for the purpose, but merely adapted to it. The pestles used are merely elongated pebbles or the hammer-stones (*toio*) described above.

A brief account is given of each mortar:

(1) This was a very good specimen with a regular series of knobs round its periphery[5]. It was found by a man named Sokari, now deceased; but, as his brother and widow survive, this could not have been so very long ago. He was hunting one day when he came on a scrub hen's mound and discovered the *duamo* underneath it while searching for eggs. Having covered it up again he returned to Yokobu, where he had a "dream" in which he saw some *aroa* bark (the main constituent of the *Usi* medicines) being pounded in it. After this he brought it to the village and it was thenceforward used for the purpose indicated.

(2) The Tugiri example is a plain one, and not of very regular shape. It was found by Sinigana while searching for his pig which had strayed at the foot of the hills on the opposite shore of the lake. It is likewise used for the *Usi* medicines. Sinigana is a man in his thirties.

(3) The specimen seen at Kesiki is broken, but was evidently fashioned with some care, having a sort of waist in the middle (Fig. 5). This one alone has a long history. It was allegedly "made" by a man named Gofo, an immigrant from Kafa who settled first at a site formerly occupied by the Kesiki people, and later on at Kara. When he died the *duamo* was for some forgotten reason carried away and hidden by a man named Fagena; and only in comparatively recent years was it rediscovered, lying upside down in the bush. The discoverer was the father of my informant, himself an old man; and Gofo, the original "maker" turns out to be the great-great-grandfather of a man now living at Kafa. If this story is to be believed— if indeed it was the same *duamo* that was lost and found—it can be traced back for perhaps 125 years, which, all said and done, may not signify much.

(4) The Fimaga mortar is a small but well formed specimen 6½ ins. high and 7 ins. in diameter. Unlike the others this is not used in the *Usi* ritual (the base for pounding the medicines was supplied

by a large, slightly concave, slab of limestone). The little mortar was black and greasy. It served as a bowl, standing at one end of the men's house and in common use, for *tigaso*, the oil which is rubbed on hair and body. Its history is quite recent. It was brought in by a present member of the Fimaga society named Tabi, who found it in the bed of Warere Creek while diving for fish. It is surmized that it was originally the property of a *kuruka*, who used it as a drum, beating the open end.

No one thinks of making *duamo* on the lake in these days. It is plain that they are here, as elsewhere, survivals of a forgotten past.

Musical Instruments

Kutubu drums (*sapo*) are of two types : one is the familiar "fish-mouth" (though the "mouth" is called *sapo-kesa*, "drum-treefork") ; the other might be called the "goblet" type. The carved

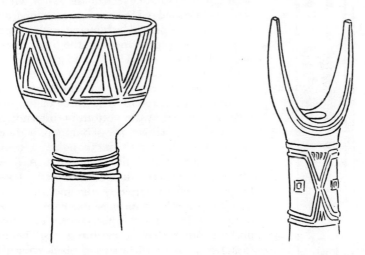

Fig. 6. Two types of Kutubu drum.

decoration in each case varies very little from the specimens shown in the sketches (Fig. 6).

The drum is about 2 ft. 6 ins. long, and without a handle. It is slenderly made and when not in use is carefully wrapped in bark-cloth and hung up. It is evidently a valued possession and I did not succeed in buying one.

It has already been mentioned that drums are never used except in connection with the *Usane* cult which deals with the curing of certain sicknesses. It is only as a culmination to a long course of treatment that a village holds an *usanehabu*, i.e. feast accompanied by a dance with drums. It is said that this cult has found its way to Kutubu from the Mubi via Fimaga, Foi, Segaro and Turigi. I do not know where the last two places would appear on the map, but they are seemingly away to the south-east. Some informants volunteered the opinion that the drums (of both kinds) had been introduced to Kutubu with the cult.

Before that happened it appeared that the local natives danced to the noise of rattles, *gasoro*. These make a livelier noise than might be supposed. They consist of several long seed pods (with the seeds loose inside) bound together. Sometimes a small handle is attached.

The set of pan-pipes (*seoro*) illustrated in the sketch (Fig. 7) was one seen on the Mubi, where it was acknowledged to be an importation from the Wage. It is played by blowing on the upper edges of the pipes, moving the instrument about slightly as one does so, and gives forth a gentle aeolian sort of sound. It is the same instrument as recorded on the Morehead, though in the present case three of the five pipes are closed at the bottom by internodes.

Jew's harps (*damoro*) are of bamboo. Natives are fond of playing them, though my trade stock of metal ones did not "go." A most interesting variant based, like the Jew's harp, on the principle of the mouth-cavity as an adjustable sounding-box, came to my notice at Herebu on the Mubi. This was nothing other than a captured sago-beetle (*huka-tama*), which is a strong black creature with a horn in its nose. While interpreting for me Girigi diverted himself by catching one of these beetles and as conversation proceeded I watched him break off the lower joint of one of its powerful forelimbs and insert a pliant piece of sago midrib in the remaining upper part. Then he shook the

Fig. 7. Left. Panpipes
(*seoro*). Length 12 ins.
(approx.)

midrib until the tormented insect began to buzz its wings with the speed of an aeroplane propeller, when he held it near his lips, mounting as if he were performing on the Jew's harp. The noise is the same, though very soft. Both Girigi and the beetle seemed prepared to go on for ever. I subsequently saw the same trick performed with other insects.

A primitive stringed instrument is also illustrated. It is made of the dry midrib of a sago frond with a strip of the bark wedged up. It produces two notes being struck alternately on right and left with a little stick (Fig. 8).

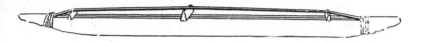

Fig. 8. Stringed instrument of dry sago midrib. Length 4 ft.

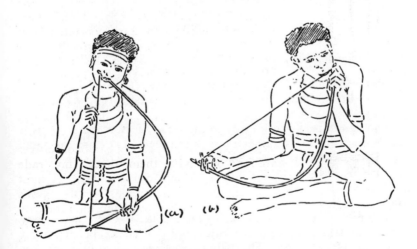

Fig. 9. *Teiboro.*

Two methods of playing the "musical bow" (*teiboro*) are illustrated in Fig. 9. In each case the player mouths as he plucks the string, thus varying the note. In the second, however, where he holds his lips lightly over the string, he begins by playing in the ordinary way; then, after a moment or two, he draws his breath in as long and as hard as he can, and in so doing manages to produce something like a soft violin note. The mechanics of this sound beat me completely. A good performer can make it last between two and three seconds.

Fig. 10. Spinning Top.

Toys

One unimportant item of material culture deserves mention if only because of its ubiquity. This is the spinning-top (*suku*) consisting of the half-shell, hard and thick, of a spherical fruit with a length of stick fixed in a hole in the bottom (Fig. 10). The stick being twisted between the palms, the top is allowed to fall and spin on the ground. A great deal of skill is shown in the spinning and in directing the fall. Several boys will play together trying to knock one another's tops over.

Counting

Fig. 11 shows the method of counting, to which reference will be made in subsequent chapters. It is used with rather remarkable accuracy, especially as providing a timetable for feasts, etc. The important numbers in this connection are 5 (*kaba*, left thumb); 19 (*kisi*, lit. "middle," the nose); and 37 (*kenagi*, right hand little finger).

The names belong primarily to the bodily features and are used as checks to memory rather than as numbers. They are the same on right and left with the sole exception of the little finger—I, *menagi*; 37, *kenagi*.

Sago

The Kutubu are eaters of sago (*kwi*), a fact which goes a long way to explain their cultural affinities with the coastal people rather than the Grasslanders. The palms grow very plentifully on the Mubi River and in certain areas about the lake itself, particularly about Samaga, at the south-east end. There is never any question of food shortage as among the Grasslanders who depend on sweet potatoes.

The method of making sago has nothing distinctive about it. Two midribs are laid end to end on trestles so that their widespreading butts form a trough for the pith.

One of the midribs is given a slightly downward tilt so that the water which is used in the process may drain slowly off at the thin end which has the natural form of a spout. The pith is beaten with a stick, water being added from time to time, whereby the actual sago is separated out and carried down in suspension. Having passed

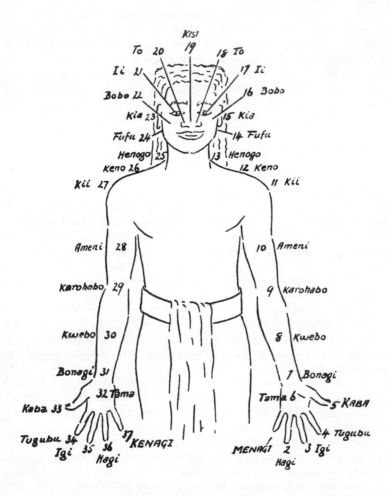

Fig. 11. Method of counting.

through a strainer (in the form of an *arera* bag) fixed near the end of
the midrib, the stream falls into a tank of palm spathe where the
sago solidifies into a block. When the day's work is over this block is
broken up into lumps and packed into a large *arera*, or else com-
pressed into a cylindrical package (*kwi-boroka*) about 3 ft. long which
is neatly bound with sago leaves. In this form great quantities are
continually brought to the Police Camp to be bartered for shells,

knives or axes. It will keep a long time in the *kwi-boroka*, especially
if it is buried underground.

Women do the whole work of sago-making apart from the actual
felling and splitting of the tree. They scrape the pith out of the trunk
with the *wasa* and beat it in the trough with sticks (*furera*). I was
much impressed by a thin little woman whom I once saw at work.
She seemed to be fairly cluttered with belongings hanging about her
person under the bark-cloth cloak, and small muffled cries revealed
the surprising fact that a baby was among them. I think, however,
that she worked thus in full marching order merely because she saw
me and wanted to take care of her possessions. Ordinarily they are
hung on convenient branches.

Gardens

Gardening is surprisingly ill-developed, even on the rich land of the
Mubi. On the lake itself the gardens, small and rather untidy, are
frequently perched on the most inaccessible slopes overlooking the
water, and this although better sites are not wanting. The Yokobu
people, e.g. had ample good land in the vicinity of the camp, but
they had mostly neglected it for the steep slopes on the southern
shore. The only intelligible reason given was that the situation
largely saved them the labour of fencing.

But gardening can elsewhere be done on a fairly large scale. The
felling of timber on Wasemi has been mentioned. It was making
possible a common garden in which thirty-two men were co-
operating, each having his own plot within a common fence. I am
assured that this is no new fashion, though the acquisition of steel
has made the undertaking easier. Common gardens are formed
under the leadership of an individual, the *kusaga*, who possesses
certain magic which he uses on behalf of all, and who is said to take
the lead by planting the first sweet potatoes.

The gardening cycle is as follows: (1) the cutting of undergrowth
and preliminary clearing (done by women); (2) the felling or ring-
barking of trees; (3) the fencing (*mafe*), with short palings;
(4) clearing and burning—the fallen trunks are dragged aside and
heaped against the fence; branches, leaves and undergrowth are
burnt; (5) planting—the digging-stick, *asu*, is of palm or wood,
about 3 ft. long.

The gardens are far from neat and weeding is perfunctory. There
is no tillage and it is obvious that plants are largely left to look after
themselves. All products are said to be planted at one and the same
time. The main ones are sweet potato (*agira*), taro (*penabo*), small
palms (*wasia*—2 or 3 ft. high, supplying edible shoots), sugar-cane
(*magi*), and bananas (*ga*). The two last-mentioned are the latest in

ripening. When their time is over the garden is simply left to be overgrown by the bush, and the site is not replanted until a good many years have passed.

Additional cultivated products are cucumbers (*anumu*), two kinds of "yam" (*yatafa* and *hogo*) and various "cabbages" (*gagana, harase, garubaio, veriveri* and *sagai*—I have not identified them); while young breadfruit (*uki*), red pandanus (*abari*), and white pandanus (*waio*) are planted in the gardens to remain as the owner's property after the land has turned back to bush.

Among the wild edible products are the leaves of *haginamo* and *hainya* trees; several kinds of fruit; bamboo shoots (*konya*) and palm shoots (*metari*). It is to be noted that the Kutubu have a very wide range of "greens," cultivated and uncultivated, and depend on them to quite a large extent.

Despite this variety of products it must be said that the natives are poor gardeners, in which they stand in sorry contrast to the Grasslanders. The great success of the camp gardens has no doubt given them some lessons in method, and if they have not taken all these to heart they have at any rate profited by the distribution of corn and melon seeds and the cuttings of imported sweet potato vines.

Hunting

Meat diet, here as so often elsewhere, is extremely restricted, amounting to a rarely enjoyed luxury. The people are dependent (1) on their village pigs which are comparatively speaking not numerous, and (2) on the game of the district, which is at least hard to catch. Game is said, however, to be more plentiful in the southeast region than in the north-west, when I was at the lake. As in the case of fishing, interest in the chase seems out of all proportion to the results obtained. Perhaps the sheer want of meat is what makes it so engrossing. It is at any rate illuminating to watch the sharing out of the wretched portions of rat and bandicoot which constitute the bag, and the avid way in which they are eaten.

The generic term for wild animals (excluding the pig) is *aso*, which seems to cover everything from a wallaby to a flying phalanger. I have enumerated eleven terrestrial species and thirteen arboreal, but have seen very few of them except in the form of smoke-dried carcases. These are presumably all marsupials except for some kinds of rat. The most important of them is the cuscus. Wild pig seems to be relatively scarce, but there are plenty of cassowary and various kinds of megapod, especially in the wet season. Large snakes and lizards are also caught, and rightly regarded as very good food.

The methods of hunting may be listed as follows:

(1) *Springe* (simply called *sui* (cane) at Kutubu; *hefa* on the Mubi). The large trap is especially for wallaby. Small *springe* are improvised in a few moments for bandicoots. etc.

(2) *Falling-Log traps* (*kagi*). These are set for pigs over a split sago-trunk which constitutes the bait. Miniatures (*pugunu*) are laid for rats, bandicoots, etc. especially in the wet season called *Pango-hasi*,

(3) *Pit traps* (*fase*). I am told that these often have sharpened palm stakes (*konyo*) in the bottom; also that such *konyo* may be set up on the ground just inside the garden fence. I have not seen either of these devices.

(4) *Nooses*. Lizards are caught with a running noose of cane on the end of a long stick; or with a noose and trigger attached to the trunk of a tree in which a lizard has been seen.

(5) *Catch-as-catch-can*. Natives are ready to pursue anything they see. They climb trees and pelt the animals down, when their dogs chase them, the hunters following with their spears. Bows and arrows are also used, though from personal observation I should say that the Kutubu were not very good shots.

Special hunting parties go out before certain feasts for which a supply of *aso* is required. They may consist of half-a-dozen men and boys who will remain away several days, living in a hunting lodge. They bring back their catch in string bags, a queer assortment of carcases, disembowelled but with the fur remaining, and twisted into strange shapes over the fire by which they have been smoked, the lizards like dragons and the big snakes like corkscrews. It is a matter for pride and general congratulation if the bags are bulging full. A great deal of magic goes towards this difficult and not very productive phase of the food quest; and it is interesting to note how many of the legends and folk-tales tell of mighty hunters—a form, no doubt, of wish-fulfilment.

The hunter, legendary and modern, depends very largely on his dog to bring him into touch with the quarry, and often to catch it. The dogs themselves are of the ordinary Papuan type, with occasional specimens, obtained by trade, of the much heavier-coated kind which belongs to the 6000 ft. Grasslands.

The Village Pig

The relative scarcity of village pigs has already been noted, but it is perhaps a passing phase. When Mr. Claude Champion first established the Police Camp he was able to buy as many as he wanted for rations—in fact they were brought in so fast that he built a pig-pen for their accommodation and killed them off as needed. It was, the natives declare, their own extravagant dealing in 1936 which depleted the village supply and they have not had time to catch up since. In explanation of it they say (1) that they were overtempted by the trade (in steel and pearlshells) and (2)—a familiar idea—that they were much afraid of the intruders, thinking they would take their pigs anyway; so they made hay while the sun shone and hastened to dispose of them for what they could get.

Pigs are spoken of as "belonging" to the women, just as dogs "belong" to the men. The expression merely indicates—at least in the first instance—that the sex named is responsible for feeding and looking after them. The acid test of ownership in the case of a pig comes when it is decided to sell it or kill it; and the decision appears to be after all with the men. But the women play their part as custodians very conscientiously and, insofar as the pig is an affectionate animal, they at least get all its affection. They may be seen sometimes with the pigs following at their heels like dogs, and at night they give them shelter in their houses. There was one special pig-house under the Yokobu *aa* like a dog kennel, with a steep plank leading down to the ground, a gangway for a pig and its litter. But this was quite exceptional.

So far from really owning the pigs, the women even fail to get an equal share of the meat when they are killed. The head, I am told, is given them for distribution at feasts and also the guts (*nemi fako*). The latter are said to be very good to eat, but they involve the trouble of cleaning and they are definitely second-class fare. It is not to be understood that this is all the pig-meat that the women ever receive, but there is no doubt that they get far less animal protein than do their husbands. At some of the ceremonies for which *aso* are provided they are rigorously excluded and get none at all.

Pigs are too precious to be eaten on any but festive or ceremonial occasions, but for a large feast they may be killed in considerable numbers. As has been noted, such a feast develops into something like a meat-market, the guests bringing *bari* shells etc. to exchange for pork. It has also been noted that natives go long distances to procure sucking pigs from other tribes.

Fishing

The lake contains many varieties of fish which are interesting to science but poor to eat. I listed eighteen by name, of which *torobu* and *aworihibu* are said to be the best. Looking down from the cliffs of Kesi into the beautifully clear water I have seen fish that were fifteen inches or more in length; but I have never seen any such caught by a fisherman. The commonest varieties, *sisigabu* and others, however highly prized, are small and bony.

Fishing at Kutubu is as much a pastime as a serious occupation. The typical method is that of spearing, the spear (*sagari*) having a thin handle, about 7 or 8 ft. long, and five or six palm-wood prongs. The solitary fisherman stands erect in his dugout, managing it and steadying himself with a paddle while he searches the transparent waters with his eyes and holds his *sagari* in readiness. No scene is more characteristic of Kutubu and its primitive untroubled life; the fisherman drifting lazily, yet intent upon his trivial business and, when the moment comes, tense as an athlete. As a sport this seems to give exercise to all the piscatorial virtues, and to demand a somewhat greater measure of skill than does most of our own fishing. It is no wonder that some immigrants to the lake have declared that the fishing was what attracted them.

Fish are sometimes caught by the use of poison (*wami*, a shrub, and *somo*, a creeper, both with a milky sap), by which they are numbed and brought to the surface; and they are also said to be caught by hand when hiding in the rocks. Women frequently dive for prawns; it is a more exacting and probably much less amusing occupation than fishing, which is by common consent reserved for males.

The fish spear is not so much used by the Mubi natives because the river water is, more often than not, muddy as well as flowing fairly fast. On the other hand they have several contrivances which are not ordinarily seen at Kutubu, viz. (1) a circular hand net, *anogo*, of string-work suspended on a ring of cane which is used in pools of flood water when they have been bailed out; (2) *oro habusa*, "bamboo trap," a long narrow tube made of strips of bamboo with a spiral binding, which is placed in small streams, mouth against the current; and (3) *kwi-habusa*, "sago trap," a cone-shaped frame of sago-bark, with a removable interior cone making it into a sort of "lobster-pot." The *kwi-habusa* may be 3 ft. 6 ins. in length. A common sight along the banks of the Mubi is that of the rough fences (*tirigira*) erected across the mouths of small creeks emptying into the main stream; they are to hold in place the conical fish-traps described above.

I am assured that Mubi women fish with lines to which earthworms (*gi-magami*) are attached for bait—there is apparently no hook; but I was never able to induce anyone to demonstrate the method, for neither the worms nor the women were forthcoming. (For *gi-magami* as the alleged diet of fish see the story of the Lost Fish-Spear below.)

Narcotics

Tobacco is grown and cured locally. Every men's-house has a row of plants flourishing on either side of it, more or less sheltered by the eaves. The smoking tube is of bamboo with a hole through the internode at one end and a second small hole, in the side of the tube, near the other end. The first hole is to draw the smoke through; the second is for the "cigarette." These smoking tubes (*sogoro*, "tobacco bamboos") are sometimes decorated with scratched criss-cross lines, but are usually plain.

Betel chewing is so far a rare habit on the lake, being practically confined to Yokobu, where indeed it is practised by only a small proportion of the men (by none of the women). These individuals are descendants of immigrants from Fasu, whence the habit has been brought; but not all of them have seen fit to take it on. Tanumesa, whose classificatory brothers were all chewers, remained proud of his white teeth which were certainly more in harmony with the accepted modes of personal decoration. But presumably betel chewing will spread gradually throughout the lake population, as cannibalism would no doubt have done but for the coming of the whites. The Mubi, etc. do not chew at all.

A small variety of areca (*tamo*) grows wild in the district, as also does the pepper (*kisuku*). The lime (*boro*) is kept in a calabash and the imestick is a spike of palmwood (*kubu*). A further ingredient is *kosani*, a kind of nut, inedible, which seems to have the effect of thickening the mixture.

Cooking

I have observed three methods of cooking: (1) in the open fire, as of sweet potatoes, palm shoots, etc.; (2) baking in green internodes of bamboo; and (3) the hot-stone oven (*sauyubu*).

Part II

Social Organization

The Tribe

The inhabitants of Lake Kutubu together with their neighbours on the east may be spoken of as a "people." The component groups—Kutubu, Mubi, Fimaga and Ifigi—may then be regarded as "tribes." I may repeat the admission that I do not know how far the people extends: there may be other groups further east or south-east that should be included. Further, it must be confessed that the name

Ifigi is applied only loosely: it may cover more tribes than one. My personal knowledge extends only to Kutubu, Mubi and Fimaga; but these may perhaps be taken as representative.

Each of these tribes has its acknowledged territory, though only in a broad sense. Migration of individuals being of common occurrence, it may be found that a man settled on Lake Kutubu, for example, still lays claim to land on the Mubi. But such immigrants, if they settle permanently, acquire land in their new homes and their original claims come to be forgotten. The case of Fasu, although it is not strictly one of inter-tribal migration, may be taken as an example. All the Fasu men now settled in Yokobu are found to possess land of their own in the immediate neighbourhood. It was allegedly parcelled out to their ancestors (quite recently) by the chief man of Yokobu, and it remains theirs to bequeath by inheritance. They are now Kutubu men and they own Kutubu land.

Generally speaking every part of the district at large may be assigned to one tribe or another. But it is so rugged and so little used that the ownership is at best nominal, and it is fair to suppose that there are considerable tracts of which the ownership is doubtful or which remain actually unclaimed.

The best indication of tribal solidarity is the distinctive dialect, which, somewhat obviously, may be attributed to circumstances of geography. It is true that neighbouring tribes such as Fasu and Kaibu have had some effect on the Kutubu language, but the principal factor in that particular case is no doubt the ease of communication on the waters of Lake Kutubu itself. In short, its inhabitants talk to one another more often than to anyone else and so develop a distinctive way of talking. Similarly with the three villages of the Mubi; and so on.

There is, however, no set tribal organization and certainly no tribal chief. On the lake there are a few pre-eminent individuals among whom I should give pride of place to Yaru of Wasemi and his namesake, Yaru of Kesi. The former is a very grim old man of undeniable weight and dignity; the latter, still in early middle life, seems conspicuous for his energy: he is one of the brighter sort, who are not so very numerous at Kutubu. But these are merely personal impressions, and other observers would probably differ. The fact remains that there is no formally acknowledged chief of the Kutubu tribe.

There is certainly a fellow-feeling among the tribesmen as a whole, though they never unite in any common enterprise save for an occasional warlike expedition. This fellow-feeling does not, of course, imply that the Kutubu villages never fall out among themselves; but it will induce them to join forces in attacks on other tribes or on foreign enemies. Thus on fairly recent occasions the whole lake population has found itself combined against one or other of the following: Mubi, Fimaga, Eragahugu, Fasu and Enabo (the last-mentioned in the north-west). It is worthy of note that Kutubu, together with the nearer tribes of Mubi and Fimaga, seems to have been frequently at enmity with Ifigi, the most distant.

Village and Village Chief

The local group of prime importance is the village, which, with its men's house and attendant *kanya*, is a very compact unit. The villagers are ready to unite in taking up arms, in giving large feasts, and in performing ceremonies (e.g. for initiations, for the building of an *aa*, for mourning and for success in the food quest); they may make common gardens; and they recognize a definitely-bounded tract as their immediate territory.

There is still some difficulty in naming the "chief" even of so small a unit. The older and more important members are collectively spoken of as *eresabu*, which means "home-keepers"—though this does not imply that they are too old to go on *kimisi*. It probably means simply that they are entitled to sit about in the *aa* while the younger men do the hard work abroad. But the term implies some obligation also. It is naively asserted that the *eresabu* "look after" the men's house: they note if the building is in bad repair or the grounds untidy, and they recommend improvements.

But apart from these privileged old men there are individuals who may be described as chief men of the several villages. It is true that the inhabitants of the villages concerned are often in doubt when it comes to naming them, and sometimes find it difficult to restrict themselves to one per village—all of which indicates that the institution of chieftainship is very ill-developed. But the following list might perhaps meet with general approval. In Wasemi, Yaru; Tugiri, Kabebe; Yokobu, Neti; Kesi, Yaru; Keseki, Aibore.

The now-accepted word in the Kutubu language for "chief" is *gi-aba*; but it is only a few years old. It is allegedly an importation from Foi, and dates from the time when Mr. Claude Champion arrived at the lake accompanied by some natives from that district (my informants assured me that they were "Village Policemen", though I do not know whether Foi yet boasts any such officers). When Mr. Champion was selecting the site for the camp near Tugiri, these Foi men introduced Kabebe as the *gi-aba* of that village; and since then, with the sanction of the armed constabulary to back it, the word has established itself firmly in the local language. It was not till I went to the Mubi that I learned that it was bad Kutubuan.

Gi-aba[6] should mean "land-father," i.e. land-owner. But the

Kutubu (as well as Mubi) phrase is *gi-gamma*, as the principal land-owner of Herebu told me with every sign of irritation. Either word, *aba* or *gamma*, may stand for "owner." You may say *oro-gamma*, owner of a bamboo clump; *nemi-aba*, *kesaba*, owner of pig or house; but not *gi-aba*. It happens to be unidiomatic.

Apart from the trivial question of form it is of more consequence to note that the literal meaning of the word does not make it solely applicable to the "village chief." While he is probably the largest land-owner in the community he is still only one of many; for the land is divided up among the various clans of the village, and, further still, among the families that make up the clans; and the senior male of each family is *ipso facto* a *gi-gamma* (or *gi-aba*).

There is a better term for "chief" available, *kabe-ga*, which means "the man (*kabe*) at the base" (I have met the word *ga* in several other connections: *usane-ga* is the principal in the *usanehabu*, the feast with drums and dancing; a sorcerer is *yekako-ga*, a man who deals in *yekako*—the source of the trouble, so to speak). And the *kabe-ga* is properly the leading male descendant in the direct patrilineal line of that clan which claims to be the first established in the village. The common mode of succession is from elder brother to younger brother, or brothers, and then back to the son of the eldest, who becomes known as the *kabe-ga* as soon as he is old and important enough to supplant the "ruling" uncle. There is of course nothing like a formal take-over, and that is one of the reasons why an ordinary villager is sometimes at a loss to say who is the real chief at any given time. Kabebe, man of about thirty-five, is by common consent the *kabe-ga* of Tugiri. His predecessor, Eraga, an old man now, has given place to him or perhaps rather faded into the background. Both belong to Paremahugu, the basic clan of the village, as did also the sequence of six *kabe-ga* (which is as far as present memory goes) who went before them.

A village chief is treated with some respect, though there is nothing to distinguish him in his personal appearance. The most strikingly authoritative in his manner that I met was Heno of Herebu, who was unmistakably the first man of his village. Others are not so easy to pick out, much of course depending on personality; but they all act for the community in various ways, providing in their persons a sort of focus for its will. The *kabe-ga* is said to give the word for the building of a new *aa*, or for an *usanehabu*; he will be personally approached by a war party requiring allies, or by a man who wishes to marry off his son (when he will probably contribute generously to the bride-price which the whole village gets together). When a member of his *aa* dies he will kill a pig, if he has one (expecting, of course, to be able to dispose a good deal of it for *bari*), and will contribute to the gift which the deceased's kinsmen must make to his maternal uncle. He also entertains visitors and sponsors immigrants, receiving from them a gift of ornaments, called *asaigabu-hafinibu* because they are laid out on his *asaigabu*, or sleeping-place. He will probably give such an immigrant some land, since as *gigamma* of the original clan, he nominally has far more of it than anyone else.

Altogether chieftainship conforms to the common Papuan pattern—the notion of an office and its functions being rather vague, but some individual being nevertheless recognized, by right of succession, as leader and spokesman.

Amindoba Clans

The subdivisions of the floor space in the *aa* would be expected at first glance to give some clue to a further social organization. But a painstaking examination conducted on these lines gave negative results. It was not perhaps a waste of labour to discover that the hearths are occupied at haphazard. There is no position of honour; the sleeping places belong to their occupants by right of usage, but their allocation seems just to have happened.

A further organization, however, over and above that of mere local grouping, is not wanting. This consists of a lineal grouping into units called *amindoba* which we may speak of as clans. While it is found that the *amindoba* are largely localized, the division still cuts right across village, tribe and people; that is to say, you may find representatives of one and the same clan in Kutubu, Mubi and Fimaga.

The word *amindoba* is fairly obviously a blend of *amina* (man) and *dobo*—which I cannot translate. The actual names of the several clans almost invariably end in *-dobo*, e.g. Orodobo, Kwidobo, etc., so that *dobo* may itself mean "clan," though I never succeeded in getting any informant to say so. *Amindoba* is spelt with a final *a* for the simple reason that I always heard it pronounced that way. (Two of the clan names end in *-hugu*, whatever that may mean. Informants said that in these cases the termination *-dobo* would sound ridiculous.)

The distribution, covering five Kutubu, two Mubi, and two Fimaga villages, is shown in the accompanying table (p. 208).

In all there are twenty-four, twenty-one being found in the Kutubu villages, only eight in the Mubi villages, and only five in those of Fimaga—which points again to the composite nature of the lake population which has apparently received many immigrants from different parts.

The most widely distributed clans it will be seen are Momahugu

Amindoba.	Wa-semi.	Tu-giri.	Yo-kobu.	Kesi.	Ke-siki.	Boru-tage.	He-rebu.	Fi-maga.
Orodobo	x				x	x		x
Kabuge	x							
Sogonidobo	x					x		
Sarigi	x							
Sanumahia	x		x					
Ekadabo	x			x	x			x
Kwidobo	x	x			x	x	x	
Paremahugu	x	x						
Momahugu		x	x	x	x		x	x
Tirifadobo		x	x					
Waru Serigi		x			x			
Kesadobo		x	x					
Hainyadobo (Aidobo)		x	x		x		x	
Komondobo		x				x		
Keruduri		x						
Baiari			x					
Iwa			x					
Aio			x					
Yarubi			x					
Haginama			x					
Soarigebu			x					
Kibidobo							x	x
Weidobo								x
Suidobo						x		
24	**8**	**9**	**11**	**2**	**6**	**5**	**4**	**5**

(six villages), Kwidobo (five), Orodobu and Ekadobo (four each). It is worth noting that the clans represented only in one village apiece are found mainly in the three largest communities, where migration from Kaibu and Fasu has been commonest. It is to be assumed that a parallel organization into clans obtains in these two localities.

Membership of the *amindoba* is determined by patrilineal descent. It has always been my experience to find that such rules of determination are subject to exception, but here the exceptions seem comparatively rare. Although deliberately seeking them, I have but one instance in which the children had been absorbed into their maternal uncle's clan (a case of orphans brought up in their widowed mother's village). The other exceptions are provided by cases of immigration, where solitary individuals (probably flying from their homes because of some quarrel) are content to be absorbed into the clan of the man who gives them hospitality. Even so they are by no means always ready to give up their old affinities. Arisa at a late stage of my investigations, when the general scheme of clan organization seemed clear, staggered me by saying that some men, himself included, belonged to two *amindoba*. His own case-history made the matter plain, however. His grand-father, Gunagi, was a Hainyadobu man of Fasu who settled in Wasemi, living with Kagerogo of the Paremahugu clan. This man's son, Pumena, brought up by Kagerogo, came to be spoken of as Paremaguhu; and Pumena's son, viz. my informant, also. He belonged to one clan by descent and the other by virtue of absorption, and maintained his loyalty to both.

Totems

The *amindoba* is exogamous (though some cases show that the prohibition need not stand when the parties belong to different ribes) and it possesses a series of totems, a major (sometimes eponymous) totem and half a dozen subsidiary ones. The four *amindoba* of Herebu are given as examples. Kwidibo; *Kwi* (sago) together with *tombi* (a banana), *mare* (a banana), *yakabo* (a bird), *yataso* (a bird), *tawa* (wallaby), *wasago* (a fish) : Momahugu; *yakwai* (bird of paradise) together with *dameni-hua* (a bird), *savesigiri* (a bird), *kamogu gurinobo* (a cuscus), *agira tabura* (red sweet potato), *magi senaga* (a sugar-cane), *tugaro* (a bean), *gakana* (a "cabbage"), *gari* (prawn), *nafa* (a fish); Kibidobo; *patamu* (a kind of tree) together with *eka* (a taro), *baragi* (a cucumber), *hamano* (a yam), *agira siakaro* (white sweet potato), *eraro* (a banana), *irihuba* (a fish), *tai* (a bird) *kumaka* (rock-dwelling marsupial): Hainyadobo; *hainya* (a "cabbage") together with *hiwi* (wild edible plant), *bako* (small burrowing marsupial), *tabura hua* (scrub hen), *barubami* (a fish), *isakami* (red prawn).

Lists from the other villages show that each clan has a similar array of totems. But the situation, as far as the minor ones are concerned, is not devoid of confusion. Some species appear more than once, claimed as totems by different clans; and one and the same clan, as represented in several villages, may prove to have a very variable list. It is evident that certain clans have subdivided, as in the case of Momahugu, which admits two branches, associated respectively with *yakwai* (bird of paradise) and *piaka* (black palm). This process has no doubt been a common one though it is beyond the scope of living memory to trace the subdivision to its source. By the same token it is to be assumed that certain clans would possess mutual affinities, the twenty-two of them sorting themselves into a few major groups. But, although some of my older informants addressed themselves to this problem very seriously, they never succeeded in reaching agreement, nor could they agree as to which was the original clan, or place them in any accepted order of priority. Such questions are obviously of no practical importance to them, and cannot be of much to us.

The main totems, in all cases examined, proved to be regarded as ancestors. Any clan, in any village, will be able to count back the ancestors of its local leader for half a dozen generations, the last of them being the totem itself. Thus for Kwi-dobo ("Sago Clan") Heno of Herebu gives the following: himself, son of Korabe, son of Orove, son of Wabirabo, son of Eregasai, son of Karoba, son of Foreabe, who was born from a sago shoot. For Orodobo ("Rattan-cane Clan") Nekinagu counts back six generations to Unubu (the 7th) which is a flying-fox. (One of many hanging head-down in a cave gave birth to a human child. This was the connection in which Neginagu swore by his beard, as mentioned above.) Similarly the first Ekadobu was born from a kind of taro called *eka*, the first Paremahugu man from the egg of a hawk, *parema*, and so on.

More significant perhaps is the fact that informants are always ready to name the place in which this miraculous birth took place or at least to ascribe a local origin to their own clans. While there is no lack of disagreement among informants of different villages in respect of one and the same clan, it seems quite likely that the clans themselves did have a local origin. The places named, however, are often obscure hills, etc., which it is impossible to place on the map. The fact that versions are so often at variance merely indicates that informants know only the traditional birthplace of the branches they happen to represent.

It is very difficult to allot any meaning or function to the totems, main or subsidiary. They are subject to no kind of taboo,[7] nor is there anything monopolistic about them. A member of the Yakwai branch of the Momahugu clan may kill a bird of paradise, eat it, and wear its feathers, and so may the members of every other clan. Despite vigorous pumping I was never able to obtain any hint that the clan members exercised any magical control over their totem species. The attitude, practical and emotional, seems to be one of indifference. Asked what he *did* about sago (*kwi*), a prominent member of the Kwidobo clan answered, "I eat it!"

Altogether I have been able to discover only two real uses of the totems, and they are not very important. Both show that it is regarded as a distinguishing mark or means of recognition.[8]

Firstly, it is a recognized practice to leave a piece of your totem, after the style of a visiting card, to show that you have done something or been somewhere. In this capacity it is called *senega*. Thus, quoting an informant's hypothetical instance, if you take a piece of meat as a present to a man in his garden-house and find it unoccupied, you hang the meat up and leave your *senega* in some conspicuous place near it. Then he knows whom he has to thank. Or, if you help yourself to a friend's bananas, sweet potatoes, sugar-cane, or pandanus, you tie some leaves together nearby to attract his attention and affix your *senega* so that he will know that it is not theft but a mere friendly act of appropriation. An Orodobo man leaves a piece of bamboo-leaf; Hainyadobo, a piece of *hainya* leaf; Suidobu, a piece of split cane. Obviously this is not a very complete address; but the recipient is supposed to put two and two together and guess correctly which individual among the various possibilities has left the message. The *senega*, it is said, may be one of the minor totems as well. If an Ekadobu man could not lay his hands on a piece of taro leaf, he might leave instead a cockatoo feather.

The other use of the totem as a sign is in the fantastic method of divination known as *fifiri-di-fakabu*, which will be described later. It is the fragment of his totem discovered on the chest of the corpse that reveals the *amindoba* of the sorcerer.

The Family

The relationship of prime importance in Kutubu society is clearly that between father and son, and I have nowhere else seen such marked evidence of close association between the two. After perhaps two years—no doubt highly important ones in the formative sense—during which the little boy sleeps with his mother in the *kanya*, he passes into the charge of his father, and, for the rest of his boyhood, seems to go with him everywhere. Little sons are treated with obvious affection, and literally cling to their fathers' aprons. Tosabo of Borutage, undoubtedly the fiercest spirit I met in the Kutubu district, brought both his little sons with him when he visited the police camp and was at pains to show them round, disregarding all others while he did so. He spent much time peering through the high fence of the fowlyard and showing the two small boys the strange birds which they had not seen before. I noted many cases of father-and-son inseparables.

The practice of adoption (*karinibu*) is common. In Wesemi, Tugiri and Yokobu, the sons of immigrants who have died are found in many cases to have adoptive fathers among the villagers, and any man who is without male issue may undertake the responsibility. Kabebe, the *kabe-ga* of Tugiri, had adopted his *kabusi* (wife's younger brother), not a very likely-looking boy, but as constant in his attendance as if he had been a true son.

There being no regular puberty seclusion and no formal transition from boyhood to manhood, the younger generation mix freely with their elders from the beginning. It is noteworthy that quite small boys will accompany a hunting expedition, which is unquestionably an arduous undertaking. They have free access to the men's house at all times exept during an *Usi* ceremony, to which they are allowed admittance only if they are already initiated. While still very young they sleep with their fathers; later on two or three lads will be found sharing a hearth.

Daughters sleep in the *kanya* with their mothers, who are, if possible, still more exclusively attached to them. This report deals mostly with the male side of Kutubu society and I am not in a position to say much about the lives of the females, young or old. But it is obvious that from the beginning daughters are accustomed to the highly restricted life of their sex. In the morning they go off with their mothers, and just as closely hooded, to the gardens or sago-swamps; and when they return at evening they immediately make for the *kanya*. I hardly ever saw any of them at play with boys of their own age. I am prepared to believe that they are really more prominent in village life than actually appeared (the smaller girls remained somewhat scared of me throughout, which probably cramped their usual style); but there is no doubt that they are schooled from infancy to occupy a position of retirement.

Status of Woman

The status of women is undeniably low. As in so many Papuan societies there is a marked separation of masculine and feminine interests, typified by the men's house to which women are denied entry except on certain specified occasions. At an *usanehabu* (which I did not have the luck to see) they are said to throng the two sides of the interior, dressed in their poor best, while they watch the male dancers. They may hold dry bamboo torches for a better view, and the young men's glances, flashing in the red light, are said to fascinate the girls into eventual matrimony. The other occasion on which females are allowed in the men's house is the funeral, when they appear in a very different mood, dim, hooded figures crouched about the corpse and wailing—both sight and sound impressively dismal.

As a strange exception to the rule of seclusion I used to see a charming little girl named Yegiame, three or four years old, running freely about the *aa* of Herebu. She was the daughter of Aranobo who was taking charge of her while her mother was away for several days at sago-making. A very intelligent, if silent, little girl, she would go at her father's bidding to fetch things from his sleeping place as if she knew all about the interior of the *aa*. It was said that it did not matter that she should have the freedom of the place as she was so young; but later on it would not be allowable. It might seem, then, that this was a permissible practice, though it must at least be a very rare one. It may be noted incidentally that there are ordinarily no secret objects in the *aa* to be specially hidden from women's view.

Women are the principal food-getters, because they do most of the work in making sago, which is the principal food. Men cut down the palms and prize off the bark; the rest of the business— scraping out the pith, beating it, and carrying home the sago starch —belongs to the women, and takes much longer. In the gardens men fell or ringbark the trees and make the fences. Women clear the undergrowth, do all the planting, and give the growing garden whatever subsequent attention it receives. They carry the loads; they feed and tend the pigs; they look after the babies; they fetch most of the wood and water; and they do most of the cooking. For creative tasks they have bark-cloth beating and a monopoly of string-work.

As for men, over and above their share in sago-making and gardening, they do all the building; they make canoes and paddles; they hunt; they fight; and they make wooden dishes, fish-traps, axe-handles and weapons. While the tasks which they specially perform are those which require a higher degree of strength and daring, they are by and large the more interesting and less incessant. It is often said that native women carry the loads, so that their husbands, free and unencumbered, may be in a better position to meet sudden attack from enemies. It is my general impression that the typical division of labour in primitive societies is largely attributable to quite other motives: the women, as weaker vessels, are given the drudgery; and they certainly have much less leisure. However, it must be said that they mostly do their work very willingly.

It is in keeping with their generally low status that Kutubu women should own very little property. Their alleged ownership of pigs we have already dismissed as a fiction. The same would hold good regarding their alleged ownership of the plants in their gardens. But about land, sago-palms, and trees there is not even a fiction: it is clearly stated by informants of both sexes that these belong to males only; and I could discover no case in which they were inherited by females. Girls "cut bamboos" from the clumps of their fathers; women from those of their husbands; and this expression may be taken to stand for all their claims on the land.

It is only in respect of their personal belongings, feminine things, that their right of ownership is undisputed—*kou* and *area* bags, mats (*asagabu*), string-skirts (*hau*), and a few others. Even shell ornaments, which they wear frequently enough, are nearly always said to belong to the men. Thus of four women who provided me with an interesting session at Herebu two said outright that theirs belonged to their husbands; one, who wore a big pearlshell and a string of cowries, said that the former belonged to her husband, the latter to her son; and the fourth, a widow, said that her sons owned everything she had. It is as if the women were caretakers, the ornaments being perhaps safer on their necks than anywhere else. At the same time, it is admitted that the caretakers are sometimes reluctant to give up the goods entrusted to them and I came across one case, incidentally, in which a woman had been guilty of appropriation. A faction fight involving the whole *aa* had arisen over the question of a bride-price, a perennial source of strife. Dagi had brought up his wife's two younger sisters, Diaso and Genumaka. The latter had been bespoken by Terebore as a bride for his younger brother, and Terebore had given some *bari* as part of the preliminary payment (*yegigibu*). When it came to the major payment (*bunuka*) Dagi alleged he had never received the item in question. Terebore, righteously angry, said he was lying, and matters led up to a fight in which partisans were involved on both sides. When they had fought it out, they found that the *bari* in dispute had actually been given to the elder sister, Diaso, for transmission to her foster-father but had never reached him because she had been overcome by the temptation to keep it. This example is enough to show that such valuables may sometimes be virtually in the possession of women, though it is plain that the contrary holds good as a general rule.

The fact that women are expected to work hard for their masters is best demonstrated by the exceptions: they occasionally protest, and protest may be met with a beating The further fact that for the most part they readily acquiesce in their duties is indicated by the fortunate rareness of such interludes. I did not have the luck, anthropologically speaking, to witness a wife-beating, but give a few remembered cases. Sometimes they have their cause in some disagreement of a casual nature. Yarimi, the second of Heno's four surviving wives (he has had six) once earned a beating because she differed with her husband regarding the procedure in clearing a garden: she went on gathering the rubbish when he had told her to begin burning. Another woman had left her baby in the house while she was catching the pig at sundown; the child fell into the fire and scorched its arm, whereupon the husband thrashed his wife for negligence. These are merely examples of husbandly exasperation, justifiable or unjustifiable. But the great majority of beatings are due to imputed laziness. Yarimi, above referred to, remembered two other occasions. On one of them,

returning from a day in the sago-swamps, she had been told to
hurry with the evening meal and had retorted that she was tired
and needed a rest; on the other her husband had demanded sago
and cooked palm-shoots, but she said she had been able to bring
in no more than a load of firewood. Heno had chastised her each
time. (It is interesting to note that wives appear to bear no malice:
both she and Heno found these memories amusing.) Again, Tari,
a delicate little woman, wife of the formidable Tosabo, had incurred
his displeasure and a beating for not having his food ready on
time, though she protested that her baby was ill and she was too
busy attending to it. Asked if she had resisted, she said plaintively
that it was useless, he was so big and strong, at which everyone,
herself included, went off into fits of laughter.

It is worth noting, however, that resistance is a usual feature
of these engagements, for the worm will turn and a Kutubu woman
will fight when her blood is up; the men admit in particular that
the women can make good use of their teeth. Thus Yaru of Kesi,
a redoubtable character, though I should think a fond husband, had
had occasion to chastise his wife Butia, but she had given a very
good account of herself and he showed the old scar on top of his
head as though he was proud of it. Metopo of the same village
said that she had many stand-up fights with her husband, pointing
to the field of battle—there is very little space on the rocky island
of Kesi—and the husband in question looked a little sheepish
when she declared that she had had the best of it. It is interesting
to note the case of a younger woman who was present at the time
I was asking these questions. She was not long married and exceptionally good-looking. When I asked if she had ever had a beating
she was far too shy to answer for herself, but the others said,
"Not yet: she is too young; by and by!" When husbands are
upbraiding their wives for laziness they are said to run over the
items of the bride-price in a loud voice, justifying their wrath and
putting their spouses to shame as not worth the money.

Exogamy

Marriage is subject to *amindoba* exogamy; it is patrilocal; and it is
negotiated by purchase (in two stages, the first called *yegige-gibu*,
the giving of a betrothal-price; the second, *bunuka-gibu*, the giving
of the bride-price).

The exogamy of the paternal *amindoba* clan is insisted on as a
rule, and among all the cases examined I found not one exception.
The prohibition extends to the *amindoba* of the mother also, and
here I discovered only two exceptions.

The reasons alleged against marriage with a girl of one's own

clan are, first, that she is an *ana*, or "sister"—which merely amounts
to a restatement of the case; the second, that such a marriage
would keep the bride-price within the *amindoba*, as if the clan
should be paying itself. It is not to be supposed that the bride-price,
which we shall discuss more fully later on, is divided among all
the members of the girl's *amindoba*, wherever they are living; it is,
on the contrary, given to the local or tribal representatives of the
clan, who form a group of patrilineal kinsmen. So the second
argument will not stand in the way of marriage within the clan
provided the girl comes from a distance, e.g. from another tribe:
and this, indeed, is admitted to be permissible in theory. But if the
girl belonged to the group of *amindoba* kinsmen who would normally
assist in getting together the bride-price on behalf of the husband,
then it would amount merely to shuffling the valuables among its
members: the paying of a bride-price seems to be a matter of
importance in itself, and under these conditions it would lose
much of its point.

In the normal instance, when the rule of exogamy is obeyed,
there are four clans involved. On the one side the bride-price
(*bunuka*) is got together by both paternal and maternal clans of
the groom: they are the donors. On the other side, it is divided
(in exactly equal proportions[9]) between the paternal and maternal
clans of the bride: they are the recipients.

But if the bride and bridegroom belong to the same *amindoba*
(whether on the patrilineal or matrilineal side) then the clans
involved are reduced to three, and one of them would be merely
paying itself, or making no payment at all. That a clan should be
at once liable for and entitled to payment in respect of the same girl is
regarded as absurd and as undesirable, because it would lead to
dissatisfaction and disputes about the bride-price. It is as if the
bride-price had become the matter of major importance.

I discovered only two breaches of the rule of *amindoba* exogamy.
In one of them the groom belonged to Herebu (Mubi) and the
bride to Kesiki (Kutubu) and this was excused on grounds of
distance, so that it may be dismissed. The other, however, was
declared to be "wrong." The groom belonged to the maternal clan
of the bride and one of the latter's maternal uncles was very much
annoyed because he had not received payment at all. I attacked the
problem of this particular marriage—the only one I know of that
was condemned—more than once, and the only grounds for
condemning it appeared to be that there was a hitch in the matter
of payment.

I discovered no hint of any supernatural sanction in favour of
clan exogamy, and the question of incest, and any attitude towards

it, cannot be satisfactorily discussed in the absence of acknowledged cases. When I once asked whether the unmarried were ever guilty of fornicating with members of their own clans, I was seriously assured that there was no such thing as premarital intercouse among the Kutubu people. This proves somewhat wide of the mark as a generalization, for informants, once they had loosened up, could cite many instances, not omitting those in which they had themselves been concerned. But it remains true that they seemed unable to recall any local cases of an incestuous nature. The only one they could think of happened at Kafa, which is beyond our limits (to the south-east). A youth named Nogimena had been caught in sin with his clan "sister." The matter was reported to the girl's true brother who had been very angry, fought with the culprit, and obtained from him a pig and some *bari* as compensation. It seems fairly clear that Nogimena's offence was in taking something that did not belong to him rather than in breaking a taboo. Any sort of premarital intercourse, incestuous or otherwise, would have led to similar retribution.

There is no positive regulation of marriage. Youths and maidens are fancy-free, except in so far as matrimonial arrangements have been made for them in their infancy. There is no grouping of the *amindoba* into larger exogamous groups: it is permissible to marry into any clan other than the father's or mother's. The only hint of any such grouping of clans was heard at Herebu, where some men maintained that Kibidobo should not marry Kwidobo. This alleged prohibition broke down under the weight of exceptions, and the reason why it was suggested became clear enough. The Herebu *aa* is divided almost solely between these two *amindoba*, and such is the traffic in valuables when a marriage has to be put through, all the members of the *aa* contributing or lending, that a union between Kwidobo and Kibidobo would tend once more to be a mere shuffling of possessions in the Herebu men's house. They really prefer to give their daughters in marriage elsewhere. At the same time, they do not care to send them too far, nor do the girls themselves approve of the notion. (It is largely their reluctance to go too far afield which accounts for the exceptions, which are not infrequent, to the patrilocal rule.) Mubi informants said that they liked to marry between their own three villages; and, if it is not too obvious to note, each tribe tends to constitute a regional endogamous unit.

It is suggested that we see here a compromise between two conflicting tendencies. On the one hand, there is the urge to establish contact and alliance with other groups by means of giving them your daughters in marriage—with the implication that you will receive theirs in return. This may constitute the basic reason for exogamy.[10] (Where marriage is by purchase, the bride-price comes to possess an intrinsic interest, so that the argument applies to the shell ornaments and axes as much as to the girls themselves: it is better to give them away and receive the like in return, for so you bind the other group to your own. To keep them, the brides or the bride-price, by you, would be to isolate yourselves and incidentally to forgo an activity, that of exchange—mere reciprocal transfer without economic motive—which seems, at least in Papua, to have developed an intense interest in itself.)

The other tendency, which to some extent counteracts the above, is to keep your girls at home, or at any rate maintain touch with them. It appears to be primarily a case of sentimental attachment, which is reciprocated by the girls themselves. Neither they nor their parents desire that they should sever their connection with home. So a solution is found by marrying, not *at* home, but reasonably *near* home.

Courtship

Kutubu girls, veiled as they are like harem ladies, may be very timid and retiring, but it seems they often take the initiative in proposals of marriage. The recognized time and place for the making of love matches are provided by the *usanehabu*, when girls can exchange glances with those youths who take their fancy. Once they have marked their man they adopt some indirect method of communication, often confiding, it is said, in his *karegi* (brother's wife) when they creep in beside her at night. The elder brother is probably the best man to take the action required, and in due course he notifies the youth, who I am assured always acquiesces. (I have a case in which a man rejected such a proposal, and his death, which followed soon after he had married another girl, was attributed to poisoning—the revenge of a woman scorned.) This is, of course, from verbal accounts. There are no doubt many and various ways in which youths and girls manage their courting in secret; but it may certainly be said that on the whole they see little of one another before marriage.

There is no such thing as free intercourse between the unmarried; no visiting of girls in their houses by night. If sexual intercourse between the unmarried takes place, as it sometimes does, it is without the consent of society—which is what informants mean when they say that there is no premarital intercourse.

My Kutubu informants at Augu told of successful and undetected exploits with evident pride. Fareape told how he had seduced the girl whom he eventually married. Finding her at work sago-making and ready to pack up and go home, he had stolen up and taken her stick while her back was turned. After searching for it high and low she had finally seen it poking up near the heap of sago fibres, and behind the heap found Fareape himself—an excellent joke which quite melted her heart. Girigi was proudest of his affair with a married woman in which she had played the part of temptress; she would go off into uncontrollable laughter, he said, whenever she saw him afterwards. Hemeno told of an episode of his boyhood where he had found himself sleeping alone in a garden-house while a girl slept in the other end, reserved for women. It shows (as do various legends) that the women's end of the house is not inviolable, for during the night Hameno entered it and woke the girl. She screamed and Hameno fled at once, taking refuge in a tree, where he waited till all was clear. But in the morning, it being plainly deducible that he was the offender, he was chastened by the girl's paternal uncle, and his elder brother paid over some *bari* in compensation.

This incident is typical in that it shows that philandering is not allowed free, but means punishment or compensation if the parties are found out. This is the case with unmarried, as well as married, offenders. A girl's fathers and brothers have a proprietary interest in her, and no man can enjoy her for nothing. I have recorded a number of cases in which the matter has been brought to light, and in every one of them the patrilineal kinsmen of the girl have taken action: there has been a quarrel, with or without violence; and the matter has ended either by compensation or by the payment of a bride-price and the marriage of the two concerned.

As for sex morality at large there is no reason to suppose that the Kutubu native is better or worse than others. But this at least may be said, that, while there are many individual lapses, the socially approved rules on the subject are strict. Premarital intercourse is forbidden, nor have I found evidence that licentiousness of any kind is socially condoned.

In a proportion of cases—I do not know how large—there is no preliminary courtship at all, the match having been arranged during early childhood, or at least during that of the girl. It is said that such contracts usually reach finality and turn into satisfactory marriages; but the bride-to-be may have objections, and in one recorded case at any rate she got her way. A girl named Tegemaka of Fimaga had been bespoken on behalf of Abusi by the latter's brother. When the time came to go to him she refused. Her elder brother hauled her off in the desired direction, but she first clung to the house-post, then cast herself on the ground, and was thus dragged to the landing, bundled into a canoe, and taken down

the Mubi to Tunahugu, her bridegroom's village. When she
escaped by night and made her way home to her mother, her
father sent her off again. But when she fled home a second time
he gave up and refunded the bride-price.

This was spoken of as an unusual case. Few girls are so strong-
minded in their objections, and we may suppose that, even if they
are, they seldom achieve their end. Kano, a girl of Tugiri, found
herself betrothed to Hagibu of Yokobu, a man a good deal older
than herself. Irahibu, the chief man of Yokobu, came on behalf of
Hagibu, delivered the *bunuka*, or final bride-price, which was
duly received and distributed; and Kano was taken to her husband's
village, being quartered *pro tempore* in the house of one of his relatives.
After howling lustily through the earlier part of the night she crept
out when all was quiet and slipped round the point in a canoe to
find shelter with her mother. But some days later it was arranged
that Hagibu should come and get her a second time. Her wrists
were bound, and she was carried off in a canoe as far as Yokobu,
whence, to make sure that there should be no further escape,
Hagibu conducted her, with her wrists still bound, across the
mountains to Fasu. The girl now lives with him as his wife.

The Betrothal Price

An advance payment, *yegige-gibu*, is given in order to bespeak a girl,
usually some years before actual marriage, and sometimes in her
infancy. It is much smaller than the final bride-price. In the only
case where I obtained a count of the items, it comprised seven pearlshells and five steel axes—apparently a larger payment than was
customary a few years ago before steel implements were common
at Kutubu. This payment is got together nominally by the father
and elder brothers of the bridegroom, and it is given nominally
to the father of the girl. But on both sides it is found that many
individuals, variously related to the principals, give or receive
respectively. For while payment is nominally made from one
amindoba to the other, it is the accepted thing that any and every
member of the *aa* may contribute one or more items. Such contributions are viewed as individual transactions: if A. gives B. a
pearlshell for the betrothal price of B.'s son, then, when the time
comes, B. will give A. a pearlshell for the betrothal price of A.'s son.
The getting together of the valuables on the one hand, and their
distribution on the other, are thus found to involve a number of
persons who are not directly concerned in the marriage contract.
The betrothal price above referred to was distributed among ten
people (the father kept two pearlshells for himself); and the ten

were variously classed as his *mae, kabusi, pasi, tana, abia* and *kaua* (only one of the recipients incidentally was a woman: a sister of the bride, who received an axe). These recipients were divided among five different *amindoba;* yet the payment was nominally to the *amindoba* of the bride's father only, and it was for him to distribute them as he pleased in settlement of his own obligations. It is to be noted that nothing was given to the bride's *abia*, or maternal uncles: for the rule that half the items are to be made over to the maternal clan of the girl applies only to the *bunuka*, or real bride-price. The betrothal price, a purely preliminary affair, is at the disposal of the paternal *amindoba*.

The Bride-Price

The *bunuka-gibu* takes place when the girl is virtually of a marriageable age, about fourteen years. I can give no accurate estimate of the amount of payment. It comprises pearlshells and *bari* (strings of cowries) as the main items, but also *sosere* (shell frontlets), stone axes, and one or more pigs. In these times steel axes and knives are commonly added.

Kutubu arithmetic is remarkably accurate up to a point, so that one is bound to think that the items of the bride-price may be enumerated with some care when they are actually handed over; yet I found it very difficult to get anyone to give a satisfactory account from memory. (I did not have the opportunity of seeing a *bunuka-gibu*.) Most informants clutch their fists and say they gave "five" of each kind of ornament. One man said he had given two string bags full of *bari*. And one said that he (his kinsmen for him) "had given strings of *bari* right up the left side to the nose, which was a pig." This seemingly cryptic utterance has its explanation in the Kutubu system of counting which proceeds from the little finger of the left hand, along to the thumb, thence up the arm, shoulder, and face, to the tip of the nose and down again on the other side (Fig. 11). My informant meant precisely that he gave eighteen strings of *bari* (perhaps 50 ft. in all) plus a pig; but one cannot be sure that he had not forgotten some other particulars.

A list given to me at Kesiki may be more or less correct because the transaction was a recent one and had been the subject of a dispute which might serve to imprint it in my informant's memories. A Kesiki man had married a Fimaga girl and he had been allowed to bring her to his home only under protest, the bride-price being regarded as inadequate. The Kesiki people had given their pledge to make good the deficiency but, delaying overlong, had received a message from Fimaga to the effect that a party would come to clean them up. The Kesiki people, a small community in comparison, had abandoned their village in expectation of an attack, and it was only when I arrived at Kutubu that they were beginning to occupy it again. The deficit (an axe, a pearlshell, three strings of *bari*, and a pig) had been made up and Fimaga satisfied. The total was apparently seven pearlshells, seven strings of *bari*, four shell frontlets, six steel axes, two trade knives, and three pigs.

It is generally agreed that the amount of the *bunuka* has leapt up since supplies of pearlshells, knives and axes have been brought by the Europeans (thus early is the common tendency showing itself at Kutubu); and this explains, according to the natives themselves, why Gosi, who recently married the widowed daughter of Nekinagu, paid considerably more for her as a widow (with three children) than her first husband gave for her as a girl.

The provision of the *bunuka*, like that of the betrothal price, is primarily the concern of the youth's father and his *amindoba* kinsmen (though the *amindoba* of the *abia* contributes, and things are further complicated by many private lendings from outsiders); and it is handed over to the girl's father or elder brother, or to the leading man of her *amindoba*. But unlike the betrothal-payment it is not wholly theirs to do with as they like. They always give half to her mother's *amindoba*, i.e. her *abia's* kinsmen. It is important for those about to marry to remember this element in the situation. For the bride's maternal clan will make very active protests if their share is not handed over immediately (what almost amounted to a war occurred between Herebu and Fimaga on these grounds); and if the maternal uncle is in any way dissatisfied he will take a more subtle revenge by causing his niece to be ill. This threat of sorcery seems to be a prominent factor in the life of the Kutubuans; they are vastly concerned with sickness and its cure, and whenever anyone falls ill, their first thought is "What of the *abia*?" In the present connection this supplies an argument not only for handing over its due share to the bride's maternal clan, but also for full and prompt payment to her paternal clan in the first place; for her brothers are *abia* to her prospective children.

Once again it is this notion, added to a general desire to keep on good terms, which provides the ostensible reason for the subsequent gifts to the *kabusi* (wife's brother) *kaua* (wife's father or maternal uncle) and *yumu* (wife's mother). The marriage-relatives would be likely to make one's wife and children sick if they were not placated from time to time. The consequent necessity for making the gifts supplies an excuse—as if the Kutubu native needed one—for the *kimisi* or "walk-about." They take the form of an occasional present of *bari* or of animals caught in the chase and may perhaps be regarded as extensions of the bride-price. The recipients make no return except in the way of ordinary hospitality.

It should be pointed out that the Kutubu bride-price does not involve an exchange of presents between the contracting parties, a custom which is common in many other parts of Papua. The price is paid down and the girl is delivered over: there is no return gift of shell ornaments, etc., from her people to those of the bridegroom.

The bride-price is usually handed over in the *aa* of the bride's father, though sometimes her people may go and collect it. It is laid out on the floor and scrutinized, the local women crowding inquisitively round the entrance. If it passes muster, the girl is conducted to the bridegroom's village. I am told that she is painted for the occasion, but I cannot get any hint of definite nuptial ceremonies. Since no marriage took place during my stay it was impossible to check this negative evidence, but after a good deal of pumping I am disposed to think it is true. The girl is lodged in the *kanya* of some relative of the bridegroom, e.g. his mother, his elder brother's wife, or his foster-mother, and she assists the elder woman in her daily work. Sexual relations do not commence until some time has passed—it is said that her husband waits for a private tip from the bride's temporary guardian. Then he will take her off alone in a canoe to work in the garden and the village will draw its conclusions. In these circumstances it seems we may say that child-marriage is not practised, though girls certainly marry young. Incidentally, it may be observed that at Kutubu there is no spinster problem.

Husband and Wife

The relations of wives with their husbands have been touched upon already. As far as I was able to observe they got on well together despite (or because of) the seldom-disputed mastery of the male. Polygamous wives live together in the same *kanya*. Heno's surviving four (two of whom are sisters) say they do not quarrel: and, if they did, they would be afraid to fight because it would annoy their husband. Yaro of Kesi's two admit to having had but one serious difference. It occurred when the junior of them, Bukia, complained that the senior, Muri, had not given her any of the fish she had caught. The former, a personable and jolly woman, related how she went for Muri in a rage, and in the ensuing combat, which was fought out with *kaminu* staffs before the *kanya*, was knocked over and defeated. Their husband and other men had tried to separate them, and when it was all over Muri had given her some of the fish.

Although I was assured more than once that adultery was unknown at Kutubu the cases are as numerous as elsewhere. One comes upon them incidentally. (It is easy for a native to forget a generalization and give you an exception in the next breath without connecting the two.) Sexual intercourse, both legal and illegal, takes place in the bush or the gardens; so opportunity is not very hard to find.

If anyone sees a couple *in delicto* he is instantly moved to go home and tell about them. Among a number of cases I came across only one in which the husband had divorced (*fuguwabu*) his wife as a result of her misconduct. The adulterer, named Gose, had been found out; he had been attacked in the men's house by the husband, Erebu, and had paid compensation of a pig and some ornaments to the latter's father, a man of importance, who so to speak, represented the aggrieved faction. The husband divorced his wife, and Gose refused to marry her. She went back to her brothers, who refunded Erebu's bride-price and subsequently married her off to a man of Foi. A more ordinary course was for the husband to content himself with beating his wife; but I have one case in which, the woman having gone off with her lover to live in a huntinghouse, they were tracked down by the husband and his friends and both put to death.

Other alleged grounds for bringing a marriage to an end were laziness on the part of the wife and cruelty on the part of the husband. I much doubt whether the first is ever sufficient in itself, although husbands often complain of it, justly or unjustly. Only one man actually gave it as his reason for throwing away his wife; but, as it appears that she had already shown a preference for someone else, it may be rather that she threw him away. However, he got his bride-price back and the third party paid another to her brothers.

Persistent ill-treatment by a husband may provoke the wife's brothers to interfere, though I heard of only three cases. In one of them a brother had assaulted the husband while in the act of beating the wife; this had settled itself in a conciliatory exchange of *bari* between the two men concerned, and, we may hope, a gentler mood on the part of the husband. In the second case the wife's brother, a boy, had gone so far as to poke a long stick into the door of a *kanya* where his sister was being beaten by her husband; but this interference, as much as his size and courage allowed him to make, seems only to have excited amusement. In the third, the woman, too frequently beaten, had sought refuge in her brother's village and stayed there till she married elsewhere, the original bride-price being refunded to her first husband. It is clear that thoughts of the bride-price largely govern the matter. If the brothers of the woman were sufficiently moved by their sister's plight to restore it, the husband would have to let her go. But it is to be assumed that they would show themselves very hard-hearted unless they had the prospect of marrying her to someone else and thus recouping themselves. Women have a fairly hard time, and it is evidently a husband's privilege to beat his wife if he thinks it necessary. Evidence of protective interference by her kinsmen is very hard to come by.

Remarriage of Widows

On the husband's death, however, the widow goes back to her brothers. It is emphatically stated that she never marries her deceased husband's brother, nor does his *amindoba* have any share in the payment if she marries again. This is made to her brother as representing her patrilineal kin, and half is given, in the usual way, to her matrilineal kin. Thus there is no such thing as the levirate at Kutubu, nor any recompense to the deceased husband's *amindoba* for the loss of a woman who once worked for it. The marriage contract comes to an end with the husband's death. For this, which among patrilineal organizations in Papua is rather surprising, there is ample evidence, and I have found no exceptions. The widow is certainly not allowed complete sexual freedom (though it may well be that offences are regarded more leniently than if they were girls: thus in perhaps the first "case" at Kutubu, where an armed constable was charged with indecently assaulting a woman, the complainants had said, "it is not as if she were a widow"). Native cases show that her brothers maintain a proprietary interest in her, and if anyone is discovered in misconduct with her he will have to meet their displeasure and make compensation or pay for the woman and marry her. It is thus to be noted that when a woman marries more than once her kin are paid more than once.

There is no sororate either. A man may marry his deceased wife's sister; but he has to pay for her, even if the wife whom she replaces has died soon after marriage. I have no case in which a refund of the bride-price was made on account of a bride's early death. (Cases of adelphic polygyny are not entirely rare. They would seem sometimes to have their origin in the fact that husbands may look after their wives' little sisters, perhaps orphans. I have several cases in which such a situation led to the eventual seduction of the younger girl and thus, after payment, to her formal inclusion in the household.)

Name Taboos and Avoidances

We have mentioned the gifts which a man must occasionally make
to his wife's brothers (*kabusi*) and parents (*kaua* and *yumu*). They
are accepted as proofs of the continued friendship which is recognized
as desirable. Men frequently visit their wives' villages, sometimes
living there temporarily; and, as we have seen, cases of matrilocal
marriage are not uncommon.

While association is friendly and free, however, there are certain
formal restrictions in the behaviour of relatives by marriage. Thus a
man may not use the personal names of his wife's parents (*kaua* and
yumu), nor of his wife's brother's wife (*yumu*), and in the case of the
women he must not be allowed to look them in the face. Women
on the other hand may not use the name of their husbands,
brothers (*karegi*) or husbands' sisters' husbands (*yumu*) and of
course they may not look them in the face. (It is to be noted that
women can use the names of their husband's parents and men of
their wife's brothers.) Neither man nor woman may use the spouse's
name. It is customary for them to address and speak of each other
as *ka-nao*, "my wife" or "my woman," and *kabe-nao*, "my man."
Another method is to call them "Father of ...," or "Mother
of ..." (naming their own child).

The reason for these name taboos, which are sometimes evidently
a little tiresome to the natives themselves, remains, as far as I am
concerned, a mystery. The native will tell you that it would affect
both sides concerned with shame (*tukutibu*) if a breach occurred;
but breaches can be mended by a conciliatory gift of *bari*, and
are not regarded as very grievous. Yet it is almost as bad to hear
the forbidden name spoken as to speak it oneself, and both men
and women will be seen stopping their ears with their fingers
when it crops up in conversation. The habit of covering the face
is explained similarly. Women will snatch at the *kosaka*, dragging it
across their averted faces, when their husband's brothers are near.
They would be ashamed to look at them or be seen by them.

It is to be assumed that these observances are meant rather to
preserve some proper distance between the parties concerned than
to express any existent antagonism. It might be thought, since the
people concerned are mostly of opposite sexes, that the concealment
of faces, if not the name avoidances, represented an extension of the
sex taboo; a prophylactic measure as it were. Yet it is rather striking
that, in one of the few instances of rape which I was able to collect'
the victim was no other than the offender's mother-in-law. He had
fled from the scene to confide in one of his paternal uncles (my
informant) who had squared the matter with a pearlshell and some
bari as compensation. The father-in-law and son-in-law, both

contemporary residents of Borutage, had avoided one another for
some time after the incident, but are now on speaking terms again.
A single instance is of no significance in itself; but I was rather struck
by the fact that my informants seemed indifferent to the relationship: they were recalling a case of rape and did not advert to the
special enormity, or absurdity, of raping one's mother-in-law.

It is also worth recalling the case of Dugami of Wasemi who
married a widow and brought up her little daugher in his household·
When she was old enough he began sex relations with the daughter,
and these being discovered, suffered assault at the hands of her
brothers. But they accepted payment for her and Dugami now has
for polygamous wives a mother and daughter—that is to say, his
first wife is the mother-in-law of his second. While this is the only
case of its kind in my notes, I doubt whether it is an isolated one;
and the real point is that my informants seemed to see nothing
outrageous in the situation: once the bride-price was paid over it
became regular.

In view of these cases one may be permitted to doubt whether the
avoidances between in-laws at Kutubu have anything to do with the
taboo on sex relations. It can at least be said that there is no very
strong feeling against such relations with the mother-in-law —not of
a sort that cannot be allayed by shell ornaments.

As for the name-taboos it seems obvious that sex cannot be made
to account for them, for they are in force (1) as between males, viz.,
son-in-law and father-in-law, and (2) as between husband and wife.
Further it is worth noting that, while there is no absolute prohibition,
a person is extremely reluctant to use his *abia's* name; and that he
will hardly under any inducement utter his own. The reason
alleged in these cases, however, is of a different nature: it is said to
be a question not of shame, but of fear. In the case of the
maternal uncle's name the thing is fairly plain: you do not utter it
lest you offered him, and are made ill in consequence. But the
reason for refusing to utter one's own name is a very curious one,
of which there are several versions. (It is not a matter of mere
modesty.) Most people have a living *yako*, or namesake, somewhere
or other, and there is a strange compulsory avoidance between the
two (they may not touch one another or sit down together till they
have made a formal exchange-gift of *bari*), and it is said that you
dare not utter your own name for fear the spirit of a deceased
namesake should hear you and "look up," when he would be
annoyed and punish you by sickness. There is also an extraordinary
belief (not held by, or even known to, everybody at Kutubu) that
each living person has a sort of spiritual counterpart in the sky,
whose life runs somehow parallel with us. Some thought that to

utter one's own name would be to annoy the spiritual counterpart and suffer illness in consequence. These somewhat obscure notions were the only explanations I could obtain for a practice which is deeply rooted in the mind of every Kutubuan.

It need not be assumed, of course, that precisely the same motive underlies all cases of name taboo; but we may perhaps say that the use of a personal name always implies familiarity and therefore possible disrespect; and the persons whose names are tabooed are, in any society, those to whom respect, for whatever reason, is considered specially due. The reasons for attributing respect (or not attributing it) are various; and in some cases they are plain, and in others not. It might be that a deeper study of Katubu society would make them all plain. But it is also possible that while the taboos are still practised the reasons for them are lost and gone forever, and that we must remain as ignorant of them as are the women who plug their ears and veil their faces.

The Maternal Uncle

We have noted the closeness of the personal relation between father and son; there is no doubt that in all normal cases their mutual affection is very strong, and in early years the son is essentially the father's dependent. The relation between nephew and maternal uncle (*abia*) is markedly different. There is no such thing as a rule by which the boy must live part of the time with his *abia*, though it happens often enough that the father and mother go to live for indefinite periods in the latter's village, when the boy will have some of his *abia's* society; and often, of course, father and *abia* belong to one and the same village. But in any case the boy remains in his father's charge. The *abia* has small formative influence upon him.

It would be absurd to say that a nephew never feels affection for his maternal uncle; but the attitude is best summed up in the word "respect," and there can be no doubt that the respect is tinged with apprehensiveness. It is said that one must never speak strongly to one's *abia*; and, as already noted, there is always in the back of the Kutubuan's mind the notion that his *abia* may afflict him with illness.

Among the many kinds of illness to which the Kutubuans are subject one of the commonest is *yesibu-rumu-hubu*, which means, "being struck by a *yesibu*" (or spirit of the dead). The spirit is in nine cases out of ten that of a deceased relative (e.g. father or mother) of the victim's *abia*; and the cause is some supposed affront or injury to the *abia* himself. It is he who undertakes the curative treatment, and he is paid a fee for it. The putting off of responsibility on to the spirits of the dead makes no real difference to the issue. They are supposedly avenging a wrong done to the *abia*, i.e. their son, and it is really he who is to be feared and placated.

The placation takes the form of a series of gifts, mainly of food and typically of animals caught in the hunt. There is no call for *bari* or other shell ornaments unless the *abia* is called upon to annul the work of the *yesibu*. (The particular treatment, *kehugabu*, by which he does so is described later.) But if he is not regularly supplied with lesser favours the necessity for *kehugabu* will assuredly arise. It is therefore sensible to keep on the good side of one's *abia*. One of the commonest reasons for his displeasure is a shortcoming in the bride-price for his niece.

The *abia's* ceremonial duties are very few. He does not pierce his nephew's or niece's ears and nose (which comes rather as a surprise), and he is not expected to play the part of initiator. As far as I can discover his ceremonial obligations are limited to the occasion of his nephew's or niece's funeral. (If, as must usually be the case, he has died previously, then his obligations are assumed by his son—the deceased's *kumiai*.) They consist of preparations for burial, particularly the building of the *deve*, or exposure platform, and the wrapping up and carrying out of the corpse. Needless to say these obligations are fulfilled in a more or less perfunctory manner: the *abia* and any of his kinsmen who are present bear the nominal responsibility, but they are helped by all and sundry.

On the fifth day after death, at the celebration called *kabai-yahabu*, or "thumbfeast, " the maternal uncle receives his final gift called *abia-i-gibu*, "giving to the *abia*." The father, brother or representative of the deceased's paternal kin will kill a pig. In the usual manner of Kutubu feasts the meat is virtually sold for *bari*, etc. to visitors and others, and the shell ornaments thus acquired are made over to the *abia*. This brings the relation between maternal uncle and nephew to an end. The *abia-i-gibu* is referred to as *fugubi*, "compensation," or "buying off." If it were not made it is to be assumed that the deceased's maternal kin would still find someone to punish.

Rights and Wrongs

Property

A discussion of property at Kutubu, as in most primitive settings, should begin with the question of land. As already pointed out, each village as such possesses its territory, though it is not always one contiguous area but may be found in several tracts here and there about the lake. Among a people who are obviously of somewhat mixed composition and where individuals are still prone to migrate from one village to another, it is not surprising that the ownership of outlying tracts should be involved in some confusion. But about the garden land nearer the villages, as well as the sago-swamps, which are much more important, there is no dispute. It is found that such areas are split up into a number of named tracts, and these are distributed among the *amindoba* clans which compose the village population, each probably possessing two or three which may be allocated to lesser kin-groups within them.

But the clan shares are by no means equal. Every village has its first-established, or foundation, *amindoba* (whose eldest capable male is acknowledged as the village headman); and his foundation *amindoba* probably owns by far the largest share of the village land. At Yokobu, for example, I enumerated 43 tracts, of which 27 belonged to Tirifadobo, the foundation clan, while the remainder were divided between Kesadobo, Sanumahia, Iwa, Momahugu, Soarigebu, Paiari, Aio, Hainya and Haginamo. These latter clans are said to have acquired their tracts by purchase, i.e. for pearlshells, *bari*, axes and knives, paid over by the settlers to the headman of Tirifadobo.

The term for land-owner or land-controller we have already noted —*gi-gamma*. Neti, the present headman of Yokobu, is referred to as *gi-gamma* of the village land as a whole; but each and every headman of the individual *amindoba* is also a *gi-gamma* of the land which the clan owns in particular.

In spite of this normal ownership individual gardens are by no means restricted to the tracts of their respective *amindoba*. At Yokobu the total male strength of Tirifadobo amounts to three adults and four or more boys. Tirifadobu land is far in excess of all the possible needs of this small group, and the remainder of the village population from time to time makes use of it. It is said that any man of another clan who proposed to make a garden on Tirifadobu soil would get Neti's consent ; but, on the other hand, Neti "would not be angry" if the garden were made without it. It is certainly a fact that existent gardens are found very much at haphazard, the gardener seldom being actually on his own ground. Further, when the village undertakes a common garden within one fence, all the clans will be necessarily using a tract of land which belongs to only one of them.

The sago-swamps are similarly owned by *amindoba* within the village. Where, as is often the case, they are shared between several, they are subdivided by tracks cut through them. It is not very easy for the European to recognize these boundaries—in ploughing through the unspeakable morass he may be excused for not looking very hard—and even the native may be sometimes in doubt as to the ownership of a particular tree. One of my best informants told of a dispute over a tree which was decided in his favour after he had

Kinship Terms

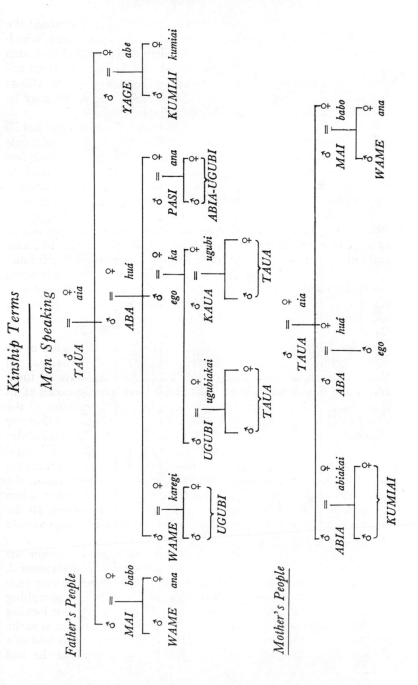

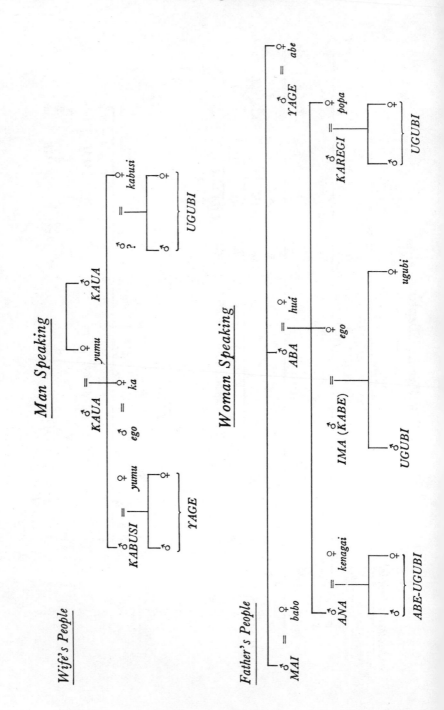

Woman Speaking

Mother's People

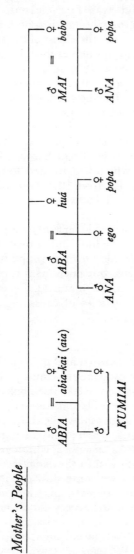

Husband's People

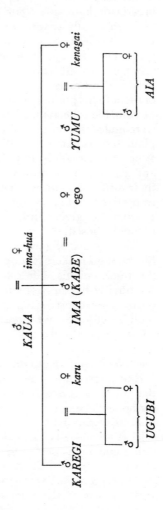

seized his adversary by the hair and downed him (one of those
relatively unusual cases in which the aggressor, though admitting he
was in the wrong, made no mention of compensation).

The sago palms themselves, as well as any trees of value growing
on the old garden sites, are personal property. Such trees (pandanus,
breadfruit, bamboos, *tigaso*, *haginamo*, etc.), have either been planted
or intentionally spared when the ground was first cleared, and
they are inherited by sons from fathers, or younger brothers from
elder. Their produce belongs to the owner, i.e. the eldest of the small
group of brothers who have inherited them; though as these brothers
grow up and marry it is customary for the eldest to make over some
of them to his juniors. Thus Irahibu received four clumps of bamboo
(a valuable inheritance) from his father. During his boyhood they
were under the control of his paternal uncle, now deceased. Irahibu
planted five clumps himself, thus becoming owner of nine altogether.
When his younger brother married he gave him two of these clumps,
and kept seven. Irahibu's two wives are entitled to cut bamboo from
their husband's clumps (i.e. from those which are allotted to them
respectively); his younger brother's wife, from the two which
Irahibu has given him, as well as from any others he may have
planted himself.

The produce of gardens is owned by the gardeners; likewise sago
by the sago-makers (though in both cases the husband appropriates
the results of his wife's work). Pigs are also owned individually
(nominally by the women who feed them, but once again really
by their husbands). The rather meagre list of material objects in
Kutubu culture—weapons, implements articles of dress, etc., are
owned individually.

Individual and Group Ownership

It is thus seen that ownership is largely individual and personal; but
that in some cases it is vested in groups, whether family, local
segment of clan, or village. We might say that the lake itself belonged
to the Kutubu tribe; there are certainly no private fishing rights or
rules of trespass. The *aa* belongs to the village as a whole. Land, in a
rough and ready sense, to the village as a whole; and in a more
particular sense to the various segments of *amindoba* which reside
in it; or again to lesser groups of kinsmen within the *amindoba*. The
same applies to the sago-swamps. When we come down to useful
trees, gardens and their produce, movable objects, pigs and dogs,
ownership is definitely individual. It would be very far from the
truth, then, to speak of Kutubu society as communistic; though
we might be justified in speaking of "communal ownership" in
certain of the connections indicated. We can at least speak of

group-ownership in these and other connections, the group being variously constituted—e.g. family, minor kin-group, clan, village or tribe. Although perhaps neither its constitution nor its rights are clearly defined, the group will reveal a strong proprietary interest when a question of ownership arises.

I should hardly hesitate to speak of Kutubu women as *owned* by their menfolk, whether husbands or kinsmen. A married woman belongs to her husband as an individual (and his kinsmen will back him up if this ownership is called in question); an unmarried girl or widow, to her patrilineal and matrilineal kin. I confess I am not able to say how far the rights of ownership are felt to extend within these groups; in practice the *bunuka* goes nominally to the immediate family on both sides, but it is fairly widely distributed. And once again, if there is defalcation, the kin at large may be literally up in arms.

Theft

Stealing is probably not very common. There are no means of locking up one's chattels, and there seems to be little attempt to hide them. A man's more precious possessions, e.g. his ornaments, may be wrapped up and put away in a corner of his wife's *kanya* (they are often worn by his wife about her neck, apparently for safe keeping); but various of his belongings are simply stuck about in the wall behind his sleeping place in the *aa*, where they are on view and unprotected. Altogether it is rather hard to come by examples of theft. The commonest would certainly be thefts from the garden—of a bunch of bananas or a few stems of sugar-cane; I have several cases of theft of sago or other prepared food; and several—much more serious—of theft of pigs, the animal being killed and eaten on the sly.

But, if we are justified in viewing women as the property of their menfolk, we may add to the cases of theft by including among them offences against sexual morality. It has been pointed out that all extramarital intercourse is against the law. A man who thus misconducts himself with another's wife is enjoying what are supposed to be that other's exclusive privileges; and if he misconducts himself with an unmarried girl or widow, he is seizing a right for which he has made no recompense. That is to say, a woman's sexual favours, whether to enjoy or to dispose of, belong to her menfolk, and extramarital intercourse is tantamount to theft.

It would be possible without any great stretch to place a similar construction on murder, that is if we laid sufficient stress on the spirit which holds together the group (however constituted) of which the victim is a member. The loss of a man, whether killed outright or supposedly killed by sorcery, has a marked effect on the group's solidarity and it might be maintained that its surviving members feel that they have, so to speak, been robbed of a man. Without being too insistent on the analogy of theft, we may at least say that murder (or imputed murder) is viewed by the group of the victim as an attack on its integrity. It is only on some such assumption, I think, that we can understand the primitive insistence on collective revenge.

Primitive Wrongs and their Redress

Without expounding the notion at any length in this place, it is submitted that nearly all wrong acts in a society as primitive as that of Kutubu, are wrongs against some particular party—individual or group; and further that they are committed especially against individuals or groups external to the group to which the wrong-doer himself belongs. There is nearly always an inner group of some sort whose sympathies will lie with the wrong-doer, and a similar group who will take up the cause of the person or persons wronged. It is not often that an individual commits a wrong against his group as a whole: his wrong usually consists in *infringing the rights* of another individual or of some of other group.

Thus not only theft but sexual offences and murder itself are wrong only because they involve an infringement of other's rights. There is of course no notion of intrinsic wrongfulness in sexual intercourse; but unless legalized by marriage, which entails direct payment, it is an offence against the woman's owners, who either use her or dispose of her, i.e. an infringement of their property rights. Similarly it would appear that the taking of human life becomes a wrong and calls for punishment only when there is some group of sympathisers to take offence and action. Thus infanticide, which is alleged to be common and of which I recorded five cases (all of children born in matrimony) was dismissed as entirely guiltless. It is not so much that the infant child is a worthless little object, but that there is nobody to take its part. If an outsider killed it, the case would be very different: it would become murder, an attack on the integrity of the family, and it would assuredly be a case for revenge.

Owing to the sentimental bond which unites the individuals of the group, however constituted, and makes so strongly for solidarity, even the wrongs done by individuals against individuals tend to embroil sympathizers and supporters on either side, so that the case becomes typically one of group *versus* group—family against family, village against village, tribe against tribe. But even if the reaction to a wrong comes to involve the whole community, we do not commonly find the community acting as a whole against the offender. It is rather split by rival sympathies. So that, however many may participate, it is still a case of a quarrel rather than a judgment. That is to say primitive wrongs come mostly under the definition of civil wrongs. Notions of crime and criminal justice belong typically to a more advanced culture.

What then are the means of setting these wrongs to rights? In the general absence of any conception of criminal justice the wronged party (with the aid of its supporters) is left to look after itself; and the means adopted is, in a word, that of *redress*. Now, while primitive wrongs appear usually to involve some infringement of rights— whether of property, privilege or status—and thus call for some measurable form of redress, e.g. restitution or reinstatement, it is important to bear in mind also their psychological aspect. It seems that they usually evoke a more or less strong emotional reaction—one of indignation with, perhaps invariably a latent sense of humiliation. The self-esteem of the victim is injured; he has been put upon. And this in itself cries out for redress also.

In view of the importance of the psychological aspect one might go so far as to say that all wrongs in such a society as Kutubu were, first and foremost, *affronts*. Whether or no they can be said to involve any infringement of right, they at least involve some injury to feelings; and as such they demand psychological redress over and above any reparation that may be made for more concrete damage. Punitive action, therefore, is inspired, not by a desire to maintain and enforce the law, but by an insistence or rights, reinforced by vengefulness. It is a case of restoring the material and psychological balance, perhaps with a bit extra; of "getting back on" the offender.

Compensation

Cases of compensation, or *fugubi*, are constantly turning up in the affairs of Kutubu. They range from those small conciliatory gifts made to fathers-in-law, which somehow enable the latter to save face when their sons-in-law have uttered their names, to very considerable payments by way of compounding for murder.

Fugubi is much in evidence in connection with sexual misdemeanours, which, as we have seen, are closely akin to theft, but where the harm done is presumably no more than psychological. It is the owners of the women concerned who are considered to suffer the harm, and who consequently receive the compensation. They are jealous of their rights, and their feelings have to be salved. To take a thoroughly typical case of adultery—Tawabi, cruising round alone in his canoe and spearing fish, lands at his garden whither his wife has gone earlier in order to work. He surprises her there in adultery with Kasagarira, who does not stay to endure the husband's reprobations

but leaves the scene as quickly as possible. Tawabi stays long enough
to give his wife a thrashing; then returns to the men's house, where
later in the day, the culprit having come home, he assaults him with
a quarter-staff. Kasagarira, although plainly in the wrong, is not
without supporters, and the thing turns into a faction fight. It is often
suggested that in such fights the right will prevail, and in the present
case this is what happens. Kasagarira and his supporters are worsted
and "driven into the water." And subsequently the adulterer pays
the husband a *fugubi* of some ornaments and a pig. The wife is not
divorced.

Intercourse with unmarried girls is equally regarded as misconduct, but the *fugubi* then goes to their fathers and brothers. What
must be a somewhat unusual case is worth mentioning, the compensation (a retrospective one) having gone to the man whom the girl in
the case subsequently married. She had carried on a clandestine
affair with a youth named Serekwi, and from some motive of her
own felt bound to make a clean breast of it to her young husband
(allegedly because she expected that the lover would visit her again
and she wished to avoid a scene). Her husband forgave her, but
vented his indignation upon Serekwi. He demanded a pig in compensation and received it—a plain case of damages for injured feelings.

Even rape seems to be viewed as a wrong solely against the
victim's owners. In the few cases that I was able to discover, the
feelings of the woman did not evoke any compassionate comment,
and in one of them, so far from sympathizing, the husband by way of
an outlet for his emotion actually debated the idea of killing her.
The story was told to me in some detail by Arisa. He had been
engaged with four men in the bush, hollowing a dugout canoe. One
of them, a bachelor named Sigiba, had left his companions in order
to procure some sugar-cane in a garden, and rather surprised them
by his long absence. The explanation was that he had chanced upon
the woman Murimu fishing in a small creek, had crept up behind,
seized her, possessed her, and left her screaming while he fled into
the bush. Murimu ran to her village and informed her husband, who
was thrown into a state of distress so violent as to verge on the comic
—at least my informants seem to remember it in that light. He rolled
himself in the mud, and thus smothered from head to foot, gave out
that he would kill the unhappy woman except that he was sorry for
his children. In the meantime Suguba's brother brought forward
some ornaments and a pig as compensation; the husband cooled
down; and eventually Suguba himself ventured back and the
episode was closed.

I have recorded several cases in which compensation has been
obtained for a false accusation. Siwi, now one of the older men of

Wasemi, had been accused of rape by the wife of Kakate, a fellow villager. Kakate charged him with the offence; Siwi denied it; Kakate assaulted him; and almost the whole of Wasemi became involved in the subsequent brawl. When Siwi's side won, dispersing their opponents with the *kaminu*, Kakate withdrew the charge and gave as compensation two pearlshells and a small pig. Another case was that of my hard-bitten friend Fareape who successfully (though with doubtful honesty) rebutted a charge of theft and received two strings of *bari* as damages for libel.

It is seen that *fugubi*, which is such a common means of righting wrongs at Kutubu, may be applied in all sorts of cases, serious and trivial, and is as much in point for purely psychological as for material wrongs. Its use is of course wholly in keeping with the view that law cases in this culture are essentially civil cases.

Retaliation

But not every case is settled by this peaceful means. There is the alternative of retaliation or revenge, which is equally a means of redressing the balance, with or without something extra.

Compensation may succeed in forestalling revenge, even for murder. A Herebu man married to a Wage woman murdered her by repeatedly jumping on her in a rage because she refused to grant him his marital rights. He fled, but would not have escaped vengeance unless he had squared the matter off by a heavy payment of four pearlshells, two axes, and two pigs to her brothers. Another man who had accidentally poisoned his wife and children (or was supposed to have done so) made immediate payment to her father, brothers, and maternal kin and thus escaped any further penalty. Similarly imputed acts of sorcery may be compounded. A man who is accused may judge it expedient to pretend he is guilty rather than face the consequences of a denial.

But the offender, or his kinsmen for him, must be fairly prompt either in offering compensation or in acceding to the demand for it; for violent retaliation on the part of the victim is a very natural reaction at Kutubu, and it does not always wait on any discussion of *fugubi*. It is very common for the fight to come first and the compensation after.

It would seem that violent quarrels are of fairly frequent occurrence, though I certainly saw none during my four months stay in the district. While it may happen that both parties to the quarrel think they are in the right, it must also happen frequently that one side knows it is in the wrong; and where this is the case that side starts under some moral disadvantage. There is an apparent belief (and I have heard it openly expressed by some) that in such a

combat the right will win out. Certainly there is a tendency to
conclude that the side which loses must after all have been in the
wrong—witness the case of Heno of Herebu,[11] where, in view of his
reputed ill-success, it is generally thought that he *was* really guilty
of the supposed act of sorcery with which the feud began.

Among a number of slighter cases which lend support to this
notion I give that of the old man Aragai of Hegisu. The Borutage
people had been giving some feast to which Hegisu was invited.
Chief among the food items was a python which was, in the usual
way, cooked, cut up into sections, and distributed among all the
important men present. Kanya, a Borutage man, had put his share
aside, but when, at the end of the day, the guests had dispersed, he
found that his section of cooked snake had disappeared with them.
A piece of meat is a thing worth making a fuss about, and an accusation was brought against Aragai of Hegisu. Aragai saw fit to deny it,
and Hegisu, highly indignant, went in a body to Borutage armed
with their *kaminu.* An exchange of recriminations turned into a first-
class *yaka-enibu* in which the visitors were badly beaten. They
returned home thinking that their man was a thief after all—an
impression which Aragai subsequently confirmed by admitting it.[12]
While there is, of course, no such thing as trial by combat, there are
many indications, such as this, that the issue of a combat is felt to
show where the right lies. One of the reasons, therefore, for refrain-
ing from wrongdoing is said to be simply the fear of a quarrel; for
one thing quarrels are deprecated in themselves; for another it is
perhaps felt that the odds will be against the offender.

Collective Revenge

For minor offences such as theft and adultery, voilent retaliation
takes a comparatively mild form. As a rule such offences occur near
home, so to speak, probably among fellow villagers; and in these
circumstances it is not customary to resort to killing methods. It is a
matter of bare fists or quarter-staffs. But when a man dies, the
retaliation meted out by his group is in keeping with the nature of
the offence, or implied offence. Apart from cases of out-and-out
murder by violence there is the ever-present suspicion of sorcery.
For here as elsewhere there is usually somebody who thinks that the
death of his friend or kinsman is due to this cause, and there are
always many ready to accept his belief and join him in seeking
revenge, which is nothing less than a life for a life.

Where sorcery is suspected the vengeance of the damaged group
may take effect in an expedition in which a whole village, or perhaps
several villages, combine to kill the supposed sorcerer. The work is
carried out in a very deliberate manner, so that for this kind of

collective revenge which is so striking a feature of Kutubu life we may fitly use the expression "judicial murder."

Several examples, in the briefest form, are given here; another, in more detail, is reserved for the chapter on sorcery. Several points—appearing in some, but not all, of the cases dealt with—may be noted in advance: (*a*) the payment of a compensation or indemnity to the alleged sorcerer's group after the action has been carried out; (*b*) the fact that the revenge expedition is an extra-tribal affair; and (*c*) the acquiescence, real or apparent, on the part of the alleged sorcerer's group in the justice of the punishment.

The examples are as follows: (1) Fae, of Kara, died, and Kadanu of the Mubi tribe was accused of sorcery (Kadanu was supposed to have intrigued with Fae's wife and to have put him out of the way in order that he might marry her). An expedition from Lake Kutubu went to the Mubi to kill Kadanu. They intimated their intention to some of the Mubi people who were likely to be found in company with Kadanu, and these are said to have left him to his fate, saying it was "his fault" and a fair thing. The avengers found Kadanu alone in a house, being confined there by an injury to his foot. He fled at their approach and jumped into the river but was overtaken, speared in the back by a man of Wasemi, and killed. Others of the Mubi tribe were far from acquiescing in the justice of the killing, but there was apparently no attempt at reprisal. I did not ascertain whether an indemnification was made.

(2) Sigina of Kesi died, and Kasuabe of the Mubi tribe was accused of sorcery. (It was alleged that Kasuabe had actually admitted bewitching him for the surprising and surely inadequate reason that he was "so good-looking"—which may however imply some occasion for sexual jealousy. Sigina had not long previously been on a visit to the Mubi.) Word was sent by the avengers in advance, saying that they were only after Kasuabe's blood; and it is said that the victim had actually told his fellow villagers to go away and leave him to his fate. He was shot while sitting in the men's house and despatched with a stone axe. The avenging party paid an indemnity to his people.

(3) Agoia of Wasemi died, and Modogo of Yogari (to the west of Kutubu) was thought guilty (because Agoia had, while visiting Yagari, sometime previously, stolen one of his pigs). When later Modogo was on a visit to wasemi he was set upon and killed while sleeping in the men's house. Wasemi paid indemnity to Yagari.

(4) Ateke of Samaga died and Sai of Fimaga was accused of sorcery (a third party alleging that he had seen him pour *yekako* on to the deceased). Kesi, with the help of all the villagers of Lake

Kutubu, went out to kill Sai. They sent a message ahead to a man named Sana, who was living with Sai; and Sana, saying, "All right, it was his fault," deserted him. The victim was surprised in a small garden house and there killed, a man of Yokobu striking the first blow. The avengers left the scene shouting that the Fimaga people would find the sorcerer's body in such and such a place and that they could go and fetch it. The victim's kinsmen however were far from acquiescing. They denied Sai's guilt and later paid a visit to Samaga, killing one man, wounding another (Yaru, the present chief man of Kesi) and burning the men's house. The Samaga people first settled as fugitives in Yokobu and finally colonized the little island of Kesi. Then they organized a counter expedition with the help of other Kutubu villages and succeeded in killing a solitary Fimaga man who was engaged in damming a small stream, Yaru being responsible for the kill. On the way home they shouted to the Fimaga people that this made the account square, and Fimaga was content to let things rest.

These short notes give no idea of the surprising brutality of these murders (it was customary for almost every man in the party to strike a blow at the victim's corpse). They constituted a drastic punishment indeed for an act of sorcery, and it seems that even in the eyes of the avengers the punishment went further than necessary. For it was apparently usual to pay an indemnity or compensation to the group of the victim in order to appease them. It is as if outright slaying amounted to something more than killing by sorcery and thus the judicial murder left the murderers with an embarrassing credit balance.

The fact that, in six[13] out of seven cases recorded in my notes, the alleged sorcerer belonged to a tribe other than that of his murderers is of significance in illustrating the point that the more serious offences are supposed to be directed against victims beyond the limits of the group. Sorcerers are not ordinarily expected to operate against those who are near them in a local or kinship sense; and the suspect in connection with any death is almost invariably found beyond the limits of the village and usually beyond those of the tribe. It is impossible to imagine that any Kutubu village could take the sort of punitive action here described against one of its own men.

Still the average expedition has a sufficiently formal cast. It is not a case of lashing out in a fury, but is carefully planned, and the participants are at pains to show that its purpose is to obtain redress for a wrong done. By way of affidavit the material evidences resulting from divination may be left on the victim's corpse: they are supposed to explain the reason for the expedition to his sympathizers and convince them of its justice.

The fact that in some cases sympathizers, or potential sympathizers, withdraw their sympathy, even before the stroke of vengeance, is of great significance. It is probable that in some instances their inaction is the result of intimidation: they are overawed at the prospect of invasion by a large force and think of their own skins first. But in so far as they acquiesce in the justice of the revenge and really mean it when they say, "It was his fault," they give proof that even at Kutubu offences can be regarded as offences against society as a whole rather than against a mere party within it. There is no mechanism by which society as a whole (whether represented by people, tribe, village or kin) can take punitive action against any of its constituent members. It is still a matter of redress, one party against another. But in this factor of acquiescence on the part of the wrongdoer's sympathizers we may perhaps see the germ of criminal justice.

Part III

Magic

Magic and Common Sense

This chapter will deal with those occult practices, designed to bring about wished-for results, which we would speak of as magical. It is quite obvious that the native makes a general distinction between such occult methods and the practical works of common sense, though we may find it hard to decide where, in his judgment, the one ends and the other begins. But I have very often detected, here at Kutubu as well as elsewhere, a certain tell-tale change of attitude, or of emotional tone, when informants come to speak of magic. In the case of harmless or "white" magic, what I fancy I have noticed is a hint of humour in the informant's manner, as if he were sharing a subtle joke with you, one that just verged on forbidden ground. Such an attitude would be more pronounced if the European party to the conversation showed any tendency to ridicule, or even to disbelieve, in magic. But one may take it that most ethnographers try to avoid giving any such impression, and I trust that I never did anything to disabuse the Kutubuans of their faith. The humorous touch was, I fancy, their own. It was as if white magic had a suggestion of playfulness in it. It would interest the writer to learn whether any other ethnographers have recorded a similar impression in other quarters.

In the case of black magic, the humorous side, if it possess one at all, is over-shadowed by some feeling of fear, present, prospective, or retrospective. It is almost always somebody else's black magic that a man talks about; and when he does so he is liable to bate his breath a little and open his eyes a shade wider. One might say that his manner contained a suggestion of awe.

There are impressions, set down for what they may be worth. But it does seem to the writer that the presence in references to magic, white or black, of some characteristic emotional colouring would be enough in itself to indicate that the native sets them aside in a class of their own.

Symbol and "Specific"

The occult practices which we class as magical (and I exclude dealings with spirits or other personal powers) seem to be analysable into two groups according to the theory of their effectiveness. On the one hand are the practices which may be lumped together as imitative magic; on the other, those which depend for their efficacy on the use of some potent substance, a "medicine," or, as I have called it elsewhere, a "specific."[14] Very often these two methods may be used to supplement each other: a rite or spell of imitative magic may be rendered effective, or more effective, by the use of a specific[15]; vice versa a specific, which might be expected to work of itself, may be given a little-extra "kick" by an imitative rite or spell; so that it is by no means always possible to say that any particular act is wholly of one sort or of the other.

But it so happens that at Kutubu, in so far as I have been able to understand them, white magic appears to fall mainly into the first class and black magic into the second. It is true that in pronouncing one of his harmless imitative spells, for gardening or what not, the magician chews ginger or some other strong herb (*takasivi, patamu*, etc.) to infuse some extra pep into the spell, and spits it over the object he is addressing as if to rouse it to action. This is in the nature of a medicine. But there is, in Kutubu white magic, no such reliance on medicines or specifics as in that of the Orokaiva. The imitative magic is here expected to work mainly by itself. By the same token, in black magic, while there is some employment of symbols, i.e. of the imitative principle, the typical method seems to depend almost directly on a magical substance or specific, something which possesses an intrinsic power, something for which the logic of imitative magic affords no apparent explanation.

I shall first deal briefly with this imitative principle as exemplified mainly in the white magic of Kutubu, and in the next chapter pass on to a longer discussion of black magic. It is hardly necessary to draw a distinction between magic white and black. It is only by what might be called cultural chance that their respective methods happen to be largely distinguishable at Kutubu. The permanent distinction between them rests on motive. White magic is harmless, neutral, or well-intention; black magic is anti-social—it aims at injury. In pursuance of my practice elsewhere I shall make the latter synonymous with sorcery and deal with it under that head.

Imitative Magic

In white magic at Kutubu the emphasis rests largely on spells; manual rites, which are so much in evidence among the Orokaiva, seem here to play a relatively small part. I cannot profess to have made anything like a complete study of the subject in the present setting, and the manual aspect of the magic may be really better developed than it appeared to be; but it can at least be said that informants left it almost entirely out of account; so that this general antithesis between Orokaiva and Kutubu magic probably holds good. But despite the absence of imitative actions or the use of what are clearly resemblance-symbols, the magic still retains its imitative character. The essence of the spell is to state a resemblance which somehow represents the wished-for result.

In a more elementary form the wish may be stated in direct, or almost direct, language. For example, my young informant-interpreter Hameno ran through a spell, learnt from his maternal uncle, to be uttered when pulling down a length of rattan cane to be used in setting a spring-trap. His spell (and I am quite confident that he gave it in full, concealing nothing) consisted of a catalogue of the animals and birds which he might catch. He reeled them off as if he had learnt the sequence by heart, as no doubt he had. There were no substitute names and no extra words. He was merely expressing in a general, inclusive manner his hopes for the success of his spring-trap: one at least among such a number would fall victim.

Girigi gave me another spell for the same purpose. He nailed his faith more particularly on the cassowary, and his spell began with a list of the places—hills, valleys, etc.—from which the cassowary were expected to come; and it went on with a list of the various fruits, etc., which they are accustomed to feed on (the trap is set in the neighbourhood of such fruits); and concluded with the curious formula, "March flies and blowflies, I put them here."

I thought that the march flies and blowflies would turn out somehow to be substitute-words and symbols for the cassowaries themselves, but Girigi provided a more direct explanation. He had seen how the march flies settled on a cassowary caught in a trap to torment it while it was still alive, and how the blowflies (of which there are many in the uncontrolled area) swarmed about it when it was dead; and this was just what he wanted to find when he came on his round of inspection (the fact that the cassowary might be dead would be no consequence unless too long dead). Girigi, in pronouncing this spell is for the most part merely saying what he wants to happen.

Such more or less straightforward statements of the hoped-for results commonly form part of the spell, though most of it may be couched in the figurative, indirect language which is typical. A fighting spell which employs the language of the garden, comparing the enemy to so many bunches of ripe bananas waiting to be cut, finishes with the words "we shoot and shoot; they fly"—the garden simile is dropped and the last words deal directly with the matter in hand—arrows and men. Similarly in a hunting spell: after what might almost be called a rigmarole wherein the bow is referred to as a special kind of palm, the spear as a bamboo shoot, the hunting-bag as a garden-bag, and the quarry as lengths of sugar-cane which will be cut up and stuffed into it, the hunter still fills out his formula with much that is only a direct expression of what he hopes will happen. "To-morrow," he says, "I and my wife and child will go to our bush house; I will thrust and the quarry will fall; I will cut it up with a bamboo knife; to-morrow I go to my hunting-place, and I kill."

It is plain, then, that the spell in essence consists in a statement, a setting forth, of the hoped-for result as if it were sure to happen; but in so far as this is a plain statement it seems very doubtful if anyone would be prepared to call it magic. It is in a certain roundaboutness that the spell finds its characteristic magical value. The component factors in the situation are represented by symbols— in the manual rite by natural symbols or symbolic actions; in the spell by verbal symbols, substitutive words. It would be a thesis worth propounding that magic in this verbal guise was simply metaphor with a purpose. The symbol used is something which the magic-maker desires to emulate, to copy, to reproduce in action or being; it is a substitute on a larger scale, or in some more potent sense, for the actuality of the moment. He wishes things to turn out that way, so he imagines, makes believe that they do.

Illustration is afforded by some simple examples from Kutubu horticulture. Planting his cuttings the gardener mutters, "This is

not sugar-cane; it is *kaveraro*." *Kaveraro* is a useless kind of cane,
very similar to sugar-cane, which in many places lines the shores
of the lake. What the gardener hopes when he compares his garden
plant to this wild useless stuff is simply that it may thrive as
abundantly. When he plants his sweet-potato he calls it *mekori
tameka*, a species of wild vine. He wishes his potato vine to grow
as strongly. When he plants a banana he says, "This is not a
banana, it is *hamaro*"—nothing more than a wild plant with great
broad leaves which is rather a pest than a thing of value but yet
provides a model of luxuriance.[16]

So setting a *buguni* or miniature animal-trap and putting in the
bait, a *pango*-fruit, a man will say, "This is not a *pango*; it is the
head of a bandicoot." Or, sharpening the prongs of his fish-spear
(*sagari*), he will say, "This is not a fish-spear, it is a *ya-huaribu
saboko*"—a shag's bill (to the inveterate, but not very successful,
fishermen of Kutubu the shag must seem to possess a most enviable
skill). Or again, fitting the points to his bird-bolt, he may say,
"I am binding on the talons of *aiyabo*, the hawk."

A few examples of food avoidance will illustrate the fact that
taboo, as "negative magic," employs the same principle, only
inverted. Symbols of what you want to happen, you use, whether
in a material sense or by merely naming them; symbols of what
you do not want to happen, you put away from you. If any kind
of food, by virtue of some point of similarity, brings to the mind
an unwelcome association, then the thing to do is to put it away
from you in the sense that you do not eat it. Young unmarried
men feel the usual concern for their figures, and take great pride
in their appearance. They are therefore ready to deny themselves
some kinds of good food merely because they convey a suggestion
of falling-off in respect of manly strength and beauty. *Kwi-huka*
(sago-grubs) and *ira-huka* (tree grubs) are avoided by such, because
of their wringled bodies; also *kumaka* (a rock-dwelling marsupial)
and *bukabo* (a kind of cuscus) because of their white fur which
makes one think of premature greyness. Prawns (*gari*) are dangerous
to young men interested in the growth of their hair, because they
seize things and pull them with their claws; and it makes one
think of having one's hair plucked out.[17] And two kinds of fish,
sesegabu and *derobu*, are avoided because, according to current
explanation, they pant so heavily landed; a youth who ate them
would have no wind for climbing mountains.

The Magic of Impersonation
What I have elsewhere spoken of as the "Magic of Impersonation"[18]
fits readily into the view of imitative magic in general. Not only

the ends and objects dealt with by the magician, but the magician himself comes to be represented by a symbol, some substitute that seems to represent success or ability to cope with the situation.

The symbol may be provided by some natural creature. It may seem rather like bathos for the man-killer to compare himself to a cucumber; but when he says, "I am not a man; I am a *baragi*," he is, I am assured, thinking of the invisibility and immobility of the cucumber lying under its broad leaves. Thus he lies in ambush. A hunting spell, given me by Arisa of Wasemi, identifies the hunter with a bird of prey: "I am not Arisa; I am Baimave. My dog is not a dog; it is Aiave. I hold the bone-wing of Baimave." (*Baimave* and *aiave* are two species of hawk, and the bone-wing representing the hunter's arrow.)

In Elema magic where the principle of impersonation is the *leit-motif*, it implies a close association between magic and myth: the character impersonated is actually a character in mythology, and the identification is effected by assuming his name. Of this I have found only the slightest trace at Kutubu though a deeper study than I could make might have revealed more of it. (Needless to say this sort of magic is deeply covered secrecy.) The trace consisted in the use, in several spells recorded, of the name Piruru, and it remains rather obscure because of the variety of interpretations which the name is made to bear. Thus, e.g. in a war spell: "I am not a man; I am Piruru lying here. *Karahua* chick, tremble; *Ga* chick, tremble; *Siakara* chick, tremble; . . . *Brrrr!*" The list of chicks runs to quite a length. They represent the enemy surprised and terrified by Piruru, the bird.[19]

Elsewhere Piruru appears as a kind of pandanus. When Heno of Herebu gave himself the name "Piruru" in a hunting spell my informant Kavarepa translated the word as "pandanus" and considered the point consisted in the fact that *piruru*, as a tree, was silent, motionless, and scentless—as Heno would, or should, be in ambush. But Heno himself gave a different explanation. Piruru was in the first place (before he turned into a tree) a legendary hunter and the point of the comparison or identification lay in the fact that he was always miraculously successful.

This is exactly on a par with the Elema Magic of Impersonation; though, to repeat, it is the only case I can bring forward in which the magic-maker professed to be impersonating a mythical character; and, furthermore, it may be mentioned that in Kutubu mythology Piruru remains a somewhat obscure person.[20] There are, however, numerous myths and stories which must be taken to possess a magical value, such as those which deal with hunting, killing, curing, food-getting and the acquisition of shell valuables.

I have not succeeded in establishing many direct connections between these myths and the magic actually used for the purposes indicated; but there can be no doubt that the two are intimately connected.[21] Further, the elaborate secrecy regarding the names of the characters in some of the stories lends itself well to the impersonation hypothesis. Different tellers of one and the same myth are found to employ different names for the characters[22]; and these names they guard with utmost jealousy, as if they were private knowledge or property. This is because they use them for private magic. On the Impersonation hypothesis this would mean that the magic-maker actually adopts the name; he steps into the hero's shoes and plays his part in a modern context.

Wish Fulfilment

The explanation of imitative magic which appeals to the present writer proceeds along psychological lines. Such magic is a universal phenomenon, in time as well as geographical space. If we ourselves can "see the point of it" it is because we, in our weaker moments, are prone to use it, or at least come very near to using it. It is true that it may easily become conventionalized, when the point is perhaps no longer to be seen. A man may adopt the name of "Piruru" as he draws his bow without having the least idea of why he does so. It is just a name, which, he has been taught, will help him to shoot straight. And the gardener who, planting his taro-offset, says, "This is not a taro, but an echidna's head," probably sees no more point in that absurd formula than we do. But someone saw a point in it once, or it would never have come into being.

It is in spontaneous magic, or at least in magic which has not travelled so far along the road of conventionalism as to have left its *rationale* beyond guessing distance, that we discern a sort of fitness that makes it understandable. In the spell, as well as in the manual rite, imitative magic is in essence a symbolic representation of a hoped-for result, and thus it gives the magic-maker some satisfaction in advance; he at any rate achieves results in imagination. His mistake in supposing that it gives him results in reality is potentially rather a serious one, for it may stand in the way of methods that really are effective. But, on the whole, magic is no more than supplementary to routines or common-sense courses of action; and as such it probably does the magic-maker some good. Like saying his prayers, it presumably gives him some extra confidence and at any rate prevents him from worrying.

Sorcery

The Sorcerer's Technique

The sorcery of Kutubu, as already stated, is mainly dependent on the use of certain "medicines" or "specifics," that is to say it is magic of a class distinct from that which we have been discussing. Whether the specifics used were originally symbols such as belong to imitative magic is a question we need not worry about: nowadays they are merely substances with an unexplained supernatural power; they are taken on trust, and any associative link which may once have accounted for their use, giving it a sort of reasonableness, is gone and forgotten.

The substances are grouped together under the name *yekako*, which one is tempted to translate "poison." Some of them may actually be poisonous—of which more hereafter—but others certainly are not, nor is the general mode of application such as to justify our using the word. It will be best to continue calling them simply *yekako*.

There are several different sorcery techniques:

(*a*) *Yekako-hubu*, "striking with *yekako*." The sorcerer is supposed to possess some *yekako* which he keeps in a bamboo tube. He secretly contrives to bring it into contact with his victim, perhaps while sitting beside him in conversation or by creeping upon him in his sleep. He is extremely careful not to touch the *yekako* with his own fingers; he either pours or shakes a little of it out of the bamboo upon his victim's bare skin, or else inserts a stick into the tube and touches his man lightly with the end of it. Any part of the body will do; the *yekako* is extremely potent, and the man will dies This, of "striking with *yekako*," is, in native belief, the sorcerer'. commonest technique.

(*b*) *Kimari mahamigibu*. "Giving in the midst of food." This method, which simply means mixing the *yekako* in the victim's food, is rarely mentioned.

(*c*) *Fanabu*. This is a variety of "personal leavings" magic. Some contact-symbol of the intended victim, e.g. a morsel of chewed and spat-out sugar-cane, is introduced into the sorcerer's *yakakora* (*yekako*-bamboo). A variety of magical substances is already stored in this receptacle, such as *or-uriri*, *anum-uriri*, *magi-uriri* (the minute "hairs" scraped from the shoots of bamboo), *anumu* and sugar-cane— I do not understand what the connection is or why they are suitable to the purpose—and *piripa*, drippings obtained from a decomposing corpse on a *deve* platform. The personal leavings are stowed in a bamboo with such substance as these and on the top of them is placed some *yekako*. The *fanaboro* and its contents are left to do their work unaided; the victim sickens and will die unless the sorcerer relents and empties the mixture out.

It will be seen that the basis of all these sorcery techniques is the *yekako*. This is a very secret thing; and while informants will talk about it I never succeeded in inducing anyone to show me a specimen. Needless to say it is always the other fellow who keeps it. Most men profess to have none themselves—and I have little doubt that in this they are usually speaking the truth. It may take various forms— it may be "like stone," or "like earth"—and the word is sometimes applied to the *piripa*, or juices of decomposing corpse. Fareape (who kept his small stock in a hole in a tree rather than in his house, where its discovery might incriminate him) said that his was like beeswax. Others spoke of *yekako* as if it were properly and originally the phosphorescent fungus which is seen glowing on damp and decaying wood in the forest. (I could not induce anyone to join me in a search for it.)

This last sounds as if it might be really a poison, and it is not impossible that it may sometimes be used as such. Speaking of the powers of *yekako* an informant at Herebu launched forth on the following story. A man named Girigimena, of the same village was living with his wife and four children in a garden house. While, he was absent on some business of his own the wife and children returned from work in the garden, and the mother proceeded to cook a meal. Rather than send to the river for water she entered her husband's end of the house and took some from his supply, kept in the usual way in a bamboo internode. After eating their meal, the mother and all the children began to vomit, and Girigimena returned to find them all very ill. He brought them across to Herebu, where my informant saw them all die, one after another, on the same day. The inference was that Girigimena had been privately preparing *yekako* in the bamboo water-vessel; and he made compensation to the paternal and maternal kin of his wife.[23] But, while this looks very much like a case of poisoning it is of course by no means proved that the poison came out of the water-vessel. This, by the way, is the only actual case of *mahamigibu* that I ever heard of, and, at that, it was accidental; so we shall probably be right in saying that the poisoning of food is at least an uncommon technique in Kutubu sorcery.

Divination

Here, as elsewhere, the belief in sorcery seems to be out of all proportion to the practice of it. What that practice may be, how often the Kutubuans really make magic to kill or injure, we have no means of knowing. But it is certain that they are very often supposed to be doing so. It has been remarked already that deaths are, by someone or other, usually attributed to sorcery; and this inevitably means that there are all sorts of allegations against individuals. In some cases—probably very few indeed—the allegations are true; in the great majority it must be assumed that they are based on imagination, false reasoning or malice.

There is a recognized form of divination, so fantastic as to be specially interesting, called *"Fifiridi fakabu,"* or "Fragments on the chest." While the corpse lies in the men's house before the funeral the older men sit round it, and one of their number plies it with questions—or rather he addresses his questions to the *aminterare,* or ghost. He runs through the names of the *amindoba* in such and such a village and then lifts the bark-cloth with which the body is covered and examines its chest. If nothing is found, he proceeds to name the *amindoba* in another village, and looks again. Sooner or later in one of these inspections he will find a fragment of a certain totem plant—a little piece of taro-leaf for Ekadobo, a piece of cane-leaf for Orodobo, etc. The fragment has ostensibly been placed there by the deceased's *aminterare,* and it is taken to indicate the sorcerer's clan. This gives the diviners a very substantial clue; and the principal is then in a position to proceed to the second phase. He must procure a small bird—any sort will do. Its liver (*gamogu*) is extracted and placed in a small bamboo container which he carries to the *deve,* or mortuary platform, where the deceased's body is lying. Here he takes out the bird's liver and cautiously cuts at it with a bamboo knife, as if worrying it, meanwhile he is listening intently for a bird-call in the neighbourhood. It is said to be the little bird *sito* that gives the call, but I am not sure that any bird might not do as well. If it is always a *sito* this little creature must have a fairly wide repertoire, for the diviner hears in its call the name of some individual belonging to the village and *amindoba* already ascertained. This clinches the matter. He brings back the news, and the sympathizers have enough data to direct and justify an expedition of revenge. One of the signs left on the victim's battered body is the bamboo knife with which the bird's liver was cut. It is carefully decorated with streaks of the bird's blood; and to it is bound the tell-tale fragment which was found on the dead man's chest. It is a sign; and the band of avengers leave the scene hoping very much that the friends and relatives of their victim will agree with them about the justness of the retribution. (They are ready to square them subsequently, however, in case they do not.)

Of this method of divination, complicated and bizarre as it as, I have had several accounts, which agree pretty closely, so that it is at least generally recognized. We need not suppose that it is always put into effect, or that every death leads to an avenging expedition. The Kutubu would speedily wipe themselves out if that were the case. But the revenge expeditions are nevertheless all too common, and some of them at any rate are preceded by this grisly kind of detective work. It is very obvious that it lends itself to victimization.

The Social Role of Sorcery

We can safely say that the sorcerer is both feared and detested in Kutubu society. Some individuals (Yaru of Kesi was one of them; Yaru of Wasemi another) enjoy a special reputation; but I was never able to unearth any concrete evidence to justify it. I think it is mainly due to the fact that they are otherwise influential men; i.e. I think the reputation for sorcery is more the effect than the cause of their general influence. The fact is that every man is a potential sorcerer in public estimation. If, when anyone dies, it is recalled that so and so (almost invariably from another locality) had a just grievance or a grudge against him or was jealous of him, or that he had merely been in his company of late, then that man falls under suspicion. No one hesitates to believe that such a man possesses his own *yekako*, and no one, except among his sympathizers, will be very critical towards the notion that he has used it. He is well advised therefore, when taxed with guilt, to pay compensation if he is given the chance, and avoid what may be terrible consequences.

Sorcery, here as everywhere else, also plays the good role of a guardian of rights. A man is deterred from harming another by the fear that the other may retaliate by bewitching him. This is true of all sorts of offences as is apparent from the constructions which the native is so ready to place on cases retrospectively: A. dies; B. must be the sorcerer because A. stole B.'s pig, or committed adultery with his wife, and so on. And in particular the threat of sorcery is allegedly implied in those taboo marks placed on fruiting trees and the like : you touch them at the risk of a dreadful disease called *dorobagi*.[24]

But whatever the excuse, whatever the previous injury or injustice, retaliation by sorcery is a thing which public opinion at Kutubu does not seem willing to tolerate. The tacit threat of sorcery is permissible; but the act of sorcery, real or supposed, will, whatever its antecedents, kindle the fire of revenge.

In the foregoing chapter it was maintained that in such a primitive society as that of Kutubu wrongs were characteristically civil rather than criminal. But if there is any kind of wrong which comes near to being a crime it is that of sorcery. For not only is it an outrage upon the victim and his immediate sympathizers, but it may rouse the antagonism of the whole society concerned. The revenge expeditions which I have spoken of as "judicial murders" draw in a surprisingly large number of confederates, many of them but remotely connected with the victim; and the fact that they look for acquiescence from the sorcerer's group, even if they do not always receive it, shows in itself that sorcery is regarded as something to be condemned by everyone: the sympathizers of the sorcerer, if they do not co-operate in the business of punishment, should stand aside and let it take its course. If anyone in native estimation is a criminal, it is surely the sorcerer.

Revenge on the Sorcerer

By way of illustrating some of the foregoing, I propose to give a detailed account of a case of imputed sorcery and the revenge which followed it. It is of rather special interest in that it took place under the very nose of the police camp.

The alleged sorcerer was a man named Kawa. At the time he was living in Tugiri, only five minutes' walk from the police camp; and prior to this he had lived at Wasemi. But he was originally a man of Hegisu on the Mubi, and thus really a foreigner to the Kutubu tribe proper, so he provided no exception to the general rule that accusations of sorcery fall beyond the bounds of the village and usually beyond the bounds of the tribe. He had married twice, under matrilocal conditions. The first union, the one that was to bring him all the trouble, was with a widow of Wasemi who already had two sons and a daughter by her first marriage. When she died he took another wife, a woman of Tugiri and went to live with her in that village.

While he was still residing in Wasemi, Kawa's step-daughter Sukuri had married Aiamena; and, on this man's early death, Kawa the step-father, made provision for the feast and the *abia-gibu*. In this he received no help from her two grown-up brothers, wherein he seems to have felt that he had a grievance. When later on Sukuri married a second time, these two brothers appropriated the brideprice and gave none to Kawa. As he belonged neither to her paternal nor maternal clan, he was strictly not entitled to any share, but since he had previously undertaken responsibilities as her step-father he felt that he had been neglected and put upon; and when later he moved to Tugiri he carried his resentment with him. These grievances were understood to have afforded him motives for bewitching one of the brothers. No doubt he had aired them sufficiently to make them well known.

The victim of the supposed sorcery was Hegemai, the elder of the two. It so happened that he was one of five Wasemi men who had volunteered to go on a long patrol with Mr. Champion. Everything was ready for a start on the following day, and these men had come to sleep in one of the houses at the camp (or possibly in the neighbouring village Tugiri, I am not sure), so that they could move off with the party in the morning. During the night Hegemai saw (or thought he saw, or perhaps he dreamt it, or perhaps merely alleged it) Kawa creep into the house and pour some *yekako* on to his body. This, he says, gave him a severe fright, and next morning, instead of going off with the patrol, he returned to his village. Whatever the cause he there fell ill and died.

Hegemai had given out the story that Kawa had bewitched him, but the rite of *fifiridi fakabu* was performed over his dead body and the results of it served to verify the suspicions that had fallen on Kawa. On the chest was found a little piece of the palm leaf *tirifa*, which showed that the sorcerer belonged to Kawa's clan, Tirifadobo; and with it a fragment of a *kosaka*, which showed that the case had to do with a woman—obviously Sukuri, about whose marriage payment Kawa had been nursing a grievance. On top of this the rite of *orokibu* was carried out, and the little *sito* bird was heard calling, "*kawau, kawau!*" Thus indubitably was Kawa fixed.

The revenge expedition, when one is undertaken, is delayed until after the *Kigi-yahabu* ceremony; and in the present case Mr. Champion had returned and was at the police camp, while Mr. Adamson was patrolling at Fasu. The station police were engaged in making a large dugout canoe on the Soru River, going and returning each day; and they happened to be at Wasemi, which lies half-way, when they saw a fleet of five canoes approaching the island from Kara. They were fully manned, and the paddlers were making a great *wowadibu*, a sort of concerted cheering accompanied by drumming on the sides of their dugouts. "It sounds as if they had killed someone." said the police, familiar with the spirit of triumph which belongs to that circumstance. But their friends on Wasemi assured them that the men had that morning dragged down a newly-made dugout to the lake, and were now merely rejoicing in their strength; and quite satisfied with this explanation the police had gone on to their day's work.

But the villagers of Wasemi had actually killed their man. It was known that Kawa was sleeping at a sago-place on the north shore of the lake together with a friend named Yamo; and the Wasemi party had crossed under cover of night and surrounded them. At a convenient moment in the morning they had made their attack. Yamo was pinioned for fear he should resist and Kawa was set upon with cries of "*Hegemai pagama!*" "Hegemai, seize him!" This probably was all the notice which the unfortunate man received of his execution: he heard the name of his alleged victim, and the next instant fell beneath the spears and trade-axes of the executioners.

They did their work with considerable thoroughness: among a score or more, not one, it is said, failed to blood his weapon. Then leaving the evidence of the divination—the *orokibu* bamboo and the fragments of *tirifa* and bark-cloth—on the body as evidence and justification, they returned. Vengeance had been satisfied and a sorcerer dealt with as he deserved.

The people of Tugiri, duly notified, crossed over to claim the body, but found it so hacked about that decent disposal was out of the question: it was put away in a hole in the rocks. They received as compensation, or as a sort of insurance against retaliation, two bagfuls of *bari* shells, part of which was sent to the deceased's true kin at Hegisu. Whether the people of Hegisu would have been satisfied with this price had the affair occurred a year earlier is a question. They would not be quite so ready as the Kutubu people to believe that Kawa was really a sorcerer, and they might have thought it worth while to begin a feud. But the government was established on the lake, and such undertakings were now attended with extra difficulties. The manner of Kawa's death was therefore kept a secret by common consent. The chief man of Tugiri came to Mr. Champion to inform him that one of his villagers had unfortunately been killed while felling a sago tree.

Disease and Its Treatment

It has been often observed that cultures tend to develop distinctive "interests," due, not to any innate propensity on the part of the people concerned, but rather to some influence of environment, or perhaps to an historical accident. Thus fathered and encouraged, the interest comes to engross a special share of attention until it may give the culture in question a definitely distinctive character. It is not impossible, of course, that some of the distinctive characters so confidently attributed to various cultures owe something to the vagaries of ethnographers. An investigator may find his attention caught by some particular phase of the culture, perhaps at an early stage of his work; and thereafter his mind may recur to the subject more frequently than it deserves, with the result that it bulks altogether too large in the final summing-up. Recognizing the possibility of this error, however, the present writer believes that the Kutubu people have developed a kind of cultural speciality, and that it consists in their excessive preoccupation with bodily disease, its causes, prevention, and treatment. It is not that their health falls below the average; they seem reasonably prosperous and content.

Yet so frequent are the references to the subject of disease, so much else seems to hinge on it, and so deeply do the people seem to be concerned about it, that one may say that it has given a characteristic colouring to their whole life. In the present case we might almost speak of a valetudinarian culture.

Causes of Disease

Illnesses are legion. The general terms, between which there seems to be no set distinction, are *garebo* (or *magagarebo*) and *kagoribu*. The specific terms will only be mentioned as they turn up incidentally. It would be merely tiresome to present a catalogue of diseases according to their symptoms, and we may best begin, on a more significant basis, by classifying them according to their imputed causes.

(1) *Direct Contraction.* Nearly all illnesses are thought to have some ulterior, i.e. supernatural, causes. But just as some treatments fall into line with our notion of common sense, so also do some ideas of causation, at least in so far as they dispense with the supernatural. Thus a man may fall ill because he worked too hard in the sun or rain; an epidemic of coughs and colds (*magami-hasi*) is thought to come of itself—I could discover no spirit theory to account for it; a man may contract illness merely by sitting near one who is hot and perspiring; and he may get stomachache (*fago-nibu*) and diarrhoea (*kotorobo*) by eating too much fish and prawns.

It is true that ulterior causes may be brought to light if such illnesses are raked over in discussion. Thus the diarrhoea is said to ensure if you eat your fish and prawns in certain special circumstances, such as soon after cutting down a big tree.[25] One of my informants drew attention to the continual drip of the sap from certain trees when newly felled—a purely magical idea; but there was also some notion of an emanation which passed over from the tree into the woodman's body. Here, as in the other cases, one might unearth a supernatural explanation by pressing one's enquiries; but it seems likely that the native himself is likely to pass it over, accepting the notion of direct contraction.

This at any rate seems to hold largely for that most common of all Kutubuan ills, "sago-sickness"—*kwi-rumu-hubu,* "being struck by the sago." It gives rise to a considerable variety of symptoms (boils are often mentioned), so that it seems obvious that the imputed cause is the only thing common to a large class of ills. This cause consists in some evil property which belongs to sago and the sago-swamps (happily it is not always present, since sago is the people's main livelihood), and it may be ingested with a meal of "bad" sago. But the usual idea is that it enters the body as a sort of emanation from the swamp, a miasma. It is like steam or smoke, and one is particularly liable to attack in the early morning (when the mists are hanging about). Once again it will be found, when we come to examine the treatment of *kwi-rumu-hubu*, that there is really, in the knowledge of some at any rate, a deeper explanation of its cause; but it may be safely said that to the ordinary man and woman this explanation remains out of mind. Sago-sickness comes straight from sago.

(2) *Sorcery.* One general cause of illness in popular belief is sorcery, the occult agency of living human beings. It is especially the "swift" illness, *fulfuta magarebo*, i.e. one with a very sudden onset, which lends itself to this explanation. Again the cases of possible leprosy are supposedly caused by the sorcerer's revenge for the breach of a tree-taboo; and there is the specific case of my man Kavarepa's illness which was put down to the action of a sorcerer on the Mubi. But it so happens that in the course of my enquiries on the subject of sickness, as such, there was very little reference to sorcery as the cause of it. Once a man has actually died it is a different matter; then the thoughts of his kinsmen readily turn to sorcery and revenge. But while, among the interminable list of Kutubu ailments, most have their specific causes, it must be remarked that sorcery hardly ever turned up as one of them.

(3) *Supernatural Beings.* It should be hardly necessary to point out that the definition of sorcery here adopted has no reference to the direct influence of spirits or supernatural beings. These are in popular belief the commonest agents of disease. They are mainly spirits of the dead, but there are also certain independent beings credited with the same sort of power.

Taubu-hubu, or *Ganaro-hubu*, results from being "seized" or shot" by the kind of supernatural monster called *taubu* or *ganaro* (the terms are apparently synonymous). A cramp, a pain in the side, a wasted body with sunken eyes, may all be ascribed to the *taubu*. It is an invisible creature, seen only in dreams, such a vision invariably presaging illness to the dreamer; but it may shoot an invisible arrow into any victim at any time.

Another Kutubu bugbear is the phantom cassowary, Magagai. Merely to see its form in the half-light means sickness. It is supposed to pick at the vitals of women and cause what are known as female ailments.

A third agent of evil is the *ii*, or *siago*, which causes the kinds of sickness classed as *ii-rumu-hubu*. Whether this should be classed under the present heading seems somewhat doubtful. It was described to me a number of times as something like a lizard which inhabited the tops of trees; but I found it impossible to picture what it could be until later on at Augu the local natives brought me a giant phasmid, or stick-insect. My Kutubu boys identified it as a *siago*. What associations this remarkable insect may possess, or what, beyond its certainly fearsome appearance, makes it an object of fear, I am unable to say. But it is averred that if a *siago* drops a fragment of bark or leaf on to a man beneath, or if it merely looks down on him, he will fall ill with *ii-rumu-hubu*. This is triviality in the extreme; but the illnesses resulting from this fantastic cause are apparently very common and they are dealt with very seriously by means of a long sequence of treatments.

(4) *Spirits of the Dead.* By far the commonest agents of disease are the spirits of the dead. Under a variety of names (*aminterare, yesibu,* etc.) they are said to "strike" (*hubu*) the victim, whereupon he becomes ill (the precise method of their attack is not specified). The spirit of any dead man, relative or otherwise, is a danger; but it is specially those of the deceased relatives of one's *abia* (maternal uncle) who are to be feared. The significance of this belief will be dealt with below. Another kind of particularly dangerous *aminterare* is that of the *yako* or namesake.

But standing in a class of their own, and most dangerous of all, are the spirits of the slain (*pauave* or *husahua*). It is said they leave the victim's body only at sundown, when they ascend with a screech to remain thenceforward in the upper air.[26] Sometimes they are compared to, or identified with, the black cockatoo; but they are obviously thought of in the main as disembodied spirits. They are said to seize their victims unawares, "like the wind," thereby afflicting them with illness. It would appear they are quite undiscriminating, being just as likely to seize their kinsmen as the enemies who have slain them.

The Punitive Aspect of Disease

It is evident that in the Kutubuan view a large number of illnesses are simply bad luck. If a man or woman breaks out in boils it is probably regarded as a case of *kwi-rumu-hubu* and all in a day's work; if he catches a cold, it may be a case of *magami-hasi*, the epidemic, which indeed he would be lucky to evade; or if he is seized by internal pains, it may be that one of the invisible arrows of a *taubu* has lodged in his vitals—a misfortune that might happen to anyone. But it is equally evident that a large number of illnesses are viewed as the result of some misdeed on the part of the sufferer, an error of commission or omission. That is to say, if a man falls ill it is very commonly assumed that he has "bought it." This often applied to those cases ascribed to sorcery. It is true that the sorcery may have been motivated by private malice, perhaps by jealousy. It would be altogether too naive to assume that every supposed victim of sorcery was also supposed to have deserved it. But it is very often concluded that the sorcerer has gone to work in a spirit of revenge, that his action has been provoked, if never wholly excused, by some injury or slight. And in so far as this is a common assumption it may be said that sorcery is here a sanction of good conduct. You must be careful not to injure people or slight them, lest you fall ill and die in consequence.[27]

But the idea of illness as punishment or revenge has a much wider application. It applies to nearly all those cases—the widest category in the medical science of Kutubu—which are attributed to the spirits of the dead. These may be leading ancestors of long ago who have retained their power to harm. Thus, if a man raises his voice unduly in the precincts of the *piaka-aa*, the presiding spirit, sometimes visible in the form of the small lizard called *hibi-ninyi*, may punish him with *i-nibu*, or sore eyes (all of which comes very close to the idea of actual sin—desecration carrying a supernatural punishment).

But the longer a ghost exists the less dangerous it seems to grow. It is the spirits of the recently dead that are really to be feared, and the ordinary offences for which they see fit to exact penalty are those committed against contemporary human beings. The avenging spirits are the recently deceased relatives of the persons wronged. It has been noted in particular that one has to be very careful to observe all one's obligations toward the *abia*. The reason, as generally stated, is that the *abia*, if wronged or neglected, will take the revenge of making his niece or nephew ill. This, however, which has been quoted earlier in the present report, proves to be a somewhat loose statement of the belief in question. It appears that the punishment of illness is inflicted directly by the *abia's* deceased relatives. They are protecting his interests and avenging any wrong, positive or negative, against him. He does not himself need to invoke them, though the fact that he is able to remove the sickness might be taken to imply that he was instrumental in inflicting it. In the course of a number of discussions directly devoted to the question, however, it became evident that the active agents are considered to be spirits of the *abia's* deceased kin, his parents or others. He himself can rest assured of their championship, so that he is in theory absolved from the guilt of sorcery. But this is a point of little moment. The significant matter is that a man must continually make presents to his maternal uncle, and to his wife's brother who is the prospective maternal uncle of his children; and he must in particular see that his wife's family is satisfied in the matter of the bride-price. So also must the bride's parents see that her maternal relatives receive their due half-share, or she herself will be liable to sickness. In all these matters the spirits of the *abia's* deceased relatives stand guard over the fulfilment of social obligations.

Nor is it only in respect of the *abia* that the spirits of the dead exercise these disciplinary powers. Any *aminterare* may "strike" any man, and it is expressly stated that it is liable to do so in requital for a wrong against its living relative. If anyone falls sick and thinks back for a possible cause, he may recall that he tampered with a neighbour's garden. In such a case it is the neighbour who will be asked to perform the curing rite of *kehugabu* (with the necessary fee which compensates him for the damage done); for it is his deceased relative who took action.

The most interesting manifestation of this general idea is found in the theory of *auamo* which provides the basis of a kind of trial by ordeal. A very common expression in the Kutubuan's mouth is *"Auamo gai !"* an oath of veracity. A man may use it in denying a charge of theft, or, for a more specific instance, in disclaiming any share in a distribution. If he is really guilty, or if he subsequently changes his mind and demands the share, then he is afflicted with the peculiar form of disease known as *auamo-siagabo*. This ranges from a stiff neck to mumps or facial paralysis. At any rate, it involves some affection of the jaws or throat, as if the man's lie had chocked him.

At Yokobu there is a fossil shell (Fig. 12) of spiral shape known as the *auamo-kana* (stone); and at Hegusu a lump of stone known as *auamo-gi* (earth).[28] It is the function of each of these (there are no doubt others of a similar nature) to provide an object to swear by. A supposed thief or adulterer may be challenged to deny his guilt while holding the *auamo*-stone in his hand. If he can do so truthfully he fears no evil, and the case goes no further. If he is lying, he will fall ill (the illness should be of the typical *auamo* variety, but this is not too heavily stressed) and he must appeal to the owner of the stone to go through the requisite curing process.

Fig. 12. Fossil shell (*auamo kana*)

Among quite a number of well-remembered cases I give just one example. Gegeno of Yokobu (my informant) lost his pig and went looking for it. Coming in the course of his search to the house of Heavi he saw traces of recent cooking and questioned the man's son, Heavi himself being absent. The little boy innocently explained that his father had yesterday killed a strange pig. On the strength of this clue Gegeno came again next morning and directly charged

Heavi, who replied that he had been cooking only cabbage. Gegeno now procured the *auamo-kana* and in company with other men repaired to Heavi's house and challenged him to restate his denial with the fossil-shell in his hand. Heavi did this and subsequently became ill. He recovered when he had made compensation to Gegeno and paid for a fumigation treatment at the hands of Kai, the old man of Yokobu who owns the fossil and thus gets occasional profit out of it.

There is some possibility that the word *auamo* has come to Kutubu, like the two oath-stones, from the south. The history of the acquisition of both the latter is recent enough to be easily recalled: they came originally from Fasu. But the idea, even if it is a foreign one, is in keeping with Kutubu philosophy. *Auamo* is explained as meaning "spirits of deceased parents"; and this is borne out by the fact that there is an alternative expression used in precisely similar circumstances—*aba-gai, hua-gai,* "by my father and mother." It is the outraged spirits of the dead who are thought to punish a man for forswearing himself.

Treatments

The treatments are almost as varied as the diseases, and it is out of the question to describe them all. It will be enough to draw attention to a few leading ideas and then to give a few detailed examples.

Common Sense and Magic. Some of the methods are recommended by what we should agree is common sense. An accepted treatment for boils, for example, is to have them lanced—though to be sure the lancing is rather superficial and has little regard for asepsis. There are also numerous herbal treatments: boils and sores may be poulticed with leaves; and the stinging nettle (*nigi*) is used, as so often in Papua, as a counter-irritant. There are doubtless some really sound remedies in the native pharmacopoeia, discovered empirically; and one general method which may be of real value is that of fumigation, or the sweat-bath.

But common sense fades very readily into magic; and the possible efficacy of herbs, barks, etc., may be sometimes ruled out by the method of application: one way of treating boils is to chew *barima* bark and spit on them. This might be an effective method of application, and the *barima* bark might be an effective medicine (I confess I have not had it identified). But the presumption is surely otherwise. My own experience of Papuan drugs and herbs is that they are used almost invariably because of some potency which turns out to be merely magical. A course of treatment for diarrhoea may be given as fairly typical. It is known as *bauru imifisibu*, and is carried out in two stages. In the first of them the packet (*bauru*) consists of a bundle of leaves, barks, etc., the trees *kofe* and *tabia* and the creeper *murokamia* being specially named. This is heated in the ashes and then, while the patient squats, is held directly under his anus so that the vapours may do their work. Alternatively he may inhale them through his open mouth. In the second stage the packet consists of the barks of *fasina*, *ima*, *magaru*, etc.—seven trees were named. The method of application is the same. It would be sheer presumption to suggest that any of these ingredients were any good at all in a practical sense; though it would be fair to suppose that each of them was originally recommended by some magical property, if only it could be discovered. All my informants could think of by way of explanation was that the trees named in the second list were all solid, hard timber. They were brought into use when the patient's condition was already improving, as if to confirm the result of the initial treatment. It might be difficult to assume, in the case cited, that the process possessed even psychological value for the patient; but in the generality of native treatments this is what mainly recommends them.

There are a number of prescribed treatments, almost ritual in character, in which (for some kinds of illness, at any rate) the psychological value may be considerable. In an attempt to analyse the leading ideas these ritual treatments may be said to aim at symbolic expulsion, transference, or extraction. Further, as a means of prophylaxis, certain ceremonies involve the placation of the spiritual beings who are responsible for the people's general welfare. I shall go on to give examples of certain treatments both to illustrate these principles and to show to what lengths Kutubu culture is carried by its obsession with disease.

Kehugabu. The *abia* is the person naturally fitted to deal with those cases of illness which are associated with him. He uses a routine treatment known as *kehugabu*, which consists principally in making circular passes round the patient's head with a burning torch. The patient in the typical case is an ailing child, one who is ill or undeveloped because its father has been remiss in making gifts to his brother-in-law (the child's *abia*). The parent must now bring forward a substantial gift, in the form of *bari* shells, to make up for previous shortcomings. These he hands to the *abia* together with a feather of the black bird *gagako*. The *abia* lights a torch of dry bamboo, passes it round and round the patient's head, holding the feather in flame so that it is quite burnt up. Meanwhile he utters an appropriate spell, "Leave him now; let his body grow light (i.e. lose the 'heaviness' associated with illness); let him grow big and strong."

This spell is addressed to the spirit which has afflicted (or perhaps possessed) the patient. It is usually referred to in this connection as a *yesibu*, and the various illnesses due to the *abia* as *yesibu-rumu-hubu*. Informants never succeeded in making consistent distinctions between the alternative expressions used for the spirits of the dead, but it was claimed that, whereas *aminterare* were bodiless beings, *yesibu* appeared in the guise of rats and birds; and the feather of the *gagako* bird was used in *kehugabu* because the *yesibu* which afflicted the patient would have taken that form. It seems almost unfair to press a savage too hard for explanations of practices which he carries out by rote, and too much persistence may evoke merely *ad hoc* explanations, provided by those rarer individuals who possess imagination or are willing to give the matter thought. I cannot say for certain, then, that the implied notion that the *gagako* feather represents the *yesibu* is really established as a Kutubuan belief. But, if it is, it looks almost as if the *yesibu* were being burnt up—somewhat hard treatment for the spirit of one's father and mother. It is perhaps rather merely burnt *out*. We are left to our own surmises for a precise explanation; but it seems fairly clear that, by and large, *kehugabu* is a rite of expulsion or casting-out.

Treatments of Sago-Sickness. The first steps in the treatment of boils, which are the commonest manifestations of *kwi-rumu-hibu*, are the practical ones of lancing, or nicking them and poulticing them with leaves. But if the boils fail to respond quickly and if the case is definitely diagnosed as one of sago-sickness, a most elaborate course of treatment may ensue. The first episode is a ritual, that of *soga-bogo-mitenabu*, "showing the decorated *soga*." Two practitioners with the necessary medical knowledge are hired to carry it out. They prepare the *soga* in private, a short length of the pithy midrib of a sago frond transfixed with a number of midribs of the individual leaves. These latter, projecting at right angles, are called its limbs; and a single spike stuck in vertically at the end is called its head. Unconvincing as these features are, there is no doubt that the *soga* is meant to be anthropomorphic. It is decorated with stripes of red paint, but remains an extremely rough and primitive model of the human frame.

Since I have never seen the rite of *soga-mitenabu* I cannot pretend to give a full account of it. But it appears that the two practitioners make a show of creeping on the patient unawares. The "dancing-man," who is fully decorated and befeathered, carries two *soga*, one in each hand; the other, who is really the principal, carries two twigs of *paiaka* (the nettle-like leaf which is used for touching or massaging the bodies of the sick). The patient sits awaiting their visitation, but is nevertheless supposed to start with surprise when they confront him. The dancer, hopping on both feet, moves noisily round and round, while the *paiakamina* (nettle-man) strokes or flicks the patient alternately with the nettle leaves, meanwhile uttering his spell.

When this has reached an end the dancer drops the two *soga* on the floor and the *paiakamina*, picking them up, places them on the front wall of the men's house, to remain there till thoroughly dried out, when, it is said, they are merely thrown away.

One *paiakamina* gave me his spell, though I cannot pretend to translate it accurately. It began with the words *Kwi-hogobi, kwi-au burisera, kwi-nai, kwi-au burisera,* and went on at great length with continual repetition of the last phrase, running through the names of various trees whose barks are used for medicines, until it finished thus: *Arurubu, kwi-au burisera, Sinanume, kwi-au burisera, Haga-kaiagi, kwi-au burisera. Kwi-hogobi* and *kwi-nai* are two particular varieties of sago, and the words *kwi-au burisera* mean, "The sago, oh, it flies away" (or vanishes). The last words, given above, may be translated "Arububu and Sinanume, the pair of them, they vanish."

Now, although the story of Arurubu and Sinanume does not appear to be very well known at Kutubu it was generally agreed that they belonged originally to some place further east, near Foi; that they were man and wife; that they were the first to suffer from sago-sickness, their limbs being swollen like tree-trunks; and that after much hard thought they themselves devised the course of treatment by which the disease can be cured at the present time. It was said (though others at another time denied it) that they respectively turned into the two particular varieties of sago named *kwi-hogobi* and *kwi-nai*. It was never suggested that Arurubu and his wife Sinanume, or their immortal spirits, actually caused the sickness, though it might perhaps be implied, especially from the fact that *kwi-hogobi* and *kwi-nai* are avoided as food by young men and girls. (They are quite wholesome but potentially dangerous as being liable to cause *kwi-rumu-hubu*. Only older people will take the risk.) But there was no doubt in the minds of my informants that the two anthropomorphic *soga* represented Arurubu and Sinanume. And the gist of the rite was expressly said to be a dragging out (*fogomabu*) of the sickness by means of them. The precise *rationale* of the practice was never formulated for me in words: it may be that the sickness is being symbolically transferred to the *soga*; or it may be that the *soga* are held up as magical examples, the patient being induced to throw off the sickness just as these two characters which the *soga* represents themselves threw it off in the legend.

This "showing of the *soga*" is only the first stage of the treatment, though if it is effective there will be no necessity to go further. It is probably followed, however, by a course of fumigations—first the *kwi-mogofumahabu* and then the *ira-mogofumahabu*, i.e. the sago-leaf and tree-leaf fumigations, each repeated time and again. The general method is the same. The patient squats on a little platform about a foot high; the green leaves, barks, or other substances used are placed beneath him on hot fire-stones; and he is then enveloped in a bark-cloth cloak which reaches to the ground. For the earlier *kwi-mogofumahabu* the leaves are said to be those of *hogobi* and *nai*, the kinds of sago associated with Arurubu and Sinanume. In the *ira-mogofumahubu* the ingredients are a whole series of leaves and barks which are thought to possess some medicinal or magical value. All these fumigation treatments "cost money," in the form of *bari* shells; but, if they still leave the patient unimproved, he or some responsible relative will stake a full-grown pig on a final throw, which is nothing less than a *kwi-usane-habu*, or "sago-dance." This is an affair of considerable dimensions, to which guests are invited from far-away tribes. Others, of the host-village, not immediately concerned with the patient, will kill pigs of their own, and there will ensue the usual lively barter of pork for ornaments. But it is still the case that an *usane-habu*, the major dance of the Kutubu people and the only one in which drums are beaten, can only take place as the direct result of a case of sickness. It represents the culmination of a long series of treatments, and if it fails I do not know if the Kutubu doctors have any further resort.

The curing ritual which precedes the dance is very similar to the *sago-mitenabu* already described, but with a different material symbol. This time it is a small plaque of palm spathe called *bodo* (Fig. 13), painted in stripes and with a fixture at the rear which enables the dancer to hold it in his teeth, whence the whole rite comes to be

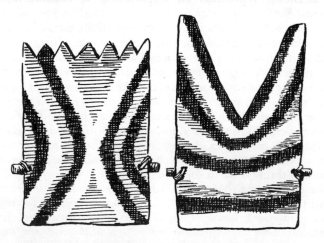

Fig. 13. Examples of *bodo*: about 8in. and 10in. in height.
Painted red, yellow and black.

called *bodo-gavirabo*, or "biting the *bodo*." Once again there are two practitioners. The principal carries a pair of *bodo* and a switch of *paiaka* leaves. He hands one of the *bodo* to the dancer who accompanies him, and this man moves round about the patient while the principal strokes the latter's body with the prickly leaves, now and again turning to bring them in contact with the *bodo*. Finally the dancer allows the first *bodo* to fall from his mouth in front of the patient, and the performance is repeated with the second. Then the principal picks up both and affixes them to the front wall of the men's house, where they remain indefinitely, probably until the *aa* itself is demolished. They are to be seen in every man's house stuck up like tiny coloured shields on either side of the entrance.[29] It is said that they must remain there in order to make certain of a cure; but, quite apart from any concern for the patient, they serve the function of *aa-sanubu* or ornament; and beyond that they are trophies, for an *usane-hubu* is a big thing for a village to carry through.

The two *bodo*, like the *soga*, are explicitly said to represent Arurubu and Sinanume, but we are left to deduce the theory of their action. It seemed to me that Kutubu informants were almost unusually vague and uncertain in their explanations of *kwi-rumu-hubu* and its treatments. But on one significant point they were sure—that Arurubu and Sinanume belonged to a country away to the east or south-east of the lake. It is probably fair to assume that the whole complex which they are supposed to have originated, even including the drum itself (which is used exclusively in the dances connected with sickness), represents an importation to Kutubu from the south-east.[30]

The Usi Methods. There remains another wide class of treatments which belongs to what may be called the *Usi* cult. This cult, a large subject in itself, will be dealt with in the next chapter; but it may be said here that its central theme and purpose is the curing, or pretended curing, of sickness; and we may at the present point give one or two examples to show it in operation.

Those who have been initiated to *Usi* are empowered to deal with the illnesses caused by spirits of the dead, whether of those who have, so to speak, died "in their beds" (i.e. *aminterare, yesibu*), or of those who have been slain (*pauave, husahua*). The usual technique (called *usi-fogubu*) is the familiar one of sucking the patient's body and revealing to him the objects, in some manner representing the cause of his illness, which have been allegedly extracted from it. This always involves some sleight of hand. In the present case it is very transparent, and the objects sucked out would seem to be of an impossible size—stones as big as one's fist to represent the *aminterare*, and pieces of wood up to eighteen inches long to represent the *pauave*.

(The distinction is not always strictly observed: I have seen a case in which the *pauave* appeared as stones.) The treatment is nevertheless carried out in all seriousness. Patients readily submit themselves, which implies they have faith; and it would be wrong to suppose that the practitioners themselves were wholly tricksters.

As the first example I give the case of a woman Gagoeni, who as a widow had married Sinigana of Tugiri. She was obviously very ill. The real cause of her illness I do not pretend to know (I gave her on chance a packet of Epsom salts which may have contributed more than the *Usi* treatment towards her ultimate recovery); but it was confidently diagnosed by the villagers as a case of *pauave-hubu*. Gagoeni herself was ready to endorse this diagnosis, or perhaps she originated it. At any rate she declared that some time previously, while working on the further shore of the lake, she had seen a "very red man," who seized her, thus making her ill. The red man was a *pauave*, the spirit of some person unidentified who had died by violence.

She had undergone *Usi* treatment more than once before the occasion here described, and the first hint I had of the affair on hand was the sight of a number of pieces of wood heaped together at one spot in the village. They were rough twisted pieces, up to fifteen inches long, of the timber called *ima*, and all were painted red. These were called simply *pauave*, and they were the result of earlier operations by *Usi* practitioners on the same case, all having been ostensibly extracted from Gagoeni's body. (It seemed likely that they might represent bones—though of rather superhuman size—particularly as seizure or striking by the spirits of the dead is sometimes called *amina-kiki-hubu*, "being stricken by a man's bones." But informants said nothing to support this idea: the sticks—or elsewhere the stones—were simply *pauave* or *aminterare*).

On the present occasion the two operators were Fareape and Yobe, the latter a true son of the patient by a former marriage. (Each received a payment of *bari* from Sinigaga, the husband.) They were making their preparations in a corner of the men's house, a small enclosure, walled off for concealment from the uninitiated and called the *usi-aa*. Here, with the assistance of some older men, they had pounded the mixture of barks which together constitute the real *usi*, using the ancient stone bowl of Tugiri for the purpose. In the *usi-aa* a considerable pile of freshly painted *ima* sticks had been collected, and all was in readiness for the operation, which would be carried out as soon as it was dark enough.

The young men poured some water into the nasty red mess already prepared in the bowl, and each took two long draughts, using for drinking-vessel the half-coconut shell which belongs by right to the *Usi* cult. Having on one occasion sampled an infusion of *aroa*, which is always the main constituent of *usi*, I can say with certainty that it is thoroughly disagreeable, but I have my doubts whether it possesses any of the intoxicating properties ascribed to it. At any rate, neither of the two young men appeared to be in the slightest degree affected: the only thing I noticed—and I noticed it at other times in the same circumstances—was that each as he put down the coconut vessel emitted a prodigious eructation. It is worth mentioning the unpleasantness, both to sight and taste, of the *usi* mixture, for it seems that the practitioner, when he consents to drink it, must, if only to that extent, be taking his preparations seriously.

I obtained in advance the spell which is supposed to be uttered just before or just after drinking the *usi*. It contains references to Somaia and Hobo (or to the woman Yabame) to whom the origin of the *Usi* cult is ascribed, and it should name the patient, expressing a wish to make him well, reduce his fever, give him sound sleep, etc. But, as so often, when it came to the point the spell remained unspoken. Neither of the two young operators uttered a word. They went about their preparations very deliberately, however. Each arranged a bark-cloth cloak over his left shoulder; then picked over the pieces of red wood, selecting those that suited him best and trying a few in advance under the left armpit; and finally fitted a branch of Cordyline in the plaited band on his left arm. Both the bark-cloth and the Cordyline were obviously meant to conceal the *ima* wood which he would presently have to "palm" in his armpit.

Meanwhile the patient, looking very sick and miserable, was sitting in Sinigana's house, some thirty yards away. The house was in darkness, but occupied by Sinigana's two other wives and their children. Gagoeni herself sat near the entrance, leaning back of her arms as props and for once without the bark-cloth cloak.

Sinigana now called to Fareape, who was still in the *usi-aa*. There followed sounds of stamping on the floor and presently Fareape came running across, visible against the sky-line, his cassowary plumes waving, and his shell ornaments ajingle. He sprang up the steps, stooped over the woman and planted his lips somewhere on her anatomy, apparently the stomach. Then he staggered back, reeling in a half circle, and uttering a sort of whine, or cry of pain. There was a heavy thud and one of the pieces of reddened wood fell to the floor. Fareape had succeeded in sucking out and somehow passing through his body the first *pauave*. He turned immediately and ran back to the men's-house, ostensibly to renew his magical preparations but really to obtain a second piece of wood. On the way he met and passed the second operator, Yobe, who proceeded to extract a second *pauave* from the patient in exactly the same way, except that he put rather more vim into his sucking, reeling, and crying out. So they continued, turn and turn about, until about a dozen *pauave* had fallen; and then on their last trips they brought two apiece, so that in all there were about sixteen. The woman bore it all in patience, though she winced and whimpered occasionally at a specially severe suck or bite.

There is little doubt that she, her husband, and the *Usi* operators all repose some faith in the treatment. The sleight of hand is indeed so clumsy and the objects extracted so preposterously large that we can hardly assume that the patient literally believes them to have come out of her body. Yet she and her husband still think it is worth the expense and trouble. The actual rite of extraction may in fact be merely symbolic, as if the *Usi* magicians should say, "This is how we get the real *pauave* out of you." In popular belief the effectiveness of these men as curers is supposed to reside in the power and knowledge which they have acquired as members of the *Usi* cult and which are not revealed to the layman. Yet it is not only the laymen who trust in *Usi*. As already suggested, the practitioners go to so much trouble behind the scenes that we must assume that they themselves believe their method has something in it.

The above description illustrates the *Usi* treatment in its simple form. But a course of *usi-fogubu*, if unsuccessful, may be followed by a large-scale attack on the *pauave* involving the participation of a number of initiates and the killing of a pig. I was fortunate enough to witness such a performance, though many details in a long story will have to be omitted or treated lightly in the following description. The patient, Yamabu of Fimaga, was suffering from an ulcer, almost covering the instep of one foot, which had been inflicted on him by the *pauave* of Dabea, not long previously killed by the people of Yokobu in revenge for supposed sorcery. Yamabu had undergone the sucking-treatment on at least three previous occasions. He had now been brought to Tugiri and a pig was to be paid to Kabebe, the principal man of the village, for organizing and conducting the ritual.

There were at least twelve other participants, all *Usi* initiates but mostly youths or boys. Part of the men's-house had been walled off for them, and here, from the afternoon onwards, they spent the whole night except for intervals of dancing. They were all dosed from time to time with the *usi* mixture and sang continuously the songs appropriate to the matter in hand. (They deal with the myths of Somaia and Yabame, the originators of the cult.) Then they would emerge all together to perform the remarkable dance, if such it can be called, which belongs to *Usi*; and, having worked off their energy for the time being, would crowd back into the *usi-aa*, almost

tumbling over each other, to renew their singing. It was not till dawn
was breaking that they finally emerged for their real attack on the
pauave. The dancers now carried sticks and branches of Cordyline, in
the leaves of which were concealed numbers of reddened stones
which were to represent the spirits who were afflicting the patient.
(Although one *pauave* had been named in particular they were subsequently spoken of in the plural.) The dancers had by this time
worked themselves up into a state of some excitement, or at any rate
abandon, and the dance surged back and forth from end to end of
the men's-house while bystanders edged away in order to avoid
receiving food-humoured blows from the sticks. After several turns
the dancers lined up in front of the alcove where the patient was
sitting, and simultaneously struck the rail above his head with their
sticks, at the same time letting fall their stones (or most of them). By
this act they dislodged and scattered the *pauave* which had been
sitting perched on the rail and gloating over their victim beneath.
Since it was still dark, except for torch and firelight, and since the
attack on the *pauave* was conducted amid a great uproar of sounds,
no one would notice the stones falling. As a matter of fact the dancers
had scattered some of them already in different parts of the *aa*,
while others they still kept in hand. Finally they burst out of the far
entrance and trooped into the women's houses. Here they carried on
their dance for a while, dropping the remainder of the stones, and
then returned in a body to the *usi-aa*. The numerous red stones were
collected in daylight and displayed for all to see—a very satisfactory
bag of *pauave*.

The subsequent proceedings need not be described in detail. The
pig, which was killed by Kabebe and his foster-son (who acted as his
principal assistant) served in part to provide what was apparently a
feast of reconciliation between the kin of the patient and those of the
late Dabea, whose *pauave* was held mainly responsible for Yamabu's
condition. A parcel of its flesh, specially cooked in a green bamboo,
was laid out on a dish and attached to a strip of bast, fully eighteen
yards in length. One end of this strip was held at various points by
the patient and his kin, the other end by the kin of the man Dabea,
the parcel of meat being in the middle. Then Kabebe, after pronouncing an interminable spell, during which he seemed to saw at
the parcel with his knife, suddenly cut it in halves; and the halves
were changed over so that each side ate the portions which had been
attached to the string held by the other. This might seem to have
little to do with the business of curing, unless indirectly, in that it
was meant to make up the quarrel between the two kin involved and
so to remove any grounds the *pauave* might have for continuing to
persecute Yamabu. Nevertheless the long spell pronounced by

Kawabe was still concerned with the *pauave*: he was naming all the bones of the deceased Dabea, his skull, arms, fingers, ribs, etc., with constant repetition of the word *furage*—which was translated to me as "I close up." This was alleged to be scaring the *pauave* away, or at least inducing it not to return. When the parcel was finally cut in two its anger was said to be finished; it would come no more.

It does not seem clear that this parcel of meat was regarded as an offering to the *pauave*; certainly no informant said so. But the rite which immediately preceded it can hardly be viewed in any other light. The red stones, which are definitely said to be the *pauave*, having been collected, were heaped together on a sheet of palm spathe and carefully covered with Cordyline leaves, little sticks of the tree called *ira-kanega*, soft fern-like leaves called *buifofore* and some broad leaves called *patamu*. These are said to be common in the place (somewhere in the upper regions) of the *pauave*, and to be somehow associated with them—*patamu*, e.g. are the leaves they affect in their armlets, and the palm-like *buifofore* serve them for feather decorations. But it seems hardly necessary to look for evidence for identifying the stones with the *pauave*, since the identification is clearly stated already. The offering consisted, sufficiently obviously, in the blood of the pig. When Kabebe's assistant had killed it with a blow from a heavy bark-cloth beater on the back of the head, Kabebe himself held it down over the stones until they were liberally sprinkled with the blood which poured from its nose.[31] Then the spathe with the stones inside it was carefully bound up and stowed away under the floor of the men's house, among similar parcels which told of similar ceremonies in the past.

Summary
One could write almost endlessly on Kutubu belief and practice in relation to disease; what has been written here is merely a clipped presentation of the material gathered during a short stay. Indeed, had I made a fuller study of the people, sufficient to justify it, I think the best method of expounding the culture of Kutubu would be to write a book on this subject in particular, bringing all the rest, or as much as was necessary, into relation with it. It would be quite feasible, and would do no injustice to the culture at large, to present the beliefs and practices connected with disease as its leading motive.

No general subject could be said to give the Kutubuan more to think about, for sickness is a breach of routine, not to be dealt with by purely routine process, and there are numerous possibilities by way of diagnosis and treatment that call for decision or trial. It is thus a main source of intellectual interest. We have seen also that current theories bring it into close relation with morality, since cases are so often regarded as the result of wrong-doing or neglect. Further, certain of the best-recognized lines of treatment are bound up with mythology and esoterics; and it may be said of the *Usi* cult that the curing of disease—partly the pretence of curing it, but also the desire to cure it—provides the *raison d'être* for the most spectacular phase of Kutubu ceremonial life. It is a noteworthy fact also that sickness affords continual excuse for the minor feasts associated with the ritual of curing, and the only excuse for *usane-habu*, which is the most pretentious of Kutubu feasts and dances. Even the drum is silent unless there is a sick man to beat it for. So it appears that the men and women of Kutubu grow sociable and even make merry over curing one another's ailments.

But while it is far from being always a solemn preoccupation the attitude towards disease and cure is perhaps predominantly a religious one, for it touches at so many points on the relations with the spirit world. In view of these facts it seems permissible to say that this special interest, or perhaps the over-development of it, has sufficed to give the culture of Kutubu its own air of distinction.

Part IV

The Secret Life

Certain departments of Kutubu knowledge and practice are reserved for privileged sections of society. It is true that these sections may be very wide, even embracing the whole male half of the population; but the members still move in a mysterious way to perform the rites involved, and therefore we may speak of an esoteric department of Kutubu culture, or of the Kutubuan's "secret life."

Apart from private secrecies, of magic and so on, there are at least three collective sub-departments of this secret life which may be spoken of as cults. They are (1) *Amaga*, the bullroarer, (2) *Usi* (certain aspects of which have already been discussed), and (3) *Piaka Gwabu*, or the Arrow-Head.

1. *The Bullroarer*

The bullroarer may be dismissed very briefly. This cult is of minor importance, since it appears to be altogether unknown to some villages of the Kutubu group. Its local headquarters is Wasemi, where alone I was able to see a specimen of the actual *amaga*—a small slat of palmwood, ill-shapen and devoid of ornament.

Among my interpreters there was only one, Waipi, who had been initiated and was therefore available to discuss the subject. But neither he nor the older initiates whom we consulted seemed able to give any but the barest account of the rites, much less an explanation of them. There was apparently no accepted theory such as I have always found elsewhere in connection with this cult, the bullroarer representing some kind of noisy monster or supernatural being which continually demands food. The only thing they could speak of with any certainty was its introduction to the lake, which was relatively recent. It had occurred in the boyhood of the old man Yaru, who was said to have been the first Kutubuan initiate; and the initiators had been invited for the purpose from Kaibu. It is plain then that the bullroarer, like betel-chewing and cannibalism, is a foreign introduction which has not yet fully established itself in Kutubu culture.

What it may mean or amount to at Kaibu I cannot say. But as far as Kutubu is concerned it seems like another example of the absorption of a foreign triat without much regard for, or concern about, its significance; a case of superficial copying wherein form takes precedence over function. It is to be supposed that it has come to stay; that in the ordinary course of events it will spread throughout the Kutubu group; and that its functions will develop in the process. But at present it may be said to bear no essential relation to Kutubu culture as a whole: it could be dropped without making any difference worth mentioning. Except to make this point, I should not consider it necessary to write of the bullroarer at all. In a short and necessarily selective account of Kutubu culture it might not unfairly be left out of the picture.

2. *The Usi Cult*

It is probable that the *usi* cult is also an introduction, though in this case it has brought with it a large body of mythical associations[32] and there is no lack of meaning and theory in it. There is no occasion to suppose that the cult, even if introduced, is anything but an ancient one at Kutubu, and it has certainly established itself as one of the people's leading interests.

Whenever we began to discuss anything in connection with *usi*, some of the men and boys who usually gathered about my camp-stool in the men's-house would take their departure, hurriedly and almost in alarm. But a good proportion remained, including young boys. (Females of course were never present: they know nothing of the inner workings of the cult.) I concluded that *usi* belonged to an extensive secret society, comprising perhaps half the males.

Its ostensible purpose, as we have seen, is to cure sickness. *Usi* is the general name for the "medicines," a strange mixture, which are drunk from time to time by the initiates. Having been taught how to prepare and drink such medicines, and having undergone some very rigorous preliminaries by way of training, the novice is qualified to treat sickness by the extraction technique already described. There is no doubt that he believes in his power to cure; but it is important to note that his motives are not wholly altruistic. He has an eye to profits in the form of fees; indeed, in the preparatory magic a great deal of stress is laid on this aspect of the matter, so much so that it may seem that the cult is directed as much towards the enrichment of the doctors as the cure of their patients. Needless to say a candidate for initiation has to pay a price for it.

No initiation took place during my stay at Kutubu, but a number of verbal accounts correspond well enough to justify an attempt at description. The business is a long one, with many episodes; but, to venture a summary, it may be said in essence to constitute a recapitulation of the experiences of the mythical founder of the cult. This is by no means to say that there are no extraneous features in it; indeed there are important episodes that have no reflection in the main myth or in any other that I know of. But the gist of present-day procedure does seem to be a recapitulation or re-enactment of a mythical procedure. Whether or not the cart precedes the horse we may begin, then, by narrating the myth of origin.

The Myth of Somaia and Hobo. There are as usual a number of different versions and it is not possible to deal with them all. But it is worth noting that there are two main variants, in one which the principal part is played by a woman, Yabame, in the other by two brothers, Somaia and Hobo.[33] These correspond with the division of the cult into two slightly different forms, *kaa-usi* and *amina-usi*, i.e. "female" and "male." The former was brought by Yabame to Ifigi, Eragahugu, Borutage, Hegisu, Kesi (in part), Tugiri, Yokobu, and Wasemi; the latter by Hobo to Fimaga, Kenahagu, Kesi (in part), and Kesiki. The differences, as far as I could ascertain, amount to very little. I shall confine the present description in respect of both myth and ritual, to *amina-usi* because the best accounts I received were of that version of the cult.

Somaia and his younger brother Hobo lived at Soborutiki, far away to the east or south-east. The elder brother used to be away from morn till eve, but he never brought anything home, either animal or vegetable. Hobo alone was the food-getter. He gardened and hunted with great diligence, and whenever Somaia returned there was half an animal waiting for him ready cooked; though even so he would not turn up till it was cold. Hobo grew very tired of all this and determined to find out what his brother was up to in his absences. So one morning, instead of being the first to leave home as was his custom, he feigned illness and waited. Then, when Somaia went off, he secretly followed him.

He was led by devious tracks which he had not previously explored to a clearing in the bush, a place of beautiful "red" ground (i.e. clay), neat and clean and planted about with ornamental shrubs. Here, keeping himself hidden in the bush, Hobo settled down to spy upon his brother.

Somaia entered a little house which stood in the midst of the clearing and emerged bearing an internode of bamboo together with a bunch of leaves. He sat down and proceeded to chant a song:

Neme buru, kirau[34] *hoke; dame soka, karau hoke*	
Dark skinned pig	parcel of salt
Baribarima, kirau hoke; situma kura kirau hoke	
Bari shells	smoked cuscus
Nemi kikekeo, kirau hake; siginabari kekeo, kirau hoke	
Leg of pig	leg of cassowary
Segere barihi, kirau hoke ; Segere kagamea, kirau hoke	
Large pearlshell	pearlshell with necklet
Nemi yumoro, kirau hoke; bari wanema, kirau hoke	
Pale skinned pig	large cowrie shell
Dame tui, kirau hoke; dame kwai, kirau hoke	
Parcel of salt	parcel of salt.

As he named each item Somaia gently and rhythmically stroked the bamboo with the leaves. Then he took some *aroa* bark and pounded it in a stone vessel; then poured water out of his bamboo on to the crushed bark, mixed them together, and drank. As if suddenly gone crazy, Somaia then began to dance, reeling about, rolling his eyes and poking out his tongue; he spat and spat and his saliva was red like blood. Finally he entered his house to rest, and Hobo, much impressed by what he had seen, hurried home in order to anticipate his return.

But though, visiting one of his springes and taking the captured cassowary, he had everything ready as usual for his brother's evening meal, the brother did not turn up. When he woke next morning there was still no Somaia, so he went boldly to the little house in the forest and entered it. There he found, not Somaia, but his bare skeleton.

Under the left arm of the skeleton was a tiny string bag. Hobo placed in it Somaia's little-finger bone together with a small stone, and slung it under his own left arm. Then he took the bamboo and went through the process of stroking it and singing Somaia's song;

then pounded the *aroa* bark in the stone mortar, poured in the mixture from the bamboo, drank, and went off raving.

He travelled from place to place in a long itinerary which led him towards the west, collecting various new herbs and further stones as he went. At each stopping place he carried out the curing treatment associated with *usi* (by biting and sucking), which he was now somehow enabled to perform. Finally he reached Fimaga in the Kutubu area, and here, in association with a man named Tamo, he seems to have conducted a school of initiation.

Together they sang the following song:

Bari kibibie; sese kura kibibie; tame kibibie.
Nemi-arami kibibie; huka boru kibibie; gagebo kibibie.

"Give us *bari*; give us smoked cuscus; give us salt; give us portions of pig; give us sago-grubs; give us axes." They were naming the price of *usi* treatment—which the people willingly paid because on all sides they found it effective.

Hobo, in this version, died at Fimaga leaving his good works behind him in the form of the *usi* cult. The large flattish concave stone which is kept, carefully wrapped up, in the Fimaga men's-house, serving when needed as a mortar for pounding the *aroa* is said to be the hero's sternum.

Initiation. We may now turn to the initiation of the modern candidates. They are presented in batches, the individuals coming from various villages to the centre where the ceremonies are to take place, and they vary in age from children to married adults. (The batch at Yokobu—where an initiation was to have taken place during my stay, but did not—comprised six boys, ranging between say ten and eighteen years, and two adults, one of whom was married.) One or two elderly men will act as initiators. They stand in no particular relationship to their charges (for once the maternal uncle is not called upon to play the initiator's part), but are merely the senior initiates in the village where the ceremonies are being staged. They will be paid in *bari* or other valuables for their services.

The initiators are known to the novices whom they severally deal with as *fagari*, a reciprocal term. That is to say, initiate and initiator address one another as "my coconut." This surely comical-sounding form of speech has its origin in the use of the half-coconut-shell as a drinking vessel for the *usi* mixture, the novice receiving his first draught in such a cup at the hands of the old man officiating. The fact that coconuts (*fagari*) do not grow on the lake supports the generally accepted view that *usi* is an importation. The cups, such as are to be seen, come from some less elevated region, as presumably did the cult itself.

The initiates are led into a closed compartment called *akaura*, formed by walling off part or the whole of one side of the interior of the men's-house. Here they are stripped of their belts, armlets and ornaments, and are given their first draught of the *usi*.

The mixture has been prepared in advance. Its ingredients are various barks, shoots, herbs, etc. which it would be futile to enumerate since I have not had them identified. But the main one is the bark called *aroa*, the mixture being sometimes referred to by that name alone; another is tobacco (*sogo*); and another a kind of herb called *yiragai*. This last at any rate must have some potency. It is not an invariable component of the mixture, but may be included when the apparent effects of drinking are meant to be especially striking. A youth, one of a group which, with some zest, was enacting the story of Hobo for me, consented to take a dose of it. Small pieces being dropped into his open mouth, he proceeded to behave as if taking a fit, bending his body backwards, turning up his eyes and clenching his teeth, while a red foam appeared upon his lips and ran down his throat and chest—an unpleasant sight altogether and a good simulation of epilepsy. He was master of himself throughout, however, and in a moment emerged smiling.

It may be that *yiragai* is the real essence of the *usi*. The whole mixture is said to be disagreeable, hot in the mouth and nauseating; but it is expressly denied that it causes the seemingly drunken behaviour that ensues on taking it. This is said always to be *korafe*, or "pretence"; though the copious salivation which may accompany it (the spittle being more or less red) is evidently to some extent a direct result of the medicine.

Having received his formal dose the novice behaves as Hobo is supposed to have behaved when he first sampled his brother's *usi*. The movements, though characterized by a good deal of abandon, are more or less formalized. The young man dances with his legs rather wide apart, rocking from foot to foot, and with stiff arms and clawing fingers, his tongue lolling out of his mouth, and his eyes rolling upwards. The whole, together with a certain amount of uncontrolled lurching and staggering, is called *mosuiabo*, and the novice, having often seen initiates in action, knows well how to proceed from the outset. It is said that his *fagari* assures him that it is all pretence (a fact which the uninitiated are not supposed to realize), but urges him to give a good vigorous performance.

Now, two or three at a time, the novices are brought out into the open, and there follows a part of their initiation which seems to have no suggestion of a counter part in the myth of Hobo. Each must be given, or must find for himself, his "*usi-a-kaa*" or "*usi*-wife." Some initiate (not necessarily his *fagari*) who is shepherding him through the village or bush, presses into his palm a few crushed leaves, picked at random, naming some animal, bird, or reptile, and saying "That is your *usi-a-kaa*." Or alternatively the older initiate may say, "There goes *fukabo* or *mamia* (naming some such creature)! After it !" Whereupon the novice dashes to grasp a dead leaf or a cobweb or anything that happens to attract his attention. With this clutched in his hand he is led back to the men's-house: he has acquired a spiritual wife.

The *usi-a-kaa*, i.e. the species which he happens to have got hold of (it may be a hornbill, *ya-fore*; a hawk, *aiyabo*; a rat; or any kind of marsupial) is thenceforward a sort of ally or familiar to him, an individual totem. He must not eat it for fear of wasting away, and it may be that he really depends upon it in some way for assistance. On this last point, however, I have no positive information. In practice, as far as I could discover, the *usi-a-kaa* is really a blind, providing a false explanation to put the uninitiated off the scent. As we shall see, the latter are encouraged to believe that these familiars are responsible for the initiate's power to cure, whereas the initiate himself knows that he derives that power from another source.

After the acquisition of the *usi-a-kaa* the novices return to the enclosure within the men's-house, to be dosed many times more during the ensuing days with the *usi* and to make periodical excursions, practising the *mosuiabo*. This probationary term lasts five days, during which the novices undergo a severe fast: they eat no "proper" food, and it is declared, somewhat incredibly, that they live on *usi* alone. Every night is spent in singing, the theme of the songs being the history of Somaia and Hobo, and during these long sessions the novices are not supposed to sleep: if one of them drops off he is jogged into wakefulness and told that sleeping is a sign of present and future weakness. Laughing is forbidden: they must take their work seriously. Altogether it is a period of considerable hardship, a test of endurance.

In the meantime the younger men of the village have been out hunting. They return on the eve of the fifth, or "thumb," day when there takes place the lesser feast and the ceremony called *soro-gibu*. The novices are led from their virtual seclusion to a place in the bush where the older initiates have prepared to meet them and give them a surprise. These older initiates are fully painted and befeathered and they employ various devices to make themselves appear impressive or terrifying or merely ugly. Among them is the trick of threading a strand of creeper through the hole in the nasal septum passing it over the ears and tying it behind the head. The novices, escorted by their *fagari* and a troupe of initiates, all performing *mosuiabo*, approach a barrier of branches and are pushed through, to be leapt upon by these older men who are waiting in ambush. They are supposed to be terrified, but I failed to discover whether the older men, in their more or less grotesque get-up, were intended to represent anything more than their merely human selves.

The *fagari*, who have followed the novices through the barrier, now give them a special medicine known as *yiragai barani* of which I have no explanation except regarding its purpose, which is to give the novice some kind of spiritual strength, whence the name of the ceremony. *Soro-gibu* means "giving the *soro*," and the *soro* is apparently a kind of essence (resident somewhere in the breast) which enables men to perform feats of daring and skill. They have it, or they don't have it; or they have it in greater or less degree. Its presence or otherwise is merely deducible from performance. The present ceremony, however, is meant somehow to instil it into the novice, to give him power, especially to follow the profession of the *usi* with success in curing and in collecting fees. It is to be noted, incidentally, that such success, or lack of it, may be prognosticated from the behaviour or the novice himself on this occasion; if he walks strongly after his five days of privation he will do well; if he droops he will be a failure.

At the *sogo-gibu* each new initiate receives a wand, painted red and white, known as his *dokoyoko fura*, which seems to mean literally his *"don't-talk stick,"* though it doubtless signifies more than this, for it is said that if it happened to break, the *soro* in its possessor would die. The novices carry these wands whenever they issue from the men's-house during the next fortnight. The significance of the name is simply that they must not divulge the secrets of the *usi*; the stick is in some manner a symbol of silence.

On the nineteenth, or "nose," day occurs the festival which brings the virtual seclusion of the novices to a close. Many guests are summoned and village pigs are killed. The new initiates are led out in line, fully decorated, and the women welcome them with enthusiasm and gifts of cooked sago. Each is formally presented with a miniature string bag (*usi-ware*) containing a little-finger bone and a stone, and this the new initiate hides, like Hobo, under his left arm. Further, each is given a large string bag of the kind called *arera* (the contents of which are not revealed to the public) together with a heap of food. The feasting, if modified, has gone on since the beginning and this in fact is the first occasion in nearly three weeks on which the novices will have a full meal. The course of ceremonies is brought to an end by the delivery of payment to the men who have acted as initiators.

Each of the string bags above mentioned contains a whole series of articles (bird feathers, coloured leaves, barks, creepers, ginger, etc.) the avowed purpose of which is to promote their owner's success by their magic power. The bags remain in the men's-house (I saw twenty-one of them wrapped up in bark and stacked or hanging up in a corner at Fimaga) until they are thoroughly blackened with smoke when, it is said, they are finally buried in order to dispose of them in perfect safety. I was unable to induce anyone to open a package to let me examine the contents; the owners professed to be too much afraid that the uninitiated might see what was in them.

Motives and Meaning. The new initiate is now equipped for practice. There is no denying that his training, though brief, has been very rigorous; and this in itself implies a certain sincerity in those who practise the cult. At the same time, the gulling of the uninitiated, including especially the patients under treatment, is admitted to be an essential part of the technique. No secret is made of the fact that the wild, sometimes almost paroxysmal, motions of the dancers are *korafe*, or pretence; and there is no doubt about the actual method of extraction, which is mere sleight of hand and clumsy at that.

There is throughout a strange mixture of sincerity and deceit. The operators may utter an audible spell in order to impress their patients: it refers to the *usi-a-kaa*, whatever it may chance to be, and is supposed to give them the notion that the individual totem or familiar is the source of power. But they have other spells for private use. When, or if,[35] they pronounce these they are doing so in order to stimulate or reaffirm their powers of curing, and it is a fair assumption that they are generally serious about it.

The same sort of mixture is observable in the practitioner's motives. While it is sufficiently plain that they are partly those proper to a medical man, it is worth adverting once again to the mere desire for gain, which is probably much the strongest element. While there is little doubt that the practitioner tries to cure and believes that he can cure, it is noteworthy that the magical formulae on which he to some extent relies refer largely to items of wealth. The contents of the *arera* bags mentioned above (the *usi* practitioner's magical kit) are predominantly symbols of success in getting worldly wealth. They are spoken of as *magami*-magic, i.e. things that will make their possessors become rich in *magami* or pearlshells (a general expression for the shell or other valuables that will come in as fees). A few, it is true, were made to refer to hunting—which seems somewhat irrelevant, though hunting is always a favourite theme in Kutubu magic. But never, though I had several accounts of the contents of the *arera* bag, was there any suggestion that they bore on success in the art of curing.

Even the mythical founders of the cult seem to have laid principal stress on the mercenary side of their profession. Somaia's song is a spell in which he enumerates the various kinds of wealth which the practice of *usi* may bring; and the song of Hobo (whose role is much like that of a disciple, the divine or mythical founder having passed on) has the same import, only stated a little more explicitly. There is no doubt that the *usi* cult, though it means some hardships and expense to qualify for it, is distinctly worth while to its members.

It is not justifiable to assume that in such a cult as the one we are dealing with there must be an inner meaning known to all its members. It may well be the case that such inner meaning, if there is one, is more obscure to its members than it is to an ethnographer (at any rate, it is probable that they are less concerned with it). Therefore the following interpretation must not necessarily be regarded as of general acceptance. But it is worth recording a statement that the objects extracted from the patient's body—pieces of reddened wood, stones, etc.—represented not *pauave*, or spirits of the dead, as the patients were led to believe, but really the bones of Somaia. Once again it was a case of bluffing the uninitiated. Those really in the know pretended to the patients that they were sucking out dead men's spirits; they pretended to themselves that they were sucking out the founder's bones, just as Hobo, when he began to practise, used, for sucking-object, the bone of his deceased brother's little finger (the one he had taken from the skeleton and put in his small string bag).

I have recorded a long spell,[36] uttered prior to the operation, which begins with a catalogue of the founder's bones—spine, neck-vertebrae, skull, lower jaw, shins, etc.—and it was made clear that these corresponded with the sticks and stones which would ostensibly be dragged out of the sufferer's body. I must confess that this does not make the meaning of the cult much clearer to me, unless we assume that Hobo is supposed to have used various of his dead brother's bones, large and small, for objects to suck out of his patients when he first started practice. The sticks and stones of modern times are perhaps substitutes for actual bones used by earlier practitioners, the first of whom was the mythical Hobo.

However this may be, I am prepared to suggest that the gist of the initiation ceremonies, in so far as they re-enact the story of Hobo, are of the essence of imitative magic, and of the particular kind which I have already called the magic of impersonation. That is to say the initiate is put through the same course as Hobo himself went through in order to make another Hobo of him.

3. *Piaka Gwabu, the Arrow-Head*

The third secret cult of Kutubu, *piaka gwabu*, would seem to be more ancient than *usi*, belonging to a deeper cultural stratum. It involves no initiation, and the smallest children, providing they are old enough to be sleeping in the men's-house, are admitted to its rites. It is thus another example of the dichotomy between the sexes, so typical of western Papua, which limits religious ritual almost exclusively to males.[37] And not only do the males possess a monopoly of the rite involved, but they enjoy the more practical privilege of eating all the meat provided for it.

Material Elements in the Cult. The expression *piaka gwabu* means "sliver of black palm." There is no question of a single sacred sliver; any such may be used. Further it is said that a mere slat of the proper palm-wood may serve the purpose. But wherever I have seen it it has taken the form of an arrow-head detached from the shaft, and in this there may well lie some significance. Whether the *piaka gwabu* can be said to represent anything, as if it were some sort of degenerate image, is a question to which we shall return later (though it may be said at the outset that we shall get no help from the native himself).

When a ceremony is pending the *piaka gwabu* is found attached to the end-post of a simple shelter called the *piaka-aa*, or "black-palm-house." At Herebu this was situated in a clearing on the small hill-top half a mile from the village; at Tugiri it was hidden in a garden hardly a hundred yards away; and at Wasemi it was in the village itself.[38] It is a very simple structure with a ridge-roof set on thin posts; in some cases it has no walls. The *piaka-aa* is a more or less permanent establishment, but the general air of neglect that belongs to those specimens that I have seen suggests that the ceremonies cannot be very frequent.

The *piaka-aa* is said to be inhabited by a *ho*, or "spirit." This is expressly said to be an *amina-ho*, or spirit of a deceased man, the word *ho* being an alternative, apparently without any different connotation, for *terare* (*aminterare*), *yesibu*, etc.; and in some cases, at any rate, it is that of a named individual, the founder of the village or its long-ago chief man. It is said to appear sometimes in the form of a small lizard, *maberaru*, and if you happen to see one scuttling about in the thatch you will be well advised not to touch it for fear it should "lash round with its tail" (in a purely metaphorical sense) and give you conjunctivitis. We shall see later that the rites performed in the *piaka-aa* are in part directed towards this individual, the *piaka-aa-ho*, as well as to the spirits of other dead men, so that they are in part to be interpreted as ancestor-worship or the placation of the dead.

Up to this point it might seem that the palm-wood arrow-head, if it represents anything at all, would be a symbol of the resident *ho*. But no such suggestion—nor indeed any helpful suggestion—ever came from my informants, and there are further facts which may well cast a doubt on such an interpretation. For there are two more material objects which always appear in conjunction with the *piaka-gwabu;* they are (1) a piece of the plant named *takorabu*, and (2) string made from the *haginamo* tree. The former is tied to the arrow-head by means of the latter.

Haginamo is one of the useful trees of Kutubu, for besides making string from its bark the native eats its berries and cooks its leaves for "cabbage." But I cannot identify it, and at any rate it plays a very minor part.[39]

Takorabu (also called *sagainya*) is either true *piper methysticum* (the Polynesian kava) or a kind of pepper very similar to it. As is well-known, *kava*-drinking is found in parts of western Papua,[40] but there is no such custom at Kutubu. The presence of the plant at the lake, therefore, and its association with a secret cult give rise to some rather interesting speculations. These are made more intriguing by the fact that among all the villages of the Kutubu people there are, it is alleged, only two specimens of the plant in existence. One, the parent, is at Wasemi, and the other (from a root or cutting) at Yokobu. For performances of the *piaka gwabu* rites in other villages the proper thing is to obtain portions of the real plant and I have seen a dried-up section of the stem of the original Wasemi *takorabu* kept by the chief men of Herebu on the Mubi.[41]

Now it is sufficiently obvious from evidence gathered at Wasemi itself that the plant was brought there from further west. It is said to have come originally from Hai—thence to Kasua; thence to Konihea (which is two "sleeps" from Wasemi); and thence to Kaibu. From Kaibu a specimen was allegedly brought to Wasemi by the father of one of the old men now living in the village. Beyond Kaibu the above-mentioned names cannot be placed on the map; but it is not improbable that the Wasemi *takorabu* derives ultimately from some region in western Papua where the plant is cultivated for the express purpose of kava drinking. If this is the case we have a good example of a cultural element passing from one region to another and leaving its original meaning behind it. *Piper methysticum* is surrounded by religious associations at Kutubu, but there is no trace of any knowledge that it is a potential drug or intoxicant. Instead of chewing it green and drinking the extract mixed with saliva, all the Kutubuan does is to take one perfunctory bite at a fragment of hard, dry stem.

Myth of the Takorabu Plant. We may pass on to the myth of the *piaka gwabu* and the *takorabu* plant which, however confused and garbled, provides our principal clue to the meaning of the rites. I attacked the subject seven times in different Kutubu and Mubi villages and there was even more than the usual amount of disagreement in the results. In the fullest accounts there are two individuals mainly involved, both of whom might claim to be founders[42]: one observes the other going through the rites of *piaka gwabu* and subsequently copies them, since when they have been faithfully reproduced. There is some show of secrecy about revealing their names and very little agreement when they are revealed; the first (the watcher) was in various version called Sagainya, Kiwidobo, Seramena, Kanawebi and Waita; the second (an "underground man" and the original performer) was alternatively Waki or Kewato. The best of a number of rather indifferent accounts is given here. It was taken from a man of Borutage.

Kanawebe lived in great poverty. He met with no success in his hunting; his sons and daughters were ailing and under-fed; his pig was skin and bones; his gardens produced little; and when he felled a sago palm there was no substance in it. Near his house, in the clearing, there stood a *haginamo* tree, and near the *haginamo* grew a little *metari* plant (a small palm with an edible shoot). Kanawebe was much puzzled to see smoke rising from the *metari* plant, and finally from curiosity pulled it up. By so doing he revealed a large hole in the ground and in it beheld a strange man bearing a string bag bulging with the carcases of cuscus, bandicoots, lizards, etc. This was Waki. He was stamping heavily round a fire (the smoke of which had first attracted Kanawebe's attention) and performing the other rites which belong to *piaka gwabu*. Having carefully observed all he did, including the fixing of an arrow-head to the post, Kanawebe filled in the hole, trod down the earth, and over the spot erected a small house. Then he went off to hunt and found that he met with unprecedented success. Returning with his string bag as full as Waki's he set up the arrow-head, built a fire on the ground in the middle of the shelter and marched round, etc., doing everything just as the underground man had done. Thenceforward he repeated the ritual after every hunt, with the result that his hunting never failed, his gardens and sago-palms prospered, and his children and pigs grew fat. After some time he observed a plant shooting from the bare earth just where he had trodden it down over Waki, the underground man. This plant was the true *takorabu*. He allowed it to grow and subsequently, whenever he performed the ritual, tied a piece of its stem to the arrow-head and bit it before beginning to eat his meat.

My informants were of the opinion that the *takorabu* itself *was* Waki; and it is equally deducible from other versions, if not plainly stated, that the plant represents the founder of the cult.[43] It would seem, then, that the piece of *takorabu* tied to the arrow-head is perhaps more significant as a material symbol than is the arrow-head itself. But we must not look for explicit theories from the people who perform these ceremonies. Neither the one nor the other, as far as I could discover, is consciously thought of as a symbol of anything.

The Ritual. We may now describe briefly the simple ritual of *piaka gwabu*. There are two kinds of ceremonies, (1) a general one called *gagebo ninyi* which may be performed at any time after a hunt, and (2) the principal mortuary ceremony called *kigi-yahabu* (which is also preceded by a hunt).

In either case the *piaka-aa* is made ready in advance. A fire is kindled in an oblong hearth on the ground and those who wish to attend sit around it, leaving a space or passageway between the fire and themselves. The hunters, who have been out some days, have already smoked their meat and stowed it in their string bags. They decorate themselves with paint and feathers at some place apart in the bush and when they are ready approach the *piaka-aa* in procession. When they reach it they stand in silence for a moment while the entrance while some old man detaches the arrow-head and *takorabu* from the post. Then they file in, and the old man taps each bag of meat with the arrow-head and *takorabu* as it is carried past him. He then replaces the arrow-head, etc., on the post and the hunting party proceeds to file round the hearth. Having completed one circuit quietly they perform one or two more, now stamping as heavily as they know how, and then come to a halt. The old man again takes the arrow-head and hands it to the leader, who solemnly bites the *takorabu* and hands it round to all the other hunters to do the same. Then all deposit their bags and sit down simultaneously, and the silence, hitherto broken only by the sound of tramping feet, gives place to conversation. The old man replaces the arrow-head, having first pocketed the *tokorabu* in his string bag, where it will remain till next time; and the leader of the hunters hands round pieces of the smoked meat, cutting up the smaller animals such as rats and bandicoots, or tearing them to pieces in his hands. Not until everyone present has been given a preliminary morsel do they turn to cooking the larger animals and proceed with the feast.

The routine described above belongs up to this point to both the occasions for performing *piaka gwabu* and the *kigi-yahabu* or principal mortuary ceremony; but each has something further. A description of *kigi-yahabu* will be given in the ensuing chapter, for it seems to belong rather to the mortuary cycle than to *piaka gwabu*. But the extra rites in connection with *gagebo ninyi* should be given at this point.

Although this little ceremony is said to be frequently performed I never actually saw it. Any men returning from a hunt may carry it out more or less privately and it does not attract a number of guests as does *kigi-yahabu*.

Gagebo-ninyi means "Handle of the Stone Axe."[44] Before the hunters leave they strew the stone floor of the *piaka-aa* with certain leaves (of which I do not know the significance) and among them they hide a little forked branch, a miniature axe-handle. (This incidentally is a branch of the *haginamo* tree which, we have seen, is somehow associated with the cult). On returning with their bags of animals they go through the general rites previously described and then take the miniature axe-handle, tie round it the entrails of the rats or other small animals which they have caught, and throw it on the fire.

Meaning and Purpose. We may now attempt to deal with the meaning and purpose of the *piaka gwabu* cult. It is plain, as already suggested, that it is in part concerned with ancestors or deceased relatives. We have noted that there is a sort of *genius loci* of the *piaka-aa* in the person of an ancestral spirit; and it is significant that one of the regular occasions for the ritual is that of *kigi-yahabu*, a mortuary ceremony. But we possess much more explicit evidence in the formulae used at the burning of the "axe-hand." According to one informant the person officiating addresses the *piaka-ho* by name and says, "I am placing your food on the fire." But others expressed the formula in wider terms: *I-aba, i-hua, i-wame, ta numaga*[45] (Oh fathers, mothers, brothers, this is your food). According to these informants the smoke (*ira mosugono*) rose as an offering to the spirits of the dead by which the little house was inhabited.

This seems to make it more than plain that the *piaka gwabu* is, in part at least, directed towards those spirits. But it seems equally clear that it is inspired by a further interest. It embodies a reference, whether of worship, placation or mere imitation to some mythical benefactor, the founder of the cult, who is perhaps brought on the scene by the symbolism of the *takorabu*. To be sure it was denied expressly by some that Waki, the underground man, still existed; but none the less, all are anxious to reproduce with ritual exactitude what he (or the man who first saw him) did in the myth. This seems to reach a deeper, or at any rate a different, stratum of magico-religious interest.

The purpose of the *piaka gwabu* is explicitly stated to be that of general prosperity. "We do it so that we may have plenty of food." Nearly all the versions of the myth lay emphasis on the miserable hungry condition of the founder before he began to practise the rites, and the change which ensued when he did. This then is a mythical example to follow, and it might be said that the gist of the whole ritual is for the modern performers to assimilate themselves to Kanawebe, Sagainya, Waki, or who ever first practised it, in expectation that the success and prosperity that he enjoyed in the myths would fall to them for being like him.

It remains to suggest some explanation of the arrow-head itself. The prosperity assured by the practice of the cult may take any form. (In one version the founder and his wife were spoken of as suffering from sickness rather than poverty and hunger, so that *piaka gwobu* may function as yet another Kutubuan way of dealing with disease.) But the emphasis is on the food quest and particularly on that most fascinating department of it, the hunt; further, it is noteworthy that the ceremonies are always performed after a hunt and that the hunters are themselves the main performers. This may provide us with a clue to the significance of the arrow-head, which gives its name to the whole complex. One old man gave me the formula which he would pronounce when fixing the *piaka gwabu* to the post :

Situma, kesikeri maganumagai;
A cuscus, by the tail, I shall seize;
Himavokavo, kesikeri maganumagai;
A large snake, by the tail, I shall seize;
Sepohavo, kesikeri maganumagai;
A white cuscus, by the tail, I shall seize;
Sisituba, kesikeri maganumagai;
A large wallaby, by the tail, I shall seize;
Kurigini, koragiri maganumagai;
A cassowary, by the leg, I shall seize;
Nemi ki, koragiri maganumagai;
A tusked pig, by the leg, I shall seize;
Duruwabu, koragiri maganumagai;
A cassowary, by the leg, I shall seize.

Without going so far as to say that success in hunting was the sole object of the arrow-head cult, as this formula might suggest, we may at least view it as a specific aim, and foremost in the believer's thoughts. Since we have been unable to find anything which the arrow-head in itself could be taken to represent *qua* image, it occurs to the writer that it may be nothing more than a symbol of hunting in the abstract. It serves as a focal point for the proceedings in general. Everything is, so to speak, brought to bear on the arrow-head by which the primary object of the cult is typified.

If such an interpretation is acceptable for the *piaka gwabu*, then it may serve also for the *gagebo ninyi*. The axe is the Kutubuan's all-round tool, his *vade mecum*. It may therefore stand as a symbol for manual toil and so serve as a secondary focal point whereby the ritual is brought to bear on the work of his hands in general.

But these are no more than speculative interpretations, and whether right or wrong they do not greatly signify. It is more important to appreciate the general purpose and method of the cult as a whole. It aims, to repeat, at general prosperity, more particularly in hunting; and the argument, inexplicit as it may be, which seems to justify it is that the success of the mythical hero will come to those who do exactly as he did. As in the case of Hobo and the *usi* cult the essence of *piaka gwabu* may well be described as ritual imitation, and, even though the modern performer may not be conscious of it, he is in principle relying on the magic of impersonation.

Death and the After-Life

Disposal of the Corpse

When a Kutubuan dies he is laid out for a day in the men's-house. Partly covered with a bark-cloth cloak, the body lies on a mat with arms straight down by the sides; it is undecorated; and there are no objects of special significance placed on it or near it. The women mourners gather round it shrouded in their *kosaka*, the widow sitting on her dead husband's feet. Her hand will be thrust out to receive the consolatory gift of a trade mirror and hastily withdrawn again, whereupon she becomes once more, like each of the other women mourners, a shapeless mass of brown bark-cloth.

For some time after death has occurred there is formless wailing; but this soon takes on a metrical quality and turns into a chant. The leader sings a phrase which is taken up and repeated several times by the rest, often with a number of serial beginnings so that it resembles a round, or even a chime of bells. All end on one long note, and then the leader begins the next verse.

Under such treatment the theme of the chant develops slowly and lasts a long time. It is apparently a formal one, for the men, although they do not sing, know the words. Some of them were dictated to me.

"You will eat *kawa* berries; *kosaburu* berries will be your food in the east.
You will eat *ira paigimi* fruit; you will eat *barua* fruit (etc., etc.);
Hainya will be your food in the east...
You will cling to the branches of the *tirifa* and the *senegani* palms;

You will cling to the leaf of the sugarcane, *magi-abaiu* (etc., etc.);
You will cling to the leaf of the banana, *kawa kabi*, in the
    east."

So on interminably about the cheerless board and lodging of the
disembodied spirit; though no doubt there are plenty of other
themes which I did not record to furnish forth a long course of
intermittent singing.

The men are meantime gathered about smoking and conversing
at the far end of the house. They await the arrival of the deceased's
maternal uncle, whose canoe may be seen approaching miles away.
When he finally arrives the women's voices become louder. They
are now singing of the spirit's meeting with its departed kinsfolk.
"Now your mother comes to meet you; go with her. Meet her mid-
stream at the mouth of Teraribu[46] and cross over."

The maternal uncle or the man representing his kin (probably a
humiai or cross-cousin of the deceased) proceeds, with the assistance
of other men who merely happen to be forward-coming to wrap the
body in mats and make it fast to a pole, when without further ado
it is carried down by two male bearers to the waiting canoe. One
of them, at least, should be a maternal uncle (or his representative),
for it is his nominal function to do the actual work in connection
with the mortuary procedure.

There is a great gathering of women about the several canoes
which are to form the funeral procession. But with the exception of
two or three they are left behind when the small fleet paddles away
to the place of disposal. Here the *deve*, or mortuary platform, has
been prepared in readiness. Once more it is the nominal work of the
abia and his kin to construct it, but at the only funeral I witnessed it
had been finished before any of them arrived on the scene. It has
been a common experience with me to find that such tasks are
readily performed by those who happen to be at hand and without
regard to any particular kinship obligation.

The *deve* is a rough coffin elevated about seven feet from the
ground. Two strong forked branches are set up and a single beam
is laid from one to the other. Short cross-pieces resting on this beam
form the floor of the coffin, and it is built up to take the form of an
oblong box. The space underneath it is fenced in by split palings
(*duruhabu*) about six feet high. Alongside the *deve* is a sloping log
resting on another forked branch. This serves as a means of access
to the coffin and is called *kakaru* (the same word as is used for the
rail steps leading up to a men's-house). The body is carried on its
pole to the *deve* and the *abia* and two or three assistants somehow
succeed in manhandling it up the *kakaru*. Then, having freed it from

the pole, they lay it in the coffin, still in its wrappings of bark. So far from looking forward to resurrection of the body for their deceased kinsmen, they make fast a few slats above it to prevent any such possibility, or at least to render it difficult. Finally a long springy stick (*siaka sui*) is implanted in the ground nearby and bent down towards the *deve*. The head of the corpse being uncovered, a string is tied to the *siaka sui* at one end and to the deceased's bunch of hair at the other. In due course, when decomposition has gone far enough, the scalp will be wrenched away from the skull and the stick will spring upright thereby preserving the hair intact.

When the body has been satisfactorily arranged in the *deve* some gifts are placed inside the fence underneath it. In the one case which I witnessed these gifts were put there by the deceased's true daughters, and they consisted of some cut sugar-cane, some edible leaves, a good parcel of tobacco and a bamboo pipe. The new *arera* bag in which they had been brought was hung up on the fence. It was said to be for the use of the spirit for collecting the berries, etc., on which he would henceforward have to subsist.

The body is now left to decompose under the weather. I am assured that relatives will sometimes come to perch on the *kakaru* and weep over their dead; but one may suppose that, if they ever do so, they soon grow tired of it. They content themselves with leaving small parcels of food about the *deve*. The only other visitors the corpse may possibly receive are random sorcerers who come (it is alleged) in order to fill their bamboo bottles with the drippings of decomposition.

The widow, who remains at home when the funeral leaves, goes immediately into seclusion—first in the *kasera* or women's retiring house, and then after a few days, in her own *kanya*. For mourning she blackens her face and breast and puts on numerous *karibu* (necklets and armlets of coarse twisted cane) and covers herself in a specially voluminous bark-cloth cloak. Hers is no merry widowhood. Apart from the fearfulness of her appearance, she is secluded for more than a month and may neither remove her garments nor wash her body for upwards of six months. Male mourners take things more easily. They undergo no seclusion, and their marks of mourning actually enhance their appearance (which is certainly not the case with women). They blacken their faces, wear a few more or less ornamented *karibu*, and tie a fringe of cassowary feathers round their foreheads.

Feasts and Ceremonies

There are three main mortuary feasts for each death. They are sometimes called *mutubiai-gibu*, *mutugiri-gibu* and *gamageha-gibu*, i.e.

First-giving, Middle-giving and After-giving; but more often *Kabai-yahabu*, *Kisi-yahabu* and *Kigi-yahabu*, i.e. Thumb Feast, Nose Feast, and the Little-Finger Feast. These terms contain no gruesome reference to the deceased's anatomy; they merely belong to the system of counting. The Thumb Feast takes place five days after the disposal of the corpse; the Nose Feast, nineteen days after; and the Little-Finger Feast thirty-seven days after. I was disposed to doubt whether these arbitrary-sounding dates could be observed accurately; but my diary records that I attended the funeral of Yamena on December 23 and the *kigi yahabu* for the same person on January 29, which works out exactly.

Over and above these three there is a fourth occasion—the *Yaro Feragabu*, i.e. Discarding of Mourning by the widow; and a fifth—*Kanigari Mikerabu*, i.e. Placing the Bones on the Limestone Platform. The former is purely a women's ceremony and the latter is perhaps no ceremony at all. At any rate, informants declare that the final transference of the bones from the village to the *kanigari*, or rock places, is purely matter-of-fact.

The Thumb Feast. The main feature of the first feast is the *Abia-i-gibu* or Gift to the Maternal Uncle. The father, brother, or son of the deceased provides a village pig, and the villagers and guests bring *bari* shells to trade for the meat. The takings in shell are made over as gift to the deceased's *abia*. It is said to constitute a *fugubi*, or compensation for the work he has done in connection with the funeral. If it were not forthcoming he would be angry, with the usual result of an *abia's* anger—somebody's sickness brought about by the offended spirits of the maternal kinsmen.

Small pieces of pig-flesh are spared from their meagre portions by the deceased's nearer relatives and stuck into the walls or thatching. They are for the ghost, and the practice of putting them there is called *Doromai-mikerabu*. *Doromabu* means to hail or address so that the phrase means literally "Having hailed, to place." It is said that the mourner cries, "*Aia, naga ta numaga!*" "Hey, this is your food!" as he sticks a morsel into the thatch. But without having seen the performance, I am ready to suspect that the offerings are usually made without saying anything at all.

The Nose Feast. For the *Kisi-yahabu*, as well as the greater *Kigi-yahabu*, there is no village pig. The meat provided is that of *aso*, or wild animals. On, say, the fourteenth day after death the younger men go out to hunt, returning with a mixed bag, already smoked, on the eve of the nineteenth. The feast itself is apparently a small affair. The meat is cut up and distributed among those present (there is no payment in *bari* shells); and when they have finished eating they throw the bones into the fire. The formula is said to be:

"Go now to your father. Do not stay here to make your widow or children or relatives sick. This is your food."

The Little-Finger Feast. The third feast is sometimes called *Kenagi-Yakarubu*—"to finish off with the little finger of the right hand"[47]—for, as far as male mourners are concerned, it brings the cycle for an individual death to a close. It is a much more important occasion than the two which precede it and is involved with the cult of the arrow-head. I witnessed its performance twice, at Tugiri and Kesi. The following account is of the latter occasion, which was in better style.

Kesi has no *piaka-aa*, so the ritual was carried out in the men's-house. The hunters had been out some five days and had already returned. Before they set out their leader had visited the *deve* and procured two of the bones of the deceased Yamena's little finger. These had been fixed into the cleft of a stick and carried on the expedition. (It is said that the *aminterare* itself accompanies the hunters, as if represented by these finger bones. If the stick happens to catch on a creeper as they make their way through the forest, they will halt and examine the trees nearby for a cuscus. The *aminterare* is meaning to assist them.)

When I arrived at Kesi all preparations were complete. The hunting party had stowed their catch, already smoked, in string bags, and had fully decorated themselves, and they were gathered out of sight on the far verandah of the men's-house. The interior was packed with visitors, sitting on either side in the *asaibu*, or sleeping places. Suddenly the futher entrance, hitherto blocked by sheets of bark, was thrown open and in trooped the hunters in procession, some twenty of them painted and befeathered. In the lead was the deceased's brother, Kanuhai, his body black and glossy with greased charcoal, his arms and legs coated with yellow clay. A pattern in the same colour was painted on his black face, which was framed by an imposing headdress of cassowary plumes. In one hand he carried his bow and arrows; in the other the cleft stick which held the two longer joints of his brother's little finger. After him came two or three others dressed, painted, and armed in much the same way, but holding stone axes in lieu of the leader's cleft stick; behind these perhaps a dozen young hunters painted from head to foot with red ochre; behind these again a number of boys; and in the rear of all a young man with a tall bamboo, still retaining its leaves, with which he appeared to be brushing the roof of the men's-house as the procession advanced. All these were hunters, and, except for the last few, every man in the procession carried under his left arm a string bag packed with the smoked carcases of the animals caught on the expedition.

As described in connection with the arrow-head cult, each bag of food is tapped with the *takorabu* plant as its bearer enters, the procession advancing in single file. At first they move slowly with short, shuffling steps until they have reached the opposite door. Then they wheel about and perform several complete circuits from end to end of the men's-house, tramping so heavily that the building fairly rocks. Finally they come to a halt, still in single file, with the leader standing opposite the sleeping place formerly occupied by the deceased. Here he silently ties the cleft stick to the post by the hearth, then slips the bag of meat from his shoulder, all the others following his example. Yaru, the chief man of Kesi, now takes the *takorabu* and hands it to the leader who, first having solemnly bitten it himself, hands it round to every member of his party, including the young boys. Thereupon they disperse and sit down.

The next business is that of sharing out the meat, in which Yaru and another senior man take charge, though there are many helpers, even to the smallest boys who crowd in as close as they can to such an enthralling scene. The meat is cut up with knives, axes and bamboo knives, or torn apart with fingers—even with the occasional use of toes—all to that sound of hissing between the teeth which indicates intense application. The meat is cut over wooden bowls set on mats so as to avoid the loss of blood and gravy, and all the workers pause now and again to suck their fingers. I even noticed one very small boy who had wedged in close enough to help, turn to his still smaller brother, who was squatting on the outskirts, and offer him two greasy fingers, which the little fellow lost no time in sucking clean.

Yaru was now standing up to count his guests, pointing with extended arm and talking to himself, for every one present, down to the smallest boy, must have his share of the meat. The portions were finally handed round in a large wooden bowl by a younger brother of the deceased. Yaru, who was energetic and a good host, saw to it that I received a junk of cuscus, a section of carpet snake, and a little hairy rat—far more than my due share. When this distribution was complete cooked sago was passed round and everyone fell to, though many put aside their meat, or part of it, to carry home.

After about half an hour all the hunters reassembled at the far end of the men's-house, and Yaru once more took up the arrow-head and *takorabu*. The latter he detached and put away. The former he fixed into the shaft of one of Kanuhai's arrows (displacing the arrow-head already there), and tied to it a little piece of meat. Then he stood aside and the hunters, giving voice to a startling falsetto squeal, came shuffling noisily down the length of the house. Kanuhai was in the lead with his bow fully drawn, and when they had all crowded through the narrow exit he sped his arrow far out over the lake towards Wasemi. Yaru himself volunteered the information that he fired in this direction because the *takorabu* belonged there, though, since the axis of the men's-house pointed north-west, it seemed rather an obvious direction for the shot to take. Apart from this point, however, it seemed sufficiently clear that the final act, in so far as it was directly connected with the deceased Yamena, was meant to get rid of him and send him as far away as possible. Such at any rate was the idea underlying the detail mentioned earlier—brushing the roof with a bamboo cobweb-broom. This rite is called *akiri takabu*, or "brushing away the soot." By removing the last traces of Yamena's occupation, the soot from his hearth-fire, his fellow villagers would, it was said convince him finally that he was not wanted.

The Little-Finger Feast comes to an end with the shooting of the arrow. If sun, wind and rain have done their work properly the deceased is by now a skeleton in the *deve*, and the next thing is to gather up his skull, hair and bones, and take them to the village where they are to be displayed before the widow. (This should happen on the day following the feast, but if the remains are not in a condition to be removed it may be deferred.) When the women have duly wailed over them, they are placed in a string bag which is suspended from the verandah-roof of the men's-house or, in the case of a female, from that of her *kanya*. I am told that the finger bones carried in the cleft stock—which no woman is allowed to see—are detached and smuggled into the bag so that the set will be complete.

Discarding of Mourning. Having seen her husband's bones the widow is released from seclusion. She now comes and goes, but continues to wear her bulky and unbecoming weeds until, at some ceremony arranged among the women themselves, they can be formally discarded.

Since the ceremony is a woman's affair and I was dependent on male informants, I got no well-informed account of it; but I repeat a description given by Fareape who alleged that he could speak as an eye-witness. He was hunting for a rat in its nest near the edge of the swamp when he observed a party of women approaching, among them the widow carrying a load of firewood. Being, as far as one can judge, an exceptionally lawless person, Fareape did not do the proper thing, which was to retire from the scene, but lay low and waited. He saw the women strip the widow stark naked. She made many protests, but everyone was laughing, and she had to go through with it. She took the load of firewood on her bare back, picked up all her ragged mourning garments in a bundle, and thus plunged into the swamp. She dumped the mourning in the mud, deposited the load of wood on top of it in order to hold it down, and then submitted to a thorough scrubbing at the hands of her women friends. Finally she was treated with what must surely be the strangest of cosmetics: one of the accompanying women squeezed some milk from her own breast and this was mixed into a paste with crushed sago grubs. Having been rubbed with this application (apparently in order to give a gloss to her skin) the widow was painted in stripes and dressed in a new skirt and ornaments.

It is far from certain that Fareape ever really witnessed this scene; but it is not to be supposed that the details could be entirely fabricated. The cleansing of the widow is at any rate believed to follow some such procedure as he describes. She is said, once more, to be ridding herself of her husband's *aminterare* when she buries the mourning garments in the swamp and weights them down.

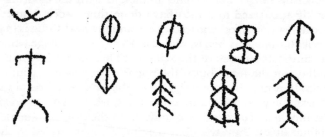

Fig. 14. Designs painted on limestone rocks at Kutubu ossuaries.

Final Disposal of the Bones. In any village one may see packages of dead men's bones, usually on the verandahs but sometimes in small detached shelters specially built for the purpose. They remain there until it is convenient to shift them all at one time to the *kanigari*, which is done, I am assured, without ceremony.

The *kanigari* are natural ledges of limestone, in some cases overlooking the lake, in others hidden among the hills. The most spectacular is Bebere on a bare white cliff quite near the Police Camp. The sloping shelf is about fifteen feet above the lake level and is difficult to get at. Some thirty-three skulls lie on it, as well as a number of miscellaneous bones, thigh bones, pelves, vertebrae, etc., all very old, for Bebere is no longer in use. The skulls must have been arranged in rows, but they are now somewhat out of order, and some may be seen in the deep clear water where they have rolled down. On the face of the rock above are scattered a few marks in red ochre, as if applied with the finger. But no informant could interpret their meaning; indeed they were not considered to have any.[48]

At Kubiritiki, one of the sites at present in use, there were more than fifty skulls, and a great showing of bones. There were also relics of the deceased—a broken drum, a paddle, belts, bamboo pipes, mouldering string bags, etc. Not a few of the more recent skulls were identified by name. It was noticeable that there were no children's skulls among them; and it turns out that juveniles have minor *kanigari* of their own. As for the smallest infants, they are said to be put anywhere. If they have no teeth at the time of their decease they are not even given exposure in a *deve* but are simply put away in a hole in the limestone and left there.

Spirits of the Dead

The Kutubuans have, or think they have, three ways of dying—by violence, by sorcery, or of old age; and the nature and fate of the surviving spirit are to some extent determined accordingly. Those who die by spear or club become *pauave* (or *husa hua*) and live thenceforward in the upper regions. There is no set idea as to their form, unless it be that they are sometimes identified with black cockatoos, *fanagainya*.[49] Mostly they are thought of simply as disembodied spirits that fly by night. The sudden screech heard in the darkness is not that of a *pauave* in bird form, but merely that of a real bird disturbed by a *pauave*. Nor is there any clear notion of the home in the sky where these spirits belong. Informants could not say whether it was a good place or a bad; though it was alleged by some that the river there was red, a colour which was associated with *pauave* in other connections and may have something to do with the thought of fresh blood. We have seen that the *pauave* are specially to be feared, for they often come down to earth, visiting people in dreams or otherwise and making them sick.

Victims of sorcery become *aminterare* (or *yesibu* or *ho*). Opinions differed as to their destination after death, some maintaining that they went up with the *pauave*, others that they remained on earth. I find it impossible to distinguish consistently between *aminterare*, *yesibu* and *ho*.[50] It may well be the case that they are words from different languages which are used without real discrimination by the composite population of Kutubu.

Besides the victims of violence and sorcery there are those who die naturally (*nena kubu*), which incidentally is an end desired by everyone, for it is equivalent to dying of old age. (An early death, unless by something as obvious as a spear thrust, is likely to be put down to sorcery). There seems to be no real distinction between the spirits of those who die by sorcery and of those who die naturally, though there is not the same uncertainty regarding the latters' destination. They all go to some place or other on the earth's surface.

There is indeed uncertainty enough as to the exact location of this place. Under the various names of Hahasurari, Hoa Gaforokoio, and, no doubt, others as well, it is merely said to be a very long way off to the east. For an idea of the native conception of this abode of the blessed the reader is referred to the story in the following section, though it is not to be assumed that this story is known to every Kutubuan. Indeed I much doubt whether it is, for in no other allusion to Hahasurari, etc., did I hear mention of an underground approach.

The spirits of the recently dead are welcomed at Hahasurari by those who have died before them. (There is no explicit notion of immortality on the one hand or of final extinction on the other, the subject not having been thought out.) But—once more without any definite formulation of doctrine—it appears that the dead are thought to spend some long time before they get there, if only because it is so far away. They perch disconsolately on banana-leaves or palm-fronds, and eat the half-edible berries they have gathered in the forest. Furthermore, they are prone to linger about the places they lived in, some, for love of their children, haunting their own houses in the form of rats. Thus squeaks, whistles, and other inexplicable noises by night are put down to *aminterare*.

Attitude of the Dead towards the Living

The ghosts or spirits of the dead behave on the whole in a thoroughly disagreeable manner towards the living. We have seen that the Kutubu regard them as responsible for a large percentage of the illnesses in which they are so interested. Apart from the *pauave*, who seem to be indiscriminately vengeful, the more peaceful spirits are liable to "strike" a man at any time, and particularly in requital for a wrong done to any of their surviving relatives. It is this which makes it possible to regard sickness as sometimes a punishment for misbehaviour, and especially as a sanction for the observance of all the rights of the maternal uncle.

In consequence of these beliefs the Kutubu, like so many other Papuans, go in real fear of the dead. This is partly, no doubt, a general vague fear of the supernatural; but this leaves unexplained the very common conviction that the dead are always up to mischief, in fact bent on killing people.

Sometimes, it would seem, they are gratuitously spiteful, and in evidence of this I cannot do better than give Hameno's story of the

Angry Corpse. (He told it with every sign of conviction, vouching for the facts, though he could not remember the names.) A man of Kafa had died and been placed in his *deve*, and a sorcerer of the same district had come to spend the night nearby, perhaps in order to obtain *piripa*, a purpose which no ghost need be expected to resent. But having comfortably settled himself for the evening he heard first a rustling sound in the *deve* and then a rending of timbers as the dead man sat up. In his haste to decamp the sorcerer had left his bark-cloth cloak lying on a log, and this the corpse mistook for a sleeping man. From the shelter of a tree trunk near by the sorcerer watched it scramble out of the *deve*, pounce on its imagined prey, and tear the bark-cloth with its teeth. At that our sorcerer fled for the river and, embarking on his canoe, paddled for dear life towards the village with the corpse in ever closer pursuit. He succeeded in reaching the men's-house, where, having taken the six rail steps of the *kakaru* in two strides, he sank exhausted on the floor. But he had saved himself only by inches. His dreadful pursuer, springing up the *kakaru*, had gripped the top rung in its teeth before it expired and fell backwards. No man stirred out of the *aa* that night; the doors were closed and the fires built up; and the men shouted across to the women's houses telling them not to dare set foot outside. In the morning the corpse was found where it had fallen. The top rung of the *kakaru* had been broken off and carried away in its fall, and was now gripped so tightly in its dead jaws that the villagers could not dislodge it. So they cut it off short on either side and carried the corpse back to the *deve*; and there, to make sure that the dead should not rise again, they heaped firewood all round and burnt it.

But there are many tales, a shade more credible than the foregoing, which reveal the dead, or at least the disembodied dead, as something less frightful. I heard at least five accounts, more or less modern ones, of kidnap by the *aminterare*, the victim having really gone into a trance or lost himself in the bush, from which predicament he was duly delivered and survived to tell of his adventures.[51] It is true that these stories do not portray the spirits very attractively (they are dwarfish, with pot bellies, clawing fingers, etc.), but informants all agree in representing them as at least kindly-intentioned. After their fashion,[52] they treated the victim with consideration; and in each case, it is significant to note, the abductors were, or included, the parents of the person abducted. It is plain that, in native belief, their motive was actually one of fondness for their child, whom they desired to take away from the land of the living in order to have him to themselves. In one case, they had, according to the victim's own story, called him by name and welcomed him with open arms; in another they had tried eagerly to talk to him, but in unintelligible voices; in another they had expressly said they had taken him because his living guardians were not looking after him with sufficient care.

Such a belief as is implied by these stories (and one meets with evidence of it elsewhere) may do something to explain the very general fear of the spirits of the dead. Apart from what may be a very natural fear of supernatural things, it seems, as already noted, that the dead are thought to be deliberately bent on harming the living. This seems to be a thoroughly unreasonable belief if their harmful intentions are thought to be quite gratuitous; but it will have some sense in it if native belief at the same time can supply the dead with a motive. As far as the Kutubu are concerned one such motive is revenge, whether for injuries done to the spirit itself while a living person, or to the relatives which it has left behind it. Another is that of fondness—when indeed the charge of malignancy disappears altogether. The curious fact is that those who most fear the spirit of a dead man are the very persons who were nearest and (probably) dearest to him in life: of all survivors they are the most liable to his attack. This becomes less unintelligible if we assume the existence of an underlying, perhaps largely forgotten, idea that the spirit will desire to keep touch with its living kin by taking them with it to the land of the dead.

Attitude of the Living towards the Dead

While such an idea may absolve the spirits, it does not make them any more popular; and in the mixed attitudes of the living towards the dead it may probably be said that the dominant feature is a desire to get rid of them. We have seen various evidences of this in the formulae used at the mortuary feasts, in the rite of brushing away the soot, and (probably) in the rite of shooting the arrow. It is apparently assumed that the danger grows less and less, and if the ceremonies are carried out properly, there comes a time when the spirit takes its departure for good and all. Indeed, by way of illustration, I heard at Kutubu what was to me a new native explanation of the seclusion of widows. It was that the husband lurked about the entrance of the *kanya*, ever ready to "strike" his wife and thus carry her off if she ventured to cross the threshold. It was only after the Little-Finger Feast that she could leave her house with safety, for by that time the husband's spirit had been induced to leave the village.

It may be this desire to get rid of the dead that makes the Kutubu (like most other Papuan peoples) so punctilious about the mortuary ceremonies. On the other hand it may be a direct concern for the spirit's own welfare—in order to ensure it a safe and speedy passage to Hahasurari—though it must be said that I have recorded no statement to such an effect. Or again it may be merely a devotion to the mortuary routine, as if the carrying out of it constituted an obligation in itself. However that may be, the natives will go to considerable trouble to do things properly, or as near properly as circumstances allow. When a Kutubu carrier died on patrol at a place called Yuma he was buried, which seemed a reasonable and convenient way of disposing of him. But it was not approved of (when they heard of it) by the people of Tugiri, where he belonged. Arrangements had to be made for exhumation, so that the bones would not rot away; and some considerable time later some Tugiri men had to make a long journey across the mountains to collect and bring them home. The people of Yuma were rewarded for having "looked after the bones" and these were duly displayed before the widow after a performance, a good deal behind schedule but otherwise in proper form, of the Little-Finger Feast.[53]

Although plainly showing a desire to remove a possible danger from their midst, the Kutubu, like other people, mourn their dead with real feeling. There are many evidences of this, and as an example I mention the rather touching sight of an old woman by the *deve* of her deceased son where she was engaged in weeding her garden. The exposure coffin was empty and derelict; her son's bones had been long since removed and actually placed on the limestone ledge, which indicates that he had died years previously. Yet she had that morning placed a fresh package of sago done up in green leaves on a stump beside the *deve*, and there were many others there in various stages of decay. According to native ideas on the subject the *aminterare* should long ago have left for Hahasurari; but the mother was still providing food for her son.

And there is evidence also that the Kutubu are interested in the After-Life and at least to some extent concerned about it. I was once in the Wasemi men's-house talking to a group while Nekinagu, slightly indisposed and also slightly bored, lay stretched on his back at my feet. Not very long previously he had lost a son, and his bones now hung in a string bag from the verandah-roof just outside. We were talking of this object when he suddenly raised himself and eyeing me keenly asked if the white men, who knew so much, were able to see the *aminterare* of their dead. I had to reply that they could not; at which he let himself down with a truly explosive sigh. When I asked him what became of the Kutubu *aminterare* (informing him, by way of a lead, that the white men's were believed to go up into the sky) he replied that they went to a place—he called it Hoa—far off in the east, and beyond their ken. Then, with another flare-up of interest, he demanded to know whether the white man had seen this place, and once more, I had to answer, "No." His disappointment, proclaimed by further sighs and exclamations, was obviously real. It would have been for any missionary *un moment psychologique.*

Part V

Kutubu Stories

The selection given in this chapter illustrates the typically wide variety of Kutubu stories, ranging from extreme simplicity, if not pointlessness, to quite elaborate myth and fiction. Some have the childishness of nursery tales; some abound in frightfulness; some are just food stories; and some are genuine myths, full of magical allusion. They have not been chosen on grounds of merit (of which some indeed may seem to possess very little), but as representative examples. However, the reader will find that they get better as he proceeds; indeed, in the writer's opinion some of the longer Kutubu stories are, by native standards, exceptionally good. It would be hard to find a neater plot for a fairy tale than that of "The Fish Spear"; while "Return from the Dead" has its strong drama, and "Moon-Man and Sun-Girl" its poetry. The burning beauty of the Sun-Girl and the cry of the Moon-Hunter calling to his dogs—these and many others are at least poetic fancies. No doubt a native storyteller could clothe them in fitly poetic Kutubuan; but this I was unable to appreciate. The stories were told to me in pidgin Motu which, despite its merits, is seldom poetic; and they are set down in English more prosaic than they deserve.

The Kutubu recognize two general types of story—the *tuni* and the *hetagho. Tuni* are usually short. They are meant to be amusing, and they are often indecent. The characters are mostly nameless and the locale of the story just anywhere. They are mostly without magical significance and are therefore told without secrecy, at any time and in any place. It is said that women are good at them (though I gathered only a few from their more bashful lips), and that they are often to be heard at nights in the *kanya.* Their function is obviously recreational.

Hetagho are longer, sometimes very long. The characters usually possess names, and the stories are staged in definite places, though in both respects different versions show a good deal of variety. It is noteworthy, however, that the names of the characters are commonly suppressed. An informant will tell you a whole long story about an old woman, a man, the man's wife, etc., scrupulously avoiding mention of their names throughout. He may give you these names later, if you ask him; but he is inclined to do so secretly, perhaps in a whisper. Sometimes he will put you off with false or substitute names, revealing the true ones only under pressure of persuasion. All this is because those names are useful to him for magic, and the knowledge of them he wishes to keep to himself.

The *hetagho* may rise to the level of true myths, when they are understood to deal with ancient events of fundamental importance and consequently possess a religious as well as a magical meaning. Certain myths have already been given briefly in connection with the various cults described in earlier chapters. But I imagine they are much fuller and more numerous than appears in this monograph. The *usi* cult in particular possesses a rich mythology, gathered together in what is called the *usi-tasi* (the "talk" of *usi*). It seems that the initiates sing, night after night, a long saga, which not only relates the adventures of Hobo or Yabame but embraces many abstruse subjects unconnected with either of them. The story of "The Return from the Dead" is said to be part of it.

Such stories are *hetagho* and not *tuni*. But it would be a mistake to assume that the Kutubuan draws a very definite line between these two categories. In the following selection the earlier specimens are certainly *tuni*, the later ones *hetagho*. But concerning those in the middle native opinions were inclined to differ. It is left to the student to say which side they belong to.

1. *The Old Woman and the Half-Cooked Snake*

An old woman caught a *barisa* snake and proceeded to bake it in the hot-stone oven. But she bungled her work; the stones were not thoroughly hot. The snake came to life, got out of the oven, and put the old woman into it. Presently she got out and put the snake in again. And so on.

Finally the snake made off into the bush, and the old woman turned into a kind of tuber called *hameno*.[54]

2. *The First Dogs*

A man lived alone with two small boys, one of whom had a pale skin, the other a very dark skin. He would go hunting while they remained at home. But while he was absent they would go hunting themselves, turning into dogs; and they were very successful. They would always turn back into little boys before reaching home.

Once when the man was returning from his hunting he stopped to ease himself, and the little boys, also returning, happened to pass nearby. They were conversing loudly, boasting of their respective kills, and the man shouted, "Not so much noise!" At this each of the two children, taken by surprise, burst into a long inarticulate howl. As they did so they became dogs again, one brown and one black, and so they remained ever after.

3. *The Secret of Fire*

A man lived alone in a house in the bush. He had no fire and had to eat his sago, fish, etc., raw. Not far away lived a little skinny boy, also alone. He visited the man and observed that he had no fire. This aroused his pity and he took the necessary appliances from his string bag and showed his friend how to produce fire and cook his food. Having revealed his secret the little boy clasped the trunk of a tree with arms and legs and became the small lizard called *ira-keragi-fegimabu* (make fire by the saw method). The man endeavoured to catch the lizard but it kept dodging round the tree out of sight. He finally let it escape because he reflected that it had been good to him.[55]

4. *The Hunter's Dream*

A man, Seramena, lived with his wife Pirimi, near Fimaga. He was a hopeless failure at hunting. He and his wife lived almost entirely on sago, and in lieu of meat, fish, and wood-grubs, he brought her the edible fungus called *kino*. She was disgusted and constantly upbraided him.

Much cast down, Seramena went away by himself and sat down by the little stream named Kerewa. Here he fell asleep and dreamt of wild animals, fish, and grubs in plenty. Next morning he met a bush pig and killed it with one shot. He left it lying where it had fallen and went to bring his wife. Keeping his secret he said, "Come with me and chop firewood."

When the woman saw the pig she was delighted. But Seramena said, "Now carry it home." She protested: "How can I carry a whole pig?" But her husband said, "Go on. You are always abusing me for not catching pigs. Now carry this one home by yourself."

This she somehow managed to do, and they singed, disembowelled, carved and cooked the pig together. Then he said, "Eat it all yourself." She protested that this was impossible, but he compelled her to obey.

After that he hunted and collected with unfailing success; pigs, cuscus, cassowary, fish, grubs—they had more than they could dispose of. They smoked some, threw some away, and ate so much that their stomachs ached.[56]

5. *The Lost Drum and the Snake-Man*

Wanagani lives with his younger brother, Sisimano. A visitor comes to tell them of an *usanehabu* dance at another village. Wanagani does not care to go, but sends his wife together with his younger brother. They carry two bags full of smoked meat, and Wanagani allows them to take his drum, telling them to look after it.

At the end of the dance, which goes on till dawn, Sisimano lies down for a sleep before returning home, placing the drum under his head for a pillow. He awakes to find it gone. After searching everywhere without success he and his sister-in-law return to tell Wanagani that his drum is lost. At first he thinks they are joking; but, finally convinced, he hits them both on the head with a stick.

Sisimano and the woman go off weeping. They travel from place to place enquiring for the drum. They can hear nothing of it until they come to a certain village where the people tell them that there was a strange drum left tied to the front wall of the men's-house; it was making a noise by itself; but now it has gone again. Encouraged by this news Sisimano and his sister-in-law go further till at last they come to a very attractive village, and there, tied to the front wall of the men's-house, is the lost drum.

Sisimano climbs up the steps to take it; but, looking in at the door before doing so, he sees that the men's-house is inhabited only by snakes. He beats a quick retreat; but as soon as he sets foot on the ground he finds he is a snake himself. He darts back on to the verandah and becomes a man again; then on to the ground, and becomes once more a snake. Thus he tries again and again, until he finally gives up in despair. He hands the drum down to his sister-in-law, saying, "You take it to my brother. I must stay here and be a snake.

The woman goes back to her husband and gives him his drum. At first she is afraid to tell him what has happened to his brother; she prevaricates, saying he is on the track behind and will shortly arrive. But at last she breaks the news, Wanagani, overwhelmed by sorrow, smashes the drum to pieces, while his wife turns into a snake and slips off into the bush.

6. *The Origin of Leeches*

A miserable little boy with a big stomach lived secretly in a *kauaru* palm at a place called Biru-Fogobu-Merave.[57] From the top of his palm he overlooked the whole neighbourhood and whenever he saw anyone stealing or committing adultery in the gardens he would shout out for all to hear. This proved a general annoyance.

Once a man was stealing some sugar-cane near the palm. The

little boy shouted as usual, and the voice was so close at hand that the man was able to locate it. He set to work to chop down the palm with his axe, but seemed to make no progress. Meanwhile the boy was crying, *"Piane, piane!"* The man took the hint and procured a crowbar of *piane* wood with which he uprooted the palm. Then, as the boy continued to cry *"piane,"* he split and opened it with his crowbar. Having discovered the little boy, he did his best to kill him with his axe, but he kept on crying out *"piane!"* So the man took the *piane* crowbar and with this at last succeeded in battering him to death.

Then he cut the boy in small pieces, which he gathered up and carried to the village. Highly pleased the people prepared to burn the boy's remains in order to rid themselves of him forever. But, going over the pieces to make sure the set was complete, they found his penis missing. The man had overlooked it. He hurried back to Biru-Fogobu-Merave, but it was nowhere to be seen. Instead the ground was alive with leeches.

7. *The Wasp Men*

Two brothers, Uhugabu and Purusuma, hunted without luck for bush pig. On the way home they chanced on a village-pig with slit ears. They were wondering to whom it belonged and whether they should kill it. Suddenly it jumped and snorted. That roused them to action and they speared it.

They carried it to a small stream where they built a bank to divert the water and, in what had been the bed of the stream, they made a hot-stone oven and cooked their meat. When all was finished they broke down the bank and the water rushed over the place obliterating all traces of their handiwork. Then they carried the meat home.

In due course the owner came looking for his pig. He followed the thieves' footprints to the stream and thence to their home. They denied the charge of theft. But the owner had seen the pig's bones stuck up on the wall of their house. He went away saying nothing. The two thieves prepared their weapons for the attack which they knew would come. The following morning was dark with rain, and the thieves woke up to find their house surrounded by men. They were accused once more but refused to confess. Then the fight began. They drove off the attackers with spears and stones, killing all of them except one light-skinned man. They shouted to him to come back if he dared, and he answered, "I will be back in a few days."

The thieves now cleared away the corpses and made ready for the second attack, their two wives helping to mend their broken arrows and make new ones. At dawn a few days later they were surrounded once more. The elder thief this time turned himself into a dog and rushed among the enemy biting them. All were killed except, once again, the light-skinned man, who went away saying he would come a third time.

In the third attack the elder thief again became a dog. But he was wounded by a spear. He retired into the house together with his younger brother. Their wives were already killed, and the two men climbed up on the roof. Here they fought on hopelessly, until they had shot away all but two of their arrows. At this stage, realizing that the fight was lost, each broke off the point of his remaining shaft, stuck it into his anus, and flew up into the air. They had become the wasps, *uhugabu* and *purusuma*.

8. *The Origin of Tobacco*

Ahoia lived with his sister Gabariya at Girarimaio, near the junction of the Augu and Mubi Rivers. They occupied respective ends of a bush house.

Ahoia would go hunting every day while his sister remained at home. One day he was specially successful, bringing home two white cuscus and a pig. He told her to roast sago and they ate their meal together. Then they retired to their sleeping quarters.

But Ahoia looked through the separating wall and admired his sister sitting by her fire. He entered her compartment and seduced her. While they were engaged in copulation the house caught fire. Gabariya warned Ahoia of what was happening but he declined to take any notice. The house was burnt over their heads and from the ashes of their genitals sprang up tobacco plants.

A man named Uapone discovered the strange plants, tried smoking their dried leaves[58] and thus started the habit.

9. *Women into Pandanus*

A number of men lived together in a men's-house. They had no wives and had to do all their own sago making. Once their chief man ran a sago thorn into his foot and this made him ill and feverish. While all the rest were sound asleep he lay in the men's-house and merely dozed, sleeping "with his eyes open." He heard a sound as of approaching rain or rushing water. While he wondered what it might be it grew louder and closer and presently he saw a large band of women enter the men's-house. The noise was that of their drums, for they were dancing. They were charmingly decorated with paint and feathers, and had bound strips of plaited cane round their breasts to keep them steady while they danced. He watched their dancing till it was nearly dawn; then he dropped off to sleep and when he woke up they were gone.

All the others were disappointed and angry because he had not roused them while the women were still present; they could have possessed themselves of wives. But he told them to feign sleep during the ensuing night, for the women were sure to return; a man would be posted to each entrance to prevent escape, and they would seize the women, each man his own. The best-looking he reserved for himself.

In due course the strange noise of drums was heard approaching; the women entered; and the men seized them. The best by pre-arrangement was the chief's; but all got someone or other—some two or three—except for the skinny man, a poor specimen, who got none at all. This man, however, made a great fuss, and it was arranged that he should have one of the extra women.

Now the men made *kanya*, separate individual dwellings, for their wives. They caused them to do the cooking and other work, and, as for sago making, they now had to do no more than fell the trees. All got on well together, and the chief warned his men to treat the women kindly and never scold them.

Before long all the women had produced children, and, when they went to the sago places, their husbands would accompany them, sitting about while their wives laboured. On one occasion the skinny man was nursing his baby when it messed itself. He called to his wife to come and clean it, but she took no notice. He called again and again, and at last in a rage shouted, "You are not a woman, you are an *abari*" (a pandanus).[59]

At that she answered and came quickly. "What was that you called me?" she asked as she took the baby. At first he refused to answer, but she insisted, and he finally repeated the words: "I said you were an *abari*." "Yes," she replied, "it is true."

In the afternoon all returned to the village. But the women were silent and unsmiling instead of laughing and talkative. The men did not fail to observe this, and they were much concerned. The chief man asked if anyone had quarrelled with his woman or spoken severely to her, and the skinny man told him of the incident in which he had been concerned. "Very well," said the chief man, "tonight we must keep watch for fear they all leave us."

But towards dawn the men all fell asleep and then the women stole away. Waking, the men set off in search of them and finally sighted them and gave chase. But by the time they had overtaken them the women were already changing shape. Their husbands seized them, and even as they did so their human arms and legs turned into the aerial roots and branches of the pandanus tree.[60]

The skinny man was blamed for it. By scolding his wife he had lost the village all its women. So he was killed, cut up into little bits and put on the fire.

10. *The Fish-Spear*

A boy lived with his sister and her husband. The husband had made himself a fine fish-spear and stowed it away in a bamboo container in his house. One day, while his brother-in-law was out hunting, the boy looked into this bamboo container and saw the fish-spear. He admired it very much and thought he would try it. So he went out alone in his canoe and, sure enough, he speared fish after fish with it. Then he saw a particularly large fish (of the kind called *nafa*) in the clear water beneath him. He threw the spear and it struck home. But then to his consternation the fish darted away carrying the spear with it under the water.

Full of apprehension the boy went home. He gave his sister the fish he had caught and she cooked them, and when the husband returned from his hunting they all ate together. After his meal, well satisfied, the husband went to examine his new fish-spear. The bamboo was empty! "Who has taken my spear?" The boy confessed. "Was it your spear then?" the husband cried, and he struck him on the head with a stick. The blood ran down the boy's face and his sister wept.

Next day, when the husband was hunting once more, the boy went down with his sister to the river. He carried a long pole. They got into their canoe, pushed off, and paddled to the place where the *nafa* fish had made off with the spear (the boy had been careful to remember the spot). Here he drove the pole into the river bottom so that it stuck there upright, with the top end above water. He instructed his sister to hold this end of the pole. For he was going to dive down in search of the fish-spear. When the pole shook in her hand she would know that he was returning. She tried to dissuade him. But he said, "Your husband was angry with me. If I die, I die." Then he plunged in and disappeared. His sister waited all day; but there was no shaking of the pole, and so she went home crying.

But at the bottom of the river the boy found what seemed like a pathway in front of him. He went on a little and it turned into a well-defined track. The water from the river was like the sky above him. On and on he went, deeper and deeper. Everything was most beautiful. There was forest on either side, and he saw numbers of large cuscus, pig and cassowary. They sat there quite tamely and his passing did not disturb them.

Presently he came to a larger road which led him to a house and garden, a charming place, well cleared, with red Cordyline and crotons growing about it. On the house verandah there sat a man, plaiting an armlet, who asked him where he had come from and what he was after. The boy did not reveal that he was searching for the fish-spear; he said he was just walking about. But the man seemed satisfied and made him welcome.

Now he prepared to give his guest some food. He cooked some sago and mixed it in a wooden bowl with some earth-worms.[61] This dish he invited the boy to share with him. But the boy was taken aback. He said he had never eaten such food. "Well," answered the man, "if you do not like it, go out on the track and kill one of those animals you saw." So the boy went and without any trouble got himself a young cassowary. This they soon cooked, and, while he ate the cassowary, his host ate the worms.

Presently there came in from the gardens a woman and a girl, both fine and handsome. These were the man's wife and sister. They also proceeded to eat sago and earthworms, while the man explained courteously that their young guest was unable to join them in eating their usual food because it was entirely strange to him.

So, always procuring his own meat by hunting, the boy continued to stay with these kind people. Some days later the man informed them that there was to be an *usane-habu* dance at his men's-house in the village. So they made ready their ornaments, armlets and feathers; washed their faces, ears and noses; and put into the last-mentioned their pencils of fine white shell. They got down the drum and fitted on to it a new snake-skin, and they prepared quantities of food as their contribution to the feast. This consisted mainly of earthworms, ready baked and stowed in bamboo containers; but to meet the special tastes of their guest the girl carried a bag of smoked cassowary meat. So they set off.

When they reached the village the boy looked about him for the pigs which would no doubt be killed for the feast. But there was no sign of them. Everyone was eating earthworms. So he called for his cassowary meat.

An hour or so before sundown the dance began. The men's-house was packed. The dance was in full swing when the boy, moving about in the crowd, saw, tied to the front wall of the men's-house, the very thing he was looking for—his lost fish-spear. And then he learnt that the fish-spear had much to do with the dance then in progress. For the man on whose behalf it was being held,[62] who now indeed lay helpless in the men's-house with a wound in his thigh, had been speared not long previously by an unknown enemy with this very weapon. In fact it seemed to the boy that the wounded man was no other than the *nafa* fish.

The boy said nothing. He danced with the rest till dawn, and then, when everyone was drowsy and unobservant, he quietly detached the fish-spear and possessed himself of it. When sometime later he returned with his host and his wife and sister, he carried the fish-spear (apparently unnoticed) with him.

Next day he announced that he must go to his own home. His real intention was to return the fish-spear to his brother-in-law; but declared that he was merely going to fetch his things, and his host allowed him to go on the promise that he would return. So he went back along the path he had come by till he reached the place where he had first dived into the river. He shook the pole, which was still standing where he had left it, and rose to the surface; and there he found his sister. She had returned each day in her canoe to weep and wait for him.

Then they went up to the house together and the husband was delighted to have his fish-spear restored to him. But next morning early the boy got together his belongings, his bark-cloth cloak, his string bag, his bows and arrows, his ornaments. He said he was going down into the water again. His sister protested but he answered, "No, your husband struck me. I am going away for ever."

At this the sister cried and the husband joined her in urging him not to go down there again; it was a bad place. But then the husband and his wife began to quarrel. She blamed him bitterly, saying it was all his fault; and soon they were at blows. When they had finished fighting she became a *kabaiame* snake and he a *sagari*, the sort of palm from which fish-spear prongs are made.

Meanwhile the boy had slipped away. He went down to the hole in the river bed and along the beautiful path till he came again to the house of his friend. He was welcomed there and the man now offered him his sister for a wife. At first he was bashful; but the girl said that she wanted him, and so they were married.

They got on well together although the boy still could not bring himself to eat the sort of food his wife gave him. While she and her people ate earthworms, he continued to kill his own meat. But one night she offered him a dish of food in the darkness, and before he knew what he had done he had eaten some cooked earthworms. He thrust the rest of it aside. But he had eaten enough. When he woke up in the morning he found that he was a fish. And his eyes were opened; he saw then that all the others were fish too.

11. *Kikiwaia, a Taubu*

Siserame,[63] a girl of Bauru on the River Mubi, went with her parents to fish on the River Dawari. On the way home she was overtaken by her periods and lagged behind on the track. When her parents were far in advance she turned and saw a big man following her. He was licking up the menstrual blood from the stones as he came along.

She was terrified. "Is this a man or an *aminterare*?" It was Kikiwaia. He carried her off to his home at Auguba and married her.

Kikiwaia supported his sister, Ariame, and brother, Ganowei. Both lived in his house, the former in an *agaro* (circular box made of bark for litters of puppies), and the latter in a *habusa* (conical fish-trap). When she first noticed these two receptacles Siserame asked her husband what he kept in them. But Kikiwaia told her not to be inquisitive; she must never look into them while he was absent from home.

Kikiwaia was a great hunter. He would bring home pigs and cassowaries; also bamboo containers full of human blood. The former he would give to his wife to cook. The latter he took off secretly. But Siserame watched him, and saw what he did with them. He went first to the dog-box and called a name. From it Siserame saw the head of a girl pop out, that of Ariame, with wide-open mouth. Kikiwaia emptied into it two bamboos full of blood. Then he went to the fish-trap from which popped up the head of Ganowei, and Kikiwaia emptied two more bamboos full of blood into his mouth. This he used to do regularly, for he killed many men from Kutubu, Ifigi, Fimaga and the whole district, bringing home their blood.

In due course Siserame gave birth to a son. When he was grown to be a little boy there took place a big dance at Bauru (Siserame's home village) and Kikiwaia allowed her to take him to it. He furnished her with the smoked flesh of three cassowaries and two pigs to take to the dance in her bag, and told her to keep a careful eye on the boy. On no account was she to let him draw attention to his father; for Kikiwaia, proposed to attend the dance also, though he would come after them and wished to remain unseen.

When Siserame and her son were at Bauru and all the people were watching the cutting up of the pigs, the little boy nudged his mother and exclaimed, "There comes father!"—pointing to Kikiwaia, who was just then stepping out of his canoe. The other guests did not pay any attention, but Siserame watched her husband from then on.

Some time later when all the people were in the men's-house, Siserame's brother, a Bauru man, went outside to tend the ovens. She was watching him through a crack in the wall, and as he bent over the oven she saw her husband shoot him with an arrow. Her brother fell, but got up immediately and returned to the men's-house as if nothing had happened. But in the morning, when the dance came to an end, he was suddenly taken ill and died.

Siserame told the villagers who had killed him—her husband. (For Kikiwaia did not shoot with real arrows. He had his own peculiar method of sorcery: he shot with an imaginary arrow and somehow extracted his victim's blood; that was how he managed to fill his bamboos.) When they heard what Siserame said the villagers made a plan with her to destroy her husband. She should go home and help from within; and on the next day but one they would all surround his house and attack him.

Siserame's first business was to dispose of Ariame and Ganowei. She heated some stones till they were actually glowing red. Then she went to the dog-box holding one of the stones in her bamboo tongs, and cried "Ariame!" The woman's head sprang up as usual, and into her mouth, wide-open for blood, Siserame dropped a red-hot stone. With a second stone she performed the same trick on Ganowei in the fish-trap, and both were killed instantly. After this she went through her husband's house and removed all his weapons, replacing them with rotten sticks; and then she waited for his return.

When he came home he deposited his catch and sat down to smoke. It was then that the general attack was launched. But Kikiwaia seemed to take no notice; unharmed by the blows of his assailants he continued to smoke. When he retaliated, the familiar weapons broke to pieces in his hands, but he himself seemed invulnerable and the fight threatened to go on for ever. But at last Siserame laid hold of a Cordyline growing near the house. "Look here!" she cried. "Ah, not that!" implored Kikiwaia, suddenly aroused. But Siserame broke the Cordyline[64] and in that instant her husband was slain.

The villagers burnt the house down over Kikiwaia, but his spirit survived and it is now a *taubu* doing invisible injury to modern Kutubuans.

12. *The Origin of the Kutubu People*

A girl was gathering firewood in the bush when she fell in with an ugly old woman. Going on together they came to a *haginamo* tree and decided to gather berries. The girl had climbed into the tree when the old woman, who stood underneath, suddenly struck the trunk. The tree sprang up to an enormous height, so that the girl could not possibly get down. She sat there crying in the branches and the old woman went away.

For several days the girl remained without food. But one morning she woke to find a great stock of provisions beside her. She ate and ate and fell asleep. Next morning there was fresh supply, and so on each day—sugar-cane, sago, meat, firewood, etc. (a long enumeration). She now stripped bark from the tree and made herself a new skirt and settled down to a solitary life.

Presently she found herself pregnant. She was very puzzled and angry about it. She could not imagine who had brought her to that condition. But in due time the child was born and nursed in the top of the tree; and after that a second child. Now she had a boy and a girl. Food continued to be supplied each day, and ornaments, *bari* shells, armlets, etc. were sometimes found with it. These she put on her children.

By now they had grown up. The boy had long hair and the girl's breasts were showing. Then one day the mother told her two children to close their eyes together. When they opened them there was no mother, no tree. They were standing on the ground beside a house.

At first they wept for their mother. But there was a supply of sago in the house, so they ate and made themselves comfortable. Then they fashioned a *toio* and a sago scraper and set about getting their own food. While the girl made sago the boy would hunt. One day they found a number of young plants set down near their house, and they proceeded to make a garden. Another day they found two piglets done up in a parcel of leaves; another day two puppies. The brother said, "You look after the pigs, and I will look after the dogs." He gave them medicines and took them out hunting and caught many animals. Brother and sister were very happy.

But the brother noticed that his sister was each day absent a long time at the sago place. He wondered what she was up to, and followed her secretly. He saw that she used to embrace a palm tree, rubbing up and down against it with her legs astride. Next day, while she was elsewhere, he wedged a sharp piece of flint in the tree trunk, and lay in hiding to see what would happen. When the girl came to embrace the tree again she cut herself, and was thus furnished with a vagina. She fell at the foot of the tree bleeding profusely. The boy did his best to stanch the blood, using various leaves (which have ever since been red or autumn-coloured).[65] Finally he thought of applying *bari* shells and pearlshells, and the bleeding stopped.

Thenceforward they lived as man and wife and their children intermarried and populated the whole Kutubu district.[66]

13. *The Place of Pearlshells*

Once there was to be a dance at Hegisu on the Mubi and the people of the neighbouring villages were getting ready to go. But one man and his wife had no pearlshells to wear. She was anxious to go whether or no; but he declared they would not disgrace themselves by attending a dance without suitable ornaments. They quarrelled and in her anger she cut off her armlets and threw away such ornaments as she had.

Then the man went off alone with his bow and arrows. He climbed the small hill behind Herebu known as Kobira Sabe, and crossed it to Koroba Sabe.[67] Here he saw a scrub hen and shot at it with a pronged arrow. He knew that he must have hit it, for when he retrieved his arrow he noticed that one of its prongs was broken off. So he followed the trail. After a while he came upon a clearing and a house; and there on the verandah sat a man engaged in extracting an arrow from his foot. It was Kobira Piwi (also called Kobira Pevere) whom the hunter had shot a few moments previously in the form of a scrub hen.

About the clearing were planted a number of beautiful trees, many of them with reddening foliage, such as *siaumu, babagu, kontabura, hiname, asoro, furubu.*[68] etc., while scattered thickly on the ground like fallen autumn leaves were fragments of shining pearlshell.

The hunter entered into conversation with Kobira and had soon told him of the forthcoming dance at Hegisu and of his quarrel with his wife. Having heard his story Kobira took him into his house and there revealed a great store of whole pearlshells of the finest quality. Four of them he gave to the hunter, two for himself and two for his wife. "Now," he said, "you will be able to attend the dance. But, one thing—you will see there a man exactly like myself. Do not speak to him or offer him any meat. And do not on any account address him by my name."

Having promised, the man returned to his house; and next day, suitably bedecked, he and his wife attended the dance. While they were feasting he noticed among the crowd his friend of the previous day, and, forgetting what he had promised, he approached him with a gift of pork saying, "Kobira Piwi, Kobira Pevere, thanks for your pearlshells."

"I gave you no pearlshells," answered Kobira (for it was he in person); "it was my double who gave them to you." Later on the man accosted him again; but once more he denied his name and hung his head as if in sorrow; and soon after that he left the dance while it was still night.

Then there was thunder and lightning and a deluge of rain which lasted till morning. When at last the guests were able to make their way home, they saw, as they approached Herebu, that the whole spur, Koroba Sabe, had disappeared. In one great landslide it had been swept down the Mubi; and with it had gone Kobira, his house and all his store of pearlshells. The Mubi had carried them right down to the Kikori in the south-east; and there they have ever since remained.[69]

14. *The Sky People*

A man named Fagena lived at Foi. One night he got up and went out to relieve himself. On returning he thought he was mounting the *kakaru* steps to his own men's-house, but he had got on to a strange set of steps and they led him into a strange house. It was full of sleeping men whom Fagena did not recognize. Presently he roused one of them and asked him his name. The man answered, "I am Fagena." They hailed one another as namesakes and Fagena discovered that he was in the men's-house of the Sky People.

Next morning when Earth-Fagena urinated he did so on the ground in the sky-village. "You must not do that here!" cried Sky-Fagena, and he hastily gathered up the ground which Earth-Fagena had defiled and threw it into the bush. "Come with me and I will show you how we do it." Earth-Fagena accompanied him to the bush and was astonished to see him shoot out fish and shrimps with his urine.

Later Earth-Fagena defecated in the open. Once more Sky-Fagena was shocked and gathered up the excrement and threw it into the bush. Then he showed Earth-Fagena how the Sky People defecated, ejecting live pigs, carpet snakes, wallaby and cuscus. (This it is explained, is how the lake and rivers and bush come to be populated with fish and animals. They descend from the sky under cover of the mists.)

Meanwhile the wife of Earth-Fagena had gone into mourning. Sky-Fagena opened a hole in the floor of the sky and permitted his friend to look down. He saw his wife all blackened, and his brother dressed up in warlike array with cloak, bag, spear, and bow and arrows (he was thinking of revenge). On the fifth day he looked down again and saw them making the Thumb Feast. These sights distressed him. "They are mistaken," he cried, "I am not dead"; and he implored his namesake to let him go down. But Sky-Fagena replied, "Not yet."

Soon after this Sky-Fagena suggested that Earth-Fagena should join him in killing somebody, and he agreed. They went together to a garden and hid there till they saw a woman and a girl approaching. They sprang on them and killed one each and then returned to the village in triumph. There was dancing and shouting and much stamping in the men's-house.

Five days later their feat was celebrated by a feast, and while it was in progress Earth-Fagena looked down again through the hole in the sky-floor and he saw that his own villagers were also making a feast. He did not know what it was for.

Immediately after the feast in the sky Fagena was allowed to return to the earth. He filled his bag with meat and stepped through the hole on to a very tall palm, by means of which he was able to descend. All the people were astonished to see him, for they thought he must have been killed or drowned. But his wife threw off mourning and everyone was overjoyed. Fagena now opened his bag to distribute his meat, but the pig had turned into *baragi* (cucumbers), the snake into a twisted creeper, the cassowary into a king of fern, and the cuscus into rotten wood.

When Fagena had got over his astonishment at these changes the villagers explained to him why they themselves had been making a feast. It was a Thumb Feast, held five days after the death of a woman and girl in one of the gardens; they had been killed by a falling tree. Fagena did not divulge what he had done five days previously; but he reflected that he and his sky-friend had been the cause of these two deaths on earth.[70]

15.   *Moon-Man and Sun-Girl*

Once in a big men's-house a discussion arose about the sun and the moon. The general opinion was that both were combined in the same person; but one man declared that the sun was a girl and the moon a man. No one agreed with him, but he was so persistent that the others finally lost their tempers, beat him and drove him out.

He fled towards the east. Day after day he travelled on, sleeping on the track. He was tired and hungry but determined to find the sun and the moon and see if he were not right. At last he came to a clearing on a little hillock. The ground was red clay; it was clean and tidy; decorative plants grew round about; and in the centre stood a pleasant garden-house. Here he found a man plaiting an armlet and surrounded by his dogs. This man enquired whence he came and what he wanted, and the traveller told him the whole story—how he had advanced the theory that the sun was a girl and the moon a man, and how his fellow-villagers had beaten him and thrown him out because of it. The man listened to him, then invited him to lodge in his house. He baked an animal and they sat down to eat.

At sundown there came to the house a most beautiful girl, the man's sister, bringing supplies of sago-grubs and fish. Of such shining beauty was the girl that when she entered the house its dark interior was lit up as if by a lamp.

By the time their meal was over it was night, and the girl retired to her end of the house, beyond the partition, to sleep there. Then the host prepared to go out. He warned the traveller not to be inquisitive, and on no account to enter the girl's end of the house. Then he went out into the night, calling his dogs to follow him, "Kimi, *ya!* Abaru, *ya!* Baiako, *ya!* Wakara, *ya!* Inuma, *ya!* Funai, *ya!*" These are star names. For he was himself the moon, and the dogs he hunted with were stars; while his sister, who had made the house bright when she entered it, was no other than the sun girl.

Meanwhile this girl was singing to herself in the house:

I have built my big canoe, I have worked hard in the garden,
  oh my neck, my neck!
I have been on a long hunt, I have cut out a big canoe, oh my
  ribs, my ribs!
I have burnt off the timber, oh my back!
I have been cutting bananas, oh my head!
I have been cutting sugar-cane, oh my back!
I have been cutting *gatove* bananas, oh my arms!
I have baled out a fishing pool, oh my legs!

The traveller listened to this song, but he obeyed the moon man
and he did not even look inside the woman's part of the house.
On the contrary, since he found it too warm, he moved his mat
and slept outside.

In the morning the sun girl went out and the moon man returned.
He praised the traveller in a very friendly fashion. He had brought
back a cassowary, a wallaby, and an echidna; and these they cooked
and ate. Then having crammed the surplus into a capacious string
bag, the moon man hung it on the traveller's shoulder, bade him
shut his eyes, and slapped him on the back. When he opened his
eyes he found himself standing in front of his own men's-house with
the string bag still on his shoulder and full of good meat.

The villagers asked him if he had found the sun and the moon,
and he said, "Yes, and I was right. The sun is a girl and the moon
is a man." "Who gave you the meat?" they asked. "The moon hunter
gave it to me and also the beautiful string bag." At this they began
to believe that what he said was true, and they wanted to know
where the sun and the moon lived. But he refused to tell them.
All he would say was that it was far away to the east.

But there was one skinny miserable sort of a man who was always
pestering him. He would wake him from his sleep and follow him
to the rear when he went to ease himself, 'always asking the same
question. At last the traveller told him. If he really wanted to find
the sun and the moon he must travel many days by a certain path
to the east until he found the house in the clearing.

And so the skinny man set off on his quest. In due course he
found the house on the hillock and the moon man was sitting there.
"Are you the same man come back?" asked the moon man."No,"
said the skinny man, "but I have come in search of the moon."
The moon man pretended to know nothing about it. "He may be
over there," he said, pointing over the hills. But since the skinny

man looked so thin and miserable he took him in and gave him some food.

At evening the sun girl came home. "Ah," thought the skinny man, "that may be the moon"; and he felt very inquisitive. But the moon man who was about to go out for the night, told him to be still. He covered him with a blanket of bark-cloth, bade him sleep well, because he looked so thin and ill, and on no account to raise the blanket or to get up and look at the girl if she should sing. Then he called his star dogs and went off on his hunting.

Presently the girl began to sing and the skinny man could not resist the temptation to peep through a hole in the partition. He beheld her, very bright and beautiful, swaying her hips and singing: "I have built my big house, oh my neck, my neck." For a moment he watched; then got up, broke through the partition, and attempted to ravish her. But she was the sun girl, and as soon as he had laid hands on her he was scorched to death.

The sun girl hid his body. When her brother the moon came home he asked, "Where is the visitor?" "He has returned to his village," lied the girl. "All right," said the moon man, also lying, "I told him to."[71]

Sometime after this the first traveller went out searching for the skinny man and so he came a second time to the moon man's dwelling; and when he learnt that the other had died, he did not go back but stayed there.

Now the moon man carried out a plan with him. Together they made a sort of receptacle of bark; they put the sun girl into it and tied it to a pole; and then they carried her down to the river and ducked her in the cold water. This served to cool her down, though it made her feel very ill. They carried her back to the house however, and gave her some salt to eat. This soon made her better, and by morning she was cool enough to be approachable. Then the moon man told the traveller to marry her, which he did.

For some time they lived together very happily. Then the villagers, since two of their number had disappeared, went out in a body to look for them, and so came to the moon man's dwelling. They proceeded forthwith to attack it and very soon their own fellow villager, now husband of the sun girl, was killed. But the moon man and the sun girl fought on. Driven into their house they climbed up to the rafters, while the enemy tried to seize their legs. At last they burst a hole for themselves through the thatching and there they stood together, at the end of the day, on the ridge of their house.

Then said the moon man to his sister, "I will go up first, and after a little while you shall follow me," and with that he sailed up

into the sky. The sun girl stayed there fighting against the men until
all her arrows had been shot away. Then she too fled up into the
sky; and it was sunrise.

16. *Return from the Dead*

A man named Tauruabu lived at Harabuio. His wife Aukuiu died
and the three death feasts were held. After the third, or Little-
Finger Feast, her bones were gathered from the exposure coffin
and placed in a string bag, and this was hung up over the door of
her house.

On the same day the husband went to visit the coffin now standing empty. Where the springy stick, *siaka sui*, had been stuck in the
ground he saw there was a large hole. He entered it and found an
underground passage. For some time he proceeded along the
passage in the darkness, but then it grew lighter and he found he
was on a good track with forest on either side. On the track he saw
his wife's fresh footprints, and he determined to follow them and
bring her back if he could.

The track led through fine country but presently he came to a
place where it was blocked by a mass of stinging nettles. These
however opened to let him pass and closed behind him. He had
surmounted the first obstacle without any difficulty at all.

But soon he found himself opposed by an enormous *gateibu*
lizard, its body the size of a tree trunk. It lay on the path facing
him, with its jaws wide open. "Are you accustomed to eat *gateibu*?"
it asked. "Yes," answered Tauruabu; whereupon the jaws closed
and, stepping on its head, Tauruabu walked along the whole length
of its body down to the tail and so continued on its way. Had he
answered "No," then he would have had to be swallowed by the
monster and passed through its body before proceeding further.
This, in fact, is an ordeal through which nearly every *aminterare*
must pass on its way to the Land of the Dead.[72]

Some distance further on Tauraubu found that the road was
barred by a great *buguni*, or falling-log trap. Instead of walking
straight into it, as the ordinary *aminterare* would do, he stood aside
and cunningly dislodged the trigger-stick, whereupon the trap fell
with a noise like thunder.

Hiding behind a tree to see what would happen, Tauraubu now
saw a beautiful girl come upon the scene. It was Berome whose
regular duty it was to attend to the trap. Each time she heard it
fall she would come to free the imprisoned *aminterare* and set the
trap again. But this time she found no *aminterare*; and when she
looked for the trigger-stick she could not find that either, for
Tauraubu still held it in his hand. At last she saw him and asked

how he, a living man, came to be there. So he told her his story and, when she learned he was in search of his wife, she promised to give him her aid. On the following day she would conduct him to her father Gaburiniki. For it was Berome's duty to despatch all the *aminterare*, after liberating them from the trap, to one or other of her parents. Only the females went to her father; the males she sent to her mother, Makorebu. In this case, however, as she explained, she would send Tauraubu direct to Gaburiniki, because it was with him that he would find his wife.

Next morning she showed him the way and gave him his instructions. She provided him with food, for, as she said, Gaburiniki would have none to give him; and she warned him that in passing Makorebu he must look the other way lest she observe and intercept him.

Tauruabu did venture a glance in passing at Makorebu and observed that she was a very big woman with ears hanging low and breasts like sheets of bark-cloth. But he got safely by and arrived at the house of Gaburiniki. It proved to be an enormously long building in the shape of a U. At one tip of the U was Gaburiniki's residence. The other was a place of congregation for the *aminterare*.[73]

Tauruabu entered the house at Gaburiniki's end and was confronted by a man in his prime, very handsome, and of gigantic size. At first the chief of the underworld was taken aback at the appearance of a living man, but when he questioned him about his business and discovered that he was in search of his wife, he also promised to give him his help. Towards evening he told him to lie down under a bark-cloth blanket and wait there till morning, when he would rouse him by shaking his leg and restore his wife to him. Then he arrayed himself in belt, ornaments and cassowary feathers, blackened his face, and began to sing a song.

As soon as the chief of the underworld began to sing, Tauraubu heard noises in the far end of the house—shouting, laughter, and loud conversation in the voices of both men and women, the howling of dogs, the grunting of pigs, the stamping of many feet; altogether a sound of jubilation. As the crowd drew near, Tauruabu distinguished the song of the *aminterare*, "Korere, Korere, Takore, Takore,"[74] etc.; and now, peeping from under his blanket he saw a throng of people and animals, all spirits. They were dancing and singing; and there, reeling limp and senseless in their midst, her head lolling from side to side, was his wife Aukuiu. They were escorting her as a new arrival into the presence of Gaburiniki.

The dance went on and on, and at last Tauruabu fell asleep under his blanket. At dawn Gaburiniki shook his leg and roused him. All the spirits were gone. But Aukuiu was still there, and Gaburiniki told him he might now take his wife. Tauruabu seized her by the arm.

"Who are you?" she asked.

"It is I, your husband."

"Why have you come? Are you dead too?"

"No."

"Are there no girls or widows at home that you should come after me?"

"I thought only of you," said Tauruabu.

At this point Gaburiniki told the woman to be content and go with her husband. He gave them for presents a special kind of sugar-cane called *magifono* and a banana called *ga-dioko* which they were to plant when they reached home. And he gave firm instructions to Tauruabu: for a certain period he was to do all the work of the household himself, make sago, fetch firewood and water, cook the meals—everything; not until he had counted thirty-seven days, to the little finger of the right hand, should he allow his wife to do a stroke of work. Then he bade them both close their eyes for a moment, and when they opened them they were standing together beside their garden-house at home.

Aukuiu remained in the garden-house and Tauruabu went to get the bag of bones from the village. For as an *aminterare* she had no bones, and it was now her business to put them all back into her body. Leaving her then to this task Tauruabu busied himself about the place. He planted the banana and the sugar-cane and watched them grow from day to day. Besides his own man's work he made sago and fetched water, cooked, fed the pigs, and did everything that his wife used to do. He guarded her well and observed Gaburiniki's instructions to the letter. And all the time Aukuiu was busy over the bones. At nights he could hear them tinkle as she sat diligently picking them over and sorting them out.

So it went on for thirty-six days, and by this time there remained only the bones of the right-hand little finger to put back. But Tauruabu was thoroughly tired of doing everything himself. He had done a day's work and was preparing to cook some sago, when he found that he lacked a few palm leaves in which to bake it. So he asked his wife to do something for him, just to cut one or two sago leaves so that he could get on with the cooking.

She hung her head for a while and then she said, "It is so nearly finished. To-day is *hagi*; to-morrow is *kenagi* and then I shall be ready." But he said, "Go and get it"; and she went.

A moment later Tauruabu heard a scream. He rushed to his wife's side and found her fainting. Her knife had slipped and cut the little finger of her right hand, the one part of her whole body that had no bone in it; and now it was bleeding so fast that nothing could stop the flow. Tauruabu held her wrist tightly, but it was in vain. As the blood flowed her body seemed to melt away, and soon there remained nothing but a fleshless pile of bones.

Tauruabu lamented his folly: "If only I had let her be just one day more." He counted over the bones on the ground and saw that just those of one finger were missing. They were still in the bag. He saw too that the magic banana and sugar-cane had disappeared from his garden. Then he gathered all the bones and put them in the bag; and carried it back and hung it again over the door of Aukuiu's house in the village. Having done that he went into the men's-house, and bade his younger brother spread a mat beside his hearth fire. He sat down on it, and the men gathered round, and he told them the whole long story; and when he had finished it he fell back and died.

The villagers were thoroughly disgusted. Had he but possessed the sense to see that last day through, he would have had his wife, and he could have shared the magic banana and sugar-cane among them all. It was the loss of these that made them so angry; for they knew that all who ate of *ga-dioko* and *magifono* would never die. In fact through Tauruabu's impatience they had lost their chance of immortality. So they laid his body in an exposure coffin, and, to express their feelings, they piled dry wood all round and burnt it.

REFERENCES

1. (Originally published in *Oceania*, XI: 121-57; 259-94; 374-401; XII: 49-74; 134-54. Reprinted as Oceania Monograph No. 6. E.S.)
2. The elevation of the lake is 2,600 ft. and the temperature ranges between about 60° and 80°.
3. Why should there be paddles, fish-spears etc. if there was no water? The native storytellers always overlooked this inconsistency.
4. *Taubada* is Motuan for "big man," "old man". It is the general form of address from native to European.
5. It was readily sold to Mr. Champion who sent it to Port Moresby. After being exhibited at the Sesquicentenary Exhibition in Sydney it is now at Canberra.
6. It is more often pronounced *kiapa*, in which fact one may probably detect the influence of Police Motuan—a case of assimilation to a familiar sound (*kiapa* string-bag in Motuan).

7. The only mention of anything of the kind came from an old man of the Momahugu clan who indicated a *moma* on a tree (viz. a fleshy kind of *Dendrobium*) and refused to touch it "for fear of sickness." It was never included in the list of Momahugu totems, however.
8. Cf. "Plant Emblem," Chapter VIII, in my *Orokaiva Society*, Oxford, 1930.
9. I failed to ascertain whether, on the groom's side, the maternal clan is due for providing actually half of the *bunuka*. But the point is immaterial. They contribute a substantial share.
10. Cf. my *Papuans of the Trans-Fly*, Oxford, pp. 166 *sqq.*
11. This was a long-drawn-out feud originating in the natural death of a man in Herebu and a resultant charge of sorcery brought against Heno. The deceased had kinsmen in Ifigi, and the two tribes, Ifigi and Mubi, became involved in war. After suffering a severe defeat Heno was virtually driven into exile; but he succeeded in inducing the people of the lake, and even some from Kaibu, to come to his assistance, and together they made an attack on Ifigi. When they were again thoroughly beaten his allies drew the conclusion that Heno had duped them: he must after all have been guilty of sorcery or they would not have failed.
12. Aragai, the oldest man in the Mubi tribe, is the deafest I have ever met anywhere. When asked in my presence to say again if he had stolen the meat he nodded cheerfully, but there is no reason to suppose that he heard the question.
13. In the seventh the alleged sorcerer and his victims were both resident in Tugiri, but one, I understand, was an immigrant and therefore to that extent beyond the pale.
14. *Orokaiva Magic*, Oxford, 1928, pp. 173 *sqq.*
15. It is argued in the writer's *Orokaiva Magic* (pp. 203-5) that in some cases the specific itself may have been originally a symbol used in imitative magic, the point of it, i.e. its suggestion-value, having vanished from memory.
16. It is also a common trick in planting a banana sucker to count *sotto voce*—*menagi, hagi, igi, tugubu, kaba, tama*. This is a more direct kind of magic. The gardener hopes the bunch will consist of at least six "hands."
17. This, at any rate, was the explanation given to me. It cannot be assumed that this was the association of ideas originally responsible for putting prawns on the black list; it may be no more than a brain-wave on the part of an imaginative modern. For negative magic can also become conventionalized and lose track of its *rationale*. The important food plant *anumu* is avoided by some young men because it is thought to make them lazy and worthless, sitting idly alone and thinking of nothing but women. I have not the least idea how such a taboo came into being; nor could any native tell me.
18. Chapter 1 of the present volume.
19. What bird exactly I do not know. One might guess a hawk; but Piruru in his avian character is supposed to eat worms, and to rise with a *brrrr!* from the grass when disturbed. It sounds rather like a quail. The point may be in the concealment and sudden surprise rather than in killing.

20. His name never cropped up independently in the myths recorded at Kutubu. It is very probable that he belongs elsewhere and is to the majority of Kutubuans only a name used in hunting or war magic. In one account he was placed at Mt. Marokari in the west; in another at Fasu in the south. He used to hunt with his two dogs, always bringing home bagfuls of game which he would bake in his bush house and then carry to his friends in the village. One day he failed to put in an appearance and after some time the villagers went to look for him. They found a pandanus (*piruru*) growing near the house, but no trace of Piruru the man. Then someone noticed the dogs snuffling and licking at one of the "legs" (aerial roots) of the pandanus and on closer examination the bark at that point was seen to be human skin. The process of transmogrification had not quite finished.

21. Cf. the myth of the Pearlshells below, with the following spell to procure pearlshells:

> *Ira furubu gamogu-rumu hasu.*
> *Konjuguri gamogu-rumu hasu.*
> *Ya Fogabu gamogu-rumu hasu.*
> *Ya Ware gamogu-rumu hasu.*
> *Ya Aba gamogu-rumu hasu.*
> *Ira Fifi gamogu-rumu hasu.*
> *Ira Tugu gamogu-rumu hasu.*
> *Kobira Piwi gamogu-rumu hasu.*

Gamogu-rumu hasu means, "I desire in my liver, I yearn." The various trees (*ira*) named are red-leaved ones such as grew about Kobira Piwi's house; Konjuguri, red cordyline, also grew there. (The birds, *ya*, do not play any part in the story as I heard it.) I cannot tell from the spell whether the speaker is actually impersonating Kobira Piwi, the mythical character who owned all the pearlshells.

22. Also the same man may give a number of alternative names for the same mythical character, a series in order of deeper and deeper secrecy. Thus Nekinagu first gave the names Tuahororo (by night) and Serasumi (by day) for the moon; then, when the others had left tent, Karudibu (by night) and Sere (by day); and finally, in a tense whisper in my ear, Figibu (by night) and Wagiabu (by day).

23. No further action was taken against him. The villagers said, "They were your wife and children."

24. This seems like leprosy. There are said to be six cases on the lake itself.

25. There was further talk of a *misihenimu*, apparently the "spirit of a tree." If glancing over your shoulder, you thought you saw two trees and found subsequently that there was only one, then you might expect to fall ill, for the second, vanishing, tree was a *misihenimu*. But this was one of those ideas which do not find general acceptance at Kutubu; no doubt it is an imported one, not fully assimilated.

26. Cf. the Orokaiva belief that the spirits of slain men reside in the upper air. *Vide Orokaiva Society*, p. 274.

27. It is worth recalling the rather curious fact that sorcery is very seldom named as the cause of illness in itself. The friends and relatives seem to

wait till the patient is dead before they call that theory into action—though then indeed they do so all too often.

28. The former was identified (from sketch and description) by Dr. M. F. Glaessner, Palaeontologist to the Australian Petroleum Co., as a calcareous internal cast of fossil gastropod, probably from Upper Tertiary limestones. The latter, which I did not see, was described as bulky, hard and yellow. I did not learn of its existence till I had left Hegisu; but I made fairly sure that it was not gold.

29. I saw one or two much larger, perhaps two feet in freight, but failed to discover whether they had any special significance.

30. The same may perhaps be true of the parallel series of treatments for the class of illness known as *ii-rumu-hubu*. Of these I have had only the barest description, but they comprise (i) *bedoro soga mitenabu* (*bedoro* being the leaf of a certain dendrobium); (ii) *ii mogofumahabu* (in which the *ii*, or *siago*, itself is used in fumigation); and a *bedoro bodo gavirabo*, followed by a dance. It is only for *kwi-usane-habu* and *ii-usane-habu* that the drums are ever used.

31. The method of curing sickness by the sacrifice of pigs has a great vogue in the Grasslands (Augu, Wela, etc.). The offering is made, I gather, to the spirits of the dead and it consists of the blood poured out of the pig's nose. The most brutal methods may be used. I have seen a long cassowary quill thrust up the animal's nostrils to make them bleed before it is killed.

32. The myths imply that the cult was brought by certain individuals to an already existent population at Kutubu, but it must remain an assumption that this is really the case. It is conceivable that the original inhabitants of Kutubu might themselves have brought the cult, together with the myths, from the region where these are supposed to have originated.

33. Yabame and Hobo may appear together, and may be represented as sister and brother.

34. *Kirau* means apparently "a *kira*, oh!" the *kira* being the "string" of *bari* shells, which is the commonest form, almost a recognized unit, of Kutubu condensed wealth; *hoke* = "stroke".

35. I do not imagine that the operator goes through such spells whenever he is practising or about to practise.

36. This happened to belong to the *Kaa-Usi*, of which the founder was Yabame, and they were Yabame's bones. In the *Amina-Usi* they would be Somaia's.

37. The only such ritual which I have heard of as belonging to women is that of cleansing after widowhood.

38. Some villages possess none at all. At Kesi, where there is admittedly very little space for building, I saw the *Piaka Gwabu* ceremonies carried out in the men's-house.

39. It is said to be on the instruction of the founder of the *Piaka Gwabu* cult that the hunter, before hunting, must neither touch, eat, nor mention the name of *haginamo*.

40. Kava is *gamoda* in the Kiwai language. See G. Landtmann, *The Kiwai Papuans of British New Guinea*, Macmillan, 1927.

41. In the absence of the real thing it is permissible to use certain varieties of the pepper vine (*keragainya* and *sigasiga*) which bear a fairly close resemblance to it. But these are plainly regarded as substitutes.

42. In others there is only one founder. There is no "underground man" as in the version given here.

43. It will be recalled that an alternative name for it is *sagainya*, and *sagainya* was in two versions given as the founder's name. In one of them he was a "big man" of Wasemi. He was the first to perform the *Piaka Gwabu* ceremony. In his day "the earth was soft, everything shook all the time, and trees fell down by themselves." After teaching the people *Sagainya* sank into the ground and afterwards came up as the *sagainya* (or *takorabu*) plant.

44. The ceremony is sometimes called *Hibu-ninyi*, which means the same thing. *Ninyi*—branch i.e. the elbow-shaped forked stick.

45. Another formula was: *aba, wamea, abai, maia, haga numaga* (fathers, maternal uncles, paternal uncles—this food is yours). My informant took the trouble to point out that the word *hua* (mothers) was omitted because the *piaka-aa* was exclusively a place for men.

46. Teraribu, near Kesi, is one of the little creeks that flow into the lake.

47. The little finger of the left hand is *menagi* (1); that of the right hand is *kenagi* (37).

48. I sketched a number freehand at the sites (see figure 14). The sizes are not recorded. The designs appear individually, not in order as shown.

49. As an interesting piece of native natural history I was assured by some informants that black cockatoos spend the night hanging by their curved beaks from the branches.

50. *Aminterare*, or *terare*, is the usual word. *Yesibu* however seemed to be always to be used in connection with the *Kehugabu* and *ho* for the spirit of the *piaka-aa*.

51. Cf. similar stories among the Orokaiva: my *Orokaiva Society*, Oxford University Press, pp. 273, 275-6.

52. In one story the spirits had carried their son through the air, resting by night in trees where they hung by their little fingers, holding him head downwards by the legs.

53. A much more difficult situation arose in regard to a man named Yola, one of those who were brought in for experience at Police Headquarters in Port Moresby. He died and was buried in that town, and Mr. Champion had to confront the people of Wasemi with the news. Nothing could satisfy them but they must have Yola's skull, asat least a representative specimen of his remains. The Government was prepared in due course to meet their wishes; but in view of compensation received the Wasemi people allowed the matter to drop.

54. Used in the popular game of *hameno viribu*. It is bowled along the ground and boys shoot little arrows at it while it is in motion.

55. Fire-making is by the saw method, with a bamboo thong and the wood

magaio. I recorded another story of the origin of fire. A man sees smoke far away in the east and goes to investigate. He finds that two branches of the tree called *magaio* are rubbing together in a high wind and that they have produced fire. He carries a burning brand home, holding it in his mouth as he swims the river.

56. Many stories tell of successful hunting—no doubt a form of wish-fulfilment. The compulsion on the woman with respect to the first pig is a typical revenge for injured feelings.

57. Buru (leech)-fogobu (cut-up)-merave (canoe-landing). This place is at Kafa, where leeches are said to be particularly numerous.

58. This is classed as a *tuni*. There is another tale of the origin of tobacco which belongs to the *Usi-tasi* (the mythology of the *Usi* cult). In this story, as I heard it, the usual places of Somaia and Hobo were reversed. Hobo was the originator and died first. He had told his brother to look under his hair tags at the back of his neck when he was dead. This Somaia did, and found a tiny bag containing tobacco seeds. This would imply that the knowledge of tobacco reached Kutubu from the east or south-east.

59. The kind of pandanus which bears a red fruit. I could not discover why this was particularly abusive. There is no doubt some missing link, but when I asked for it my informants did not seem able to see the point of the question.

60. I do not know that it throws any light on the above story to add this native statement. "The *abari* are women: therefore when the men are eating *abari* women must not talk.

61. *Gi-magami,* literally "earth-things." These are reputedly the diet of fish. The present story was heard at Herebu on the Mubi.

62. An *usanehabu* is organized only in order to cure some case of sickness.

63. In another version the girl is named Kunumaka and the *taubu* Ganaro (the latter is also used as a general term).

64. The Cordyline was a *giru-magami* or "dream thing" which, while it existed, ensured his safety. A man who dreams of a thing (either individual or representative of a species) may regard it as having some protective influence over him.

65. In another version it was said that the girl's blood was responsible for red colours in nature, the boy's semen for white colours (white leaves, stones, etc.).

  A theory of conception or the make-up of the body, is that the mother's menstrual blood makes all the soft fleshy parts (thus, if you cut yourself the blood flows); the father's semen makes the hard "white" parts—bones, teeth, finger-and toe-nails.

66. This story was one of those given me without names for the characters, my informant only supplying them after the tale was told. The mother (i.e. the girl who climbed the tree) was Saube. (She became a *marua* bird on leaving the children). The person who supplied the food, i.e. the father who revealed himself, was Ya Baia, a hawk (the imagery is obvious). The boy was Kanawebe and the girl Karako. These were said to belong to "Paremahugu" *amindoba.*

The first part of the story is one of the *amindoba* myths, representing "Paremahugu" as the original clan. The second part, the story of how the girl cut herself, etc., is a general myth. Other versions of it give the characters different names.

67. *Sabe*="nose," i.e. spur or ridge.
68. The names of these and others are used in magic for obtaining pearlshells.
69. The knowledge of this story is of value in pearlshell magic. I have several versions and they were all told me in great secrecy. Also a spell for winning pearlshells (attracting their possessors and making them ready to deal) which mentions Kobira and certain of his trees with coloured leaves. Birds with bright plumage are also named as having a magical bearing on pearlshells. I imagine that in both cases the connection lies in the highly prized coloured sheen of the gold-lip.

There is a further story of the origin of pearlshells (told me by the same informant). A little girl gives birth to them. This is staged at Mt. Kwaimu (apparently to the north-west) and the story ends with an account of a storm and landslide which carries the girl, her home, and her shells, into the River Augu.

70. This story I heard in Wasemi. It was obviously a new one to some of the Kutubu people. It bears on the belief (not held by, or known to, all of them) that each man on earth has a namesake in the sky. It was maintained that events or deeds on earth have their counterpart in the sky. If your namesake possesses a woman, so do you: if he kills someone, so do you, etc. But informants could not make up their minds whether these things happened simultaneously, or whether one was the cause of the other. In the case of the above story there was some difference of opinion. As told it appears that Fagena and his friend had killed the women in the sky-garden before the death of the two women in the earth-garden. But others suggested that the two village women had first been killed in the garden and that their spirits had then been killed in the sky. The notion of sky counterparts for all who live on earth is certainly a very striking one but quite apart from the fact that it does not seem familiar to everybody, it cannot be regarded as very important. Except for the trivial fact that a man may not utter his own name it seems to have no effect on conduct.

The sky-dwellers of this story are not identified with the *pauave*, spirits of slain people who ascend into the sky. The two beliefs are independent. The people of the story are called *Turumena* (lit., Thunder People). I was given the names of three of their villages: Kakasuru, Hehewo and Arubani. The thunder (*turu*) is the sound of their dancing and cheering. I also heard mention of an obscure person called Bane or Kabe-a-Kone (Pale-Skinned Man) who was said to dwell in the sky. The thunder was the sound of his voice crying, "Who has stolen my pig? Who has cut my sago?" etc. It was said that only the old men knew about him: but I was never able to extract anything from them. Once again I think this an unimportant belief and to the great majority of Kutubuans entirely unknown.

71. This sort of thing I take to be humorous padding.

72. The *gateibu* of the story may be the very large lizard sometimes spoken of rather credulously as a "tree-climbing crocodile." Smaller lizards called *gateibu* are found at Kutubu, but they are said to be poor food, not comparing with the monitor, *iraharabu*. Old women are said to eat them, but most people refuse to do so since it would cause their bodies to waste away. But it is a matter of indifference; some people do eat them, and Tauruabu apparently was, or pretended to be, one of these. I cannot see any point in this episode. It may contain an obscure reference to some ceremony of initiation and form of "swallowing by the monster." If so it is a foreign allusion, for there is nothing of the kind at Kutubu.

73. The U-shape was insisted on by informants, and demonstrated by a drawing on the ground.

There was some uncertainty regarding the tip of the U occupied by *aminterare*. Some thought that all the spirits of the previously dead remained there permanently. Others said that it was merely a sort of reception hall, the final abode of the spirits being somewhere else, and the meeting with Gaburiniki merely an episode on their way to it. Gaburiniki was supposed to possess each woman spirit sexually; Makorebu each man spirit. After this they plucked out the spirits' tongues and replaced them back to front, so that they could not talk intelligibly.

As will be seen, Tauruabu met Gaburiniki before the deceased woman was brought to his presence. It is not clear what she was doing in the meantime.

74. *Korere*, the west, is the place of the living; *Tahore*, the east, the place of the dead.

PART IV

5

THE VAILALA MADNESS AND THE DESTRUCTION OF NATIVE CEREMONIES IN THE GULF DIVISION[1]

Part 1

THE VAILALA MADNESS

General

During the latter months of the year 1919 there began in the Gulf Division that singular and really important movement known as the Vailala Madness.

Originating in the neighbourhood of Vailala, whence it spread rapidly through the coastal and certain of the inland villages, this movement involved, on the one hand, a set of preposterous beliefs among its victims—in particular the expectation of an early visit from their deceased relatives—and, on the other hand, collective nervous symptoms of a sometimes grotesque and idiotic nature. Hence the name Vailala Madness seems apt enough and at least conveys more meaning than any of the various alternatives.

A punctual notice of the outbreak was made in the Annual Report of 1919-1920, where there appear (p. 116) extracts from the diary of Mr. G. H. Murray, who as Acting Resident Magistrate, Kerema, was able to observe the phenomena in their earliest and possibly most virulent form; and in the same volume a further account by Mr. Murray is included in his magisterial report.[2]

Since that time the movement appears to have lost much of its energy, though there have been, and probably will be, occasional revivals of a more or less local character. However, the Vailala Madness is not dead: in a sense it has settled down. Certain of the early beliefs have been somewhat discredited, and the crazy, uncontrolled excitement of the earlier stages is now very seldom to be seen. But there still remain beliefs and practices which may be said to have consolidated into an elementary cult; and the nervous disorder which used to afflict whole villages together may still be seen, whether genuine or assumed, in individuals.[3]

Furthermore, whatever the present condition of the Vailala Madness may be, its work in one direction stands good: for where it has touched it has made a clean sweep of the ceremonies, and has destroyed almost every treasure of religion and art. This is undoubtedly the serious feature of the disturbance: compared with the wholesale destruction of native practice and tradition, the collective nervous disorder is matter of small and transitory importance.

The present report will first give a description of the Vailala Madness in its existing condition, together with some account of its origin and dissemination; and will afterwards deal with the abovementioned question, viz. The Destruction of Native Ceremonies, as one which cries out for consideration and action.

Designation

The name Vailala Madness seems the most distinctive and suitable; but the several alternatives may be mentioned—

1. The Gulf *Kavakava*: i.e., The Gulf Madness.
2. The Orokolo *Kavakava*: Though it happens that Orokolo itself is practically the one coastal village in the Gulf Division that has remained immune.
3. Head-he-go-round: The usual Pidgin-English expression. (Throughout the report this expression will be used especially for those individuals who still continue to be affected by the Madness.)
4. *Kwarana giroa*, and *kwarana dika*: The Motuan equivalents.
5. *Haro heraripi*: An Elema expression, meaning literally "Head-he-go-round."
6. *Iki haveve*: "Belly-don't-know"; this is the usual name throughout all the coastal villages in the Gulf Division.
7. *Abo abo*: To the West, in the Purari Delta (where the Madness has a very small footing), it is called *abo abo*—giddy or crazy.

Distribution

Though movements of a similar nature may have taken place in other parts of the Territory,[4] it would appear that as a complex the Vailala Madness has been practically confined to the Gulf Division.

From Nomu, at the mouth of the Alele, to Oiapu, the first village west of Cape Possession, it has taken hold of the coastal villages almost without exception. On the West, only one village has succumbed completely, viz., Apiope, a section of Maipua settled on the River Aivei. Whether, on the East, the Maiva villages have been affected to any extent I am unable to say. Inland, however, the Madness has made considerable headway, particularly on the

Vailala, where it is found in villages 60 miles up the river; and also
in the Opau group north of Kerema.

It must be understood, however, that different villages are
affected in different degrees. Orokolo and the neighbouring village
Iogu appear to have resisted the new influences successfully: and
here all the paraphernalia of the ceremonies are to be seen as in the
old days. Yet the next village of Arihava—only a mile or so removed
—has been a veritable hot-bed of the cult, and is still one of its
most active centres.

In other places there may be detected a luke-warmness. In
Karama and Koaru (where, in the early enthusiasm, everything
pertaining to the old religion had gone by the board) there are now
dances to be seen and ceremonies in preparation. The people of
Keuru, next door to the very birth-place of the movement, are
backsliders. In the Delta, the village of Kerewa (Maipua) was at
first fairly carried off its feet by the missionary zeal of Arihava; but
since coming by slow degrees to disillusionment, has gone back to the
old ways under the firm impression that it has been humbugged.

These instances must not be construed as minimizing the influence
of the Vailala Madness. They do show, however, that in some
places, or in some moods, the old culture may come by its own again;
and they may serve to indicate the method by which a misguided
and destructive movement should best be dealt with.

Method of Description

The phenomena of the Vailala Madness may be divided into two
fairly distinct categories. First, there are the purely nervous and
physical symptoms, which seem to be entirely unreasoned; second,
there are the associated ideas or doctrines, together with an elementary ritual.

Such a division runs the inevitable risks of abstraction, especially
as there is no doubt a strong interaction between the two sets of
factors. But for purposes of description it should be allowable to
deal with them separately: for it seems probable that both (1)
the characteristic behaviour, and (2) some, at least, of the
doctrines and practices are familiar enough to science or history,
as separate entities.

The Nervous and Physical Symptoms of
The Vailala Madness

In the Individual

It was not my good fortune to witness any large collective demonstrations during my journey down the Gulf coast; but individual
cases are to be seen commonly enough.

In practically every village will be found a certain number of men who are from time to time overtaken by the Madness; and, for lack of a better term, these may be called by their Pidgin-English name of "Head-he-go-round Men," an expression which has the advantage of being entirely non-committal.

A less clumsy alternative may be used, viz., Automaniac. Although, as will be seen,[5] this does not quite cover all the subjects, it will nevertheless apply to the most important and numerous class of them. The word is meant to imply a self-induced condition of nervous or mental derangement.

CERTAIN CASES
Several instances may be described as they were seen and noted:—

1. *At Nomu, April, 1922*
During a moonlight evening numbers of people were collecting in the open square of the village. A young man named Mara stood on the *eravo* platform; he was bending, swaying and tottering, hands on hips. He continually rolled his eyes and uttered exclamations, which the onlookers said were unintelligible to them. When taken inside the *eravo*, he kept peering up into the roof. Subsequently he became quiet and went down among the people, where he seemed to bear a leading part in the dancing which was going on.

When questioned soon afterwards he was almost imbecilic in appearance but quiet rational. On subsequent occasions he was normal, though possibly a little "soft" looking. Other informants said that, when there is noise or excitement, Mara's "head goes round." He is known to climb the Nomu flag-pole on occasion. Although such a silly-looking creature when under the influence of the Madness, he was by no means exposed to ridicule or disrespect. On the contrary he was the object of silent and, it seemed, rather scared interest while on the platform; and later acted as leader in the singing and dancing.

2. *At Nomu, April, 1922*
On the same evening another man, Maukape, was seen sitting on a verandah.[6] He did not declaim, but moaned and shuddered continually in a way suggestive of teeth-chattering.

Maukape is a much older man, of rather forbidding appearance but of mild and pleasant manners. He is popular in the village. He has a reputation as diviner, and possibly as *puripuri*-man.[7] There was no suggestion of imbecility in his appearance, but he had that lined face and somewhat worried expression which may possibly be associated with *puripuri* or native occultism.

3. At Arihava, April, *1922*

A man was seen delivering an exhortation from the platform of an *eravo*. Dancing and singing was going on near at hand and his voice was almost drowned, but numbers of people were gathered about the platform; watching and listening. He spoke at the top of his voice, and very rapidly: the language, I am told, was English, and was not understood by the people present. The only phrases intelligible to me were "*Ihova*"[8] (with frequent pointing to the sky); "Me wantum *kaikai*" and "He all right." The speaker was highly excited, striking himself continually on the chest. Throughout the performance his right leg trembled violently as if quite uncontrolled.

When he had finished, another man took his place. This speaker, however, seemed to lack inspiration: his right leg began to tremble, but without the same appearance of spontaneity, and finally subsided altogether.

4. At Vailala, December, *1922*

A young man, Karoa (of fine physique and appearance), was displeased because several others and myself had entered the *ahea uvi* without consulting him. He poured forth a volume of gibberish which contained a good many Pidgin-English phrases, but was intelligible to nobody.[9]

When his harangue was finished he stood aside, stuttering and mumbling in the familiar manner suggestive of teeth-chattering; he made a few symmetrical gestures with both hands, but for the most part motioned with his right hand before his solar plexus as if encouraging his stomach to rise.[10] Meanwhile he heaved long sighs, and looked genuinely distracted. Finally he moved across to the flag-pole, and stamped round and round it, shouting such phrases as—"Hurry up!" "What's-a-matter?" "Come on boy!" Many people present watched Karoa closely, and, as it seemed, with a touch of fascination.

5. At Lese, January, *1923*

About noon, a man, Eapi, made his appearance and strode rapidly up and down the village, performing sharp about-turns. Under his arm, which was jammed tightly to his side, were some small missionary text-books. He was highly excited and inclined to be hilarious; his breathing was short and panting. This man was said to be continually in an abnormal condition and was possibly a confirmed lunatic. The people of the village watched him with a sort of gloomy uneasiness; they were not by any means amused.

It should be stated that all the above cases (with the possible exception of the last), are those of recognized "Head-he-go-round

Men." Such individuals are afflicted most frequently at night-time, and one may occasionally hear their moaning and stammering as they wander through the village.

The actual feelings of the subject are not very easily understood. The common native name for the condition, *Iki haveve*, which means literally "Belly don't know," would appear to arise from the facts (1) that the seat of the strange sensations is commonly felt to be in the belly; and (2) that the subject, when overcome by them, does not know what he is about.

The stomach is certainly regarded as the source of inspiration by those especially gifted Automaniacs who can divine; and one of them has defined to me two distinct stages of the seizure: first, *iki haveve*, when he is simply dizzy or ecstatic; second, *iki pekakire*— "Belly he think," when the inspiration rises. *Pekakire* means literally, "to climb." As for the alternative name *haro heraripe*, *haro* means head, and the word *heraripe* appears to indicate a whirling motion. It is used of the wind, *bea heraripe* meaning a whirlwind.

Several men have described their own sensations. A youth of Vailala West said that when the Madness came upon him—"his legs went round........'all-a-same whisky.'......After that he did not know what he did........and finally the talk came up from his navel." Incidentally he maintained that his knowledge of whisky and its effects upon human behaviour was no more than objective. Another intelligent, and possibly more cautious, informant of Keuru said the "Head-he-go-round Men" behaved themselves "all-a-same ginger beer."

In Silo a certain Heviope had occasional seizures: he would then wander about the village, seeing nothing, and finally might fall quite senseless. His first attack, he said, had come upon him after he had been assaulted by another man. In some cases, especially where visions are being described, the subject will say that something "hits his head."[11]

The above cases are, I believe, all genuine; that is to say, they are cases in which the subject was for the time being at least, *non compos*. But there are undoubtedly individuals who assume symptoms of a similar nature for reasons of their own: indeed, impostors of this kind must constitute a fair proportion of the recognized "Head-he-go-round Men." It is noticeable that probably the majority of these recognized "Head-he-go-round Men" have been "signed on,"[12] and that they are proficient in Motuan, and even in English.

The value of a general impression cannot be disputed in such matters as these: it would be possible to weed out a proportion of laughing impostors, for the simple reason that their faces do not bear the slightest impression of trying or nerve-wracking experience. On the other hand, there are those who, one concludes at a glance, take the matter all too seriously; and who are betrayed by such symptoms as wrinkled brows, a nervous twitching of the mouth, or a somewhat harrassed and worried expression. Undoubtedly many of the more outstanding "Head-he-go-round Men" look "nervy."

It would seem likely, however, that in many cases the nervous disorder is self-induced, and to this extent the subjects are impostors. Though it must be understood that in such cases the Madness is none the less real.

There are therefore three main categories into which the "Head-he-go-round Men" may be divided:—

1. Those who fall into the condition quite involuntarily. Some of these may be in greater or less degree "mental" cases.
2. Those who, for motives of their own, simulate the Madness without giving way to it.
3. An important intermediate class of those who voluntarily induce the Madness and, for the time being, surrender completely to it.

It may be pointed out that the term Automaniac, which will be used generally as synonymous with "Head-he-go-round Man," is in strictness applicable only to the last category.

Nervous and Physical Symptoms as Collective Phenomena

As a collective phenomenon the Vailala Madness is now seen only occasionally, i.e., when circumstances are favourable to a demonstration.

In April of last year there was, for one reason or another, some little excitement in the village of Arihava. A great throng of people were joining in a dance (in which there seemed very little organization) and in other parts of the village groups of men were engaged together in "dances." One such group of six, clustered about a flagpole, were chanting vigorously, and going through various movements in time. These movements were rather exaggerated, and the performers were making hard work of them; one man seemed to be fanning his stomach continually; another revolved on one leg; but, generally, the actions of several men were in some sort of conformity. When they would pause for a moment, and the chanting ceased, the gestures of one or two of them would continue in moderated form. Of these six dancers, it was said, only two were "Head-he-go-round Men"; the others were simply "joining in."

For an idea of the Vailala Madness as a collective phenomenon, reference must be made to G. H. Murray's account. Striking features are the rapidity of its spread, the numbers of people affected, and the general similarity of the symptoms. Current accounts along the coast tell how whole villages, even little children, were afflicted simultaneously; and the majority of those who are now completely normal will admit that in the original furore they "went *kavakava*."[13]

It is said that the appearance of Mr. Hurley's plane caused in some places a fresh accession of the Madness, especially as it provided a stimulant to the flagging belief in the promised ancestral reunion; though such excitement must have been very short-lived, for, three months after the aeroplane passed, hardly any reference was made to it.[14]

However, an incident which occurred in Arihava last January will serve to show that collective demonstrations cannot be regarded as altogether things of the past. The villagers of Arihava were at first hostile toward the new idea of rice plantations; they were as yet ignorant as to their share in the work and the returns; and feeling ran very high.[15] The following extracts are from the journal for December of Mr. F. P. Mahony, Assistant Inspector and Instructor.

"On entering the main village of Arihava, I observed at one end, on a particularly clear space, a number of natives, approximately twenty, gesticulating and carrying out many antics which could only be likened to those of a lunatic. On making enquiries ......I learnt it was a renewal of what was previously known as *kavakava* or Vailala Madness."

Mr. Mahony proceeded to call the roll for the villages of Iogu and Nomu, the demonstration continuing meanwhile. Finally he commenced the roll-call for Arihava itself. "As the name of each native taking part in the *kavakava* was called, he came up, and, being unable to talk or stand quietly, sat down on the ground, trembling all over, and the eyes being badly blood-shot." The roll-call being completed the *kavakava* began again, this time on a larger scale; and subsequently Mr. Mahony was bombarded with extraordinary questions. After an interview of two hours he told the natives his throat was sore with too much talking and left them on the best of terms.

General Remarks on these Symptoms

The above somewhat fragmentary evidence, together with the accounts by G. H. Murray, may perhaps render possible a diagnosis of the purely nervous and physical symptoms—a matter which may best be left to medical opinion. One may venture, however, to offer a few remarks upon the phenomena in (1) their individual aspect; and (2) their collective aspect.

(1) The mental instability of the native generally is commonly recognized; instead of preserving a steady balance under strong emotion, he may lose command of himself and give way to excesses. As emotion must find an outlet in action, these may (if his higher controls be relaxed) even take the form of unguided and involuntary bodily movements, such as those which characterize the Vailala Madness.

The reason for this instability is no doubt in large degree a matter of nurture; where there is no strict standard or tradition of self-control, outbursts of passion or frenzy are without their strongest deterrent. But there may also be a purely racial predisposition. Such a predisposition has been said, for instance, to belong to the Malayan peoples in especial; but in various other parts of the world there has been noted a similar tendency, viz., to engage in meaningless and uncontrolled somatic movements (especially those of a mimetic character) when under the influence of, or as a result of, powerful emotion.

In certain pronounced or exaggerated forms (such as the Latah of Indonesia, and the so-called "Arctic Hysteria") this nervous affection seems more or less localized or endemic. If, as seems likely, the predisposing cause is racial rather then environmental, the difficult question then arises of how far they are strictly speaking pathological, and how far they are natural. So with the less severe manifestations the same question will confront us.

It is not impossible that we have here to deal with a genuine innate weakness of the Papuan's character.[16] And whether this be an innate tendency or no, it should be remembered that there is no tradition against such conduct. A native of the Gulf would not make a fool of himself or be regarded with aversion if he indulged in the most outrageous antics, or even fell in a fit: he would be proud rather than ashamed of himself.

(2) Secondly the phenomena of the Vailala Madness may be regarded in their collective aspect. Once begun, the madness spread with the swiftness and certainty of an epidemic throughout the coastal villages, meeting almost everywhere ready acceptance or the feeblest resistance.

The secret of this swift contagion no doubt consists largely in the imitative character of the Madness. Mobs of villagers, already excited and jubilant at the news that their ancestors were returning to them, witnessed some individuals in their midst exhibiting signs of violent emotion, and indulging in primitive gestures and actions. Unconsciously, or without any effort at inhibition, they find themselves imitating the actions, and joining in the vague emotions of the leaders; until whole villages may be, without rhyme or reason, comporting themselves like so many lunatics or epileptics. Meanwhile the outrageous beliefs and hopes promulgated by the originators of the movement are the more readily accepted by reason of the suggestibility of an excited mob which has cast aside its self-control. Such are common enough phenomena of mob psychology.[17] They have been witnessed in a form hardly less repulsive and exaggerated in many religious revivals, especially among negro christians.

An interesting parallel was provided only recently in London, when many individuals in an audience of shell-shocked soldiers fell into contortions in imitation of one of their number; and a report, received (while the present is in writing) by the Medical Department from Dr. Bellamy, T.G.M.O., East, describes a scene precisely similar which he witnessed at Raniau, in the Northern Division.

The villagers were very unwilling to take the hookworm treatment he was about to give them. The first subject, who Dr. Bellamy thinks was the village *puripuritauna*,[18] resisted all attempts to administer the oil, and both he and all the other people present were in a state of considerable excitement. "Eventually he drank; and no sooner had he done so than he turned his head sideways and started to run in circles, brandishing a stick and shouting and throwing himself into epileptoid attitudes. As each of the men following drank he did exactly the same, until the whole village seemed a mass of capering lunatics."

It appears that these people are affected by the *Baigona* cult, but have substituted the taro for the snake; they perform "frenzied dances to the taro spirit." On this occasion they were shouting that "God was speaking to them."

A few more notes from the report may be quoted: "The women not yet lined up but standing round.... seeing their men carrying on began in sympathy to do little stunts of their own....throwing their arms about....staggering gait....falling to the ground.... weird attitudes, but all silently ....no shouting from the women."

Taking into account therefore the mental instability of the native, and the ordinary effects of mob psychology (to which, indeed, his very instability particularly exposes him), the nervous and physical symptoms of the Vailala Madness are not altogether to be wondered at. Nor is it unlikely that revivals will take place in the Gulf Division, and similar disturbances in other parts of the Territory.

The Doctrines and Practices of The Vailala Madness

We may now turn to the description of the cultural aspect of the Vailala Madness, i.e., to the doctrines, practices, and material paraphernalia, which together give it the character of an elementary cult. These latter features of the movement are still much in evidence, whereas the symptoms above described have in large degree played themselves out.

The Expected Return of Deceased Relatives

Perhaps one of the most fundamental ideas was that the ancestors, or more usually the deceased relatives, of the people were shortly to return to visit them. They were expected in a large steamer, which was to be loaded with cases of gifts—tobacco, calico, knives, axes, food-stuffs, and the like.

So the people of Kerewa, a Maipuan village, had been convinced by a party from Arihava that a great steamer was soon to appear off Orokolo, manned by the *a'avaia* (or spirits) of their deceased relatives. The cargo was to be allotted to various villages, and the people of Kerewa would know their own cases by *bupu*, or marks. In the meantime they were to accumulate sago and coconuts and have everything in readiness to welcome and entertain the ghostly crew of the steamer.[19] Having promised to inform Kerewa by message the moment the steamer hove into sight, the Arihava party now left the villagers preparing in a flurry of excitement for the welcome-home.

Some time passed without news; messengers were sent to Arihava, to be informed that the vessel had not arrived, but was still expected. But as day after day passed, and the steamer was now long overdue, the villagers grew less sanguine, and finally fell to upon the sago and coconuts, concluding that they had been grievously hoaxed. The normal life was gradually resumed; the sacred objects which had been destroyed were replaced; and Kerewa now provides a happy instance of a community that has successfully shaken itself free from the Vailala Madness.

The belief in the steamer flourished in the early days of the movement, and evidently spread from end to end of the infected area. Now, naturally, it has lost its force, and is mentioned with a little shamefaced amusement. One informant, who had certainly been enthusiastic in spreading the tale, denied all personal association with it, appearing to think the matter somewhat discreditable to him; and declared that the people, having now got over their *kavakava*, no longer believed in the steamer.

In some early versions of the belief the steamer was to have on board a consignment of rifles, which would be used in driving the present white inhabitants of Papua, out of the country. It seems, however, that, in the very natural uneasiness or even alarm which the movement at first occasioned among the more or less isolated Europeans, too much stress was laid upon these and similar stories. The circulation of garbled and exaggerated accounts gave good cause at first for the fear of a general rising; but in the opinion of Mr. G. H. Murray, who made haste to look into the matter, this fear had little or no foundation of fact. Though it seems that vague ideas of Papua for the Papuans were current at the time.

Ancestors as White Men

A feature of interest and importance is that in some places the returning ancestors or relatives were expected to be white; and indeed some white men were actually claimed by the natives to be their deceased relatives returned. Several cases are told of in which a European—no doubt to his embarrassment—was warmly greeted by one of the natives as his father. According to a native story, a certain young man of one of the smaller Vailala villages when walking in the bush encountered a white man, in whom, after a close scrutiny, he recognized his deceased father. Then father and son sat down and wept together for a long time, until at last the former rose, cut some bananas, and, leaving them with his son, disappeared; while the latter returned to the village and told the story.

Where certain of the Automaniacs profess to receive visitations from the dead, these latter sometimes appear as white men. Thus a man, Laive, of Wamai, tells how his father came down from the sky and "hit his head," so that Laive fell back senseless. When he came to, there was his father standing before him as a white man.

Another Automaniac (and one of great intelligence), viz., Lai, of Motu Motu, sometimes holds converse with his deceased daughter and parents. He described their European clothes and boots; and then—possibly because he was uncertain of my own beliefs in the matter, and was anxious to be on the safe side—he added that "sometimes they have white skins, and sometimes black skins."

GENERAL REMARKS ON THIS BELIEF

It may be pointed out that there are two distinct ideas at work here. One is that the white men are the returned ancestors of the natives; the other is that the natives become white in an after-life. These two ideas are not necessarily associated.

The former is an imaginative hypothesis to explain the appearance of a totally strange variety of humanity; and it has suggested itself independently to more than one race of savages, no doubt before as well as after the time of stout Cortes and the Mexicans. Whether such a belief had any great vogue in the Gulf Division would be difficult to say, though its occasional presence is certainly beyond doubt. As far back as 1912 a member of the London Missionary Society found the natives of Moviavi on one occasion in a state of the highest excitement because they had got hold of the idea that he himself was one of their returned ancestors.

A parallel may be found in Mr. E. W. P. Chinnery's patrol report[20] in which he describes how he and his party were taken for "ghosts" when they entered a new village in the Kunimaipa Valley. Mr. N. W. Thomas remarks the prevalence of this idea among the Australian Aborigines, with the interesting observation that "in the North it is the Malay and not the white man who is regarded as the dead black."[21]

The other belief, however, viz., that in an after-life the black men will be white men, is common enough in the Gulf Division, and might easily be the result of Missionary influence, whether taught or not.

An old man, Evara, who was one of the leading spirits in the movement, and who, indeed, has more claim than any other native to being its originator, said that "brown skins were no good....he wanted the people to have white"; and although he did not commit himself to a definite opinion as to the complexion of Heaven's inhabitants, he was very obviously in favour of white. This incident, by the way, is no doubt typical of the native's desire to imitate the white man, and of that deplorable corollary—his contempt for his own race.

A picture of Heaven, *Ihova Kekere*, or Jehova's Land, was given in some detail by a prominent "Head-he-go-round Man" of Vailala West. The land was like the earth, but much better; there was no forest, as in New Guinea; the houses were built of the "ground" itself, not of stone. There was food in abundance—white man's food, such as limes, oranges, water-melons and also sugar-cane and bananas. There were sheep, and certain animals of another kind called *arivara* (apparently to be identified with the water-buffalo).[22]

Everyone wore long garments, reaching from the top of the head down to the feet, and resembling those worn by the white men[23] on Yule Island; some of these garments were red, some white and some black, i.e. any dark colour.

The chief man in Heaven was *Ihova*; under him were *Noa*, *Atamu*, and *Eva* the wife of *Atamu*; also *Mari*, daughter of *Atamu*; *Kari*, a very large man; and *Areru* and *Maupa*, both children of *Ihova*. (The last names are worth including as problems of philology at least.)

My notes do not record whether the informant thought the dwellers in his Heaven were white or not, but the description is certainly reminiscent of certain scriptural pictures; and it is easy to understand how, on one hand the wish to resemble the white man, and on the other the example of Biblical characters, might lead him to believe that in Heaven, where all wrongs are put right, his own disadvantage in colour would be rectified.

Christian Elements in the Doctrines

The strong undercurrent of Christian teaching in the doctrines of the Vailala Madness must be recognized. Some of the most prominent figures have declared that they were "Jesus Christ Men" now, and imply that they have done with their old heathen ways. The names of Jehova, Jesus, God, etc., are frequently heard from the Automaniacs, with many varieties of pronunciation, which are of course natural and excusable, though sometimes almost comic.

Certain of these men have had, and still do have, visions of God or Christ, from whom they receive instructions or messages for their fellows, usually of an ethical character.

The belief that the dead ascend into Heaven, or the sky, is an essential doctrine; though naturally a doctrine neither explicit nor entirely uniform. In Vailala West, the leader of the cult, one Biere, gave a fairly detailed and consistent account of Heaven[24] and explained how the *hae*, which is resident in a man's stomach, or rather about his solar plexus, during life, leaves him at death and ascends into the Heaven which he had described.

Old Evara, of Iori, spoke of "the Good Place" as *Hedi*—which is presumably a rather anomalous corruption of "Heaven." Kori, of Nomu, and Ua Halai, of Arihava, on the other hand refused to commit themselves as to the final destination of the departed; and were inclined to think a man might, in the common phrase, "die finish." Though they said there was reason to fear the *Haida ove*, i.e., the ghost or spirit, in the bush by night—which is, apparently, merely the old belief. But it should be noted that Kori, though undoubtedly one of the most actively and powerfully associated with the movement, at any rate in the earlier stages, is now somewhat anxious to disclaim his connection with it when questioned by the Government. Such variations, however, make it obvious that we cannot expect any thing like orthodoxy in a cult like the Vailala Madness.

At the Maipuan village of Apiope, on the outskirts of the affected area, it was stated by the several Automaniacs there that the *a'avaia* of the dead went up into the sky. My informants did not have any specific name for the place of the dead, but the principal spokesman (obviously a serious-minded and intelligent man) suggested in a very shy and tentative manner the name *Yesu*. He did not appear able to explain what *Yesu* meant: it was plainly little more than a name to him, vaguely connected with the souls of the dead and their final home. Later, however, when the village flag (a recognized insigne of the cult) was produced, and a faded but martial portrait of George V displayed to view, the spokesman confided to me in the same diffident manner, that it represented *Ihova Yesu-nu-ovaki* —"Jehova" the younger brother of Jesus."

Undoubtedly in the spread of a cult only the broadest and most obvious of the doctrines are likely to remain uniform; these, together with the practices and externals, e.g., the actual material objects, may be handed on and survive intact; the finer points, however, and the philosophy of the matter, are likely to be ignored, mis-understood, forgotten or ridiculously contorted.

Cult of the Dead

MORTUARY FEASTS

The really fundamental fact in the whole cult is the tremendous interest in the dead: and perhaps the most important regular duty connected with it is the making of mortuary feasts. In all the affected villages are to be seen roughly-made tables, usually with benches surrounding them. These tables and benches are always fixtures and usually placed in some central position in the village. The relatives of a deceased person make a series of mortuary feasts which are set out upon the tables and consumed *al fresco* by men and women alike.

In Arihava it was the custom to place the victuals of the feast upon the table and subsequently to divide them between men and women. The women and children ate their share on the ground close by, squatting or sitting in their natural way; the men sat up to the table. (It may be remarked that on no other occasion would a man voluntarily endure the discomfort of sitting up on a bench to his meals.)

Before the feast the table is decorated, the conventional ornaments being beer bottles with bunches of bright croton. Young coconuts, husked, are placed ready for drinking.

The making of these feasts is certainly regarded as obligatory. It seems likely that in some places, and by some people, they are definitely understood to be feasts made to the dead. In the Western most of the affected villages, Apiope, of the Delta, it was said that the *a'avaia* of the deceased would be angry if the appropriate feasts were not made for it, and might visit its anger upon the negligent relatives by means of a sickness. Furthermore, a sickness on the part of any man might be construed as the vengeance of the *a'avaia* of his relative; and it would be necessary for him to make a feast by way of reconciliation. In Vailala a similar idea prevailed; the word *hae* was here used to denote the soul, spirit or ghost of the departed. The *hae* would be angry if no food were put out for it but should there be plenty, it would be satisfied "and go away."

There is nothing new in the fact of these mortuary feasts in the Gulf Division; they are apparently part of the old culture; and they illustrate this keenly-felt interest in, and, to some extent, fear of the dead or rather of the spiritual entity that is believed to survive death. It would be a surprising thing if a new cult could abolish an interest so deeply grounded. Thus it would appear to be only in the highly pretentious style of arraying the feast that there has been here any great deviation from former custom.

In the matter of such feast-making, however, it must be remembered that there is always another motive besides the religious, viz., the purely social and material, one important factor in which is a good appetite. It appears to be a man's recognized social duty to provide food for the many when he happens to have a large supply. A mean individual is not playing his social part; and no doubt in former times some means or other were found to bring him to a sense of his obligations. Such means are not wanting now with the Automaniacs; they will be discussed presently under Divination.

FOOD OFFERINGS

Besides the mortuary feasts, one may see in many of the Gulf villages a daily "offering" set out in some special place. This usually consists of no more than the beer-bottle vases with their gay croton leaves, and the young coconuts. They are set out on tables in the special houses belonging to the cult, where they remain from morning until evening (and in some places apparently longer).

At Arihava it was explained that these were intended for the *hae*. Biere said that the *hae* actually came down into the house where the tables were set out, and that he was made aware of their presence by a message from his belly. (It was even said here at Vailala that a *hae* might help itself from a dish of food; but such an idea did not seem usual, nor in keeping with the common conception of a *hae* as something immaterial.) At evening, Biere, or some of his associates, would enter the building and the food which happened to be there would be distributed among any of the village people.

COMMUNICATION WITH THE DEAD

The "ahea uvi"

The above-mentioned special houses deserve description. They and the ubiquitous flag-poles both have a close connection with an important feature of the cult, viz., the supposed frequent communication between the Automaniacs and the dead.[25]

The special house is called *ahea uvi* in Arihava and the Vailala villages. The expression means literally, "hot house." Informants found a difficulty in explaining the rationale of the name, but it appears, on the information of one or two, to rest upon the supposition that, when a man enters the house he becomes "hot," i.e., inspired, afflicted with the Madness, or simply excited. In the more Easterly villages of Motu Motu and Lese, the corresponding building was called "the office."

Usually the *ahea uvi*—to use the native expression—is a square-built edifice, neat, new and well constructed. It probably stands in a central position, but may easily escape the notice of a casual visitor, because it does not differ in any great degree from the square-built type of domestic dwelling. Furthermore it is kept shut: natives are not coming and going from it; and as a rule if questioned, they will say it is so-and-so's house, in the endeavour to conceal its real function. Inside there are probably tables and benches; the former bearing the young coconuts and crotons in bottles. In one, at least, of these houses is to be seen a garishly-painted sideboard.[26]

The house is usually closed, and frequented only by the Automaniacs. A general quietness, and indeed an air of sanctity, pervades the place. Before a feast the dishes may be set out on the tables, but the actual meal is, I am told, not taken inside. As was previously mentioned, the victuals, after being allowed to remain some time in the *ahea uvi*, are distributed by the Automaniacs toward sun-down: and it was explained at Vailala that during the day the *hae* actually enter the place and partake of the feast.

But the most important function of the *ahea uvi* is that of a rendezvous between the souls of the dead and the Automaniacs; or a holy place to which the latter repair for inspiration. In some cases there is a seat on the veranda, where the subject will sit until he feels the usual sensations in his belly, and the messages rise to be spoken. The case described on page 334 above was that of a prominent Automaniac sitting in this manner on the veranda of an *ahea uvi,* and already in a state of abnormal excitement.

It is with the dead that the Automaniacs hold communication according to the popular theory. But one very reliable informant at Motu Motu said that they communed with *Goss*—presumably God; and various other individuals claim to receive messages from the same source.

Towards the Eastern end of the affected area, the "office," as it is called, was not seen so frequently as in the West, and may perhaps be of comparatively recent introduction. The above-mentioned informant of Motu Motu was anxious for information concerning the *ahea uvis* in the Vailala villages.

The Flag-pole

Besides these special houses—one might at a stretch call them temples—there is a further very typical medium of communication between the Automaniacs and the souls of the dead. This is the flag-pole.

It is not to be supposed that the flag-pole is everywhere regarded in this light, viz., as a means of intercourse between the worlds of the dead and the living. In many places it is simply a material object which has been received as part of the cult, and brings no further meaning with it. In Apiope, where the flag-pole was termed *parakke* (presumably a corruption of flag) the villagers could give no reason for its existence. Over on the Orokolo side, they said, there were flag-poles, and Kori, with the other "Head-he-go-round Men" had told them to erect one in their village.

The flag-pole appears to have been instituted by the London Missionary Society a good many years ago. The villagers were given flags, and might hoist them on any signal occasion; but particularly, I understand, on Sundays, when they were partly meant as a sign that the day should be kept. Now, however, it has certainly been adopted by the Vailala Madness as one of its cult-objects.

In many cases the pole bears a person name, and in some is possibly given a real personality. The Automaniac, Ua Halai, prominent in Arihava, had raised the flag-pole *ive kera,* and had said to it: "I have made you stand: stand firm, then, and do not let sickness come to this village." When the flag-pole was first set up, said Ua Halai, there had been no sickness; but now some people were dying. Formerly he had cared well for it, but now "too many people looked at him, and talked to him," Besides that, "some had grown tired of the flag-pole, and did not make feasts around it when they should."

The main function of the flag-pole has been mentioned: there are certain individuals who can receive messages from the dead through its agency. A group of men singing vigorously at the foot of one of these poles were unable to explain or, I believe, understand, what they were singing: something came down the flag-pole, into the ground, up into the belly of the leader, and thence into and out of his mouth: all the rest were following his lead.

In Vailala it was said that the principal Automaniacs alone could interpret the messages which travelled down the pole: these came from the sea "like the wind" and the listener heard the actual noise of creaking or swaying; "after that his belly began to talk." An Automaniac may lean with his hand against the flag-pole, or stamp impatiently round it, urging it to respond with cries of "Come on boy!" "What's-a-matter?"

A trader[27] on the coast was of opinion that the flag-poles were in the early days of the movement "wirelesses intended for sending messages to the steamer;" and had even seen a pumpkin hoisted to the top of one of them with the apparent intention of despatching it to this destination.

This explanation certainly squares with the method of "receiving" described to me at Vailala; and there is to be seen at Opau, I am informed, a highly ingenious representation of an aerial, with wires of lawyer-cane, and a small office or cabin at either end for the operators. Presumably the apparatus at Popo[28] has supplied the model in this case; but it may also be responsible for the whole idea of the flag-pole as a means of receiving messages from the sky.

Certain Ethical Points

A brief description may be given of certain ethical points which are associated with the Vailala Madness; not that they belong to it in any sense exclusively, but simply that they have been adopted by it, and are continually preached, if not practised.[29]

Thou shalt not steal, commit adultery, nor break the Sabbath, are the three commandments most frequently heard; though it is a question whether they are observed more obediently now than in former times. The cardinal sin, however, is to neglect feasting the dead: and this, no doubt, largely because it is an omission by which the community suffers.

One point is curiously stressed. In these days of enlightenment, all feasts are to be shared equally by women and men. The former practice of debarring women, which was an essential of certain ceremonies, is now regarded as thoroughly bad and out-of-fashion.

It cannot be denied that there is much good in the general code advocated by the "Head-he-go-round Men." Many of the messages they profess to receive and utter are well-meant and often laudable enough. An informant at Motu Motu (who happened to be in especially close contact with the mission teacher) occasionally fell

into the "Head-he-go-round" condition, when he saw his deceased
parents and daughter; they told him that it was wrong to steal, and
that those who did would "find big trouble on top," i.e., at the
hands of God. Old Evara, of Iori, preached the same rule with a
different sanction: those who did wrong would die. Biere, of Vailala
West, claimed to receive and pass on such messages as these: To
make a feast; to tidy the village thoroughly; to be cleanly in eating;
to wash the hands.

It seems that for any crime committed there is one recognized
way of repentance: the offender must kill a pig. Probably there is
here the underlying social obligation referred to on page 346; and
no doubt on occasion, when it is seen that a man's pigs are too fat or
too numerous, a crime is made to fit the punishment. Such long-
existent social obligation serves as a connecting link between the
present practice of atonement and past custom. Though there are
signs of a more abstract notion of sin in the new cult.

It appears that some of the Automaniacs took it upon themselves
to carry out a sort of public confessional. Kori, for instance, of
Nomu, visited the village of Kerewa, paraded the whole population,
and addressed them. The women and children were asked if they
ever stole vegetables from other folk's gardens. "No, No !" they
answered, "We have gardens of our own"; to which Kori responded
in a loud voice, "You are all liars," to the thorough confusion of the
women and children.

Describing (with no little verve and action) his own method,
Kori said that he might be called to the side of a sick man. He would
sit there for a while until the *kavakava*, i.e., the sensations of the
Madness, came over him, and the words began to rise from his
belly: at the same time he would begin to groan and shake. Now
he turns to the patient: "You have had something to do with another
man's wife," "No, Kori, never." The accuser is quiet for a moment,
until the response ascends from his stomach. Then turning again to
the sick man, he cries in a loud threatening tone, "You lie!" Hereat
the accused confesses his guilt, and is informed that he must kill a
pig for all to eat, or he will die.

In Kerewa it was suggested that Kori was nothing more than a
fraud, who assumed the "Head-he-go-round" condition so that he
could have a big pig killed whenever he saw one. This aspect of the
matter certainly deserves consideration.

Imitation of White Men

In the meantime there are two further features of the cult which
must be dealt with. One is the tendency to imitate the white man
in certain particulars; the other is the break-down of the old religion.

The first in some degree leads up to the second: it may be briefly touched upon at this stage, as mainly a matter of recapitulation. The second, however, is held over to the latter part of the report, where it will receive the full discussion which it deserves as undoubtedly the gravest feature of the Vailala Madness.

Mention has been made of an apparent preference for white skins, and the hope of being white in an after-life. It is a further curious point that the dead are not infrequently depicted in the imagination as clothed in European garments. One informant at Moviavi was visited while in the "Head-he-go-round" condition by God himself, wearing coat, shirt, trousers, hat and "foot", and addressing him in the white man's tongue. The gist of the message was that Sevese and all other "New Guinea" ceremonies should be destroyed, and that dances should be given up.

Another Automaniac (Laho, the V.C.) at Lese, when asked why the villagers had abolished certain practices, answered—"The white man doesn't do such things; why should we?" Perhaps another instance of such imitation is seen in the new habit of cropping the hair close.

There is one respect in which a very praiseworthy but sometimes amusing effort has been made; that is in the imitation of plantation, or possibly police, discipline. The "fall-in," for example, appears to have been regularly enforced upon the commonalty by the leaders.[30]

In Arihava, when a great mass of people was dancing somewhat aimlessly together, one man was regulating start and finish with whistle-blasts.

In Motu Motu the old nine o'clock curfew was in full vogue, and said to be a very fine institution; though no doubt its stringency is modified by the fact that no one is in a position to tell the time.

The Origin of The Vailala Madness

An account having been given of the essential elements of the Vailala Madness, we may consider its origin (or perhaps rather the occasion of its outbreak) and the manner of its dissemination.

It is more than possible that the trouble had been brewing for some time previous to 1919, unrealized either by the natives themselves, or by the Europeans who were watching them. As to the immediate cause, however, several suggestions have been made. One is that a sermon on the Resurrection, preached by a white missionary, was misconstrued by his congregation: an explanation which may not meet the actual case, but, which, nevertheless, contains a certain amount of ideal truth.[31]

Mr. Murray is inclined to the opinion that Kori, of Arihava and Nomu, was the originator. Another suggestion is that it was Hareha, of Vailala East. But answers to my own inquiries among the natives have pointed almost invariably to one individual, Evara, of Iori, on the lower Vailala.[32] In the outlying parts of the affected area opinions may vary, but near its acknowledged centre, Vailala, Evara may be said to enjoy the distinction by common consent.

A small, elderly man, Evara is brisk and intelligent; obviously an outstanding personality. When I interviewed him he wore a soiled coat of white duck, and a Victory medal suspended by a red tape from the top buttonhole. He was proud of his reputation as the first of the "Head-he-go-round Men," though professed that he was no longer subject to recurrences of the Madness.

It appeared, however (partly from his own account) that he was from youth up liable to some sort of ecstatic seizures. His son Kivavia, a Government interpreter, told how Evara was once alone in the bush with his bow and arrows "looking for birds"; he must have fallen into a trance, for he lay four days unconscious while the villagers were searching for him. Finally he came to himself and returned. Evara had been unable to explain the occurrence, said Kivavia, though had suggested that a *puripuri* man had ripped up his belly.

It was on the death of his father, according to Evara himself, that he had first experienced the feelings of the Madness (though he gave no description of them). This was a good many years ago, and on that occasion he had lain on the floor of his own house, and not revealed his condition to the village. Later, however, when his younger brother died, Evara had been much affected, and the Madness, or *iki haveve*, came upon him again. This time "he spoke to the others of the village, and they all got *iki haveve*."

If native accounts can be trusted, the out-break at Evara's village created considerable excitement. The news of it spread rapidly and visitors flocking to the scene were themselves quickly infected.

Whether the idea of the steamer and the returning ancestors originated here is not certain. But there was much talk at first of an aeroplane which was dropping messages from the sky; and a planter, who lives close by and has been acquainted with Evara for many years, expressed his surprise that the old man should even know of the existence of such a thing.

It is possible that this may have some connection with a curious little myth which belongs to the Vailala Madness. Informants at Arihava told me (from hearsay) that Evara had in his possession a number of "papers"—written messages that had come fluttering down from the sky during a feast in the village, and I was assured he would be willing to show them to me. Being questioned, however,

Evara seemed altogether ignorant of the portent. He had no papers, he said, but there was a book in his box. This was immediately brought, and proved to be a modern novel of 244 pages—"Love and the Aeroplane," with a very vivid portrayal on the cover of this kind of machine, with a man and woman precariously attached to it by a rope.

Another incident is worth recording. It is perhaps not so entirely trivial as it would appear. On the wall of the *ahea uvi*,[33] is an advertisement for Lifebuoy Soap, depicting a field-hospital, a motor ambulance and a number of figures in uniform. Almost the first thing Evara did was to point out one of the minor characters, a private soldier in the middle distance, and say that it was himself. This he did quite with an air of glee, patting himself on the chest. Then he proceeded to identify the other figures. The foremost (a soldier washing out his clothes) was a deceased elder brother; another, his deceased father; the doctor was a second deceased elder brother; a buxom nurse was his son Kivavia, the present station interpreter; and a patient sitting up in bed, a deceased son named Haia.

Dissemination of the Vailala Madness

The very rapid dissemination of the Vailala Madness is sometimes ascribed by the natives themselves to supernatural means. It was said to have come to Lese "like a sickness"; and the Automaniacs there denied that they had seen the symptoms in others, or even heard of them, before they were themselves affected. Others have said that the Madness came "like the wind". It may be noted that certain Automaniacs will even deny that they have acquired their knowledge of Jehova, Heaven, the Sabbath, etc., from natural sources such as the Mission School, claiming that it has come to them apocalyptically out of their stomachs.

In reality the Vailala Madness appears to have been spread in two ways: first, by the common method of acquiring ceremonies, i.e., by going to see them and then reproducing an imitation at home; and second, by the new method of active proselytism. From accounts received in various villages along the coast, it seems that, from Vailala Westwards, the most zealous spirit has been Kori, the present V. C. of Nomu; towards the East, one Harea,[34] of Haruape, Vailala West.

Kori, who, for his enterprise, might well be styled the Paul of Papua, is another rather singular personality; more than usually keen and alert, perhaps more than usually cunning, but nevertheless a very faithful and energetic friend of the Government. He gave an account of his own conversion. "The Madness had spread from

Iori down to Vailala," he said, when he and a companion went from curiousity to see it. It was evening, and they were sitting with some friends smoking and talking around a fire. Many people were capering foolishly about the village under the influence of the Madness. Kori watched them from time to time, and now it appeared to him that the fire was red in his eyes, his vision grew hazy, and he was conscious of the red fire and little else. So he turned to his friend and asked whether it were the same with him. Finding that it was, he suggested they were both getting *iki haveve;* and proposed that they should return to their village where "many other people would get *iki haveve* also." With that the pair of them arose, and made haste back to Arihava, neither resting nor eating by the way, and in this manner the Vailala Madness was brought to Arihava. Kori's zeal, however, did not permit him to rest content with this. Though he himself denied it, information from other sources proved that he had led parties of very militant enthusiasts to the Maipuan villages, and even as far as Kaimare in the Delta. In both places the villagers had been completely overawed and looked on helplessly while the sacred objects in the *ravi* were dragged out and heaped on to a bonfire. In Kerewa, it was said, one man had ventured to protest, but was seized and beaten by the apostle, for which action the latter subsequently paid a fine.

It was, at least in part, by means of such vigorous tactics that the Vailala Madness extended so rapidly. From the beginning, leaders seem to have sprung up in one village after another, and their efforts must have almost everywhere met with a ready response by virtue of the sort of reaction referred to on page 338.

The "Head-he-go-round Men" or Automaniacs

Having now discussed the Vailala Madness in its principal aspects, and having offered some suggestions as to its origin and dissemination, we are in a position to examine the type which has continually been referred to as that of the "Head-he-go-round Men," or Automaniacs.

Previously it was suggested that there were three main categories:
(1) The involuntary victims;
(2) The pure impostors;
(3) Those who voluntarily surrender themselves to the Madness condition.

In respect of the influence they exert upon the villagers, it matters little to which of these three classes they belong. Whereas in the youth of the movement any and every individual was subject to the seizures, the rank and file have now regained their normality, but some few will be pointed out in every village, who from time to time, intentionally or otherwise, lapse into the old disordered condition. These are the "Head-he-go-round Men," or, for short, the Automaniacs.

Now in certain villages, at any rate, these men enjoy very considerable power; and it sometimes appears that they have superseded the former Chiefs. In one of the villages of Vailala West, there were three leading Automaniacs named, of whom the principal was Biere. The former Chief, or *abua*, of the village was Kauka, now an old man; his proper successor, it was said, would be a younger brother named Kaivu Ko. But neither of these men was regarded as first in the village—that position belonged to Biere. Whereas Kauka had been formerly, Biere was now *karikara kiva*—responsible for the village. It was said that Biere's claim to this position rested upon the fact that he had been the first to introduce the Madness into Vailala West, but it must be admitted that he appeared a very strong character, and deserves to be a man of influence.

In other instances it was not so definitely stated, but equally obvious, that the real temporal power had been transferred from the former *abua* to the Automaniacs. The village policeman, for his part, may be rather prone to disclaim connection with the Madness, but at least in two cases there was no possibility of doubt and here the power of the individual was, of course, doubled.

In most instances there seems to be a small clique of such men in the village whose power will naturally vary according to their personalities, but who are to no small extent respected and obeyed. It is not too much to say that in many villages there is a "Head-he-go-round" regime.[35]

It is possible to view these men from another aspect, viz., as constituting an incipient priesthood. Their more or less exclusive right of entry to the *ahea uvi;* their duties of distributing the feasts; their supposed intercourse with the dead, or in some cases with Heaven, and their function as mediums of the oracle would all in some degree justify the use of such a term.

But one is tempted to apply a name usually considered less complimentary—that of Medicine Man. This charge is based especially upon certain powers generally assumed by, and accredited to, the Automaniacs, viz., those of divination.

Powers of Divination

It was expressly stated at Nomu that a certain Maukape there had no wish to be cured of the Madness, because when under its influence he was able to detect sorcerers. Should a Nomu man be *puripuried* by an Arihava man, Maukape would be consulted and could reveal the identity of the assilant. The latter would be taxed with the matter, would confess and make amends[36]. It is especially in the detection of thieves, adulterers, and so forth, that the divinatory powers of these men are exercised and the method commonly employed is highly interesting and possibly original.

In various villages[37] is to be seen—after special inquiry—a pole of considerable length and weight, with a knob at one extremity which usually shows that the pole has been used in the manner of a battering-ram. In most instances this object was kept within the *ahea uvi*, or on its veranda. No generic term for these poles was found, each bears its own personal name. Their origin remains a puzzle[38]. It is expressly stated by all, however, that the poles were not known to their ancestors, but are a new fashion pertaining to the Vailala Madness.

One specimen at Arihava was approximately thirty feet in length and six inches in diameter. Another at Vailala West was even larger, or at least heavier than this. The example shown in the illustration belongs to Silo; it is about fifteen feet long and the knob at the end represents the head of a snake.

The pole is carried on the shoulders of two or more men, it is said to move of itself, the bearers simply going where it takes them. It is by virtue of this property the divining agent. When a pig has been stolen, or some other crime committed the pole is brought forth, and, borne on the shoulders of certain men, will make for the house of the guilty party and batter against the timbers of it. Even though the bearers endeavour to take another direction, the pole will bring them forcibly back to the guilty house. The culprit, I was assured, invariably confesses and pays a pig for his crime. No explanation was forthcoming as to the real source of the power; the operation, however, appertains very distinctly to the Automaniacs.

From a display made at Vailala it seemed that there a definite personality was ascribed to the pole. In this village the people were very well disposed and rather anxious than reluctant to show their divination pole in action. Five men shouldered it and waited quietly for some moments until it should begin to move. Now the men began to walk—this way and that a few paces; once or twice they advanced to a palm and bumped it lightly. Biere, the principal Automaniac was standing by the flag-staff; the pole advanced to him and stopped; he addressed a few words to it and a moment afterwards it came and paused in front of myself.

Soon the pole began to grow somewhat more demonstrative. By this time six men were shouldering it the thing—which is virtually a tree-trunk—wheeled and whirled until the bearers were panting with their exertions. Biere meanwhile shouted exhortations: "Come on boy, come on boy!"

Having watched the antics of the pole long enough, I was returning to the rest-house when it began to follow, first at a walk, then at a run. Finally it drew up across my path and I was advised to tell it to retire to bed, which, on being requested, it did immediately.

Informants declared persistently that the pole acted automatically, or at least that the bearers did not try to influence its actions. The unanimity in the movements of the six men was certainly a little remarkable; I have not noted whether they were a "team" and accustomed to respond to the action of a leader.

On this occasion, when there was no further motive for the performance than that of obliging me, it is not necessary to suppose that all the movements of the pole and its bearers were automatic. But, on the other hand, it is possible that there should be a certain degree of automatism in the procedure when there is a tendency to excitement and loss of control among the villagers. Whether there be definitely a scheme against any one man, or whether the bearers are simply subconsciously following the subconscious lead of some individual, it is easily seen that such a form of divination could lead to the victimizing of innocent pig-owners.

At Arihava an offer was made to locate a stick of tobacco if I should "plant" it. A trial was accordingly made. Six men were placed out in an open space, one of them having a stick of tobacco secreted on his person. When all was in readiness, the pole, carried by its two regular bearers, advanced directly and without hesitation to the man with the tobacco.

The experiment was repeated, two of the placed men being eliminated because they spoke the local language, so that only my own three boys and myself took the field. Again the pole bore down immediately upon the man with the tobacco. On a third trial, however, two initial false attempts were made; and on a fourth trial, three, before the tobacco was found.

During this experiment the two bearers could be heard talking quietly to one another after making one or two false attempts. These two particular men have been specially detailed to their work by Ua Halai, who said that with other bearers the pole would be passive, or "too heavy."

Although the Automaniacs had voluntarily suggested this trial with the tobacco, there seemed to be a little uneasiness in the village while it was in progress. Kori, the V. C., was obviously anxious to have no part in the proceeding, and the audience showed a plentiful lack of enthusiasm.

It is doubtful, however, whether any manifest failure on the part of the divination pole would seriously disturb the faith which is fixed upon it; and, at any rate, the above-described tobacco test could not be considered a very fair one. In Vailala the pole was evidently thought to be infallible. A man might deny his guilt, but the instrument of divination would return again and again to his house until finally he confessed, and made due reparation by killing a pig. No accused man, it was said, ever holds out in his plea of innocence; the reason given by one informant was "That he would be frightened of gaol."

Comments on the Power of the Automaniacs

By such means as those which have been indicated, the Automaniacs have acquired and confirmed a very strong influence over the rest of the village. Moreover the mere fact of their unnatural behaviour when under the influence of the Madness earns them the respect of less-gifted folk, if it does not actually inspire them with fear. Never once was it stated that the Automaniacs were really "possessed," though their close connection with the *hae*, or spirits of the dead, is always recognized, and it is believed that the wisdom emanating from an Automaniac's belly is not his own.

The power of the possessed, and the dread that others have of them, is well known. But whether thought to be possessed or no, it seems likely that, among primitive people, a lunatic, epileptic, or super-normal, will inspire fear or respect merely by the strangeness of his conduct; and where the subject trades upon his infirmity he may easily build up a strong influence. In the earlier part of this report, several instances were noted in which the villagers looked on at the insane behaviour of the Automaniacs with every indication of awe; and although many will declare that they themselves have never been afflicted with the Madness, these men do not think of openly deriding those who are afflicted.

To sum up regarding the Automaniacs or "Head-he-go-round Men"; it would appear that there is in most of the coastal villages a small clique or cabal of those who still continue to exhibit the symptoms which were very common three years ago, but which have become dormant among the great majority; these individuals (who fill all the intermediate grades from the sincere crank to the thorough-going impostor) possess no small influence, especially by reason of their professed occult powers; in certain of them may be seen a somewhat unwholesome combination of prophet, priest and wizard;

and, indeed, the whole system is not unlike a mild and incipient Shamanism.

Whereas the majority of the natives have regained their normality after the early enthusiasm of the Vailala Madness, it might be said that they are still "bluffed" by the "Head-he-go-round Men."

Part 2

DESTRUCTION OF CEREMONIES IN THE GULF DIVISION

It is particularly in the matter of the destruction of native ceremonies that this "bluff" makes itself evident. As this aspect of the Vailala Madness provides the theme for the practical part of this report, it has been reserved until now for consideration.

It is with the utmost disappointment that one finds in village after village the devastation which this movement has caused; with disgust also, and something like incredulity, that one hears on all hands the condemnation of the old customs. It seems nothing less than preposterous that old men, who have been brought up among the ceremonies, and who have taught their sons that their prime moral duty is to carry on the ceremonies, should of their own accord come to despise and abandon them. Yet no old man has the initiative to speak a word in defence of his dishonoured tribal customs. Too often in a group of witnesses, it is the Automaniac, who, being the leading personality, acts as spokesman, while the others sit in silence, not venturing to contradict him, even if it occurred to them to do so.

It is not to be thought that the old school are secretly boiling with discontent. They have got it into their heads that the old customs are no good: they swallowed the notion wholesale in 1919, when they were mad, and they have not got it out of their systems yet.

No more thoroughly deplorable instance could be found of the power of suggestion than this, when at a time of uncontrolled excitement, age-long traditions were thrown aside in favour of the absurdities of the Vailala Madness.

Here and there may be seen welcome signs of a revival of the old ceremonies: the fact that they have not reasserted themselves more completely is in large part, I believe, due to the sometimes sincere, sometimes unscrupulous Automaniacs, who are prolonging the suggestion.

Reasons for Discontinuance of Ceremonies

If a traveller enter the Gulf Division from the Delta and move down the coast, he may first be astonished and entertained by the queer behaviour of Nomu and Arihava, should he be fortunate enough to see any demonstrations there; next, he will be delighted to find in Iogu and Orokolo the numerous artistic masks of the *Sevese*; but then, proceeding Eastwards, will be more and more exasperated to find in every village that the ceremonies have been discarded and the masks and all other paraphernalia connected with them destroyed.

To the question, "Where are your *Sevese*?" there is always the bright response, "Oh, *Taubada*, we throw 'em away," expressed in the tone of one who bears welcome news, or announces some action of his own for which he expects the approbation of the hearer. If, however, the hearer fail to offer his congratulations, the tone of the informants may alter slightly. They cannot, as a rule, bring forward any reason of a logical kind, but will in the great majority of instances say that the "Head-he-go-round Men" had told them to give up the ceremonies, and that they had done so without question.

Two other explanations are offered not infrequently: first, that the ceremonies are discouraged by the missionaries; second, that nowadays there is too much work to do for the white man.

Each of these three explanations may be examined. The first may be dealt with briefly, and mainly by way of recapitulation. The second two may be suitably discussed in this report, although the latter does not in any way bear on the subject of the Vailala Madness, and the former does so only indirectly: for they are both considerations of importance when we are dealing with the wider question of the destruction of native ceremonies.

Vailala Madness as the Principal Cause of the Discontinuance of Ceremonies

There is no doubt that the Vailala Madness has been the principal direct agent in the destruction of the Gulf culture. In discussing its effect it is necessary to make a distinction. On the one hand the vast bulk of the population have accepted the cult holus-bolus and without question: they have destroyed their ceremonies simply because they were told to, and because everybody else was doing the same. On the other hand, certain of the Automaniacs have some sort of theories upon the matter which must be given fair consideration.

In regard to the first matter enough has been said. It is only necessary to stress again the recognized instability and suggestibility of the native, and the extraordinary character of the circumstances in which the transition was made from the old cult to the new.

The actual logic of the destructive attitude is less convincing. It was asserted time and again that if the ceremonies were renewed there would be many deaths. At Arihava, for instance, it was said that if the *kovave* ceremony[39] were repeated, "twenty, thirty, or forty people would die:" on the last occasion of it there had been many deaths in the village. In Apiope the same reason was put forward. During the last few weeks of my stay in the Purari Delta, deaths were certainly numerous in many villages, possibly through some minor epidemic. The entire immunity (until that time) of Apiope was attributed by its inhabitants to the fact that they alone of all the Delta villages had done away with the former ceremonies. It was a question whether one should wish the people health and long life, or the salutary lesson of a plague.

It is significant that the logical connection between the deaths and the continuance of the ceremonies was never made plain: presumably this, again, is one of the blindly accepted doctrines of the cult.

One informant however (Kori) made an attempt to explain the association in a way which at least reflects some credit upon his ingenuity. When formerly the ceremonies took place there were a certain number, especially the women, necessarily excluded from the ceremony itself and from participation in the feast. These people would be found prying into the mysteries, or they might surreptitiously obtain some of the pig-flesh: and as a punishment or in revenge would be done to death by *puripuri*. In times long past, the informant added, the ceremonies had been conducted without this high rate of mortality, because then *puripuri* was not practised in the neighbourhood; it dated merely from the time of Kori's father, Mamu.

Another reason, in which there is more of common sense, is no doubt supplied by the tendency to imitate the white man, and to despise what is truly native—an attitude of mind which is difficult to account for except on the hypothesis that some argument or persuasion has been used; or that the native has been laughed or scolded out of his ways. An informant at Moviavi expressed the view in a memorable phrase: "Throw 'em away, bloody New Guinea somethings;" and Lai, of Motu Motu (a Christian—Vailala-Madman of sagacity and the best intentions) was informed by deceased relatives in a vision that "the first time men were bloody fools. . . .no savvy anything."

Apart from this attitude of contempt, or assumed contempt, there is a notion among some of the "Head-he-go-round Men" that the ceremonies, even the dances, are "wicked." At Silo, an astonishing doctrine—professedly acquired from a former teacher—was expressed in another phrase worth remembering: "Stop quiet along village." To notions such as these, no doubt, are due the wholesale iconoclasms and the sort of primitive Puritanism which has induced these natives to forswear their amusements, to discard their ornaments and to settle down to a life of dull prison-like regularity.[40]

Discouragement of Ceremonies by Missions

In several cases it has been expressly stated by the natives that the mission teachers have discouraged the ceremonies. Whether this is in accord, however, with the general policy of the London Missionary Society, I am not in a position to say; individual opinions and courses of action will be bound to vary in such a matter.

Further, while direct responsibility is out of the question, it cannot be denied that the mission has contributed much to the Vailala complex; and although the excesses are discountenanced, there are presumably features in the doctrinal content of the movement which would have the approval of the missions: and even the cessation of ceremonies and dances may be regarded as a means to salvation and a rare opportunity for the substitution of Christianity.

At Silo it was said that a certain teacher formerly stationed there had done his best to dissuade the people from carrying out their ceremonies, but that he had been disregarded. Finally, however, the Vailala Madness swept over the place, and the ceremonies had then been done away with. Thus it appears that here, as elsewhere, the proximal cause of the destruction of the ceremonies was the actual Vailala Madness; but it also appears that pressure had been used before discouraging the ceremonies.

Whatever may have been the attitude of the London Missionary Society regarding these matters in the Gulf Division, there is no doubt that in various parts of the Territory it has been the considered policy of certain bodies or individuals to suppress the native ceremonies; and therefore a further discussion of the rights and wrongs of such a policy is worth pursuing.

Labour for the White Man as Causing the Discontinuance of the Ceremonies

Before, however, taking up the matter in its more general aspect, it is necessary first to deal with the third cause commonly assigned for the cessation of the ceremonies. This is, that nowadays the natives have too much work to do.

The work referred to is plantation labour rather than Government labour, though the native's conscience will readily allow him to make an excuse of either.

Old Evara, of Iori, apparently anxious to please, said that the ceremonies had been dispensed with so that the people might devote more time to the cleaning of their villages and to gardening.

Altogether, the plea that Government fatigues are too heavy need not perhaps be treated very seriously. Although it has to be remembered that, owing to the ingrained dilatoriness of the native character, one cannot expect rapid or intensive work; so that, when the village is left to itself, a small task will take a long time in the doing; and thus even comparatively light duties imposed by the Government might actually crowd out the ceremonies.

Without questioning the necessity or the value of material improvements, one may argue against the mistake of multiplying them at the possible expense of the ceremonial, religious or spiritual life: and this for reasons practical as well as sentimental.

The plantation labour, however, certainly does interfere with the social life in the village. It is said to be a common experience with recruiters that, when a ceremony is pending in any village, they will display their trade in vain; and vice versa, a long delay in a ceremony or actual cessation, is sometimes due to the absence of a number of young men on the plantations.

This is especially so when a large number of men sign-on simultaneously from the same village. Thus, for instance, in Karama there was seen a taboo-platform (called *safu*) loaded with coconuts. This tabu had been declared for the ceremony and feast at which an elder age-group of men present bark belts and hornbill feathers to the younger age-group.[41] But so large a proportion of the young men concerned being away at work, the ceremony could not proceed. It is not that the delay in this instance would cause any serious dissatisfaction, but that the absence of a majority of the young men tends to make the village life very "dead." For, although they do not lead in a ceremony, they commonly supply much of the initiative and vim, as well as performing the often heavy work which it entails.

Here is certainly a difficulty for which no immediate remedy can be suggested. The needs of the plantations cannot be ignored; nor, for practical reasons, can the social life of the village.

In general terms, however, it may be suggested that there is one cardinal fault in the native character (over which the most sanguine might shake their heads) that is mainly responsible for the dead-lock, viz., the tendency known in this country as *dohore*. Whether it would be possible to speed-up the village life, especially in the conduct of ceremonies, is a matter concerning which many people will harbour no doubt whatever. Yet it will be obvious that the village would have time enough and to spare for all its ceremonies, Government fatigues, plantations work and daily labours, if it would only buck into them a little.

In particular, it may be urged that from the village point of view it is undesirable that a majority of the young men should be absent at one time; or that they should be absent for a long time.

Insufficiency of Materialistic Policy of Reform

Among those who concern themselves with natives there is an occasional tendency—indeed it amounts to a policy with strong advocates—to concentrate upon material reforms to the neglect of matters spiritual. The argument is that if we look after the native's body, his soul may be trusted to look after itself.

There is no doubt as to the need of material reforms. The only thing that should puzzle this hard-headed variety of philanthropist is that the native does not seem very keen to have them.[42]

The negligence of the villagers and their indifference to the most obvious improvements, must be the despair of many a magistrate. In the Delta, for instance, where the plank gangways would seem to be essential to reasonable comfort, it is only the periodical patrol, one may venture to assert, that keeps them in existence. Anyone who lives in a village continuously between one patrol and the next will know the hopeless state of dilapidation into which these gangways are allowed to fall before the rumour of an approaching launch rouses the people to perfunctory activity and thoughts of gaol.

Let it be imagined that the Government and all other white people should withdraw completely from the Purari Delta, and it is not inconceivable that within a very few years the villagers would be coming and going in the old style—by canoes, over slippery logs, or wading through the mud. Yet, despite the filth and discomfort, the *pairama* and *aiau* festival would still go on with all their pomp and ceremony and still be the delight of the community, and its most engrossing interest.[43]

This is merely an example (and partly hypothetical at that) but it will serve to emphasize the necessity of regarding the native's soul, or his mind, or his higher nature—however it be called—and not his body only, if we mean him well. The wrong attitude is exemplified in an extreme form by the phrase (which has many variants) "A nigger's soul is in his belly;" in which there is some truth and a good deal of coarse error.

Were it, for instance, impossible (as is not the case) that the *sevese* ceremony and the rice plantations should prosper side by side in the Gulf Division; and were it essential that one should give way, the present writer would have no hesitation in saying that the natives would derive more good from *sevese* than from rice.

Insisting, therefore, that the material welfare of the native is neither the only, nor even the first, consideration, we might ask what is best for his soul—which word is used in the widest possible sense (without any Christian connotation, or idea of a hereafter) to denote the body of sentiments associated with his higher activities, e.g., those of social intercourse, art and religion.

It is a common postulate—for the missionary, one presumes, a necessary one—that the native does not know what is good for him. By accepting this postulate we set ourselves the difficult and responsible task of deciding what is good for him.

This has been made largely a question of morality. But it is a fundamental principle of ethics that no code or creed can be laid down without regard to the psychology of those for whom it is intended and it is justifiable to ask whether the Papuan is everywhere given a proper admixture of guidance and liberty, or whether he is not sometimes hustled by the scruff of the neck up the wrong path of righteousness. For presumably a man's soul should be his own—in a sense it is himself. Yet, what with the zeal and energy of various reformers, the native's soul has sometimes an ill time of it between the upper and nether millstones of Materialism and Christianity.

Description of Certain Gulf Ceremonies

Before proceeding to advocate the continuance of the old culture, it is necessary to give some account of it, or at least of the ceremonies, which are here the main concern.

It has, of course, been impossible to witness the actual performance of any ceremony of importance in the Gulf Division, and all information has been gathered by the much more laborious and much less trustworthy method of verbal description.

The two principal ceremonies of the Elema people are (1) the *sevese*; and (2) the *harisu*.[44] They are described according to their performance among the Kaivipi people and both accounts are from information obtained at Karama and Koaru.

For both of these ceremonies, though especially the former, elaborate masks are made, upon which is expended a wealth of skill, art and humour. Several *eravo* at Orokolo are filled with the headpieces of *sevese* masks, made of bark-cloth on a framework of cane, and with decorations, in admirable taste, consisting of conventional clan designs.

The "Sevese" Ceremony

A brief explanation of the *sevese* ceremony may be given, though it can convey no idea of the spectacular and dramatic effect vouched for by many witnesses.

Some time after a man's death, his sister, may be, will approach others of the immediate family and desire them to make a *sevese* for him. Probably a brother will undertake the task and he will receive payment, especially in the form of food, from the woman's husband; that is to say, the *sevese* is made by the wife's family and paid for by the husband. Similarly, should a child die, the *sevese* is made by its maternal uncle and paid for by its father.

Matters are so arranged that a great number of *Seveses* are prepared simultaneously. The payments of food culminate in a great feast, attended by throngs of guests, when after long preparation the *sevese* are completed and promenade the village.

When all is ready, the masked figures, completely disguised, issue out with dancing and beating of drums. They are presented with huge piles of food, which they accept by dumb show, and subsequently distribute to their own people; this food being normally a gift or payment from the husband to the wife's family.

The inner meaning of the ceremony is made clear by what follows. The relatives will greet the mask as if it were the dead man himself. His sister will come and embrace it and rub her nose on it, weeping and crying, "My brother, my brother!" She will bring her children and say, "Here is your uncle (*koau*) come back." In the enthusiasm of her welcome, it is said, she will even cram fragments of food into the mouthpiece of the mask.

It does not appear, however, that the ceremony has anything of a mournful tone about it. For several days everything is feasting and gaiety; the brilliant masks constantly coming and going from the *eravo*, and dancing through the village. Each is proudly identified by those with whom it is most closely associated, bearing, as it does, the designs appropriate to the clan of the deceased.

In theory the designs on the *sevese* mask should be the clan-designs of the individual which it represents. The degree of consistency is, indeed, somewhat remarkable: among the masks seen at Orokolo it is possible for a novice (with very little previous experience) to recognize at a glance the clan which any mask represents. Furthermore, these designs appear to have a totemic meaning.

When finally the festival is over, the masks are heaped together and burnt. In parts of the Gulf Division it may be that the *sevese* is still a mystery. In Karama, however, and the adjacent villages there seems to be little secrecy. I am told that the masks are burnt in full view of the village. At the burning, some relative—properly the maternal uncle—is given a brand from the fire. This he throws away, calling on the *ove* (spirit) of the dead man to take it with him to the place where he is to abide.

Thus it will be seen that the *sevese* is apparently in essence a mortuary ceremony, representing the return of the *ove* (or spirits of the dead) their feasting and final departure; and the foregoing description, brief though it is, will serve to indicate that besides being a religious performance, it is a brilliant and artistic pageant, and an occasion for lavish hospitality and social good-will.

The "Harisu" Ceremony

A somewhat fuller account (also from Karama) may be given of the *harisu*. It does not appear that there is anything in the nature of a cycle of ceremonies among the Elema people. The *sevese* is one ceremony; the *harisu* is another, and the seclusion of boys a third matter which has no connection with either of the former. Beside these there are minor ceremonies and dances of a more or less ceremonial nature. The *harisu* may therefore be regarded separately. It is one of those secret societies in which practically everyone is in the secret except the women. But to be in the secret one must pay the price of a pig, and when, as occasion demands, a celebration is held, any number of young men may be initiated.

Initiates to the *harisu* are normally youths who have passed through the period of seclusion. They are now full-grown, and very probably married; and it is the custom that a batch of these youths (who constitute a *migiotau* because they have undergone seclusion at one time) should likewise be initiated together to *harisu*.

A young man suggests to his father that he would like to be introduced to the *harisu*. The latter tells him to go and consult the others of his *migiotau*—the young bloods of the village: this he does and when it is found that they all have pigs and are anxious to see the *harisu*, some excuse is made for a celebration.

It appears that the invariable antecedent to a *harisu* ceremony is a quarrel in the village (a matter which will be touched upon later). Further, it must be pointed out at this early stage that there is a definite *harisu* organization into two classes: on the one hand there are the *harisu oa* or owners of the *harisu*: on the other, there are the *hahoedas*, or makers of the *harisu*.

Each *harisu* has its personal name, under which it has appeared and reappeared many times; and whenever it is decided that the *harisu* shall pay a visit to the village, each particular one will be constructed by its hereditary *hahoeda*, and these latter will be paid or rewarded (in pigs and other food) by its hereditary *harisu oa*. The details of this interesting organization need not be entered into here. It is sufficient to say that, whenever the *Harisu* invade the village, it is because the matter has been amicably arranged beforehand between the *harisu oa* and the *hahoeda*, i.e., the owners and the makers; and that when there is a large batch of young men desirous of understanding the *harisu*, some pretext for a demonstration is speedily found, properly by the picking of a friendly quarrel.

All the preparations are conducted in strict secrecy. At some convenient spot in the bush slightly removed from the village, an enclosure, or small *eravo* is constructed, which shall serve as hiding-place and manufactory. The intending initiates are sent into the bush to cut sheets of coconut fibre, which are sewn into head-pieces by the old men in the enclosure, being fitted over the heads of the initiates so as properly to locate the eye-holes, which are to be burnt through. When fully prepared and painted, these head-pieces are hung on sticks outside the enclosure to dry.

The making of the masks has probably been a long and leisurely process, but now they are completed. The initiates go up into the bush and gather banana leaves, which they try upon their bodies and limbs; and then, being fitted to their satisfaction, remove and tie into bundles. Leaving these hidden, they spend the remainder of the day collecting betel-nuts, which are intended for the old men; and at sundown return in their canoes, taking the bundles of leaves and their bags of betel-nuts into the enclosure.

It is now the eve of the appearance of the *harisu*. During the evening the young men come and go in the village as if nothing were in the wind; but they have warned their wives not to expect them home that night—a ruse by which both wives and husbands are said to be greatly tickled. Later on, the initiates will foregather and spend their time talking, smoking and chewing, all in the highest of spirits. Some of their number will go out to see if the village is quiet, and soon the initiates will themselves pretend to be asleep.

But at about midnight they go stealthily to the enclosure, where the older men are awaiting them. A silent guard of these older men goes out to see that no one is spying, and then the initiates, shouldering their bundles of leaves and their head-pieces, file through the village down to the shore: palm-branches may be dragged after them to obliterate the footprints.

Now, accompanied by some of the older men, they move off Eastwards along the beach to the place called Iruku-ovo, walking through the shallow water so as to leave no traces behind them. They reach Iruku-ovo (which is only a mile or two distant) in the earliest hours of the morning. There they don their costumes and play among themselves until the dawn is beginning to break.

In the meantime the older men who remained in the village have come down to the beach and are sitting about their fires. Suddenly someone will discern the *harisu* approaching in the uncertain light of daybreak. The alarm spreads through the village, and the women and children come flocking down to the seashore.

The *harisu* advance abreast along the beach, dancing and nodding their fantastic headgear: they have been instructed to disguise their gait to avoid recognition. As they pass the small intermediate villages, they are hailed by their personal names: "Kiva, Mairi, Harovara-hari, etc., who told you to come? Do you mean to taboo our coconuts?" The *harisu* wheel to face their questioners, bow and shake as if in acquiescence, and then proceed until they are again interrupted.

Thus finally they come to the main village of Karama. Here every man, woman and child has turned out for their welcome. At first they are greeted almost derisively. "What have you come for? There is no food to spare in our village, no fish, no yams or taro. Who asked you to come? We did not."

Suddenly, however, the people change their tone: "Kiva, Mairi, you are welcome. Everyone has been eating the coconuts; none have been allowed to ripen and fall. We will entertain you one year—two years, and will not send you back to your homes." At this turn of the talk, all the people shout *"Baifuape"*; there is a tremendous cheer, and the *harisu*, which have been listening with dumb gestures, burst into a run, and, scattering everybody in flight, career through and through the village until they finally disappear into the *eravo*.

Here the initiates put off the masks, steal out to the creek behind the village and bathe. After this, by means of a wide detour, they approach the village from quite another direction, explaining that they have been absent over-night. Their wives and mothers are bubbling over with excitement and, hearing their accounts, the young men freely express their disappointment and annoyance at having missed so fine a sight; in fact they will go at once to the *eravo* and see the *harisu*. Being dissuaded by the tears of their female relatives from so risky an investigation, they finally consent to wait until the afternoon, when the *harisu* are expected to reappear, and in the meantime, since they have been very active for the last twenty-four hours and more, go to sleep.

Towards the evening certain other men will don the masks (which have been hanging meanwhile in the *eravo*) and parade the village; while the initiates, affecting to set eyes on the *harisu* now for the first time, loudly express their astonishment.

For several days the *harisu* continually sally forth from the *eravo* to scour through the village or along the shore. Perhaps on the fourth or fifth day the great feast is held. Certain men stand forth in the village and cry out the names of all the initiates, declaring that they have seen the *harisu*,[46] and must pay accordingly. The women-folk are alarmed to hear that the young men have seen the *harisu*, thinking they are doomed in consequence; but the initiates explain that, although they did catch sight of the *harisu* retiring into the bush, the payment of a pig will adjust the matter.

Meanwhile the *harisu* are again promenading, and show their impatience at the delay by going from house to house and committing acts of violence, tearing down planks and rails, demolishing house-ladders, and so forth. Finally, however, when the pigs are produced and killed, they are satisfied and grow quiet.

There are quantities of sago and betel-nut made ready also, and these, together with the pigs, are apportioned to the several *harisu*. The latter are themselves arranged in some sort of hierarchy, and occupy their several places in the *eravo* according to precedence. The food is arranged in front of them in piles, and the four principal *harisu* (worn, properly by the four senior *hahoeda*, or makers) come forward to take formal acceptance. Great quantities of meat and vegetables are thrust upon them and attached to arms, neck and shoulders, until the old men are said to stagger under the weight. Soon they disencumber themselves of the food and the costumes also, and a general distribution and feast ensues, the women and those who are uninitiated receiving some share outside the *eravo*.

The initiation has now come to an end, but the *harisu* continue to reside in the village for perhaps a year or more; during which period the masks may be worn by any and every man who pleases.

An essential feature of the *harisu* ceremony is the taboo upon the coconuts, which begins with their entry into the village and ends with their departure. The *harisu* commonly carries a rod, bow and arrows, or even a spear—weapons which, with the exception of the first, are not used in earnest; though it is the occasional delight of the wearer to pursue and belabour man, woman or child with his rod, this being no more than horse-play.

It is said, however, that the *harisu* might conspire to punish one who broke the coconut taboo. Presuming the offender be observed and informed against, a number of men may secretly arrange to administer a corrective. Early in the morning the *harisu*, in full dress, will surround the *eravo* in which the culprit is asleep. Some will creep upon the sleeper, and even prod him with their arrow-points. If he seek to escape through the hole at the rear of the *eravo*, he will be terrified to see, in the half-light of morning, a ring of these portentous figures waiting for him with their long sticks. The whole performance seems to be more in fun than in earnest, but the victim does not escape without a rough handling and a thorough fright.

It was mentioned before that the real occasion for the appearance of the *harisu* was a quarrel. In the case of a disagreement, it may be that the two parties are not on speaking terms, until one of them decides, or is prevailed upon, to summon up his *harisu*. If he be a *hahoeda* he will be responsible for making the mask himself, and will be paid or supplied with food by the *harisu oa* of that particular *harisu*; if, on the other hand, he be a *harisu oa* he will request the *hahoeda* to construct the mask, and will himself undertake to supply the food. However this may be, the other party to the dispute will be invited to partake of the subsequent feast, and a reconciliation is thus effected.

The typical instance is that of a quarrel between husband and wife. The fact that the former has chastised the latter is never likely to be hushed up in a native village, where neither men nor women hide their grievances; and it may give rise to a *harisu* invasion. The husband may be induced, it is said, to go to the trouble of having his *harisu* made (and very likely a number of other *harisu* will appear at the same time). The preparations are supposed to be kept secret, and when the *harisu* appear it is a surprise. The by-now-repentant husband calls the attention of his wife to his own particular *harisu*. "Do you see Paovikia?" he may say, "He has come to tell us we must not wrangle, or lose our tempers and fight any more."

Like the *sevese*, the *harisu* are not made "for nothing;" to express the rule in Pidgin-English—"Suppose he stop good, no make 'em *harisu*."

Thus it appears that they have the primary function of peacemakers; and that they are also to some extent guardians of the law and enforcers of the taboo, with at least the nominal right to employ measures of violence.

As for an interpretation of the masked figure and its possible symbolism, there is one belief universally accepted, viz., that the *harisu* comes out of the bush, and goes back to the bush. With the women and the uninitiated, this is supposed to be a real belief; with the men who are "in the know," it is a make-believe, i.e., the whole game is carried out as if the *harisu* were actually beings which belonged to the bush.

One or two informants have said that they were *ove* (or spirits of the dead; or rather spirits of certain individuals long since dead). But this idea is not stressed, and to the great majority of those who regularly participate in the *harisu* ceremony, the idea does not seem even to suggest itself.

However, in this connection it is perhaps significant that the word *karisu* (or *kalisu*) which exists side by side with the word *harisu*, denotes the more or less malignant and fearsome spiritual remains of a dead man, which are sometimes seen fitting about the village, or more especially the place of burial, in seemingly human form.

Moreover, the arrangement of the *harisu* into groups of a local character—each such group belonging to two or three small village units—and the further internal arrangement of these groups into hierarchies of *harisu* with personal names, may reinforce the possibility that they in some way represent spirits long departed.

Though it may be repeated that this certainly is not a generally accepted doctrine, nor one that is even thought of except by the ingenious or understanding few. If the ordinary native be asked "What is a *harisu*?" he will respond, with a mixture of amusement and impatience, that it is a *harisu*; that the men make it out of cane, leaves and so forth, and gammon to the women that it comes alive out of the bush.

Lastly it may be mentioned that there is strong supposition (for which the evidence is too detailed and tedious for this report) that the *harisu* is an imported ceremony in some manner super-imposed upon, or rather accepted by, the earlier culture of the Gulf Division.

The foregoing, probably very imperfect, account may be enough to show the importance of the *harisu* ceremony, and above all the spirit of whole-hearted enjoyment in which it is carried out. Its social complications have been lightly dealt with. Its artistic aspect cannot be fully appreciated because it has not been seen; but no one will deny that there is some dramatic skill in the mere routine.

Its religious meaning is, no doubt, somewhat obscure: the whole performance seems far from serious. But it must be remembered that the native seems capable of adopting by turns two very opposite attitudes toward his ceremony. One moment it is all a game, a *koikoi*, a "bluff" on the women; the next, our native has so lost himself in the spirit of the thing, that it has passed for the time from make-believe to true belief; and he is awe-stricken or terrified by the objects of his own devising. In cold-blooded description, however, this latter aspect is not made evident. It is necessary to watch the performers and to deduce from the far more trustworthy evidence of their behaviour and expressions, the real nature of their emotional attitude toward the ceremony.

The Value of Ceremonies in General for Emotional Satisfaction

The emotional content of primitive religion has been stressed by anthropologists; and, in general, the need for emotional satisfaction in every direction has better scientific recognition nowadays than formerly.

It may be fairly contended that native life, compared with our own, has few excitements for the individual. His interests are so vastly fewer than ours, that common daily life cannot present to him that amount of change and incident which it does to those who move in the most humdrum of civilized environments. But, like any other human, he is fundamentally a complex of emotions, which in the long run demand expression. Living, as he does, a life of little variation and comparative indolence, he finds an unconscious remedy in occasional outbursts of social excitation: it is, no doubt, a matter of the gradual heaping up of emotional energy until it overflows in some form of more or less violent activity. The native has a quiet life of it for a good time, and then, with all his mates, he "goes on the bust."

The periodicity of ceremonial life is a feature of great importance; and the ceremonies in particular may well be regarded as the principal means of emotional expression known to a primitive society. No contrast could be more striking than that between the quiet, regular, almost lethargic daily life of a Purari Delta village, and the keenness, elan and elevation of spirits which go with a ceremony; and nothing more astonishing than the mere physical energy expended at such a time—almost to the point of exhaustion—in dance and song.

Bearing in mind the above contention, we may quote once more the deservedly immortal phrase "Stop quiet along village," to insist that it is a mistake to urge such a course upon primitive folk, because it involves a real, though perhaps not a realized, hardship.

Apart from any earnestness or intensity which may exist in the heart of a native, he ought not, at any rate, to be denied his "fun." In some places it is all too evident that, in fulfilment of the proverbial warning, he is now a dull boy.

From the standpoint of the employer alone, the value of entertainment and recreation—in general of emotional satisfaction—for his native labour is self-evident; and even where such entertainment (as, for example, the beating of drums) must occasion some annoyance to the European, he might be well advised to bear with it.

An informant in the Purari Delta (where recruiting is said to have fallen off very considerably in late years) declared he had no intention of signing-on again: he described with obvious bitterness how, when a friend of his had died on the plantation, the weeping and howling of his comrades had been very abruptly checked. The planter or manager, apparently exasperated by the lugubrious strains in which, after their own fashion, the boys were venting their feelings, had requested them to mourn in silence; and finally went down and laid about him with a whip, thus very effectually enforcing his advice. No one will refuse some sympathy to the sleepless and irritated manager; but it will be readily understood that by preventing a natural and customary demonstration, especially when feelings were more or less deeply stirred, he would not be increasing his popularity or prospects as an employer.

There are those who, genuinely anxious to improve the native's condition, will argue that for him work is the prime essential—in which there is, of course, much truth. They will say "Let him come and work on the plantation; teach him to be industrious and ambitious, and to know the value of money; show him what he can buy in the stores, and how he can improve his own houses and villages." So far, so good. But some will go on to say "This is all he needs to make him prosperous and happy: don't let him waste time on foolish, childish ceremonies"; in which there is the error of the long-discredited "all work and no play" policy—a policy which is, if anything, less profitable for primitive than for civilized savages.

Suppression and Abnormality
Not only does the suppression of ceremonies, games, dances, and the like, rob the native of that zest of life which is derived from social enjoyments, but it may lead to ugly social abnormalities. It is a commonplace of psychology that energy denied its proper outlet will break loose at some unexpected point, that repression leads to abnormality; and it is not improbable that in the Vailala Madness the voluntary suppression of the ceremonies contributes something towards the repulsive and ridiculous behaviour of its victims.

The ceremonies—to say nothing of their artistic and emotional value—are *healthy* social activities which have been either evolved or accepted and modified in perfect accordance with the character and desires of the people. So long as they are allowed to follow one another regularly the feelings of the people will pursue their natural course of rising, culmination and subsidence: this is the anabolism and katabolism of collective feeling.

But hold down or stifle these purely natural activities, and you may have to deal with an objectionable case of collective hysteria. If, for the sake of analogy, it can be imagined that the Neapolitans, disapproving of the intermittent puffs of Vesuvius, could be foolish enough to fill the crater with a stopper of concrete, they might shortly witness a disturbance in some unforeseen, and possibly most undesirable direction.

One essential, at least, toward preventing further ebullitions of the Vailala Madness, or similar abnormalities in other parts of the Territory, is to give the natives some other and more wholesome means of satisfaction; and for this purpose it appears that, generally speaking, nothing can be more suitable than their own ceremonies.

Substitutes provided for the Ceremonies

It is obviously undesirable to destroy the natives ceremonies and offer him nothing in return. It remains to be considered whether the substitutes provided are in any way better than the original. This question resolves itself principally into a comparison of native religion and Christianity in respect of their suitability for the native.

Religion, in the anthropological sense, requires an extremely broad definition. The history of religion begins with the simplest elements of primitive practice and belief, and ends with the most up-to-date form of Christianity. The question, in brief, is whether, in the case of any primitive people, the former can be abolished and fitly replaced by the latter.

It may be a feature of highly evolved religion to place doctrine before ritual in importance. With primitive religion, however, it is the very reverse. No generalization is of greater importance here than that faith, doctrine and philosophy are secondary to the ritual. Where a ceremony may be carried out punctiliously in all its details and with a singular intensity of emotion, the participants may be going through it blindly, and with no realization of the meaning or symbolism which civilized observers will read into it.

The inability of the native to explain ceremonial acts is a familiar difficulty to anthropologists. It is not that he wishes to conceal anything, but that he has nothing to reveal. Where explanations are forthcoming, they are commonly obtained from either of two sources: first, those old men of chiefly rank who are the temporary holders of hereditary theory; or, secondly, from those few individuals of exceptional intelligence or imagination who will evolve an explanation out of their heads to satisfy a questioner. The rank and file have but one explanation: "We do it because our ancestors did it."

An interesting evidence of this ignorance is found in the songs which belong to certain ceremonies. In the Purari Delta it might be said that each ceremony has its appropriate songs but woe betide the hopeful investigator who thinks the song will throw any light upon the ceremony. He may succeed in puzzling out what approximates to a word-for-word translation, but his informants will have no idea of the general purport. It is, in fact, a song which they have sung many times, but always in complete ignorance of its meaning: just as some members of the congregation will sing a hymn with a fervour only equalled by their obliviousness to the verbal content.

In a ceremony named *erimunu* (the Spirit of the water)[47] recently acquired from Orokolo by the Purari people, a group of young men, hoarse and perspiring, may beat their drums for hours on end. But barely a syllable of the songs do they comprehend: they are in the Orokolo language, and the songs have been taken over with the ceremony.

So with other acquired ceremonies; the manual rites are often taken, and the explanation left—if indeed the owners of the ceremony have any explanation to offer. An interesting dance called *Apuriri* and performed at Koaru, as a favour on the part of the villagers, presented in the form of a ballet, with chorus of drum-beaters) what might well be some small incident of village history. The principal figures were a man bearing bow and arrows; two men playing the parts of women and wearing *ramis*; and a fourth, who danced backwards and forwards continually thrashing these two women with a switch of cassowary feathers.

This dance, it was said, had been acquired from Orokolo. The dramatis personae had a hereditary right to their respective parts— they even bore character-names—but not one of them appeared to have the slightest inkling of the meaning of the dance or of the history of these characters. Yet there was no mistaking the keen enjoyment of actors, chorus and spectators.

These are only illustrations of a by-now accepted principle of anthropology—that of the supreme importance in the native's mind of the ritual, and the meagreness and vagueness of the doctrine. It has been very boldly expressed in one terse phrase: "On the whole, ritual is the savage substitute for God."[48]

The principle rests upon one still more fundamental. Primitive religion, if not advanced religion, is largely a matter of the emotions: and emotion finds its satisfaction, not in belief, but primarily in action.

Hence not only the unfairness, but the actual impossibility, of abolishing ritual and substituting doctrine. It is questionable whether the native has reached that stage when he can digest any but the simplest elements of Christian teaching. Some of the pathetic absurdities in the beliefs of intelligent native Christians might well throw doubt on the matter.

It is difficult for them to assimilate a few elementary Christian doctrines to their own scheme of things, to the body of their tribal traditions, and to their whole cultural environment. But to bid them do away with all the rites to which they, and their ancestors before them, have been accustomed to "Stop quiet along village,"

and to thrive on the Holy Creed and the Ten Commandments, is
simply to ask the impossible. It is to snatch away the baby's milk-
bottle and offer it a pound of steak.

Real Differences between the Papuan and the European

Even where such a policy has apparently succeeded, it is a
question whether after these subtractions and additions, there remains over a true native or a kind of abnormality—a cultural hy-
brid. The more exaggerated type of "Jesus Christ Man" in the Gulf
Division almost literally makes one's flesh creep, as something a little
horrible and wholly pathological. Such men are denaturalized: they
have ceased to be true natives; whether or no they have become
true Christians is for those who best know them and Christianity
to decide.

Speaking, however, of the contact between white man and native
in more general terms, we might ask for an explanation of one very
striking feature in our own attitude. Why is it that those who come
frequently into touch with natives express so universally their
preference for the more primitive of them i.e., for those who have
had least to do with white men?

There are few who will disown their liking for the naked savage
when once he has got over his natural suspicion and put aside his
arrows; and many who will not deny their admiration for him,
while, on the other hand, there are as many who make no secret of
their antipathy toward certain "educated" boys.

These are very common opinions. They are not put down for their
value as opinions, but merely as facts requiring explanation. It
may be that the European unconsciously resents the steps toward
equality that the native is taking; or he may be contemptuously
amused, or even disgusted, at his imitation of the white man's ways.
But he does not—or should not—harbour any such sentiments
toward the native in his element. For the true native he can feel both
liking and respect. The type he will always despise is the imitation
white man with a black skin.

Science will yet succeed in defining the actual differences of
mentality which exist between races, as it has partially succeeded
in defining differences of physique. Whatever, or however slight,
these mental differences may prove to be, there are over and above
them vast differences of environment and culture. The Papuan and
the European are both men; but when we consider what they were
born, where and how their forbears have lived, and what they have
respectively been brought up to, we must admit the differences will
not be small.

We cannot change the real nature of the man; we cannot easily change his environment; and, before we change his culture we might ask whether the substitute we intend to provide is any better, or as well suited to his nature and environment as they exist. Furthermore is not his culture itself, or are not some parts of it, possibly worth preserving for their own sakes as a human achievement?

In Motu Motu there are now no ceremonies or dances; the people do not keep late hours, but professedly retire at 9 o'clock. But before that hour may be seen the "School."[49] Three or four lighted hurricane lamps are set in a row along some boards. On either side, sitting on the ground, are gathered a number of men, women and children—perhaps fifty in all. At one end stands the leader, clad in white singlet and *rami*. All present join in a chant; the leader prays; then, with him, all read from their books. In the pauses there is absolute hush. When the "School" is over, men, women and children disperse in silence to their homes.

Taking into consideration the native habit of mind and disabusing our own minds of all Christian prejudice, we may fairly ask whether this solemn performance is an advantageous substitute for the *sevese* or even for the wholesome and amusing obscenities of a rollicking native dance. Not that it is anything but excellent in itself indeed, an effort towards ritual, even in so simple a form, is sure of appreciation.

Without seriously advocating any such measures one might suggest that the Christianity that would succeed among the natives would be one with a minimum of perplexing doctrine, but full of sacrifice, communion feasts, baptism by immersion, processions, pageants, fastings, flagellations and the like. The poor native hates thinking, but he loves carrying on.

Adaptation, not Substitution
The main contention of the present report may be put very shortly—Adaptation, not Substitution.

If an allegorical flight be allowed, native culture is like a tree, and a very fine tree too—if we can only induce ourselves to look over the fence of our own particular cultural garden with any feeling save disapproval. A little judicious trimming and pruning will do this tree no harm: and it will, no doubt, take grafts well enough. On the whole it is worth some care and encouragement. Our business is not to back it down, or drag it up by the roots, and plant one of our own fancied varieties in its place. This is, at least, a risky experiment; and it is doubtful whether our new tree would flourish; for the soil will be of very different quality.

The thing is not to unmake and remake; but to improve what has been made already. It must be remembered that native religion is a growth or organism, the natural outcome of long-distant ante-cedents under the continual formative influence of mind and environment. It will not be perfect; it may have some evil features; but it is natural.

It can no doubt be supplemented. The simplest of new doctrinal or ethical teaching is an improvement where it adds to spiritual comfort or happiness. It may be freed from admittedly evil influences. Though here, of course, rises up the great difficulty: the danger is that we be too drastic rather than too lenient. Every feature has to be judged on its merits and impartially; our own standards are not always applicable. And it must be admitted that the worst features of a primitive civilization, from head-hunting to black magic, are seldom quite devoid of good.

Practical Questions of Renewing the Gulf Ceremonies

It is especially with the ceremonies in the Gulf Division that this report is concerned. Their various values—religious, social and artistic—have been touched upon. They are the highest product of native civilization in that region: for their own sakes they are too good to lose.

Whoever, in the name of philanthropy or of Christianity, would discourage them, is depriving the native of his best, and giving him in return some unappreciated material reforms and a smattering of strange religion—an exchange which leaves him poor indeed.

At present, owing, in the last place, to the ravages of the Vailala Madness, the ceremonies are dormant. Unless they are revived within a generation, they will be dead; for traditions cannot get over gaps.

There are, however, encouraging signs of reaction in some of the coastal villages: even the Automaniacs will describe the old healthy practices of heathendom with a gusto which is itself promising, for it shows their interest is not entirely defunct.

But these Automaniacs, I believe, hold the others in check. Whether they are sincere, or whether they are schemers, their power is a malign influence upon the village: and before the cere-monies can burst into life again, this evil restraint will have to be removed. The Vailala Madness knocked the true native head over heels, and the Automaniacs are still holding him down.

If the Government officers, and the white men in general, made it their business to ridicule and discredit these men; to drive out of the heads of the people the idea that their ceremonies are wrong or disapproved of; and to urge and encourage a revival of them; then the Gulf Division would yet struggle back to life and health.

Conclusion

Two Practical Arguments

In conclusion, there are two matters which may be dealt with very briefly; and which may, as arguments, have some weight with those who think all the foregoing to be some what too idealistic.

One is the interdependence of social functions in primitive society, which has been made a byword of anthropology. Whereas in our advanced civilization the various functions of business, art, religion, social entertainment, and so forth, are virtually independent of one another; in primitive society they are closely and essentially inter-related. So that, for instance, if one proceed to investigate the art of the Elema people he will see the clan system unfolding before his eyes, and soon find himself involved in the intricacies of totemic religion.

It follows from this general principle that one cannot delete any of the social life of a primitive people and leave the other parts unaffected. If one take exception to the ceremonies, it is not possible to say: "Have done with the ceremonies, but go on living just as you were in other respects." Only minor matters can be treated in this way, or else a thoroughly effective working substitute must be provided. Where this does not happen there may ensue the social disorganization and stagnant inactivity which cannot but be admitted evils. You have only to remove one wheel to stop the watch, or one stone from the social structure to have it tumbling about your ears.

The last matter is of still more severely practical importance. It has been recently maintained by eminent scientists that the break-up of tribal customs has far-reaching results of a more than sentimental character. And it has been argued that the principal cause of native depopulation is no other than this, viz., the destruction of native culture.[50] The medium is psychological. Leave the native something worth living for, and he may live.

REFERENCES

1. (Originally published as: 'Territory of Papua', *Anthropology Report* No. 4, 1923. E. S.)
2. (For the writings G. H. Murray on the Vailala Madness see Commonwealth of Australia 1921. Williams had them included in *Anthropology Report* No. 4 as appendixes, but for reasons of space they have not been reprinted in the present volume. E. S.)
3. Even genuine "mental" cases seem now to be, in common opinion, associated with the Vailala Madness, though originally they may have

been quite independent of it. So also on the cultural side, certain of the old practices and beliefs have been incorporated into it, and cannot be ignored in a description.

4. The Baigona cult of the Northern Division presents some striking similarities. *Annual Report*, 1912, p. 129; *Annual Report*, 1919-20, p. 63; F. E. Williams, *Orokaiva Magic*, 1928.
5. See below, pp. 354 ff.
6. Of an *ahea uvi*, see pp. 347-8, below.
7. Sorcerer or medicine-man.
8. i.e., Jehovah.
9. This language was said to be "all-a-same Djaman", i.e., German, "the language spoken at Rabaul." This strange explanation was offered independently in several places.

One informant (at Keuru), said that he had been to Rabaul and "knew German"; but this so-called German which the "Head-he-go-round Men" spoke was all humbug. It seems that numbers of natives have actually been taken to Rabaul from this neighbourhood by geologists of the Anglo-Perisian Oil Co.

It is regularly claimed that the speech comes up from the man's belly, he does not learn it: in fact, that it is "ventriloquism" in the true primitive sense with nothing of the modern parlour-trick about it (Tylor, 1873, ii, 182).

Further, there is a general idea (presumably quite groundless) that the Automaniacs can understand one another when speaking this jargon, though they are not understood by the commonalty.

The speakers usually bring out a number of Pidgin-English phrases, many of which have a plantation ring about them:—"Heave 'em up", "Come on boy", etc.

It is interesting to note (though not in connection with the Vailala Madness) a little song and dance popular with the children at Vailala. Hopping on one leg they shape up to one another and retreat again and again in a very pugilistic manner, singing meanwhile in their harsh little voices a refrain in which they do not appear to see any meaning, but which may also have a plantation ring about it. It is reproduced under thin phonetic disguise:
Ai kikki bluddi us—Heh! Heh! Heh! Heh!.

10. Both the symmetrical gestures and the "fanning" movement before the stomach have been noted in one or two other cases.
11. For a further description by an individual, *vide* the conversion of Kori, pp. 353-4.
12. Colloquial expression for indentured labourer.
13. Motuan word meaning mad.
14. It appears that accounts of the aeroplane had been received in the Gulf Division villages long before it passed over them; hence it did not occasion the excitement that might have been expected.
15. Mr. Mahony was informed that this demonstration was carried out as a protest against the rice-growing proposition; and is of opinion that it is a "forced business", with the idea of bluff behind it.

Some further description may be quoted from a personal letter kindly sent me by Mr. Mahony:—

"These natives . . . were taking a few quick steps in front of them, and would then stand, jabber, and gesticulate, at the same time swaying the head from side to side; also bending the body from side to side from the hips, the legs appearing to be held firm. Others would take the quick steps forward, and stop, placing the hands on the hips, jabbering continuously, swaying the head from side to side, and moving the trunk of the body backwards and forwards, remaining in this position for approximately a minute......"

16. The weakness is only a matter of degree: whoever jumps for joy, or beats his breast, or wrings his hands, or tears his hair, is finding satisfaction in the same way.

17. *Vide* in general William McDougall *Introduction to Social Psychology*, (1921, Chapter IV) and *The Group Mind* (McDougall, 1920, Chapter II).

18. Sorcerer.

19. It was not made clear whether the relatives were to appear as flesh and blood, or in some ethereal form. Presumably they were expected to have a corporeal appetite for the coconuts, sago, and pigs; though the word *a'avaia* (Motu *laulau*) was used. Nor did I gather how long the relatives were to stay.

20. *Annual Report*, 1916-17, p. 63 (Commonwealth of Australia 1918).

21. Thomas 1906, p. 207. It is suggested, however, that the white man is believed to be the dead black, reincarnated rather than actually returned.

22. This beast was said (in quick succession) to resemble a pig, a cow and a horse. It is to be seen in Rabaul, where it is used as a draught animal.

23. The Roman Catholic missionaries.

24. *Vide* pages 343-4 above.

25. Cf. Patrol Report by Mr. A. R. M. Rentoul, March, 1922, where he describes what is apparently an *ahea uvi*, with a table "on which were laid two bowls of rice, three bottles of flowers, and some betel-nut, and a clean rami for table cloth. Only one man was in charge, and he lay alongside under a mosquito net, as though he were on guard." This was in Vailala East. The man under the mosquito net might well be an Automaniac.

26. An interesting point is that, in some of the *ahea uvi*, separate tables or parts of the building are allotted to the separate clans who have a share in it. In one example at Arihava there were a great number of decorated bark-cloth strips, bearing the designs appropriate to the clans. Such facts indicate that the social organisation has to some extent survived the Vailala Madness, or has been adapted to it; whereas the old religious life has been to all intents and purposes ruined. The only thing that remains to the latter is the engrossing interest in the dead, which is founded too strongly in fears and affections to be given up.

27. Mr. H. Coghill, of Orokolo.

28. Wireless Station of Anglo-Persian Oil Coy.

29. *Vide* G. H. Murray in Commonwealth of Australia 1921 for access of crime while Madness was in progress.
30. This is also the opinion of Mr. Lambden, Patrol Officer, Gulf Division.
31. Many references are made to this "drilling", which at first may have lent colour to the idea of a native rising. (*Vide* official letters from A. L. Blyth, Esq., A.R.M., of 8/6/21, and 27/5/21; the former quoting H. M. Saunders, Esq., Patrol Officer; also official letter from A. Wade, Esq., Government Oilfields, of 8/9/19.)
32. *Vide* letter from A. L. Blyth, Esq., A.R.M., 27/5/21.
33. Now converted into a store-room for rice.
34. Harea, whom I unfortunately neglected to see, is evidently one of the most prominent figures associated with the cult. I cannot say whether he is to be identified with the Hareha, of Vailala East, mentioned by G. H. Murray in Commonwealth of Australia 1921 and on page 352 above. (See footnote No. 35 for another reference to Harea. E. S.)
35. It may be that there are the rudiments of an organisation among the Automaniacs of the coastal villages. From Vailala Eastwards it was agreed in many of the villages that the boss "Head-he-go-round Man" was Harea, of Vailala West (Haruape). This title arises probably from the fact that he was largely responsible for carrying the Gospel Eastwards and afterwards performed something like a tour of inspection.
36. In Arihava it was said that the Automaniacs also had power to heal. The healer rubs his palms together (the former practice of chewing hot bark and spitting on the palms has been abandoned by the cult) and then massages the limbs of the patient towards the extremities, whence he extracts the complaint—whether in any material form (as by the old custom) I am unable to say. It appears that the patient kills a pig for the village, and then rises cured. I have no evidence that direct payment is taken by the Automaniacs.
37. Examples were seen in Arihava, Vailala West, Silo and Motu Motu. I am reliably informed that they are to be found in other villages also.
38. For a striking parallel, *vide* Werner 1906, pp. 90-92. The use of these poles is only another instance of the time-honoured system of 'rhabdomancy'. Possibly the Baigona Cult (of the snake or python) in the Northern Division might be able to throw some light on these divination poles and their origin...(a mere guess). (Williams took this question up in *Orokaiva Magic*. E. S.)
39. (For a full account of the *kovave* ceremony see *Drama of Orokolo*, Chapter VII. See also in this volume, Chapter 2, footnote 10. E.S.)
40. At Lese some village children were noticed without nose and ear perforations—a rather striking break-away from custom. It was said that, now they had no further need of nosebones and ear-rings, it was not necessary to pierce noses and ears. Hair is now commonly cut short in the Gulf Division.
41. The youths who pass through the seclusion in one batch are called collectively a *migiotau;* those who pass through in the next batch (some years after) constitute the younger *migiotau*, and so on.

42. The comment of the Administrator upon a patrol report from the Gulf Division is here very much in point. The report mentions several instances in which the inhabitants of settled villages fled at the appraoch of the patrol.

    "It is regrettable that so many villagers run away on the approach of Government officials. Do you think that too much is being required of them in building, fencing, clearing large areas for coconuts and the making of numerous and lengthy roads? While the resident magistrate and patrol officer show commendable zeal in having much-needed work done, it perhaps might be better to proceed a little slower."

43. (For these festivals, see the detailed account in F. E. Williams' 'Natives of the Purari Delta' (1924). E.S.)

44. Variant pronunciations are *semese* and *hevehe* (on the West). The *harisu* ceremony, or what corresponds to it, is called *kovave* at Orokolo and the Western extremity of the coast generally; apparently *oioi* at the Eastern end. (Williams' brief account omits that in the west—see *Drama of Orokolo* and Chapter 2 of the present volume —*hevehe* ceremonies are for collective catharsis rather than a mortuary rite. While *kovave* is fully described in *Drama of Orokolo*, Chapter VII, *harisu* differs in many respects and the description in the present essay is of great ethnographic value. E. S.)

45. I do not know the meaning of the expression.

46. The "seeing" means that the initiates see the *harisu* under construction. This appears to be the essence of initiation—to see and understand, to know that the *harisu* are made (and how they are made) and that they are not strange living creatures from the bush.

47. (For *erimunu*, see "Natives of the Purari Delta" (Williams 1924), Chapter 15. E.S.

48. R. R. Marett, 1920 p. 66.

49. Whether this is a nightly performance I am unable to say.

50. An *argumentum ad verecundiam* may be permitted in a final foot-note. "Essays on the Depopulation of Melanesia", ed. by Dr. W. H. R. Rivers (Cambridge Press), is reviewed in "Nature", Feb., 1923. The volume itself is not to hand; the following quotation is from the review.

    "Sir Wm. MacGregor and Mr. C. M. Woodford, who write from the point of view of the official; and Dr. Speisef, of Basle, who writes as an anthropologist, fully bear out the contentions of the members of the Mission, i.e., the Melanesian Mission. The authors, without exception, agree that the depopulation in Melanesia is to be attributed largely to the breaking-up of custom which has followed contact with the white man......Dr. Rivers, in a concluding essay...suggests that the most important factor is psychological. The native, he maintains, has lost all interest in life through the suppression of customs such as head-hunting, with which have disappeared a large number of closely-related social activities. His suggestion that total suppression of such customs could be avoided by substitution of harmless elements is deserving of careful consideration."

    (Cf. Rivers 1922, McGregor 1922, Woodford 1922, Speiser 1922. E.S.)

6

THE VAILALA MADNESS IN RETROSPECT[1]

It is now more than twelve years since a movement known as the Vailala Madness began in the Gulf Division of Papua. It spread with the speed of an epidemic and affected with very few exceptions all the coastal villages of the Division. At the beginning there was high enthusiasm: the movement was then in native phrase, "hot". But as this heat abated the masses gradually ceased being directly affected, and the movement was only carried on by a number of specialists, or "bosses", who still were or pretended to be under its influence. Finally, it lapsed altogether, though naturally some of its results remain. I am unable to give a precise date for the expiry of the movement, since native informants are so far from reliable in such matters. But at the western end of the Gulf Coast (where this paper is being written) there was about three years ago a definite move to reinstate some of the ceremonies, and this, it is said, effectually "closed the way". During its early youth, then, the movement was very vigorous; that was the time of miraculous expectations and miraculous happenings. Then it began to die its lingering death, and by now it is no more than a memory. It is the main purpose of the present paper to compare that memory as it is with the youth of the Vailala Madness as it really was.

Summary of the Movement

An account of the movement has already been published by the Papuan Government as an Anthropological Report,[2] but its main features may be recapitulated here. The most striking of them was that of mass hysteria. Great numbers were affected by a kind of giddiness; they lost or abandoned control of their limbs and reeled about the villages, one man involuntarily following the example of another until almost the whole population of a village might be affected at the same moment. The condition was known as *haro heraripe* "one's head is turning round". It is as obvious that these symptoms were involuntary among the masses as that similar symptoms were deliberately affected by certain leaders for their own purposes. While they indulged in these antics the leaders frequently poured forth utterances in "Djaman", or "German", a language composed mostly of nonsense syllables and pidgin English which was wholly unintelligible. But at other times they took care to make themselves understood by words and actions, and thus the movement was invested with real significance.

The main teaching was that the old customs and ceremonies must be done away with. The bull-roarers and the masks worn in the *Hevehe* and *Kovave* ceremonies were cast out of the men's houses and burnt while women and uninitiated children looked on. Personal adornment was banned; feathers were snatched from the heads of vain unbelievers; and the forbidden lime-pot was dashed from their hands. In some communities the people, or certain influential men among them, were strong enough to resist the invasion and preserve their possessions and customs. But in most they were completely overpowered: they caught the *haro heraripe* and themselves joined in the work of destruction. There can be no doubt that misunderstood Mission teaching had something to do with this aspect of the Madness.

But besides mere iconoclasm there was some positive doctrine. The "bosses" declaimed against thieving and adultery. (There was no originality in this, and it certainly had no great effect, for sexual standards were noticeably relaxed for the time being.) Some of the preachers were perhaps quite sincere, though by claiming to detect wrong-doing they continually extracted atonement from the wrong-doers in the form of pigs. Further they insisted on cleanliness, on the equality of women; and, as the most important duty, on the necessity of offerings to the dead.

It is to certain prophecies and beliefs, however, that I wish to draw special attention. It was foretold and everywhere believed that the spirits of the dead would return; in some quarters they were expected to appear as white men, and indeed some Europeans were actually welcomed as the ghosts of Papuans. Universally it was believed that a steamer would come to the Gulf. The original idea was certainly that it would be full of the spirits of the Papuan dead, though many of those who looked for the vessel were not quite clear as to the nature of its passengers. The leaders were in continual communication with the dead, receiving messages in various forms, sometimes by papers that fluttered down from the sky or were held out by invisible hands, but mainly through the agency of flagpoles, the message being caught at the top and transmitted to the base, where it was received by those who had ears to hear. Everywhere preparations were made for the welcome of the dead. Food was accumulated and ripe coconuts were stacked in readiness for loading on to the steamer. In the meantime the spirits were supposed to come in invisible form and eat of the offerings that must be set out for them; and in many villages there were tables ready laid with knives and forks and floral decorations. It was principally from these offerings to the dead that the "bosses" or leaders were enabled to make their profits; for they posed as go-betweens and had sole access to the *ahea uvi*, or "hot houses", to which the spirits resorted in order to partake of the offerings made by the more simple-minded. By methods such as these, and by continuing to make or allow their heads to "go round," the leaders kept the Vailala Madness alive long after the masses had ceased to show any nervous or physical symptoms.

The Leaders

It is important to get an idea of the personal character of the leaders. Unfortunately the more prominent of them (at this western end of the Division) have since died, so that it is not possible to add much that would be reliable to what has already been said in "The Vailala Madness". Biere alone remains from among the real leaders; and further acquaintance confirms the impression that he is a strong character and a man of high intelligence; it also makes clearer the fact that he was an impostor. I think he may stand as an example of that class of leaders who deliberately used the movement for their own gain. Ua Halai, of Arihava, was, I believe, of the same class.

While some leaders, however, were cool impostors others were evidently to some extent sincere. Harea, who played a highly important part, I never met personally. He eventually became a lay preacher, but the Rev. R. A. Owen, under whom he worked, informs me that he was a strange character, fanatical in the extreme, and liable even as a lay preacher to verge upon unintelligibility. The record of Evara, to whom as an individual it is plain the movement owes its origin, has already been mentioned in "The Vailala Madness", with the significant item that he had been subject to ecstatic seizures before ever the Madness began. I have since learned that as a youth he was marked by extreme nervousness; he avoided the men's house; he would fly to the bush on the least sign of a quarrel between two villagers; and he would never come near to look on a corpse at a native funeral. When he married, his "inside hardened", but this unusual nervousness must have attracted some attention, for it was his son, born after it had disappeared, who told me of the forms it took. There is reason then for thinking that both Evara and Harea were to some extent unbalanced.

I am prepared to think that the same could be said of a number of other leaders. Hairi, of Hohoro, e.g. had come to Orokolo, where a dance was in progress, and paraded naked before the dancers

He then visited the local missionary and saw in his house the spirits of four deceased villagers. He still gives a circumstantial account of this vision, not doubting its reality. He also met other spirits on a later occasion. The same man has given me a version of a legend involving strange contortions of his own; and he is the only man from whom I have heard of a character called "New Guinea Jack". He could not give me a clear account of this person's exploits. He said he knew them when the *haro heraripe* was on, but now he had forgotten the details. Hairi seems to be perfectly sane now; but from his own account one may be inclined to believe that during the earlier days of the Vailala Madness he was deranged.

On the whole it seems likely that not a few of the doctrines of the movement originated in visions and delusions; and it cannot be doubted that they were to some extent born of the mental confusion that followed the inrush of new European ideas.[3] It is also worth observing that the central doctrine, viz. that the dead would return, represents what is normally the longing of every native; and it is significant that Evara's head "went round" previously at the death of his father, and again, when the movement was launched in 1919, at the death of his brother.

Present-Day Versions

We may now consider some present-day versions of the happenings of 1919-21, when the Vailala Madness was still "hot". I made a point of questioning younger men on this subject. Some of my informants had then been no more than children; others—and the testimony of these is specially interesting—had been away as indentured labourers and know of the earlier period only by hearsay. The accounts given by these younger informants perhaps represent the more or less consolidated memory of the real Vailala Madness.

Not only from these informants, however, but also from adult contemporaries of the movement I derived a rather surprising impression. One might have expected that the whole thing would now be regarded everywhere as a gigantic hoax bristling with impostures and unfulfilled prophecies. On the contrary I found a fairly widespread belief that the strange things which were expected to happen really did happen. It is true that some informants are sceptical, and in regard to at least one notable happening (which will be referred to later) there remains no illusion whatever. But there still lives a popular belief that those first years of the Vailala Madness constituted a brief age of miracles.

Men will tell you to-day how the ground shook and the trees

swayed twelve years ago. (They are familiar with earthquakes, but this continual movement was no earthquake.) Flowers sprang up in a day, and the air was filled with their fragrance. The spirits of the dead came and went by night—morning after morning the imprints of their European boots and even their bicycle tracks were found on the beaches. After dark they could be heard moving in the bush. In Arihava just after sundown dogs used to rise from the ground and roam the village. They belonged to the *bevehere haera*, the "cold" or dead people, and they were large black-and-white dogs like those of Europeans. The people tried to catch them but always failed. Lights flashed suddenly out of the darkness: they were the same as electric torches, but no men were seen behind them. Papers came fluttering from the sky, and excited individuals snatched at them: but the papers eluded them and vanished. Some "bosses", however, did receive papers, offered by invisible hands at night, and these were taken to the white missionary for interpretation. The coming of an aeroplane was prophesied and sure enough (by a coincidence that must have meant a great triumph) the real aeroplane appeared. Meanwhile messages continued to come down the flagpoles: an informant who might be relied upon for a sceptic tells me how he used to hear the warning hum in the pole, followed by a sort of spiritualist's knock at the base; then he would see a "boss" lay his ear to the wood, receive the message, and deliver it. The messages being mostly broadcast in "German" meant nothing to the unenlightened, but there was no doubt—and in many minds there still is no doubt—that they were received.

The Phantom Ship

We may refer in more detail to three features or incidents of the Vailala Madness. The first is that of the Phantom Ship, if such a title may be excused. This vessel was much spoken of and genuinely expected. No doubt a great number of believers were sadly disappointed over the *Sisima* (steamer), as they called it; but it would be a mistake to think that even now they have all been completely disillusioned. Some informants, indeed, have said bluntly that the steamer did not turn up, but I find an impression remaining in many quarters that the expected visit, or a number of visits, did take place even if the spirits did not materialize.

Thus a young man who was house-boy to the Magistrate at Kerema tells me how he once heard cries of "Sailoh!" from the village of Karaita just below the residency. He went out to see what boat was coming and found some of the "bosses" and others affected by the Madness running about the beach in great excitement, clapping their hands and shouting "Hippu ! Hippu !"

They were welcoming the Phantom Ship. My informant looked out over the calm waters of Kerema Bay and saw the wash of the steamer as she approached. He heard the pounding of her engines, then the rattle of her anchor-chain. He heard the dinghy lowered noisily into the water and the sound of her oars as she was rowed ashore. And not only he but all the others present (so he says) heard the same sounds, for they were communicating their impressions to one another. Soon their ears informed them that the dinghy was returning; the anchor was heaved up, the engines started, and the Phantom Ship sailed out of hearing. Not once had she been seen.

Again, one hears how a steamer (the prophecy is not nailed down to one only) entered the Vailala River at night. She had three masts and an imposing red funnel, though these perhaps were not very clearly observed; more emphasis is laid on her lights, which many saw as she passed quickly upstream. None of the passengers were visible, but when Evara paddled out alone in a canoe and came alongside they threw a token into the dug-out. It was a medal which he subsequently wore round his neck like the badge of a Village Councillor. (When I met Evara, nine years before I heard this story, I noted his Victory Medal, 1919, but he did not tell how he had come by it. I do not know that he himself professed to have received it from the steamer.)

Here at Orokolo and Arihava the steamer was sighted one morning at about 11 o'clock. The smoke was seen, but before the vessel came properly into view it was obscured by clouds. To the majority of people in Orokolo (who had escaped or resisted the Madness) the steamer was not so clearly visible, but the *haro herari̇pe* men would clutch them by the arm crying, "There, can't you see it?" and my informants appeared to have no doubt that it had really been there.

The Resurrection of Ua Halai

When at the end of 1922 I was first inquiring into the Vailala Madness at Arihava one of my best informants was Ua Halai. He was still, so to speak, practising, and was the most influential of the "bosses" in a village of some 1,500 people. I did not know then that he had been the hero of the remarkable exploit which is here recorded; perhaps everyone conspired to keep it secret, for there was a well-grounded feeling that the Vailala Madness was not viewed with favour by the Government. The exploit was nothing short of resurrection from "death".

It transpires that Ua Halai had complained of indisposition one morning, and by midday he was "dead". He had apparently foreseen this eventuality, for he had issued instructions that when his body was laid out in the usual fashion it was not to be closely approached. Further, he had said that no grave should be dug for him; his friends and relatives should wait and see what they would see. Ua Halai was so "dead" that the rats gnawed his ears. (This point is made by all who tell the story, and the disfigurement of the ears is vouched for by eye-witnesses. Some also say that his toes were attacked.) But at noon of the third day he came back to life, issued forth from the house, and began to preach in a voice of thunder, using the "German" language. Next he caused a litter to be carried from end to end of the long village of Arihava while he lay reclined upon it, waving a cassowary-plume switch and crying out that his litter was the steamer of Lavara, a legendary ancestress, come back to Papua. During his period of "death", as he gave out, he had been to the land of the dead, whence he had brought back more warnings against stealing, adultery, etc., as well as the idea of the *ahea uvi*, or "hot house", which was to be shared as a place of resort by the spirits and the "bosses".

To us, of course, it appears almost self-evident that Ua Halai's "death" was a carefully prepared hoax. It would seem likely that he had accomplices among the other "bosses", for it is said they stood guard, allegedly looking for signs of returning animation, but also enforcing their superior's wish that none should approach too near. Yet with the rank and file the hoax was a complete success; I have heard no one express any doubts, and in answer to a direct question one will be told seriously that for three days the man was dead. Had I known of this exploit when I met Ua Halai in person it would have been possible to examine his ears and see to what extent he or his accomplices had gone to provide this grisly evidence. That the ears were in some way disfigured is beyond doubt. It is, of course, conceivable that they were actually gnawed by rats during a trance, but the careful staging of the whole affair is strong evidence for the other interpretation.

Maivake's Ghost

The third incident is of a different kind in that it represents a failure on the part of the "bosses" to carry out their pretence. In Vailala West the principal "boss" was Biere, whom we have seen to be a man of outstanding intelligence and personality. He was surrounded by a small clique who long continued to exact offerings from the villagers on behalf of the dead; and someone of this clique conceived a unique method of impressing the common people. It was to provide them with the representation of one particular ghost, that of a man Maivake, who had died not long previously.

Biere and his colleagues, who like the other "bosses" assumed what might without any stretch be called the role of priesthood, placed a strict taboo on the *ahea uvi*. Two younger members of the clique, Aita and Karoa, used to take turn and turn about in impersonating the deceased Maivake. Morning and evening the ghost appeared, his face masked and his body enveloped in a garment of bark-cloth similar to that of certain grotesque figures, known as *Eharo*, which form an adjunct to the *Hevehe* ceremony. Maivake's costume, however, was treated with some kind of oil which made it soft and clinging and thus gave it an unfamiliar look. An eyewitness has described the scene as Aita paraded in his ghostly character before a crowd of women and girls who danced and sang. Towards evening the offerings of cooked food—only the good lean of the pork was acceptable to the spirit—were taken up to the *ahea uvi*, and only the young attractive women were allowed to take it up. (Some informants have declared that these young women used actually to enter the *ahea uvi*, and that some of them were interfered with in an obscene manner.) My informant did not venture too close, but he was impressed by the strange texture of the garments, and he declares, I believe sincerely, that he did not then suspect the figure to be any other than that of Maivake.

The report of this spirit spread far and wide and seems to have gained general credence among the rank and file. I am told that the "bosses" in Arihava (we need not suppose they were so thoroughly gulled) were actually preparing to follow the example of Vailala and produce a spirit of their own when they were suddenly interrupted by news of a collapse. Some suspicion must have existed in Vailala, and one evening a person of very solid character named Kaiva dared to lay his hand on the ghost. Feeling substantial flesh and bone under the bark-cloth, he tore the latter off and began to belabour the young man Aita who emerged from the disguise. Aita, in the midst of his beating, objected to bearing the sole blame, and recommended the angry villagers to go in search of Karoa. But Karoa was already half-way across the Vailala River, and it was a long time before he ventured back to his home.

Conclusions

It is not surprising that false rumours and beliefs should have been prevalent in the early days of such a movement as the Vailala Madness, but as we have seen these beliefs have outlived the Madness and are still held to a rather remarkable extent. It may be suggested, therefore, that they are already passing into the form of legends; that what were in popular estimation the miracles of those exciting days are now more or less absorbed into folk-memory. We must wait, perhaps, a good deal longer before this suggestion can be fully verified; but should it prove to be sound, then we shall have concrete evidence of how those legends had their beginning.

I do not propose to deal in this paper with the general causes of the Vailala Madness. By way of brief summary I submit they are to be found in certain effects of contact with and subjugation by a superior people. Such contact involves (1) the effort to assimilate a body of new and difficult ideas, and a resultant mental confusion; (2) the loss of customary means of social excitement; and (3) a general sense of inferiority. It is suggested that the first of these three factors was largely responsible for the emergence of the leading ideas of the movement, and that the latter two placed the masses in just the right mood for their acceptance.

It is rather, however, in the causes of certain particular beliefs connected with the movement that we are interested here. The evidence must always, of course, be far from complete, but one can cite a few historical details that will plausibly account for the emergence of certain beliefs and practices. The rite of receiving messages by the flagpoles, for instance, must be correlated with the fact that the Anglo-Persian Oil Co. had a wireless apparatus at Popo, where many Gulf boys had been at work; and the existence of the flagpoles themselves, with the fact that they had been set up in some villages with quite another purpose by the London Missionary Society. The choice of "German" as the language of inspiration may be directly due to the fact that certain Gulf boys had been to Rabaul, where the A.P.C. also operated; or, if not that, then at least to the fact that we had recently been at war with Germany. The prophecy that an aeroplane would come I should hardly hesitate to trace to Evara's possession of a book, *Love and the Aeroplane*, with a picture of the hitherto unknown flying-machine on the cover[4]; the dramatic fulfilment of the prophecy came when Capt. Hurley's plane, the first in Papua, flew over shortly after on its way to the Delta Division. And a number of doctrines and beliefs—notably that of Ua Halai's resurrection on the third day—must be traced to the Christian teaching which was being given in the Mission schools. Such antecedents, however trivial, must play an all-important part in the shaping of legend; it is this sort of thing that gives the distinctive form or the queer turn to the story. In the case of nearly all established legends the historical antecedents can only be conjectured, but it need not follow that we are always wasting our time when we try some historical reconstructions from the evidence of legend as we find it.

The part played by individual leaders in the movement is obviously of the greatest significance. The attribution of its origin

to Evara has been amply verified by my later inquiries; but some
of the other "bosses" had their own gleams of imagination. It is
obvious that movements of this kind have their starting point in the
mind of an individual, viz. in his personal reactions to those antecedents, large and small, which may be regarded as more ultimate
causes. Then other individuals begin to exert their influence, like
so many buds on an original stem from which new branches may
develop. We have briefly examined the character of a few of these
leaders. Some of them were undoubtedly cool schemers with a gift
for leadership or organization and an eye to their own interests. But
it seems that this class have in some measure proceeded by exploiting
the ideas of men who were not so well balanced. In fact it is not too
much to say that the most important ideas of the Vailala Madness
emerged originally from visions or delusions. It is certainly easier
to believe that they were the product of fevered imagination than
of cool planning.

The reaction of the populace to such ideas is in primitive society
the test of their permanency. We have seen some amazing examples
of suggestibility and credulity. While in some villages the people
stood firm against the destruction of their customs, there must have
been few out-and-out unbelievers. The most extravagant claims
were not too much for primitive gullibility, and prophecies were
accepted as facts even after they had manifestly failed. The delusion
or the pretence of one man may thus easily become the belief of
thousands and eventually appear in the guise of legend. Indeed, it
is not improbable that the miraculous exploits of many culture
heroes are no more than their delusions or pretences which have
been accepted as facts.

I have pointed out that there are degrees of scepticism and
credulity among different informants. But provided there are
sufficient believers I do not think that at the primitive level a leaven-
ing of unbelievers can prevent this kind of legend-making. There
are, in fact, varying moods of scepticism and credulity in every
individual; or to put it another way, there are moments when the
native's critical faculty, such as it may be, is awake, and others when
it is sound asleep; in truth in seems almost that he deliberately puts
it to sleep. Now, when a native is story-telling he and his audience
are in the mood of credulity; they willingly discard the trammels of
fact, and the more the miracles the better the story.

This coming and going of credulity is familiar in the native's
attitude toward his ceremonies as well; and certain features of the
Vailala Madness serve to throw light on the growth of ritual as well
as legend. It might fairly be claimed that the offerings at the *ahea
uvi* and the receipt of heavenly messages at the flagpole had the

makings of genuine ritual; but it is the experiment of Maivake's Ghost that provides the best instance. Here the "bosses" of Vailala, and those of Arihava who were about to follow their example, had all the materials at hand for the creation of a new kind of masked ceremony, one which might have replaced the *Hevehe* and *Kovave* that they themselves had cast out. There may have been other doubters besides the man who unmasked the ghost, but there were certainly a great number who believed; and had the cult but lasted long enough to develop a more liberal policy, absorbing into its midst all who paid the necessary pig, then it might conceivably have become permanent. No doubt many similar experiments have failed in the past: the circumstances attending one such attempt, however, may throw a light upon those masked ceremonies which have had a more successful run.

If the present paper has any claim to interest it is because it deals with culture on the move. The Vailala Madness came as a violent shock to the societies of the Gulf Division, and the adjustments and reactions afford material for the study of culture in a state of unusually rapid metabolism. Incidentally we have been enabled to trace with some particularity the origin of a number of beliefs and of certain practices which might have become permanent. It may be idle to speculate upon origins in a static culture; but there are more than enough native societies undergoing change at the present day, and the study of these has, I believe, a special importance, for here if anywhere we shall have a chance of discovering how elements of culture begin and how they grow.

REFERENCES

(1. Reprinted from *Essays Presented to C. G. Seligman*, eds. E. E. Evans-Pritchard and others, London, Kegan Paul, Trench, Trubner and Co., 1934, pp. 369-79. E.S.)

2. "The Vailala Madness and the Destruction of Ceremonies in the Gulf Division" (*Anthropology*, Report No. 4), by F. E. Williams (Government Printer, Port Moresby, 1923).

3. On this matter see C. G. Seligman, "Temperament, Conflict, and Psychosis in a Stone-age Population", *British Journal of Medical Psychology*, vol. ix, 1929.

4. See *Vailala Madness*, pp. 352-3 above.

7

CREED OF A GOVERNMENT ANTHROPOLOGIST[1]

The application of anthropology has been much under discussion at recent meetings of this Section. 'To-day', as J. B. S. Haldane has said, 'science is important because it is applied, and it is only the applicable portions of science which are reasonably sure of survival'.[2] It is well, then, to try to convince ourselves, as well as others, that our particular science can have some importance and that it does possess some applicable portions. There is only one danger. Anthropology as a science is still young, and some of the materials which call for its application are fading away faster than it grows. There is therefore some need for haste, and the danger is that we may try to apply our science prematurely, to begin eating our pudding before it is really cooked to an applicable turn. In fact, I think this has already happened.

The present address embodies some of the views of one who is expected to be *ex officio* concerned with anthropology on its useful side. Government anthropologists (with the stress on the first word) are still unfortunately rare birds among that large genus of queer birds to which anthropologists in general are admitted to belong. And any government anthropologist may, by virtue of a more or less close touch with administration, develop a somewhat distinct point of view. It is that point of view, developed during nearly seventeen years of work and play in this capacity, which I shall endeavour to present to you.

But I must begin with three qualifications. In the first place I do not pretend that this paper is a fully-rounded exposition. It should have been called merely 'Some Views of a Government Anthropologist'. The incautious word 'creed', to be frank, was chosen simply because it makes a more effective title. Secondly, it is a personal statement. I do not presume to nail it on the head of any other government anthropologist. And thirdly, it is unofficial. In some particulars the views here expressed may be at variance with those of the government that employs me. But happily that government is not of the totalitarian variety; and, while it may not share all the opinions of a semi-technical adviser, it raises no objection to their publication, and even goes to the generous length of paying for it. One could certainly ask no more.

I

The Applicable Portion of Anthropology

The appointment of Government Anthropologist in Papua falls under the Native Taxation scheme. You are possibly familiar with that scheme's guiding principle. All the taxes gathered from the natives are paid into a Trust Fund which is kept strictly separate from general revenue; and this fund is expended solely on objects of native welfare. It is divided into an Education Fund and a Benefits Fund; and from the latter, which is devoted to purposes having for their object 'the direct benefit of the natives of Papua', are derived the salary and expenses of the Government Anthropologist. This for a start places that functionary in a somewhat embarrassing position. My worst enemies, I believe, are ready to concede that I am moderately conscientious; and such a person in such a situation must occasionaly be visited by qualms of doubt.

To begin with he must recognize that, of the many branches of study embraced under the pretentious name of anthropology, some may, or must, be dispensed with as beyond his scope—either because no one researcher can attempt to be encyclopaedic, or, more importantly, because such departments have no demonstrable usefulness.

Thus the whole branch of Physical Anthropology in the narrower, more conventional, sense may perhaps be lopped off his tree of knowledge or research. No one would deny that in the wider sense of human biology it may be of immense practical importance; but that is a field which anthropology, except theoretically perhaps, does not pretend to cover, and few practising anthropologists have had the training which would fit them to study it. In the narrower sense, however, despite the inexhaustible scope which a country like Papua provides, physical anthropology is, to say the least, of obscure value to its inhabitants. To be autobiographical, I have long since laid aside my callipers.

Then again there is the department of Prehistory, which has cast such a spell not only over its specialists but over the lay public. There is scope enough for this study also in Papua, with its stone implements and weapons, its buried pottery, its scattered megaliths and rock carvings, and its mysterious pestles and mortars. All these provide ample food for theory and speculation. But without going so far as to say that such theory and speculation are perfectly fruitless, I feel confident that they find no proper place under the Native Benefits Fund. The stone age in Papua simply crumbles at the touch of steel; and a new Sheffield hoe in the hand of a native gardener is to a government anthropologist at least as interesting as an adze of stone, and much more significant.

Thirdly, there is that branch of our science commonly known as Ethnology. Few countries can be more closely packed with opportunity for this study than is Papua, with its endless diversity of cultures. There is scope there for many anthropological lifetimes in the sorting out of identities, resemblances, and differences, in the investigation of development and diffusion, in the tracing of migrations, cultural and human, and in the game of historical reconstruction. But while recognizing (and I speak from experience) the fascination of such studies in general, one cannot but conclude that the data are too multiplex, too confusing, and too unreliable to permit of really safe conclusions. The most ambitious and seemingly important are liable to be pricked into collapse; and one cannot fail to be impressed by the irreconcilability of conclusions reached by independent and equally painstaking investigators in one and the same field. It might be—though I hardly imagine it is—some consolation to such investigators to reflect that, whatever the outcome of their search, right or wrong, sound or unsound, it does not in any practical sense really matter. This at any rate is true as far as the native is concerned and it will provide a government anthropologist with an excuse for considering that part of his work (if he obeys the temptation to go in for it) to be inessential.

Fourthly, I may mention the handmaid of ethnology, viz., Museum Collecting. This part of my duties (if it is such) I have performed in a manner which can at best be called perfunctory. One realizes the great importance of ethnological museums, not only for those who pursue ethnology as a science, but for the public to whose education they make a highly valuable contribution. But a government anthropologist may well feel that in this connection his first duty is towards the native artists and craftsmen who make the things which fill the museum cases; and it cannot be denied that in some instances collecting has done serious, even irreparable, harm to the art or craft in its living state. This is a theme I have elaborated elsewhere. It will be enough to say that my own sympathies are only secondarily with the museum. They are first and foremost with the encouragement, adaptation, and development of artistry and handwork in the native village. What is of real value is not the product, but the skill and the will.

These departments of study which I have enumerated are to a government anthropologist rather in the nature of side-lines. They may perhaps be his hobbies, encouraged or winked at by a generous employer; but they are not his real work. I fear this is a very blunt expression of my opinion. To pay such scant respect to the chosen provinces of perhaps a majority of this audience may seem a tactless beginning, and almost calls for apology. I may have trampled on some corns already; but even if privilege (as I am glad to think) denies you the opportunity of kicking out to-day, I hope your subjects will receive their due in subsequent discussions. As for the man in the street (who has his own idea of anthropology), we may well imagine him wondering, after such a list of disclaimers, whether anything is left at all. 'If you have no interest in skulls', he might exclaim, 'or in stone implements and potsherds, or in describing, discussing, and collecting fishhooks, jew's-harps, and the like, what in the name of Anthropology do you get your money for?'

Now some of you will perceive that up to this point I have been, following the earlier lines of the notable address given by Professor Radcliffe Brown before the British Association in 1931. And, as he has made sufficiently clear, there still remains a kind of anthropology which is of real importance in theory, and which, in its application is by far the most valuable of all. There remains in fact the study of cultures and societies as they exist at present, whether virtually unchanged or in process of changing.

It is well recognized that in this sphere the most productive method consists in the intensive study, lasting over long periods, of certain specimen societies; and it should be possible for the government anthropologist to pursue this method in just the same way as his unofficial colleagues. He may indeed be gratified by official requests for his opinion—they keep his pecker up while they consume his time—but his best, and in the end most useful, work will be done in the field, where there are no messenger boys and no ringing of telephones. And I should not miss this opportunity of recording my appreciation of the ideal conditions which the Papuan Government has provided for my own work.

An anthropologist's specific knowledge of one society should obviously be useful in dealing with specific problems within that society, and probably, by analogy, with similar problems in others. But his work may have a more general value as well; for he has contributed a specimen study towards that general science which Radcliffe Brown so aptly calls Comparative Sociology. It is from this science that its students hope to derive general conclusions regarding social relations in the abstract, or culture in the abstract. And these conclusions, since the question is essentially one of how human beings contrive to live successfully together, must be one of unsurpassed importance, not only in regard to the backward peoples, but in regard to the world at large. It is sufficiently obvious that anthropology, whatever its achievements hitherto, is at least striving after something of real consequence.

This modern method of anthropological research resolves itself into a patient and largely humdrum investigation. It is not, we may be thankful, without its high-lights and its juicy morsels; but (Professor Malinowski has used some such words) it is no longer devoted expressly to the discovery and recording of the quaint, amusing, obscene, and bloodthirsty. It was just this preoccupation which condemned anthropologists in public estimation to appear slightly more ridiculous than, say, geologists. The work of the modern school may perhaps dispel that atmosphere. It is somewhat drier work, but much more serious; for it studies the given society in every aspect of its relations, in the endeavour to see it in the round or through and through, as far as such a penetrating or pervasive view is possible. In this way subjects like kinship and economics, which at first might seem dry fare indeed, become essential and, with skilful treatment, even attractive courses in a meal that never ends.

It is primarily to the Functional school that we owe this revolutionary advance in method; and it is this improved method which affords the best promise of application. Indeed, if any kind of anthropology can claim to be of practical use, it is this which we call the functional; for its subject of study is just what we have recognized as our real problem, viz. how people, whether black or white or black-*cum*-white, contrive to live together in society.

Now it so happens, for whatever reason, that I do not, as far as I can discover, belong to any modern 'school' of anthropological thought. Such independence or isolation, while I have at times found myself regretting it, has at any rate some advantages. Not the least among them is that it absolves one from any sense of loyalty—and loyalty in the intellectual sphere is plainly no virtue, but the worst of vices. If, then, I venture to criticize the functional school in respect of its primary postulate, I can do so with a pleasant sense of freedom. What I shall say may be deemed unorthodox, because functionalism holds the field. It may even be deemed presumptuous, because of the great eminence of that school's principal exponents. But it cannot be disloyal, because I have never owed the school any allegiance.

To proceed, then: while readily acknowledging the great debt of anthropology, and particularly applied anthropology, to functionalism, I feel prepared to accept that discipline in only a restricted degree. The prime postulate of functionalism lies in the conception of social or cultural integration. To quote Radcliffe Brown: 'The newer social anthropology looks at any culture as an integrated system, and studies the functions of social institutions, customs and beliefs of all kinds as parts of such a system'[3]; and Malinowski:

'The functional view of culture insists therefore upon the principle that in every type of civilization, every custom, material object, idea and belief fulfils some vital function, has some task to accomplish, represents an indispensable part within a working whole'.[4] These quotations could be amplified by many others from the pupils of these distinguished leaders. What they have in common, to repeat, is the conception of culture as an 'integrated system' or a 'working whole'.

Now, when it comes to the application of anthropology, there is undoubtedly discernible in the work of many functionalists a tendency to champion existing primitive customs against interference by Europeans. The rationale of this attitude is expressed in a moderate utterance of Professor Malinowski: 'The functional method, by showing what a culture does for a primitive community, establishes its value and thus utters a warning against too hasty interference with native belief and institutions'.[5] But elsewhere in the literature of functionalism we find evidence of a much more uncompromising attitude. It is as if the writers in question felt some sentimental bias in favour of the old against the new; for they are prone to rise in indignation if anyone ventures to condemn some feature of primitive life—sorcery, for instance—while on the other hand they may sometimes be heard to speak of things as they find them with praise and admiration. Surely, if it is unscientific to condemn, it is also unscientific to praise; each is an offence, whether conscious or unconscious, against the stern rule of objectivity. It is as if these writers adopted the assumption that 'all things work together for good' in primitive culture; and so deep and engrossing has been their study of it that it appears to have risen in their estimation to the status of an end in itself. Thus culture comes to be invested with a kind of sacrosanctity; and in its extreme form this view or attitude would seem to forbid all positive interference in the name of good government or philanthropy.

To a government anthropologist this conclusion will seem so drastic as to suggest the possibility of a fallacy somewhere in the premises; and the greater part of this address will be devoted to an endeavour to show that there is one.

II

The Question of Cultural Integration

The ultimate aim of social or cultural anthropology in its modern form is, as we have seen, to discover social laws, or more generally to reach a progressively truer conception of the nature of culture itself. That word, as necessary to anthropologists as it is sometimes irritating to outsiders, may be defined provisionally as 'the "system" of beliefs, customs, techniques, sentiments and values, which certain people hold more or less in common, being thereby enabled to live as a society in the broadest sense of that term'.

This is obviously a hazy conception, one to which it is impossible to set clear boundaries. Not only may one culture fade imperceptibly into another, but within itself it is riddled with diversity, as between the major groupings, the minor groupings, and the very individuals to whom it belongs, or who belong to it. These considerations for a start suggest that the systematism of culture may have been exaggerated. And it is this exaggeration, I shall contend, which represents the fallacy in the functional premises.

Seventeen years of experience have in fact made me more and more dubious regarding this fundamental claim that cultures are integrated systems. In 1922, when the flags of the functional method were first unfurling themselves, I emerged from my training with the new idea (amongst others) duly implanted in my mind. Almost my first work was among the Elema people of the Gulf of Papua (a district where I have since done further periods in a much more intensive style), and almost my first publication was a pamphlet called *The Vailala Madness*. At that time (1923) I was grievously alarmed at the threatened extinction of certain native ceremonies. It still seems that the continuance of these ceremonies is threatened, a situation which one does not cease to regret, though it is possible now to view it with more philosophy. But what I wish to mention is the subsequent modification of the views I then formed (or perhaps accepted) regarding both Elema culture and culture at large. In 1923 I wrote that 'You cannot delete any part of the social life of a primitive people and leave the other parts unaffected'; and, more graphically, 'You have only to remove one wheel to stop the watch, or one stone from the social structure to have it tumbling about your ears.'[6]

The first of these two statements I should not quarrel with to-day. But the second, which might have been written by the most zealous disciple of functionalism, I would, if I could, disown. For in the light of subsequent events and subsequent reflection I think those words represent a wholly exaggerated view and a false prophecy. I cannot now regard Elema culture, or any other, as a thing so easily wrecked or brought to a stop by interference or by the loss of any of its parts. And I have come round to my present more moderate view partly as a result of a much deeper study of the Elema themselves and their ceremonies than was possible when I uttered those premature opinions.[7]

The principal ceremonies are those of the *Hevehe*, or *Sevese*, cult, and resolve themselves into a tremendous cycle which continues, on and off, for anything between five and twenty-five years. They surround certain gigantic masks which come, ostensibly from the sea, to the men's house in rudimentary form. There they remain throughout this long period, being gradually built up, until at the end of it they descend for a month of brilliant masquerade. Then, their dancing over, they are destroyed and their spirits return to their element, eventually to be summoned again when the whole cycle recommences.

Owing to the fact that various independent cycles are in progress, each at a different stage, in various men's houses, it is possible to piece the episodes together and see this remarkable cycle in its sequence and as a whole. But close examination of the cycle has convinced me that it is a composite one; that certain parts of it, by no means unimportant in themselves, are interpolations; that they are inessential to the general scheme; that they merely adhere. In short I see in the *Hevehe* cycle partly a system, and partly a haphazard agglomeration. Parts of it could be dropped; and in fact in different performances parts of it are dropped. It is at best a semi-integrated system.

Now from the *Hevehe* cycle as part of Elema culture I think it is possible to argue (if only by analogy) to Elema culture as a whole. And here I think I see sufficient evidence that the larger whole also is only partly integrated. I have indeed seen junks of it disappear in the course of the last fifteen years, and this without the effects which on the functional hypothesis might be expected to follow. Witness the imposing and once universally practised custom of secluding youths. It has now virtually dropped out of existence, even in those communities which set their faces against change most firmly and which still carry the great *Hevehe* cycle through from end to end.

This, of course, is not a situation which need sting anyone into a fury, least of all a properly cold-hearted anthropologist. It is merely a phenomenon which demands our attention. It goes without saying that such a disappearance has its due causes, though I cannot enter into them here; and needless to say it cannot be without some effects All I wish to say is that those effects on the totality of the culture seem remarkably small, if not negligible. Considering its dimensions as an institution the effects of the disappearance of seclusion seem much smaller than a functionalist interpretation would have led us to expect. My own explanation is that this institution is not deeply impacted in the general mass of the culture; it is one of those features bulky, imposing, intrinsically important as they may be, which can be deleted without creating any but a slight disturbance. Just like the *Hevehe* cycle, therefore, which is only a portion or feature of it, so Elema culture as a whole is no more than semi-integrated or partially systematized. It remains in part a haphazard agglomeration.

Now having gone from an institution to a culture, I shall carry the argument a stage further and—ambitiously indeed—essay to speak of culture in the abstract.

While anthropology is discovering, or at any rate seeking, the general laws of culture, it is at liberty to form a provisional picture of the whole thing. And since it is recognized to be *sui generis*, these pictures (for quite a number have been hung before us) must take the form of analogies. Thus, for example, we hear of structures or frameworks: 'The material economy is dovetailed into the framework of the whole social structure' (a phrase of Dr. Firth's)[8]; or again of mechanisms or machines: 'Culture is merely a very complicated piece of machinery. All the different parts of the mechanism interlock and have to work together, or the machinery is of no use' (Driberg)[9] (and I might have quoted again my own similes of the watch and the building in ruins). These are, of course, analogies, and we need not do their authors the injustice of taking them too literally. But they nevertheless imply an over-stressing of the systematism of culture which I think amounts to error, even serious error.

And the same may be said of that other familiar analogy, though it comes nearer the mark, viz. of the organism: 'Every custom and belief of a primitive society plays some determinate part in the social life of the community, just as every organ of a living body plays some part in the general life of the organism' (Radcliffe Brown).[10] Although so explicitly stated this also is only an analogy and presumably should not be pressed too far. I would submit the opinion, however, that the degree of integration revealed by any organism is wholly beyond that achieved by any culture.

I shall now go on to suggest an analogy or simile of my own which goes to the opposite extreme. It amounts to gross exaggeration and is intended to be provocative, so that I am almost nervous of making it public. But I shall compare culture to the heap of rubbish in the corner of your back yard. This, I can well imagine, verges on blasphemy. Let me hasten to explain.

It is a familiar experience in our own modern world that action or change in one sphere, e.g., of politics or economics, may have wide, unforeseen, and sometimes disastrous results in other spheres. That it must have some effects is of course elementary. If we drop a pin in this room the reverberations of that tiny impact should, in theory at any rate, reach the antipodes. Similarly, if we disturb one part of a culture, however insignificant, it may be admitted that we disturb the whole. But it does not follow from this that the culture is a fully integrated whole or system. Similar effects might be observed in our pile of rubbish. Poke it with a stick, add or remove one empty jam-tin, and, however slight the change, you have affected the whole mass, through and through. Remove, let us say from its midst, a thing so great as an empty kerosene-tin, and you may create a disturbance of almost volcanic proportions. Yet this is no system. The figure is deliberately chosen to represent the opposite.

Our scandalous simile, however, is meant merely as a counterblast. I do not for one moment suggest that culture is devoid of system. My point is that it is only in part a system. It always remains to some extent a hotch-potch and a sorry tangle.

If one had to bring forward a more serious analogy one might compare culture to a human mind or personality. This is not to resuscitate the notion of a group-mind. It is merely a comparison, with special regard to the respective degrees of organization in the two things compared. Each has its gradations. Some cultures, like some minds, are organized to a relatively high degree; some on the other hand to a notably less degree. And just as a mind may harbour inconsistent beliefs, division of loyalties, emotional conflicts, etc., and yet contrive to function with reasonable or average success, so may a culture contrive to function even though it be far from fully organized.

I would submit, however, that the integration of a culture is of lower degree than the integration of an ordinary mind. And how could it be otherwise? The individual's mind is the product of a few paltry years of limited experience acting upon a quantum of inherited physical material. The culture in which he lives (and of which, indeed, he probably assimilates only a fraction) is a vague accumulation of factors contributed by countless minds in the past and present, the product of an age-long history of chance.

This analogy with the individual mind might be pushed a good deal further; but I will leave it and give you yet another—and here, I think, we draw close to a real comparison. Every human establishment—for specific example let us take an individual's house and property—is a culture in little, a culture microcosm. It is sufficiently obvious that some households are well, others ill, and none completely organized. And yet in all cases (or at least we hope so) there is some definite attempt at organization—a more rational purposive attempt than has ever been possible in the case of culture at large. If then, there is any lack of organization in household, department-store, battalion, or whatever you please, how much greater that lack is likely to be in a whole culture which to a large extent has just happened to be what it is.

Much hinges upon our interpretation of those often intrinsically unimportant things called 'survivals'. The functionalist, one understands, simply does not recognize them as such: when they cease to fulfil some function they cease to exist. Now I have a friend of some eminence in the legal profession and of undoubted domestic virtue who agrees with me (and no doubt with you) that many of us accumulate too much property. And when it comes to occasional house-cleanings he is confronted by certain domestic survivals which he calls by the name—it is one which might even find a place in our own scientific vocabulary—of *tooglies*. He does not cast them out, either because they are endeared by some association, or because they might come in handy some day, or because it would be too much trouble to get rid of them, or simply because they have been there so long that they might as well stay. I cannot help thinking that culture at large, like our own houses, is full of tooglies; in fact that it is more or less clogged by an accumulation of the superfluous, or what might be called cultural junk. (If we chose to recall the culture-mind analogy we could speak of them as miner cultural habits, habits which we still retain though they have outlasted their original significance.) All such things are undoubtedly parts of the culture as a mass, but it is surely another thing to say they are parts of a system.

The view I have expressed is intended to apply to every kind of culture, having regard to the fact (I think it obviously such) that some are better organized than others. It is true that Radcliffe Brown states explicitly that 'Occasionally the unity of a culture may be seriously disturbed by the impact of some very different culture, and so may perhaps even be destroyed or replaced'; and he observes that 'such disorganised cultures are very common at the present day all over the world'.[11] This would seem to be all too true, and not least of our own. But the lack of organization of which I speak is, as I see it, in greater or less degree inherent in every culture even those which seem to be in a relatively stable condition. The complete unity or systematism which functionalism postulates could belong only to society in some ideal world.

III

Culture Measured by Value Standards

So far I have endeavoured to consider the material of this discussion, viz. human culture, in an objective manner—as it i., or as it seems to be. But I should find it extremely difficult to pursue my work as a government anthropologist without also adopting from time to time that other method of viewing it, viz. as it should be, or as one thinks it should be. The government anthropologist, by reason of his contact with official colleagues and superiors who have on their hands the responsibilities of good government, as well as with those others who have at heart the cause of native welfare, is perhaps more liable than other anthropologists to develop and use this point of view, i.e. to think in terms of ends and values. One of the fairest of my fellow-workers—and I mean fairest in the gallant rather than the judicial sense—once accused me of showing an 'administrative streak'. It would be difficult indeed for any government anthropologist not to acquire one. He is almost inevitably a Jekyll and a Hyde. On the one hand he should be an objective observer. But on the other he may, I maintain, be a critic and even—if he is built that way—a reformer. I do not know in which capacity he is the Hyde and which the Jekyll; but all we need demand of him is that he should be able at will to keep his two personalities separate.

Nevertheless, when it comes to social problems, it is impossible to *solve* them in any practical way without appeal to ethics. As Professor Ginsberg has recently said, the social problems of deepest interest are 'just those in which questions of value and questions of fact are closely interwoven' [12]; and their effective handling involves, not indeed a fusion, but a synthesis of social science and social philosophy.[13]

I would now invite you, therefore, to look at human culture, particularly at the advanced culture to which we ourselves belong, with the eye of criticism. Is it not possible to see in its vast, baffling complexity some *confusion* as well as system? I use this word with emphasis. If we study a highly involved subject in which to common sense there is apparent confusion, must we say that the confusion is unreal, only showing the limitations of our understanding; that it is all really system, however complicated, and that a deep enough study would reveal it as such? Or may we say that the confusion actually exists? If we grant that there is any such thing as confusion anywhere, then I would submit that by every standard of order and efficiency we find it present, in greater or less degree, in every existent human culture—from the sorry social mess in which we, the civilized, find ourselves at present down to the relatively simple and static cultures which we mostly study as anthropologists.

It seems *a priori* inevitable. For, if I may be permitted to repeat myself, culture is a man-made thing, and, even at that, has had but little rational control or purposive selection. It is the product of innumerable minds, subject to innumerable chances. Things which have been shot together have somehow got stuck together. The utmost that could be expected, therefore, is some approximation to a system; and the most highly organized of cultures does no more than bungle through.

I trust this part of my address has not appeared in the light of destructive criticism only. If my point is sound, then we shall have a truer, if a less clear and artistically satisfying, picture of culture in the abstract, the thing with which as social anthropologists we are ultimately concerned; and furthermore we shall have done something to clear the way for the positive action which I believe administration is sometimes called upon to take.

After arguing the matter at such length I should be mildly content to amend our provisional definition of culture by calling in an 'approximation to a system'. Or perhaps it would meet the case to dispense with the word 'system' and speak of a 'complex', if this can convey the idea of a vast complexity of factors which is by no means devoid of system on the one hand, or of confusion and entanglement on the other.[14] As for the fallacy which, it seems to me, exists in the premises of functionalism, it is a fallacy of overstatement. The integration of culture is not a principle but merely a good idea which has been ridden too hard.

Now I am not concerned here to attack any of the specific conclusions to which, I think, the over-stressing of cultural integration has led, e.g., in the realm of primitive law, or even kinship. What I would take exception to is rather the general attitude (already referred to) which some at any rate of the functionalists have adopted when it comes to the application of anthropology. In the conservation or protection of primitive culture their work has been inestimable; for, to repeat the words of Professor Malinowski, they have 'established its value', and they have made and are making what is up to the present the most important of all contributions to applied anthropology by showing how it 'works'. But, assuming that the point of view I have expounded has something in it, I suggest they might now spend some time, and not less profitably, in discovering to what extent cultures do not work, or to what extent they work badly.

IV

Anthropology and Trusteeship

I shall now attempt to discuss—though still, I fear, in abstract terms—how anthropology may be applied in a somewhat more positive manner. We may presumably dispense with the idea of culture as something to be preserved for its own sake. I have sought to show that it is at best only partially organized; and if this be granted it would seem to follow that it is in some degree inefficient. And we may go further. It is also laden with unhappiness no less than with happiness. For if man is born to sorrow it is largely sorrow of his own making, and he is far from being solely responsible as an individual. Many at least of his sorrows are prepared for him by the culture into which he is born; he is condemned thereby to some suffering, and the luckiest of the lucky will not escape entirely. And I should go further still. Culture is plainly a thing which has nowhere reached its potential limits of development. Some, notably those which we study as anthropologists, are more backward, more restricted, than others. It is notorious that within our own society there are individuals who do not get their fair chance; but, more than this, there are whole societies which have not had their chance. As I see it, then, the best of cultures is not devoid of muddlement; it carries the seeds of unhappiness; and it is only the embryo of what it might be.

Now according to the modern notion of trusteeship it is the duty of the administrator, as it has long been the self-appointed duty of the missionary, to try to improve things. In view of the extreme difficulty and danger of deciding for other people what is good for them, it is a duty which we trust they will always face with proper humility; but it is one which they are not likely to shirk. It becomes necessary for anthropologists, therefore, to recognize this obligation on the part of others even if they decline to participate in it themselves. As for a government anthropologist, he might even be expected as part of his duty to participate. At any rate I think he would make himself more useful if, besides observing and recording things merely as they are, he could also, in his other character, consider them with respect to their value. He might even feel called upon to set things right himself, though I feel sure he would approach that task with all the reluctance of Hamlet. But fortunately for everyone, perhaps, the actual responsibility is not his. His advice may be taken or left.

Assuming, however, the practical necessity for judgments of value, I should begin by declaring an article of faith, viz. that in the application of anthropology, as in any other phase of social work, the primary, indefeasible values are those of the individual human personality. To the administrator, trustee for their welfare, the human animals under his care, both European and native, represent the end; their various cultures are merely means, good, bad, or indifferent, for the satisfaction of their needs and the expression of their potentialities.

This, which seems to me a fundamental postulate, provides him with his charter. For cultures, obviously imperfect and changeable things, are no more than the best means evolved hitherto by the societies to which they belong; and there can be no denying that they stand in need of tidying-up, purging, reconciling, blending, and developing. To this task, tremendous both in difficulty and responsibility, the administrator and the missionary are already actually addressing themselves. The extent to which their interference is justifiable is certainly debatable, and to that point I shall return. But it falls in with the view I am trying to expound that they have some right at least, indeed that some interference amounts to a necessity. And, whether this be so or not, the policy of interference has come without doubt to stay, so that the anthropologist, even if he disapproves, might bow gracefully to the inevitable and do his best service by criticism, constructive as well as destructive, of its methods.

I have elsewhere stated[15] what seem to me the three general tasks of native education in the broadest sense of that word—which might indeed be taken to embrace all the essentials of a native policy. They are the tasks of Maintenance, Expurgation, and Expansion—not perfectly suitable words, but the best I could think of. I shall go over these briefly and in the reverse order.

First, then, regarding Expansion, by which I mean the enrichment of a culture both by development and by the introduction of new factors. There are, of course, arguments against the introduction of new things—so-called gifts of Western civilization—or at least cautions to be observed. For they may do more harm than good. But I am bound to think that it is the duty of the educator, and through him of the administrator, to give the native a chance of fuller development than has hitherto been possible for him. To take literacy for a concrete example, I cannot think the arguments against it, though they may dictate caution, can absolve us from the responsibility of giving it ultimately to the native as his right. And there are many possible advances in the spheres of economics, politics, art, and religion towards which we might assist him. I would dare say of morality also, except for its suggestion of the pot and the kettle and the fear that anthropologists might think I was thrusting this unfamiliar burden on them. Ideally speaking, however, it is the anthropologist, provided he will deign to think sometimes in terms of value, who is best qualified both to criticize and to suggest the ways and means of adding to an existent primitive culture; for not only should he be the best judge of what is suitable and assimilable, but he should be best aware of the shortcomings of the culture as it stands.

Now for the more ticklish and contentious subject of Expurgation.

Allow me first to point out that the theory of culture as a semi-integrated, imperfect whole will allow for the process of expurgation (as well as expansion) in a way that seems hardly possible if we postulate a full, or even a very high, degree of integration. Experience surely shows that cultures possess a good deal of plasticity; that they possess the power to change, to slough or forget old things on the one hand, and to absorb or find room for new things on the other. It is only necessary to give due heed to the warnings which the functionalists have uttered regarding the danger of disruption, the upsetting of balance, and so on, without going so far as to admit such perfection of balance or integration as would seem to make any interference a disaster. For culture as I now see it is the kind of watch that does not necessarily stop for the removal of a reasonably small wheel, but may on the contrary go all the better.

It is true that some things are so deeply embedded and possess so many ramifications that they may justly be called 'indispensable' or 'vital'. And here, unless adequate substitutes can be provided, our interference is likely to bring about serious dislocation—a prospect which should certainly give us pause. But I cannot concede the functionalist plea that everything is vital. There are many things for which no such claim can be made and which would probably be better away. When we seek to eliminate them we may perhaps trust to the adaptive or recuperative powers of the culture to enable it to heal over the breach and survive, when it will be all the better for the change.

While I believe it justifiable to eliminate some things from the primitive cultures that lie, so to speak, at our mercy, I should not dream of suggesting that we should do so merely because they 'outraged civilised notions of propriety'. That common argument is itself an outrage on propriety. But there may be good reasons of other kinds. Our much wider experience and scientific knowledge may enable us to see defects which remain hidden from the native himself. It may be something that hinders the satisfactory living-together of black man and white man which we have to aim at and which certainly requires some adjustment on both sides—for it must be remembered that the white man also has his rights in applied anthropology. But what concerns us more obviously are the defects within the bounds of the primitive culture itself. A time-honoured but mistaken method of agriculture or stock-raising, for example, may be eating into a community's resources; an equally time-honoured method of sanitation may be a danger to its health. Such things are fit subjects for expurgation.

In these cases, however, it is the whole community that suffers through its own age-long mistake embodied in its culture; and I want to draw your attention to a sort of defect that may not be quite so obvious. I have declared my own belief in the primary rights of the human personality, and I think accordingly that wherever we detect the existence of abuse, injustice, exploitation, repression, pain, and suffering—in short, the victimization of the individual by the society—then once more we are called upon to interfere. I should say from my own observations that sorcery (to use a somewhat threadbare subject for illustration) despite its functional connections is responsible for much more harm than good. It is the prime source of suspicion, fear, dissension, and strife—things which seem the very negation of satisfactory living-together and which undoubtedly entail unhappiness. I think we are called upon to remove this form of victimization by the best means in our power.

Similarly with head-hunting, by way of a more extreme and equally hackneyed example. A good defence on functional lines can be made out for this also; no one will deny that it may play a highly important part in a general way of living on the Middle Fly.[16] But, to adopt the individual's rights as a criterion, what of those unfortunates who play the less desirable part of the two roles necessary to a head-hunting scene? Can any more drastic infringement of a man's rights be conceived than to fall on him in his sleep and cut off his head?

Whether, then, in the interests of the whole community or of certain individuals within it, I am bound to think that some interference may be justified. And if it is I should regard it as good service on the part of anthropologists in general, and even as the duty of government anthropologists, to lend their aid. For once again they are in a very favourable position to detect abuses. While it is happily beyond their scope to perform cultural excisions or amputations, they should not hesitate to recommend them where they think fit; for they, in theory at least, are the best qualified not only to diagnose the complaint but to judge whether the general constitution of the patient will stand an operation.

Thirdly, we come to the task of Maintenance. In this anthropologists have always willingly lent their assistance, and the primitive peoples of the world, if they realized it, might perhaps be grateful to those field-workers who must so insufferably have bored them. In fact I repeat that this providing of argument for maintaining existent cultures has been the greatest contribution hitherto made by applied anthropology. And incidentally I think it the best general result of a training in our science that it should broaden the student's mind, teaching him liberality and tolerance, so that he realizes there are other ways than our own, possibly as good and possibly better.

The anthropologist's tendency to cherish the old cultures is so common and so strong that one suspects, as I have mentioned already, a sentimental bias in their favour—for anthropologists are seldom so cold-hearted as they would like to be. I do not imagine that I am wholly free from this bias myself. But there are some very good reasons for maintenance other than sentimental ones.

In the first place there is the general argument of the functionalist that culture represents a working whole in which interference may bring about stoppage or dislocation. One may appreciate the value of this argument without following it to a logical extreme.

The second reason lies in the intrinsic merits of backward cultures as we find them. Those researchers who have cut themselves off from their own world for long periods and immersed themselves in the strangely different world of the so-called primitives always, I believe, find much therein that is truly admirable. They admire it more than do outsiders for the simple reason that they know it better; and they are not necessarily cranks for doing so. Further than this, the sharp comparison which all are able to make between Western civilization and primitive culture is not in the eyes of anthropologists, who see both sides, so unquestionably favourable to the former. In short, primitive cultures may seem worthy of preservation, as far as may be, for their own sakes.

V

Cultural Self-Determination

But there is still another reason for preserving them—or, to put it more cautiously, for letting them be—and this brings me to my final point, in which perhaps we step right out of the accepted sphere of anthropology as a science.

We may in wisdom or in arrogance believe that the native and his culture stand in need of reform. But let us never forget that he is himself and his culture is his own. The very fact that we may feel bound to provide scope for a fuller development of the native's personality should imply, one presumes, a genuine respect for that personality. And this means first and foremost a recognition of his right to freedom. By this, of course, I mean nothing so crudely obvious as the denial of slavery. I mean the right to live as he himself thinks good; and this implies also the right of a primitive society as such to enjoy its own culture.

I can conjure up only two justifications for repressive or destructive interference. One is that the culture itself contains abuses which stifle or frustrate the human personality. The other is that in its wider relations it may infringe the rights of others, whether native or European, with whose interests it must be reconciled. Granted, however, that liberty of individual or group must stop short of making itself a nuisance to others, it remains a principle which we choose to regard as sacred. If this is really so, then the native's liberty is no less sacred than our own. He also should have that right, which we prize so highly, of self-determination.

It is mainly on these ethical grounds that I would protest against any definite policy of moulding the native after our own pattern. This policy is sometimes justified on the assumption that we are all moving in the direction of a single united world civilization, to which is added the further tacit assumption that our civilization will provide its model. Even if this be the case I cannot see how it is compatible with the principle of freedom to set about deliberately working for conformity—though to be sure, if the native chooses in the long run to copy our model, then we shall all no doubt be satisfied. There may, however, be quite a different and perhaps more satisfactory future in store for us, viz. one of unity in diversity; and if the vast native populations of the world choose to remain something very different from us it is doubtful whether we should question their right—as it is wholly doubtful whether we should question their taste.

Nevertheless there is a widespread campaign, explicit or inexplicit, direct or indirect, to do away with the native's old way of life and substitute our own. Needless to say it may be motivated by good intentions, even by altruism. But it often appears that the native may have but little say in his own future; for though coercion may be absent, he is nevertheless carried helplessly along with the tide of propaganda and suggestion. In so far as the choice lies between the two extremes of remaining as he is or becoming Europeanized I think that, under certain conditions at present in existence, he is bound to veer strongly towards the latter because the two alternatives are not placed before him fairly.

Let us for a moment try the boots on our own feet and see how we should like to wear them. It is a fact unquestioned that we are deeply and strongly attached to the institutions of our own culture, e.g., private ownership, democracy, and individual liberty. Each one of these institutions or ideals is now subject to attack by rival systems to whose propagandists we should be unjust if we denied their true missionary zeal. Thus we find Fascist on one side and Communist on the other both pouring scorn on the outworn system of democracy.

It is happily unnecessary to declare one's personal opinions upon any of these rival systems, though it seems obvious that our present civilization is so far from being a satisfactorily working whole as to demand some fundamental readjustments. Whatever these may be, however, it is certain that we shall fight hard against any interference with the system we are used to.

I ask you now to imagine hypothetically a band of missionaries, whether Fascist or Communist, in our midst. They are armed with overpowering influence and prestige; and they have sole control of the weapons of education and propaganda. Picture our initial resentment and indignation, but recognize that these in due course would die down; that certain of our cherished ideals would disappear; and that our children would eventually embrace the new order with open arms, convinced that it was their free choice to do so. This hypothetical parallel may throw some light on the justice of similar methods in so far as they involve the displacement of primitive cultures.

The Devil may quote Scripture to his purpose, and I give you another parallel. I recently listened to a sermon on the following text: 'Be watchful, and strengthen the things which remain, that you are ready to die'. It was taken from St. John's inspired admonition to the church in Sardis, and the preacher succeeded in giving this somewhat obscure utterance a plausible interpretation. The Church, which had forgotten the essentials of the Christian faith, was to hold fast, pending its rejuvenation, to the superficialities, the mere rites, material emblems, and so forth, which had their value and which were themselves threatened with extinction. An inattentive anthropologist might well reflect that this advice was applicable in a wider sphere. Nearly 2,000 years have passed since the shrewd apostle wrote those words; and by now, in some widely represented opinions, the essentials of Christian faith have themselves become superficialities, trimmings on the face of civilization—something which it might, if it wished, cast off. Indeed revolution in one country and another is at this moment engaged in casting it off.

Once again it is happily unnecessary to declare one's own opinion as to whether a changing civilization could fittingly dispense with the Christian faith; though I would go so far as to assume that that faith has no divine protection to ensure its continuance. That, or its decay and extinction, must depend solely on the present and future generations of humanity; and one may prophesy a long struggle between those who are for it and those who, with perhaps equal sincerity, are against it.

Its vast importance, historically and now, both in our civilization and those of other so-called Christian nations, goes without saying. Nor need I draw attention to the place it holds in the people's affections and all their conservative sentiments. Its maintenance or otherwise is therefore a burning question of applied anthropology—though somewhat bigger than we are accustomed to tackle—and a functionalist from Mars could hardly do other than echo the apostle's words, 'Strengthen the things which remain'. Whatever their religion or lack of it, that is a policy which most anthropologists, if they could transfer their spirit of championship from primitive cultures to advanced civilization, might feel bound to endorse.

But let us imagine once again a situation in which the enemies of Christianity were politically dominant and in absolute control of education and propaganda. They would possibly succeed in blotting Christian belief out of the people's mind; and strange to say the generation which saw it disappear would believe that they had freely willed its disappearance.

Now this would be cultural displacement; it would at least create a serious void; it would be the end of a great human achievement for which no one, whatever his beliefs, would deny admiration; and—which is my point—it would be a denial of self-determination. The ordinary citizen, so strong a champion of his own institutions, might therefore, if he could change places in imagination, question the methods which are sometimes brought to bear against the weaker, more defenceless, cultures of the backward peoples.

All our positive efforts for the welfare of native peoples, therefore, have to reckon with this right to personal freedom and self-determination. I do not think it is a solid wall against which they must all dash themselves to pieces. I believe on the other hand that our scientific knowledge and our wider experience of social rights and obligations should qualify us to help, advise, and perhaps to guide; though the very experience which gives us such an advantage should have taught us how hard it is to know what is good for ourselves, and how more than hard to know what is good for others.

Freedom, the right to think for ourselves and to do what seems good to us, we regard as the highest prize of our civilization. But the possession of it, as we know too well, is insecure: it depends on two complementary factors. On one hand, as we are told, the price of freedom is eternal vigilance; and no one deserves to keep it who has not the courage to fight for it. On the other hand, it can only live by tolerance; and this, in the present connection, is plainly the aspect which we have to consider. The limits which we impose on native liberties are not to be dictated by our own arbitrary sense of propriety, but by consideration for the rights, in fact the liberties, of others, whether individuals or societies. While, then, we undertake the high-sounding obligations of trusteeship, we should impose those limits with a hand as light as it is firm, recognizing that the native's way of living is his own, that he is much devoted to it, and that, if it does nobody any harm, he has a right to it.

If, as I suggested earlier, the native chooses in the long run to conform to our pattern, we should of course be prepared to abide by his choice. It seems wholly probable that he will conform to greater or less extent; and while it would be unfair to lead him deliberately away from a path that might suit him better. I think we should not deny him the opportunity of conforming. Our course then—and it seems to me the most vital part of a native policy—is to educate him. And by education I mean far more than is meant by the word in popular currency; in fact the sort of liberal education which relates itself both to the new things of Western civilization and to the existent things of his native condition. It would well become the anthropologist to co-operate with the educator in formulating the ideal methods which would make, not for any specific type of our own choosing, but rather for straight and independent thinking, critical appreciation, and, in the spheres of action and conduct, vigour, efficiency, and consideration for others. However distant and idealistic these may sound, it is only as the native advances along the path towards them that he will become fit, or indeed able, to choose his future for himself.

Should anyone ask, 'What are you aiming at? What are you trying to make of the native?' I think the only proper way to answer this at-first-staggering question is to side-step it. Our purpose need be no more than to give him, by education and by respect for his rights, a chance to make something of himself. Provided he plays the game by respecting others' right, then he can make of himself just what he pleases.

It may seem as if what was said in the earlier parts of this address has been unsaid in the last. But I do not think this is the case. I was at pains to show that things may be far from right in any primitive culture. It needs no pains to show that they are far from right in the world at large. Administrators engage in a bigger field of operations than, as a rule, do anthropologists; they have a wider variety of factors to consider than may occur to us: they recognize that the native problem is only part of a larger one; and they are pledged to the everlasting, if not hopeless, task of reconciling rights. While, then, we might be only too glad to let the native go his own way, it is not wholly possible. His way of life must somehow enter into relation with the affairs of the world. It is to be hoped that we may leave him his fair share of freedom; but to leave him entirely to himself would be to funk the issue and neglect our duty.

REFERENCES

(1. Reprinted from the Report of the Australian and New Zealand Association for the Advancement of Science, Canberra Meeting, January 1939, Vol XXIV: 145-59. The paper was originally presented as a Presidential Address to Section F, Anthropology, at that Meeting. E.S.)

2. Haldane 1937, page 66.
3. Radcliffe Brown 1931, page 154.
4. Malinowski 1926b, page 133.
5. Malinowski, ibid.
6. F. E. Williams, *The Vailala Madness*. (Reprinted as Chapter 5 of the present volume; the passage quoted here appears on page 380. E.S.)
7. (The evidence to which Williams refers is presented partly in his *Drama of Orokolo*, 1940, partly in three papers reprinted as chapters 1, 2 and 6 of the present volume. E. S.)
8. Firth 1929, page 27.
9. Driberg 1932, page 14.
10. Radcliffe Brown 1922, page 229.
11. Radcliffe Brown 1931, page 158.
12. Ginsberg 1937, page 322.
13. Ginsberg 1937, page 328.
14. *Involved* and the somewhat unusual abstract noun *involution* might be made to convey the required meaning.
15. Williams 1935, *The Blending of Cultures*.
16. (The reference is to Wedgwood 1930. For a full discussion, see Williams, *Papuans of the Trans-Fly*, 1936, Chapter XV. E.S.)

F. E. WILLIAMS' ACCOUNT OF HIS STUDY IN EUROPE

In the academic year 1933-4 Williams undertook a study tour, supported by a Rockefeller Fellowship. On his return he wrote an account of the tour. It was published in the Annual Report of the Administrator of the Territory of Papua for 1933-4 (Murray 1935, pages 8 and 9). We reprint it here, to make up to some extent for the rarity of the available biographical data.

The Rockefeller Fellowships are granted to certain accredited workers in (1) the Natural Sciences, (2) Medical Sciences, (3) Social Sciences, and (4) the Humanities. Anthropology comes under the third heading. Applicants must have a decent record and a fairly strong backing as the number of Fellowships in any country is of course limited; the Foundation has to be satisfied that the recipient is the sort of person who will, through his Fellowship, bring benefit to the branch of science which he studies. The object of the Foundation in awarding such a Fellowship as mine is to give the student opportunity to bring his knowledge and technique into line with the latest and best developments. Mine would have enabled me to study at any anthropological school or schools in England, America or Europe.

As things turned out I spent the whole of my time in England and most of it at the London School of Economics, where I studied under Professor Malinowski. It was my main object to acquaint myself at first hand with the aims and methods of the Functional School, and having spent $2\frac{1}{2}$ terms in Malinowski's seminar I feel I have come somewhere near achieving it. The intellectual stimulus of contact with Dr. Malinowski and his electrical seminar could not be valued too highly.

When at the London School of Economics I attended lectures by Professors Ginsberg (Psychology), Seligman (Ethnology) and Coatman (Comparative Administration), and others. The London School of Economics is as keen and busy as a nest of red ants.

It was something of a relief to get away to Oxford for the latter part of the third term. I had taken with me the notes and partly written MSS of a book on the Morehead, and soon after reaching England secured permission to submit it as a thesis for the B.Sc. degree. Completing the book took a good part of my spare time throughout the year and was rather a dead weight. But I finished it off at Oxford and was able to take a degree on 4th August. It is in the hands of Oxford press and will be published under the title *Papuans of the Trans-Fly*, with an introduction by Dr. Haddon. My old tutor, Dr. Marett, was my "Supervisor" and I had the benefit of many conversations with him—hardly once on the special subject of my book. I also saw something of my former instructors Mr. Balfour and Dr. Buxton at Oxford.

I twice visited Cambridge as the guest of Dr. Haddon (who retains his immense enthusiasm for everything Papuan) and was able to meet a good many of the leading British anthropologists in London.

An extension of leave made it possible for me to attend the International Congress of Anthropology and Ethnology at London, 4th-10th August. This Congress, organised by Professor Myers, was a very good show. It was divided in the usual way into a large number of sections. My own interest was chiefly in the Sociological Section (President, Professor Seligman) which had 'Ritual' as its main topic. I read a paper here on the Mask Ceremonies of the Papuan Gulf.[1] I also read a paper on Papuan Sorcery in the General Ethnology Section (President, Dr. Haddon)[2], and in the same section gave a talk on Applied Anthropology.

During the year I gave a paper on Exchange Marriage and Exogamy at the Royal Anthropological Institute.[3] I cannot say that I was otherwise rushed with invitations to speak in public.

The Wellcome Medal essay was written late in 1933 and rather as an afterthought, indeed I was hard at it during a Christmas holiday in Dublin and had to apply for an extension of a week in order to finish it[4]. It arose out of the report on Native Education which I had written earlier in the year and was called Education and Culture Contact. The terms of the competition require a "research essay on the application of anthropological methods to the problems of native peoples, particularly those arising from the intercourse between native peoples, or between primitive natives and civilised races". The essays are submitted anonymously to a Medal Committee as adjudicators. I do not know who the adjudicators were nor who else entered for the competition. I was particularly pleased to get the medal as the Application of Anthropology to problems of native welfare is presumably the *raison d'être* of my job; further it gave me the chance to attack what I think to be a certain extravagance of anthropological theory. If the test of applicability leads to a *reductio ad absurdum* then there must be something wrong with the theory.

The whole trip was well worth while. It has knocked off some of the accumulated rust of 12 years.

REFERENCES

1. Abstract published in Congres International des Sciences Anthropologiques et Ethnologiques 1, 1934, p. 274. E. S.
2. Abstract published in Congres International des Sciences Anthropologiques et Ethnologiques 1, 1934, p. 203. The paper appeared in 1935 as 'Some Aspects of Papuan Sorcery', *Sociological Review* XXVII: 220-31. E. S.
3. Abstract published in *Man* (1934, vol 34, p. 110), under the title 'Exchange Marriage and Exogamy. Summary of a Communication Presented by Mr. F. E. Williams'. E. S.
4. It appeared under the title of 'The Blending of Cultures: An Essay on the Aims of Native Education', Territory of Papua, *Anthropology Report* No. 16, 1935. E. S.

BIBLIOGRAPHIES

1. *Works by F. E. Williams*

1923   'The Pairama ceremony in the Purari Delta, Papua', Royal Anthropological Institute of Great Britain and Ireland, *Journal*, 53: 361-87.

1923*a*   'The collection of curios and the preservation of native culture (with a preface by W. M. Strong)', Territory of Papua, *Anthropology Report* No. 3. Port Moresby, Government Printer, 20 pp.

1923*b*   'The Vailala madness and the destruction of native ceremonies in in the Gulf Division' (with an introduction by W. M. Strong), Territory of Papua, *Anthropology Report* No. 4. Port Moresby, Government Printer, xiii, 78 pp.

1924   'The natives of the Purari Delta' (with an introduction by J. H. P. Murray), Territory of Papua, *Anthropology Report* No. 5. Port Moresby, Government Printer, vi, 283 pp.

1925   'Plant emblems among the Orokaiva', Royal Anthropological Institute of Great Britain and Ireland, *Journal*, 55: 405-24.

1926   Anthropology, Papua. *Annual Report for* 1924-25, 28.

1928   *Orokaiva Magic* (with a foreword by R. R. Marett), Territory of Papua, *Anthropology Reports* Nos. 6-8. London, Oxford University Press, xii, 231 pp.

1928*a*   'Native education; the language of instruction and intellectual education', Territory of Papua, *Anthropology Report* No. 9, Port Moresby, Government Printer, 25 pp.

1928*b*   'A Binandele drill', *Man*, XXVIII: 12-3.

1928*c*   'Report', in Commonwealth of Australia, Territory of Papua. *Annual Report for the Year 1926-7*, 57.

1929   'Rainmaking on the river Morehead', Royal Anthropological Institute of Great Britain and Ireland, *Journal*, 59: 379-97.

1929*a*   'The blending of native and European cultures', Australian and New Zealand Association for the Advancement of Science, *Report of 19th meeting, 1928*, 19: 371-6.

1929*b*   'Report' in Commonwealth of Australia, Territory of Papua, *Annual Report for the Year 1927-8*, p. 16.

1929/42   (Ed.) *The Papuan Villager*, Port Moresby, Government Printer.

1930   *Orokaiva Society* (with an introduction by Sir Hubert Murray), Territory of Papua, Anthropology Report No. 10. London, Oxford University Press, xxiii. 355 pp.

1931   'Bwara Awana houses on Normanby Island', *Man*, XXXI: 174-8.

1931a 'Papuan petrographs', Royal Anthropological Institute of Great
        Britain and Ireland, *Journal*, 61: 121-55.
1932   'Sentiments and leading ideas in native society' (with an introduction
        by Sir Hubert Murray), Territory of Papua, *Anthropology Report*
        No. 12. Port Moresby, Government Printer, iii, 16 pp.
1932a 'Sex affiliation and its implications', Royal Anthropological
        Institute of Great Britain and Ireland, *Journal*, 62: 51-81.
1932/3 'Trading voyages from the Gulf of Papua'. *Oceania*, 3(2): 139-66.
1932/3a 'Depopulation and administration', *Oceania*, 3: 219-26.
1933   'Physical paternity in the Morehead district, Papua', *Man*,
        XXXIII: 123-4.
1933a 'Depopulation of the Suau district', Territory of Papua,
        Anthropology Report No. 13. Port Moresby, Government Printer,
        75 pp.
1933b 'Practical education: the reform of native horticulture', Territory
        of Papua, *Anthropology Report* No. 14. Port Moresby, Government
        Printer, 64 pp.
1934   'The Vailala madness in retrospect', in E. E. Evans-Pritchard and
        others (eds.), *Essays presented to C. G. Seligman*: 369-79. London,
        Kegan Paul, Trench, Trubner and Co., 385 pp.
1934a 'Mask Ceremonies in the Papuan Gulf', *CISAE* (Congrès
        International des Sciences anthropologiques et ethnologiques),
        1: 274.
1934b 'Some Aspects of Papuan Sorcery', *CISAE*, 1: 203.
1934c 'Exchange Marriage and Exogamy. Summary of a Communica-
        tion', *Man*, XXXIV: 110.
1935   Some effects of European influence on the natives of Papua',
        Australian and New Zealand Association for the Advancement
        of Science, *Report of 22nd meeting*, Melbourne: 215-22; also
        Abstract in Fifth Pacific Science Congress 1933, Canada, Pro-
        ceedings, 4: 2885.
1935a 'The blending of cultures: an essay on the aims of native education',
        Territory of Papua, *Anthropology Report* No. 16. Port Moresby,
        Government Printer, 44 pp.; also 1951 Papua and New Guinea,
        Department of Education, Official Research Publication No. 1.
1935b 'Some Aspects of Papuan Sorcery', *Sociological Review*, Vol. 27:
        220-31.
1935c Account of Study in Europe. In Commonwealth of Australia,
        Territory of Papua, *Annual Report for the Year 1933-4*, 8-9.
1936   'Papuan dream interpretations', *Mankind*, 2: 29-39.
1936a *Papuans of the Trans-Fly* (with an introduction by A. C. Haddon),
        Territory of Papua, *Anthropology Report* No. 15. Oxford,
        Clarendon Press, XXXVI 452 pp.; and also Papua. *Annual
        Report for 1934-5*: 34-6.
1936b 'Bull-roarers in the Papuan Gulf', Territory of Papua, *Anthropology
        Report* No. 17. Port Moresby, Government Printer, 55 pp.
1936c 'Arts and crafts of Papua', Papua, *Annual Report for 1934-5*: 33-4.

1936d 'The natives of the Morehead district', Papua. *Annual Report for 1934-5*: 34-6.

1936e ' "Little Stonehenge" of a forgotten race', *Pacific Islands Monthly*, 6(11): 32.

1937 'The hornbill feather in the Abau district', Papua, *Annual Report for 1935-6* : 19-20.

1937a 'Native art and education', Australian and New Zealand, Association for the Advancement of Science, *Report of 23rd meeting*, Auckland: 191-6.

1937b 'The natives of Mount Hagen, Papua: further notes', *Man*, XXXVII: 90-6.

1938 'Recently discovered megaliths in the Trobriand Islands', Papua, *Annual Report for 1936-7*: 34-5.

1938/9 'Seclusion and age grouping in the Gulf of Papua', *Oceania*, 9(4): 359-81.

1939 'Creed of a government anthropologist', Australian and New Zealand Association for the Advancement of Science, *Report of 24th meeting*: 145-59.

1939a 'The reminiscences of Ahuia Ova', Royal Anthropological Institute of Great Britain and Ireland, *Journal*, 69: 11-44.

1939b 'A cycle of ceremonies in Orokolo Bay, Papua', *Mankind*, 2: 145-55.

1939c 'The Kaiamunu-Ebiha-Gi cult in Papua', *Man*, XXXIX: 48.

1940 'Report on the grasslanders', Papua, *Annual Report for 1938-9* : 39-67.

1940a *Drama of Orokolo: the social and ceremonial life of the Elema* (foreword by C. G. Seligman), Territory of Papua, *Anthropology Report No. 18*. Oxford, Clarendon Press, 464 pp.

1941 'Group sentiment and primitive justice', *American Anthropologist*, 43: 523-39.

1940/41 & 1941/42: 'Natives of Lake Kutubu, Papua', *Oceania*, 11: 121-57, 259-94, 374-401; 12: 49-74, 134-54; also *Oceania Monograph No. 6*.

1944/45 'Mission influence amongst the Keveri of South-East Papua', *Oceania*, 15: 89-141.

2. *Other Works Referred to*

Barnes, J. A., 1962: 'African Models in the New Guinea Highlands', *Man*, LXII, No. 2.

Barton, F. R., 1910: 'The Annual Trading Expedition to the Papuan Gulf', in Seligman 1910, 96-120 (Ch. VIII) and Plates XII, XIII.

Buchler, Ira R. and Henry A. Selby, 1967: *Kinship and Social Organisation*, New York, Macmillan.

Burridge, K. O. L., 1960: *Mambu: a Melanesian Millennium*, London, Methuen.

— , 1969a : *New Heaven New Earth*, Oxford, Basil Blackwell.

— , 1969b : *Tangu Traditions*, Oxford, Clarendon Press.

— , 1973 : *Encountering Aborigines*, Oxford, Pergamon Press.

Commonwealth of Australia, Territory of Papua, 1912:
Annual Report for the year 1910-11.

—, 1918 : *Annual Report for the year 1916-17.*
—, 1921 : *Annual Report for the year 1919-20.*
—, 1935 : *Annual Report for the year 1933-34.*
Driberg, J. H., 1932: *At Home with the Savage*, London, Routledge.
Durkheim, Emile, 1912: *Les formes élémentaires de la vie religieuse*, Paris.
Dutton, T. E., 1969: 'The Peopling of Central Papua: Some Preliminary Observations', *Pacific Linguistics*, Series B, No. 9.
Elkin, A. P., 1943: 'F. E. Williams—Government Anthropologist, Papua', *Oceania*, XIV, 91-103.
Firth, R., 1929: *Primitive Economics of the New Zealand Maori*, London, Routledge.
—, 1952: 'Notes on the Social Structure of Some South-Eastern New Guinea Communities', Part II: Koita, *Man*, LII: 86-9.
Forge, Anthony, 1967: 'The Abelam Artist' in *Social Organisation: Essays Presented to Raymond Firth* (Ed. M. Freedman).
—, 1973: *Primitive Art and Society*, Oxford University Press.
Frazer, Sir James George, 1915: *The Golden Bough: A Study in Magic and Religion*, 3rd Edition. In twelve volumes, London, Macmillan.
Ginsberg, Morris, 1937: 'Social Science and Social Philosophy, *Sociological Review*, Oct.
Glasse, R. and Meggitt, M. J. (Eds.), 1969: *Pigs, Pearlshells and Women*, Englewood Cliffs, N. J., Prentice-Hall.
Haldane, J. B. S., 1937: *The Inequality of Man*, Pelican Books.
Hogbin, H. Ian, 1936: Review of 'Papuans of the Trans-Fly', *Man*, XXXVI.
Holmes, J. H., 1902: 'Initiation Ceremonies of Natives of the Papuan Gulf', *Journal of Royal Anthropological Institute*, XXXII.
—, 1924: *In Primitive New Guinea*, London, Seeley Service.
Landtmann, G., 1927: *The Kiwai Papuans of British New Guinea*, Macmillan.
Lévi-Strauss, C., 1962a: *Le totémisme aujourd'hui*, Paris, Presses Universitaires de France.
—, 1962b: *La pénsee sauvage*, Paris, Plon.
—, 1967: *Les structures élémentaires de la parenté*, 2nd Edition, The Hague, Mouton.
—, 1971: *L' Homme nu*, Paris, Plon.
—, 1973: *Anthropologie structurale deux*, Paris, Plon.
McDougall, Wm., 1920: *The Group Mind*, Cambridge University Press.
—, 1921: *An Introduction to Social Psychology* (16th Edition). First published 1908, London, Methuen.
MacGregor, Sir Wm., 1922: 'Disease and its Treatment', in Rivers 1922, pp. 78-83
Malinowski, B., 1920: 'Kula: The Circulating Exchange of Valuables in the Archipelagoes of Eastern New Guinea', *Man*, LI.
—, 1922: *Argonauts of the Western Pacific*, London, Routledge and Kegan Paul.
—, 1926a: 'Myth in Primitive Psychology', *Psyche Miniatures*, No. 6, London.

—, 1926*b*: 'Anthropology', *Encyclopaedia Britannica*, 13th Edition, New Vol.

Marett, R. R., 1920: *Psychology and Folklore*, London, Methuen.

Murray, J. H. P. (Sir Hubert), 1921: 'The Government of Subject Races', in: Commonwealth of Australia, *Papua Annual Report for 1919-20*.

—, 1923: 'Comments' in Williams 1923*b*.

Needham, Rodney, 1971: *Rethinking Kinship and Marriage*, A. S. A. Monographs No. 11, London, Tavistock.

Oppitz, Michael, 1974: 'Shangri-la, le panneau de marque d'un flipper. Analyse semiologique d'un mythe visuel', *L'Homme*, XIV (3-4), 59-84.

Piddington, Ralph, 1938: Review of 'Bull-Roarers in the Papuan Gulf', *Man*, XXXVIII.

Pouwer, J., 1966: 'Towards a Configurational Approach to Society and Culture in New Guinea', *Journal of the Polynesian Society*, 78: 267-86.

Radcliffe-Brown, A. R., 1922: *The Andaman Islanders*, Cambridge University Press.

—, 1931: 'The Present Position of Anthropological Studies', Presidential Address to Section H, British Association for the Advancement of Science, Centenary Meeting in London. Published in *Proceedings of the British Association for the Advancement of Science*. Reprinted as Chapter III of A. R. Radcliffe-Brown, *Method in Social Anthropology*, University of Chicago Press, 1958.

Rappaport, R. A., 1969: 'Marriage Among the Maring' in Glasse and Meggitt, 1969.

Ray, S. H., 1929: The Languages of the Central Division of Papua', *J. R. A. I.*, LIX: 65-96.

Rivers, W. H. R. (ed.), 1922: *Essays in the Depopulation of Melanesia*, Cambridge University Press.

Rosman, A. and Rubel, P. G., 1973: 'Marriage Rules and the Structure Relationships Between Groups in New Guinea Societies' (Paper delivered at the Colloquium on Ecology and Society in Melanesia, Paris, May 1973).

Saussure, F. de, 1916: *Course de linguistique générale*, Paris.

Schwimmer, Erik, 1973: *Exchange in the Social Structure of the Orokaiva*, London, Hurst.

—, 1974*a*: 'Objects of Mediation: Myth and Praxis' in *The Unconscious in Culture* (Ed. Ino Rossi), New York, E. P. Dutton, pp. 209-37.

—, 1974*b*: 'Les Orokaiva s'interrogent sur l'origine de l'échange'. Address delivered at Colloque Informatique et Ethnologie France-Canada II, Paris, May 1974.

—, 1974*c*: 'The Aesthetics of the Aika', Paper given at symposium on The Art of Oceania, McMaster University, Hamilton, Ontario.

—, 1975: 'Friendship and Kinship', in *The Compact: Anthropological Approaches to Friendship* (Ed. Elliott Leyton), Memorial University of Newfoundland, ISER Press.

Seigman, C. G., 1910: *The Melanesians of British New Guinea*, Cambridge University Press.

—, 1929: 'Temperament, Conflict and Psychosis in a Stone-Age Population', *British Journal of Medical Psychology*, IX, Part 3.

Speiser, Felix, 1922: 'Decadence and Preservation in the New Hebrides', in Rivers, 1922, pp. 25-61.

—, 1929: *Über Initiationen in Australien und Neu-Guinea*, Basel, Emil Berkhausen.

Sperber, D., 1974: *Le symbolisme en général*, Paris, Hermann.

Strathern, Andrew, 1969: 'Descent and Alliance in the New Guinea Highlands', *Proceedings of the Royal Anthropological Institute for 1968*, pp.37-52.

Thomas, N. W., 1906: *Natives of Australia*, London, Constable.

Turner, Victor W., 1969: *The Ritual Process*, London, Routledge and Kegan Paul.

Tylor, Edward B., 1873: *Primitive Culture: Researches into the Development of Mythology, Philosophy, Religion, Language, Art and Custom.* 2nd ed., 2 vols, London, John Murray.

Watson, J. B., 1970: 'Society as Organised Flow', *South Western Journal of Anthropology*, June.

Wedgwood, Camilla H., 1930: 'Some Aspects of Warfare in Melanesia', *Oceania*, vol. I (1).

Werner, Alice, 1906: *The Natives of British Central Africa*, London, Constable.

Wirz, Paul, 1934: *Beitrage zur Ethnographie des Papua Golfes*, Leipzig, Teubner.

—, 1937: 'The Kaiamunu-Ebiha-Gi Cult in the Delta Region and Western Division of Papua', *J. R. A. I.*, LXVII: 407-14.

Woodford, C. M., 1922: 'The Solomon Islands', in Rivers, 1922: 69-77.

INDEX